Praise for Mel Ayton's *Hunting the President: Threats, Plots, and Assassination Attempts—From* FDR *to Obama*

"A true scholar and a real pro, Mel understands what many of today's nonfiction authors simply miss: That the sensational does not need to be sensationalized. . . . With his wonderful writing style, he knows how to tell a great story while remaining faithful to the historian's primary tasks to be accurate, credible, and trustworthy. Mel is the embodiment of all of those qualities."
—DAN MOLDEA, author of *The Hoffa Wars: Teamsters, Rebels, Politicians, and the Mob*

"I love the book. . . . It's a great read."
—PETER BOYLES, host of *The Peter Boyles Show*

"A fascinating and very important book which I heartily recommend. . . . Even for people who know American history; even for people who have a special expertise in the history of presidential assassinations; you're going to learn a great deal from [this] new book."
—MICHAEL MEDVED, host of *The Michael Medved Show*

"A fascinating book. . . . A terrific story."
—ROB SCHILLING, host of *The Schilling Show*

"Readers who pick up *Hunting the President* will take away much they didn't know before about many who've stalked presidents with murder in mind."
—ALAN WALLACE, *Pittsburgh Tribune Review*

"[Mel Ayton] has provided a comprehensive account of all these assassination attempts plus more made against the modern presidents. . . . I've got to tell you, I couldn't put this book down. It is absolutely fabulous."
—CHUCK WILDER, host of *The Chuck Wilder Show*

PLOTTING TO KILL

THE PRESIDENT

PLOTTING TO KILL THE PRESIDENT

Assassination Attempts from
Washington to Hoover

MEL AYTON

POTOMAC BOOKS   *An imprint of the University of Nebraska Press*

Library of Congress Cataloging-in-Publication Data
Names: Ayton, Mel, author.
Title: Plotting to kill the president: assassination
attempts from Washington to Hoover / Mel Ayton.
Description: Lincoln: Potomac Books, An imprint
of the University of Nebraska Press, 2017. | Includes
bibliographical references and index.
Identifiers: LCCN 2016022227
ISBN 9781612348568 (cloth: alk. paper)
ISBN 9781612348797 (epub)
ISBN 9781612348803 (mobi)
ISBN 9781612348810 (pdf)
Subjects: LCSH: Presidents—Assassination—United
States—History. | Presidents—Assassination attempts—
United States—History. | Presidents—United
States—Biography. | Assassins—United States—Biography.
| BISAC: HISTORY / United States / General.
Classification: LCC E176.1 .A887 2017 | DDC 973.09/9—dc23
LC record available at https://lccn.loc.gov/2016022227

Set in New Baskerville ITC by Rachel Gould.
Designed by N. Putens.

CONTENTS

ILLUSTRATIONS

PREFACE

New Revelations

Plotting to Kill the President is a corrective to the many history books and biographies that have ignored or overlooked numerous threats American presidents have faced; some serious enough to have placed the chief executive within a hairsbreadth of assassination. Many stories within this study have remained largely hidden from the public; some are buried in newspaper archives and others in government reports, presidential memoirs, bodyguard memoirs, Secret Service agents' memoirs, Library of Congress records, National Archives documents, and presidential libraries.

From the time of America's first president there have been groups of organized plotters or individuals, acting out of personal or political reasons, who have been determined to assassinate the chief executive.

During the period covered by this book, three American presidents were assassinated (Abraham Lincoln, James Garfield, and William McKinley) and, according to official publications, only one other president, Andrew Jackson, survived an assassination attempt.

Plotting to Kill the President addresses these historical events but also reveals the numerous never-before-told incidents when the president's life was put in danger, including stories of attempted stabbings, shootings, and bombings.

Unknown to the general public, most of America's presidents have survived "near lethal approaches" in which would-be assassins have breached the president's security but the assassination attempt has been thwarted, either by presidential guards, White House guards, White House doorkeepers, Secret Service agents, or local law enforcement officers. As the *Minneapolis Journal* stated in 1901, "There are more of the . . . dangerous cranks than the public ever hears anything about."[1]

Most of the would-be assassins researched for this book were individuals bent on achieving infamy. A central and overriding motive for many presidential assassins and would-be assassins has been a craving for notoriety after living a life built on constant failure. The assassins believed their acts would propel them into the history books and they would be recognized as important people.

Plotting to Kill the President reveals many previously unknown or little-known assassination attempts against American presidents that have occurred from the inception of the republic to the time of the Great Depression. Most shocking are the revelations about the assassination attempts against Presidents Arthur, Hayes, Cleveland, Harrison, Roosevelt, Taft, Wilson, and Hoover, which are revealed here for the first time. Chester A. Arthur was the victim of two assassination attempts. The first attempt was made at the Butler Mansion in Washington DC, and the second attempt occurred at the White House. A gunman stalked President-elect Hayes and plotted to kill him during the inauguration ceremonies at the Capitol. Harrison and Cleveland were the victims of previously unknown assassination attempts by lone gunmen. A serious assassination plot to kill William McKinley was hatched four years before his actual murder in 1901. A plot to blow up William Howard Taft's train was foiled by local law enforcement officers, and a gunman stalked Taft with the intention of killing him. A man who had stockpiled bombs, dynamite, and nitroglycerine in his hotel room in Hoboken, New Jersey, confessed he was plotting, along with fourteen others, to assassinate Woodrow Wilson. In 1919, an insane man, armed with a .32-caliber pistol, stalked Wilson, intending to kill him and "save the world."

The assassination attempt against former president Theodore Roosevelt by John Schrank, in 1912, is widely regarded as the only serious assassination attempt Roosevelt suffered. However, the commonly accepted notion among presidential historians that Roosevelt was never the victim of an assassination attempt while in office is now seriously undermined. There were at least three occasions when armed assassins breached the president's security, placing Roosevelt within seconds of assassination. Two attempts to kill him were made at his summer home and one attempt occurred at the White House.

Many presidents, including Grover Cleveland and Chester Arthur, conspired with their White House aides to conceal from the public the true natures of their illnesses. In Cleveland's case, he believed public knowledge of his cancer would be harmful to the perilous state of the nation's economy. In Arthur's case, he kept his illness, Bright's disease, from the public because he was concerned about public confidence.

Plotting to Kill the President also reveals that, at least since the time of Lincoln's assassination, presidential aides and friends conspired to cover up numerous assassination attempts against American presidents. In 1901 a "clerical employee" at the White House told a newspaper reporter, "Few persons realize how vital a subject at the White House the possibility of presidential assassination always has been. Of course, nothing of this discussion gets out except in the cases where a shot is actually fired or some other overt act committed which startles the country. Of the larger number of seemingly suspicious cases that, whether alarming or not, are nipped in the bud, little is ever known."[2]

White House guard William Henry Crook noted in his memoirs, "Episodes of [violent behavior] were a frequent occurrence in the White House. We dealt with them quietly and they rarely got into the newspapers."[3] The plot to assassinate Rutherford B. Hayes during his inauguration was "kept from the public" by "his request."[4] Even before he became president, Ulysses S. Grant was the subject of assassination attempts and his reaction was to tell his aides to keep them secret, as he believed it would lead to further attacks.[5]

The assassination attempts against Grover Cleveland were covered up partly due to the intervention of Henry T. Thurber, the president's secretary during his second term. President Cleveland's aides believed publicity would only inspire copycat attacks. Following an assassination attempt in New York in 1892, shortly before Cleveland's election to a second term as president, New York Police Superintendant Thomas J. Byrnes and Cleveland's doctor, Joseph D. Bryant, conspired to keep the incident a secret. However, the details of the assassination attempt were revealed by a doctor friend of Bryant's who attended the president when he was attacked. An acclaimed journalist of his time, Frank G. Carpenter, of the *Deseret Weekly*, wrote, "Through Dr. Bryant and Superintendent Byrnes the matter was kept out of the papers and today no one but the president and his most intimate friends know the exact facts of the case."[6]

Additionally, a statement that Henry Thurber made a few years before his death in 1904 partly supports the claims of a cover-up. "Nobody will ever know," Thurber said, "the extent of my efforts to protect President Cleveland unless he should be assassinated."[7]

In Benjamin Harrison's case, the president was unaware of the plot to kill him as, according to U.S. Secret Service chief John S. Bell, the president's aides and political friends kept the incident from the president and were sworn to secrecy. Supportive evidence of the cover-up resides in the discovery by this author that the president's private secretary, Elijah Halford, had been lying when he told the press that the assassination story was false.

During Theodore Roosevelt's administration, William Loeb, secretary to the president, also attempted to cover up assassination attempts. In September 1903, he said that Henry Weilbrenner's attack on the president had the effect of "arousing all the mental freaks" that held the president responsible for "everything that happens" and that it was for this reason that "many frustrated attempts upon the life of the president [were] kept secret."[8]

In October 1903, Loeb met with Secret Service chief John E. Wilkie about how the agency could effectively carry out its protection duties. Loeb announced his intention to suppress every fact in connection with the arrest of "cranks" at the White House. Loeb also said he would "make trouble" for any police officer or Secret Service agent who failed to observe his orders in this respect. The diktat was extended to the Washington police force. The *Washington Times* stated, "The police authorities have decided not to give out reports of cranks or insane persons who have been hanging around the White House for the possible purpose of injuring the president."[9] A newspaper report of 1897 stated, "The policemen and doorkeepers at the executive mansion do everything in their power to suppress news of cranks."[10]

However, in an open democracy like that of the United States, it was often difficult to keep many attempted assassination stories from the public, especially when reporters often spent a good deal of their time in the White House front-door vestibule and were able to observe the efforts of White House doorkeepers in keeping mentally unstable individuals or political fanatics from attempting to approach the president. Additionally, personal papers and diaries kept by presidential secretaries, obscure government reports, and newspaper archives have confirmed the efforts made to hide the risks presidents have always taken when carrying out their duties.

PLOTTING TO KILL

THE PRESIDENT

CHAPTER 1

————

Guarding the Early Presidents

[There is] a solid layer of savagery beneath the surface of society, unaffected by the superficial changes of religion and culture.

—Sir James Frazer, *The Golden Bough*

No man who ever held the office of president would congratulate a friend on obtaining it. He will make one man grateful and a hundred men his enemies, for every office he can bestow.

—John Adams

At the founding of the United States, Americans were proud that their chief executive was not surrounded by an armed guard or the presence of regal trappings. They saw Europe as a place where monarchs and dictators feared their subjects and required armed protection when they exited their palaces. Americans believed in the exceptional nature of their government, and to accept protection for the president would be to acknowledge that America was no different from the despotic regimes in Europe.

America's leaders also feared they would be perceived as having erected barriers between themselves and the people if they chose to have bodyguards. A children's primer that was popular during the Civil War illustrated American "exceptionalism" with reference to how the president was protected:

How are emperors and kings protected?

By great troops of guards; so that it is difficult to approach them.

How is the president guarded?

He needs no guards at all; he may be visited by any persons like a
   private citizen.[1]

The nature of presidential protection in the early nineteenth century
was therefore virtually nonexistent. Although the early presidents were
at times the objects of abuse and received numerous threatening letters,
they did not, on the whole, take the threats seriously and moved about
freely without protective escorts.

The American republic and its leaders were, from the beginning,
split on the issue of how the American president should interact with
his constituency. Although George Washington and Thomas Jefferson
shared a view of where the capital of the new American republic should
be located, they had very different opinions about the nature of the
presidency. Should the president act as a king or a commoner? By 1791,
for example, Washington came under severe criticism for his receptions
at the White House, which were described as "monarchical." However,
the first president believed that sumptuous state ceremonies enhanced
respect for the new republic among other nations.[2] Jefferson, on the
other hand, was "careful in every particular of his personal conduct to
inculcate upon the people his . . . unwillingness to admit the smallest
distinction that may separate him from the mass of his fellow citizens,"
according to a British diplomat.[3]

An early dispute about the role of the "first citizen" centered on
the chief executive's new home. The original plans for the new city of
Washington DC called for a "presidential palace" five times the size of
the building we now know as the White House. The plan reflected the
Federalist Party's monarchical idea of the presidency. Federalist Party
leaders argued that Americans wanted their president to act as a kind
of elected king, set apart from the people. The republican opposition,
led by Jefferson, despised any notion that the president should act as a
monarch or that he should live in a home with aristocratic airs like the
European monarchs. Jefferson's political principles sought to deflect the
aristocratic and elitist attitudes of the Federalists and portray instead the

openness and liberty that was associated with the common American. Jefferson's Democratic-Republican Party (as it was then known) characterized the Federalist position as unbefitting a true democracy based on equality and a classless society. A modest way of living, they believed, reflected the spirit of the age. "Kings live in parks," they argued, and "presidents live on streets."[4] (In 1800, Jefferson was elected, in part, by publicizing fears about the Federalists' "monarchical aspirations."[5])

Because the Democratic-Republicans considered the idea of a presidential palace antidemocratic, they rejected any effort to deny public entry to the "People's House," and access was, from the beginning, a security problem. Even while the White House was being built, the public wandered in and out without being challenged. In Jefferson's time, and for generations afterward, citizens used the White House grounds for picnics, walks, and even public fairs.

Foreign travel for a president was also considered to be against the ideals of the nation because citizens were fearful that their president might be seduced into imitating the ways of European monarchy if he visited their palaces.[6] As well, the idea of stationing guards in and around the White House was considered wholly inappropriate to the nation's character. However, although the American people and their leaders prided themselves on the absence of a royal guard at the White House, it gradually became imperative that some form of security should be installed. Unruly visitors and office seekers, who were taking up the president's time, mandated it. Beginning in the first quarter of the nineteenth century, increasing restrictions on public access to the White House were imposed, due largely to concerns for the personal security of the president and his family.

However, for a century after John Adams first moved into the White House, the protection of the mansion and its residents remained a relatively minor concern, except during wartime. As time passed, various combinations of police officers, guards, and soldiers furnished security for the president's home.

Until early in the twentieth century, security for the president at the White House consisted mainly of guards in civilian dress. In addition to the guards, a doorkeeper was assigned to maintain watch in the entrance hall. John Adams, John Quincy Adams, and Andrew Jackson were against it. James Monroe was in favor of the security.[7] Although the doorkeeper was not armed, he always had firearms close to hand. It was not until the Tyler administration that a permanent company of guards was established to protect the president and the White House.

―――――

The arguments about how the president should live and how the White House should be secured soon extended to how the president's person should be protected. Today, protection is seen as a form of "legitimacy." In the time of the founding fathers, the idea of a bodyguard was viewed as a weakness. Citizens were also concerned that the introduction of a Praetorian Guard in the style of ancient Rome might embolden the president to use it as a standing army against his opponents.

From the beginning, American presidents wanted to avoid the martial displays that were common in other countries when it came to protecting a head of state. The aim was for a president to lead an independent life that simple citizenship secured, going and coming just like every other American—walking abroad, strolling through the streets, driving with his family and unattended by guards or detectives. The presidents also believed that America was different from European nations and therefore should not fear that one of its citizens would kill their democratically elected leader.

The absence of any fear for the president's safety also resided in the fact that the country had only a small population. The year Jefferson entered the White House, the population of the United States was 5,308,473, nine-tenths of which resided east of the Alleghenies.[8] Eighty percent of the population lived in the countryside, and the absence of public transport for the common man resulted in only a small number of people who could travel to meet with the president.

The early presidents also did not go electioneering, as the public considered it unseemly. This meant that the president did not place himself in harm's way by exposing himself to danger in large crowds. It was indeed a paradox. The American people did not want their president acting like a king, but neither did they want him campaigning like an ordinary politician.

Additionally, while the lives of the presidents were widely publicized, their faces were not. They went about their business unrecognized for most of the time. Each day at 1:00 p.m., Thomas Jefferson liked to go horseback riding, usually riding alone. Few knew his identity when he often stopped to converse with locals. On one occasion, a man who did not recognize Jefferson told him how angry he was with the president. Jefferson invited him to the White House.[9] In 1817 James Monroe and his aides called at an inn in Altona, New York, and went unrecognized until the president revealed his identity during supper. On a visit to New York City in 1847, James Polk was frequently mistaken for his traveling companion, Alabama senator Dixon Hall.[10] However, with the advent of new inventions like the daguerreotype and photography and the publication of the presidents' portraits in the press, the risk of assassination increased. The first photograph of a president was not taken until the 1840s, however, and not until the end of the nineteenth century did the press publish the president's photograph.[11]

————

Despite the belief among American citizens and their leaders in Congress that the president need not fear assassination, threats on the lives of American presidents were a constant. Individuals or groups who attempted to kill American leaders or threatened assassination can be traced back to the time of George Washington.

Washington did not hire personal guards, even though he received his fair share of abuse and threatening letters. An article published in a New York newspaper accused him of being a thief, allegedly overdrawing his salary by $5,000. During one presidential campaign he was accused of being a murderer, and John Randolph of Roanoke once toasted Washington with, "George Washington, may he be damned."[12]

Washington was deeply hurt by some letters that impugned his character. He wrote, "Every act of my administration had been attacked in such exaggerated and indecent terms as could scarcely be a Nero . . . or even a common pickpocket."[13] Washington was also excoriated in the press. By the end of his term he "was beset by unmerited censures of the vilest kind."[14]

Although no overt attempts were made to kill Washington during his two terms as president, he did place himself in harm's way when he personally led a federalized militia force of approximately fifteen thousand troops to quell the Whiskey Rebellion during his second term. But in the relatively bloodless conflict, Washington was not present during any of the skirmishing.

Washington also eschewed any efforts to protect him on his travels. When a Charleston artillery battalion offered to guard the president during his visit to the city in 1791, Washington declined, saying he "considered himself perfectly safe in the affection and amicable attachment of the people."[15]

However, Washington had many brushes with death long before he became commander in chief of the revolutionary army and president of the republic. In 1753, during the French and Indian War, the twenty-two-year-old Washington volunteered to be the messenger who would deliver to the French an ultimatum demanding they cease encroaching on English-held territory. On his journey to Pittsburgh, the crude raft on which Washington and his party hoped to float to the French-held Fort LeBoeuf began to sink. Washington, a nonswimmer, escaped death as the raft sank in the icy waters of the Alleghany River. Later, during the expedition, an Indian guide, who had been secretly allied with the French, pointed his rifle at Washington and fired. However, the shot missed.

The following year, during the same conflict, Lt. Col. Washington volunteered to lead a party of men to establish an outpost against the French. Leading a surprise attack, a man close to him was killed and several others wounded.[16]

Months later, Washington fought with Gen. Edward Braddock during his crushing defeat by the French in the Battle of Fort Duquesne (Pittsburgh) in 1755. As Washington continued to fight in the battle, Braddock was killed and Washington took command of the troops as all the other officers had been killed or disabled. Washington's hat was knocked off his head by a bullet, and two horses shot from under him. At the end of the campaign his clothing had four bullet holes.[17] Washington wrote to his brother, "By the all-powerful dispensations of Providence I have been protected beyond all human probability or expectation; for I had four bullets through my coat, and two horses shot under me, yet I escaped unhurt, although death was leveling my companions on every side."[18]

Fifteen years later, in 1770, Washington returned to the same Pennsylvania woods where the battle was fought. There he met one of his adversaries, an Indian chief who had traveled a great distance to meet his opponent. The chief told Washington that a "mightier power" had shielded Washington during the battle when Indian warriors had him in their sights. "The Great Spirit protects that man," the chief said, "and guides his destinies—he will become the chief of nations and a people yet unborn will hail him as the founder of a mighty empire."[19]

However, Washington's closest call, it can be argued, occurred when he was leading American forces in the War of Independence. On September 11, 1777, an army of 12,500 British troops marched through Pennsylvania toward Philadelphia. Capt. Patrick Ferguson, a thirty-three-year-old Scotsman, commanded the British sharpshooters. He was reputed to be the Redcoats' best shot. When Ferguson spotted a group of soldiers, he aimed his rifle at Washington but decided not to shoot because "it was not pleasant to fire at the back of an unoffending individual, who was acquitting himself very coolly of his duty." Ferguson said he could have "lodged half a dozen balls in or about him before Washington was out of his reach," but he "let him alone."[20]

As leader of the revolutionary army, Washington was the target of an alleged assassination/kidnap plot. In June 1776, the battles at Lexington, Concord, Bunker Hill, and Ticonderoga had been decided. But still undecided was the question of what the battles were really all about. Were the colonies fighting to secure a more enlightened British rule, or were they fighting to become a free and independent nation?

Washington was aware of the divided sentiments of his fellow citizens and was also fully aware that many of them, including the mayor of New York, felt loyalty to the Crown. However, Washington was unaware that there were British sympathizers within the Continental army, also serving close to him in high positions.

Washington's personal guard, which had been formed in 1776, had been handpicked not only for their skills as soldiers but also because they were considered to be devoted to the American cause. The strength of the guard was usually around 180 men.

In the spring of 1776, Washington and his army marched to New York City for an anticipated attempt by the British to occupy the city. When they arrived in New York, two of Washington's honor guards, Thomas Hickey and Michael Lynch, were arrested for passing counterfeit money.

During their incarceration, the two men confessed to prisoners Israel Youngs and Isaac Ketchum that they were British loyalists and had secretly enlisted in the British army. They said the Royal Navy was soon to invade New York and American defectors like themselves were going to blow up the King's Bridge, which was the only route to the mainland. Other conspirators, including another eight soldiers in the honor guard, would raid munitions depots. Washington's forces would be trapped on Manhattan Island, surrounded by thirty thousand British soldiers and several hundred ships. David Matthews, the mayor of the city, and William Tryon, the governor of New York, were allegedly part of the conspiracy and had financed the plot.

Isaac Ketchum informed the authorities, and the Provincial Congress of New York acted quickly. By June 22 every known conspirator was rounded up, including New York's mayor, but the governor had fled and Washington's troops were unable to find him. Over the course of the next three days, Michael Lynch and two other accomplices agreed to give evidence against Thomas Hickey in exchange for leniency. At the court martial they gave sworn testimony that Hickey had joined the conspiracy and tried to recruit additional participants.[21] However, the trial proceedings indicate that Hickey had only a minor role in the conspiracy. Hickey himself said he was only participating in the plot as a ruse and insurance against being executed if the British overran the city.

Although all the conspirators were arrested, Hickey was the only one put on trial. At Hickey's court-martial he was found guilty of treason. He was hanged on a wooden scaffold near New York's Bowery on June 28, 1776, before a crowd of twenty thousand spectators. Many members of the crowd were soldiers instructed by Washington to observe the execution as a warning to any potential traitors. Hickey was the first American executed for treason.[22]

Although there is little doubt that the plot did in fact take place, historians are divided as to whether Hickey played an important part. One man gave evidence that Hickey was merely playing along as a way to foil the plot. Some twenty arrests were made in the case and many of them turned state's evidence to implicate Hickey. Only one man was accused of organizing the kidnapping of Washington, but there is no record of any charges against him. Other conspirators who escaped justice were the governor and the mayor.[23]

Historians are also divided about the alleged plan by Hickey to murder Washington by serving him poisoned peas at the Fraunces Tavern, which was frequented by the general and his staff. The alleged plot, for which there is only sparse evidence, may have been exaggerated throughout the years. The murder attempt was hatched when Hickey began a relationship with Phoebe Fraunces, the daughter of the tavern's owner, and it reached its climax as she served dinner one evening to Washington and his staff. Hickey entered the kitchen and allegedly sprinkled belladonna on a dish of peas his lover was about to serve Washington. She had told Hickey that peas were one of the general's favorite dishes.[24]

The story, which some historians say is apocryphal, goes on to relate how Hickey watched from the kitchen door as Fraunces served the meal. However, as Washington began to eat she loudly announced that the peas had been poisoned. Washington's aides immediately seized Hickey, and one of the officers scattered the peas in the garden. They were eaten by chickens and one of them died shortly afterward.

However, there is no mention of poisoned peas in the transcript of Hickey's court-martial record. Additionally, there are a number of weaknesses in the story of the alleged plot. For example, the owner of the tavern definitely had a daughter, but she was named Elizabeth and was only ten years old at the time the plot was supposedly hatched.[25]

John Adams was the first president officially to live in Washington. He arrived in the city on June 3, 1800, and was met by a large body of citizens on horseback. He was escorted to Georgetown, where he lived until moving into the partially completed White House a short time later.

John Adams did not provide for any security for the mansion. Nor did he have any personal protection except for his servants and staff, despite receiving many threats to his life. The threatening letters Adams received included one from a "ruined merchant," who wrote:

Myself and my family are ruined by the French. If you do not pro-
cure satisfaction for my losses, when a treaty is made with them, I am
undone forever and you must be a villain to your country!!! Assassination shall be your lot, if restitution is lost to America through your
means, or if ever you agree to a peace without it. The subsistence of
thousands, who have lost their all, depends on it. A ruined merchant,
Alas! With ten children!!! Made beggars by the French.[26]

When Adams submitted the name of William Van Murray to Congress
as minister plenipotentiary to France, empowered to negotiate a settlement putting an end to the Quasi-War, federalist newspapers became
abusive. Numerous threats of assassination followed, but he ignored
them and continued his strolls around Washington and his early morning swims in the Potomac unguarded.[27]

When Thomas Jefferson succeeded John Adams as president in 1801,
he insisted on being called "Mr. Jefferson," not "Mr. President." He also
eschewed the customary horse and carriage and walked to the Capitol
from his boarding house on the morning of his inauguration. He wanted
to show he shunned the accoutrements of monarchy and dramatize his
"republican simplicity." He also rarely traveled by carriage but instead
rode his horse, accompanied by a single servant, because he insisted
on "mingling with the people."[28]

Following Jefferson's inauguration, however, it became apparent that
additional police protection was needed, and accordingly, in 1802, the
mayor of Washington was given general police authority. He made no
immediate use of this power, and it was not until three years later that a high
constable and forty deputy constables were appointed to police the city.[29]

During the presidencies of Washington and Adams, guests at the White
House showed their respect by bowing rather than shaking hands with
the president. When Jefferson took office he abandoned the tradition
and, at an Independence Day event, made a point of shaking hands
with the guests to show his "common-man" credentials.[30]

Like Washington, Jefferson had also been a target for British soldiers
during the War of Independence. On June 3, 1781, a plot to kidnap him

was foiled by Virginia Militia captain Jack Jouett. At a tavern, Jouett overheard Col. Banastre Tarleton and other British soldiers discuss a plan to capture Jefferson, who was governor of Virginia at the time. They also planned to kidnap other Virginia legislators.

Jouett rode forty miles through the night to warn Jefferson, and the future president escaped to safety. Tarleton arrived in Charlottesville a short time later but was too late to put his kidnapping plans into effect. Although his primary target eluded him, Tarleton was successful in capturing a few legislators and the famous Daniel Boone. The British released them on parole after a few days in captivity.

The third president had assisted in drawing up plans for the Executive Mansion. He had given security some thought. In his plan for the grounds of the White House, Jefferson provided for gate lodges, in which guards could be stationed, but the guards were never supplied. However, the new police authority, instituted in 1805, and which appointed a chief constable and forty deputy constables, added additional support.[31]

———————

Although a personal bodyguard for the president was not provided by Congress until the time of John Tyler, most presidents had servants and aides who could come to their defense if the chief executive was attacked. A number of early presidents also hired guards for the White House grounds, and a doorkeeper was present at the entrance hall to the mansion.

When James Madison succeeded Jefferson, he did not hire a bodyguard as such, but he did have a "body servant," named Paul Jennings, who sometimes assumed the role. Jennings was a slave, and after Madison's death, in 1836, he was sold by Dolly Madison to Daniel Webster to pay off her debts. Webster loaned him money at eight dollars a month for his service. Jennings lived as a freeman in Washington until his death in 1870.[32]

Madison's most serious brush with death and apprehension about being taken hostage occurred when America had declared war on Britain over control of the seas. The conflict was partly to do with trade restrictions resulting from Britain's war with France, but also because America had ambitions to control Canada.

Even though war had been declared in 1812, Britain had been occupied by the conflict with Napoleon. Only when the French emperor was exiled to Elba, in the spring of 1814, did the British government feel able to free enough forces to meet the American challenge. Its popular commander, Maj. Gen. Robert Ross, had helped the Duke of Wellington win the Peninsular War. He had a reputation for courage verging on recklessness. His orders were to give the Americans "a good drubbing." His Royal Navy comrade in arms, Rear Adm. George Cockburn, a ruthless sailor, urged Ross to land the army, march the fifty miles to Washington, and burn the city to the ground. As the Americans had burned legislative buildings in Toronto, it was inevitable that similar attacks would be made in the American capital.

Some 4,500 British veterans, who had fought under Wellington and defeated the French in Spain, arrived in Chesapeake Bay near Washington DC in the summer of 1814.

Madison stationed one hundred militiamen around the White House and they camped on the North Lawn of the mansion, positioning cannon at the north gate. President Madison rode toward the battlefield on August 23.[33]

When the news reached Washington that a large British army had joined up with Cockburn, there was pandemonium. Families piled their furniture on carts and headed out of town. Unfortunately, most of America's small regular army was attempting to invade British Canada, so Madison would be left mainly with part-timers, many of them poorly trained.

The two armies met at Bladensburg, five miles northeast of Washington. The British sweltered in their woolly red tunics. Many British soldiers had been left behind, expiring from the heat, on the march from the ships. But they were confident that they could defeat these Yankees, just as they had defeated Napoleon.

When Madison arrived at Bladensburg he became incensed by the American general's incompetence. The Americans were full of spirit but clumsily spaced out in three lines of troops that were too far apart to support each other. By late afternoon the U.S. Army had either run away or been withdrawn, and only a valiant stand by the third line did something to redeem American honor. Madison personally assumed command of the only remaining viable American force, a navy battery commanded by Commodore Joshua Barney. However, his efforts to rally the troops were unsuccessful. The road to the capital was now wide open. Madison sent a message to his wife, Dolly, telling her to prepare to leave the White House before he traveled to the capital by carriage. Before she fled, Dolly Madison insisted on taking the time to remove her favorite red curtains and a portrait of George Washington, which she made sure was carted off to safety.

When British troops arrived in the city, and with George Cockburn urging him on, Ross ordered the burning of both houses of Congress in the ornate U.S. Capitol building. Their next target was the White House. The volunteer American soldiers retreated before the British entered Washington, and Madison ended up wandering around the swamp-infested forests in the Washington countryside for four days. The British thus faced no resistance. Cockburn, Ross, and their staff explored the fourteen-year-old mansion.

At the White House, British troops proceeded to destroy the mansion. Fifty soldiers were stationed outside, and when the order was given, they smashed the windows and hurled in torches. In minutes, the blaze swept through the main reception rooms, destroying all the treasures that remained. Cockburn and Ross were unrepentant and now set their sights on Baltimore, one of America's richest cities, thirty miles to the northeast.

On September 12, Ross and Cockburn landed the army at North Point, fifteen miles from Baltimore. However, as Ross had insisted on leading his army from the front, he became the target for an American militiaman who shot him in the chest, fatally wounding him. Although it was a heavy blow to the army's morale, they pressed on, beating back the U.S. force in their path.

The British had advanced to within reach of the strongly manned entrenchments at the edge of Baltimore. From the sea, Royal Navy frigates and gunboats armed with mortars subjected Fort McHenry to a massive bombardment that lasted twenty-five hours. However, the British eventually abandoned their attack.

The war continued for only four more months, with no real gains for either side. It ended on December 24, 1814, and did not accomplish one purpose for which it was initiated. No new territory was gained by either side, and Madison had failed to address the issues of impressments of American sailors and ships and the rights of neutral shipping. When Andrew Jackson defeated the British in New Orleans, the war had already ended.

James and Dolly Madison never returned to the White House. It took three years of rebuilding before the next president, James Monroe, could move in and another twelve to add the fine porticos on the north and south of the building that we see today.

———

James Monroe succeeded Madison in 1817 and became the fifth president of the United States (1817–25). He had served in the Continental army from 1776 to 1778 and rose to the rank of major. Monroe crossed the Delaware with Washington and was wounded at the Battle of Trenton, nearly dying from his injuries as a bullet grazed the left side of his chest and then hit his shoulder, injuring the major artery bringing blood to the arm. Monroe's life was saved by a doctor who stopped the bleeding by sticking his index finger into the wound and applying pressure to the artery. Surgeons operated later to remove the bullet but could not find it. Monroe recovered from the wound in eleven weeks, but carried the bullet in his shoulder the rest of his life.[34]

Shortly after he became president, Monroe made two long tours of the country in 1817 to build national trust. Frequent stops on these tours allowed innumerable ceremonies of welcome and expressions of good will. When he traveled he was anxious to avoid criticisms of "royal progress" so he announced he would travel as a "private citizen" to assuage fears he would be acting as a "monarch."[35]

During his tours he was praised by the American press for not having guards to protect him. He traveled with only his personal secretary and one government official, as well as two servants. The *American Telegraph* contrasted James Monroe's tour with the "situation of an European sovereign . . . guarded by thousands of slaves . . . [living in constant dread of] the pistol and the poniard of the lurking assassin." The newspaper noted that Monroe was attended only by a "few of his particular friends" and made a journey of two thousand miles, "not only with security, but without fear and molestation." The president's "only bodyguard" was "the love the people bear their government and its officers." The *George-town Manager* noted the difference between European powers, built on despotism, and the liberty afforded the young American republic, which led to a president journeying through several states "unprotected save by the affection which surrounds him."[36]

During one of his tours, the citizens of Frankfurt, Kentucky, introduced President Monroe as the "unbiased choice of a free people. Guarded by their love, he needs no other protection." The people of Boston welcomed Monroe as a president who "required no other protection than what arises from the affections of his fellow citizens."[37]

However, this tranquil image of a president free to mingle with "the people" without facing danger was deceptive. Recognizing that security around the White House may have been too lax, attempts were made to control the number of visitors. The president also barred members of the public from walking around the mansion unattended.[38]

Despite the image that Monroe portrayed as a president free from any danger, he was fearful of assassination. He hired guards to protect the White House. They dressed in civilian clothes and were recruited for Monroe by the marshal of the District of Columbia. On special occasions the guard was increased. These measures were in addition to a doorkeeper who was always on duty in the entrance hall to the mansion and had the responsibility of admitting visitors to the White House and denying them admission, if necessary.[39]

Monroe also hid sharpshooters in the trees of the White House, and in 1818 he had an iron fence constructed around the grounds. Gates with heavy locks were installed on the north side of the mansion. During special days when the White House was opened up to the public, including the Fourth of July, the number of guards increased but they were directed to remain hidden around the grounds.[40]

The White House doorkeeper, always on duty in the entrance hall, kept firearms close at hand in a small lodge room off the hall. He had the authority to admit or refuse nearly anyone who appeared. But this did not prevent thieves from entering the mansion, joining a party in the president's drawing room celebrating the election of John Quincy Adams, and stealing General Scott's wallet containing $800.[41]

However, there was some criticism about Monroe's practice of keeping the White House open to the public. According to the novelist James Fenimore Cooper:

> I have known a cartman to leave his horse in the street and go to a reception room to shake hands with the President. He offended the good taste of all present, because it was not thought decent that a laborer should come in dirty dress on such an occasion; but while he made a trifling mistake in this particular he proved how well he understood the difference between government and society. He knew that a levee was a sort of homage paid to political equality in the person of the first magistrate, but he would not have presumed to enter the house of the same person as a private individual without being invited.[42]

Unruly public visitors were not the only danger Monroe confronted. During a dinner party at the White House, an argument between the British and French ministers resulted in the drawing of swords. Monroe confronted both men, drew his own sword, and ordered them to leave the mansion.[43] In another incident, Monroe was physically threatened by his secretary of the treasury, William Crawford. The two men had argued about patronage recommendations, to which the president objected. Crawford raised his cane, calling Monroe a "damned infernal old scoundrel." In response the president picked up a set of fire tongs and cursed Crawford before the secretary calmed down and left the White House.[44]

————

Monroe was succeeded by John Quincy Adams, an austere and aloof man, the son of the second president, who was relatively secluded from the public. Adams was a quiet and studious man who eschewed lavish social occasions. But he was accessible to American citizens, and the White House door was always open to all during the day. He would breakfast for an hour, "from 9 to 10," then "have a succession of visitors upon business in search of a place, solicitors for donation, or mere curiosity from 11 till between 4 or 5 o'clock."[45]

Unlike his predecessor, Adams did not hire guards, because he "did not favor the practice."[46] Usually alone, he would take long walks through the streets of Washington in the early hours of the morning, which lasted for two hours. He walked around four miles, returning to the White House to watch the sunrise from the windows of the East Room before reading his Bible. And in the summer he would usually walk down to the banks of the Potomac alone, shed his clothes, and swim nude across the river at a place where it was a mile wide. He rejected all offers of protection during his swims and strolls.

On June 13, 1825, Adams very nearly drowned in the Potomac during one of his swims. He was accompanied by his steward, Antoine Guista. The two men paddled a leaky canoe across the river with the intention of swimming back. However, the canoe filled with water during a squall and sank. As Adams was wearing a loose shirt, it impeded his ability to stay afloat as the sleeves filled with water. By the time Adams reached shore he was exhausted. Adams sat naked on a rock while his servant procured a carriage to return them to the White House.[47]

Word had spread that the president had drowned, and news of his death reached the White House. After Adams returned to the mansion his wife urged him to give up his morning swims, but to no avail.[48]

Although Adams eschewed security measures, calling them "pretentious and undemocratic," he would at times be confronted by a less-than-agreeable White House visitor who would cause alarm to the president's staff.[49] One individual who managed to meet the president, Peter McDermott, told Adams he was a messenger from God. He was quickly shown the door.[50]

Adams also granted an interview to a man who had threatened to kill him. Dr. George P. Todson, an assistant surgeon in the army, had been court-martialed and discharged. He petitioned the president to reinstate him, but when Adams refused he became incensed. Todson responded by threatening to assassinate the president.

Todson visited the White House several times over the period of a few months, each time pressing his case and attempting to persuade the president of the injustice of it, but without success. Todson's lawyer warned Adams about the threat but the president agreed to meet Todson once more, on December 16, 1826. During the meeting, Adams once more refused Todson's request that he overturn the court's verdict. However, the president managed to calm his threatener by finding Todson an assignment for work on the frontier.[51]

On another occasion a court-martialed army sergeant walked into the White House and demanded that Adams have him reinstated. The president asked him for proof that the verdict had been wrong, and when the army sergeant said he could not provide it, his request was turned down. A few days later the discharged army sergeant again came to the White House and told the president he had a choice—either be assassinated or order his reinstatement. President Adams paid no attention to the threat and continued to walk about unguarded, both during the daytime and at night.

The would-be assassin hung around in the vicinity of the White House, and finally one day he came up to Adams and stated that his threat had been a joke. He requested that the president give him enough money to pay his way home. The president gave him the money.[52]

The country was increasing in population by the time Adams handed the presidency over to Andrew Jackson. It was also becoming more democratic. However, the culture that existed in nineteenth-century America, preventing the formation of personal presidential protection, began to create severe problems for the safety of the chief executive. As the country's population grew, so did the threats to the president's safety as mentally unstable individuals and political malcontents decided to act. And the growing differences between America's regions, especially between the North and South, exacerbated the problem.

Even as late as the 1890s, Americans were so confident their country was different from European nations that they did not believe the president required constant personal security—despite the assassinations of Presidents Lincoln and Garfield, and the attempted assassination of President Jackson. Accordingly, presidential protection remained lackadaisical. The *Pittsburgh Press* opined in 1890, "The news cabled across the ocean from time to time indicates a feeling of unrest and dissatisfaction on the part of the masses and a feeling of uneasiness on the part of the aristocracy. The people of this country have looked with much horror and some amazement at the spectacle of the trembling czar fearing death at any moment by the hands of the nihilists in Russia. The chosen rulers of us Americans know no such fears."[53]

Three years later, the *Lewiston Daily Sun* White House correspondent wrote,

Strangers from other countries are amazed at the freedom with which our public men go to and fro and receive persons who are unknown to them. Most of our presidents have been in the habit of taking walks in the White House grounds or adjacent streets absolutely unprotected and sometimes alone. Such a thing is not known among the royalty of Europe. Europeans who visit Washington can scarcely believe their eyes and ears when a president is pointed out to them strolling along the streets unaccompanied by guards or outriders.[54]

Even after the nation was traumatized by the assassination of William McKinley in 1901, legislators balked at providing a presidential protective guard. Florida Democratic senator Stephen Mallory said a presidential guard was "antagonistic to our traditions" and such protection would appear to be a "Praetorian Guard similar to the monarchs of the continent of Europe." The president, Mallory said, "should not be surrounded with all the pomp and ceremony of an autocrat."[55]

CHAPTER 2

—————

The First Attack on an American President

Damn him, he does not know his enemy; I will put a pistol . . . erect a gallows. . . .
Damn General Jackson!
—Would-be Jackson assassin, Richard Lawrence

Andrew Jackson, who succeeded John Quincy Adams in 1827, was swept
into office on his reputation as a military commander and by a hero's role
in the War of 1812. He is known for ushering in a new age in American
history. His time in office and beyond was called "the Age of Jackson"
and noted in terms of the passing of political power from established
elites to ordinary voters organized into political parties.

With Jackson's election in 1828 came the birth of populism and the
emergence of formal political parties. The 1820s was a time when states
began opening the elections up to all (white male) citizens and he was
the first president to style himself as a "man of the people." In effect,
Jackson demonstrated that ordinary people could govern themselves.

It was also the beginning of a long period, running through most of
the nineteenth century, in which average people were very interested in
politics. American citizens were wildly patriotic, but not particularly rever-
ent about their elected officials. New Englanders, for example, considered
Jackson to be a somewhat unlettered and brutish ignoramus, and said so.

Throughout his life, Jackson was criticized for his unbending opinions
and autocratic manner. But he had a number of noted successes. At

the beginning of his second term in office he held the Union together when no one else could. He forced South Carolina to remain in the Union by threatening to send an army of two hundred thousand to the state. He will also be remembered for saving the Union by winning the Battle of New Orleans in 1815. If the British had succeeded in the War of 1812 they would have marched up the Mississippi valley, met up with the British in Canada, and given away the land west of the Mississippi to either Spain or the Indian tribes.

In 1833 Jackson was successful in destroying the Second Bank's federal charter. It was a private bank that held the government's money, and its charter was due to be renewed in 1836. Jackson believed the bank concentrated the financial strength of America into a single institution, making the rich richer, threatening America's sovereignty by its potential to be controlled by foreign interests, and favoring the northeastern states over those in the South and West.

Jackson has been criticized by historians because he signed the Indian Removal Act, which eventually led to the Trail of Tears when tribes were expelled from Georgia and force-marched to land west of the Mississippi. However, although Jackson was fully responsible for the policy of Indian removal, it should be remembered that it was also the policy of the United States. At the time, there was a strong belief that the conflict between Native Americans and white settlers could not be settled. It was also politically impossible for powerful tribes such as the Cherokees to remain in Georgia. Additionally, Jackson believed that the policy benefitted the Native peoples by guaranteeing their continued existence.

————

Jackson was the son of Irish immigrants, Andrew and Elizabeth Jackson, and was born in the backwoods of the Carolinas—what was then considered the frontier of America. His father died shortly before Andrew's birth and his mother tried to raise him to be educated. Jackson resisted, and without a father figure, he became a wild young boy who liked to bully his peers.

The Revolutionary War affected the teenage Jackson in a personal way, leaving him forever bitter toward the British. When the war came to his area, his oldest brother, Hugh, enlisted and was killed during a battle.

Jackson worked as a courier for the commander of the local patriot regiment and was taken captive by British troops along with his other brother, Robert. After a small engagement between opposing forces, Jackson and his remaining brother hid in the house of their relative, Thomas Crawford. After British dragoons discovered the two, they began to destroy the house. The British commander ordered Andrew to clean the mud from the soldiers' boots. Jackson refused: "Sir, I am a prisoner of war and claim to be treated as such," he replied. Angered at Jackson's impudence, the soldier raised his sword and swung it at Jackson's head. The boy managed to deflect part of the blow with his left hand, but he received a serious gash on that hand and another on his head—two scars he would bear for the rest of his life. When Robert also refused to clean the boots, he was hit with the broadside of an officer's sword.

The British took Andrew and Robert Jackson and twenty other prisoners from the battle to Camden. There the British placed all of them into a small prisoner camp with 250 other men, with no medicine, no beds, and only a small amount of bread for food. Both boys became infected with smallpox and would have likely died had their mother, Elizabeth, not helped to arrange a prisoner transfer—the patriots turned over thirteen redcoats and the British freed seven prisoners, including the two Jacksons. Andrew walked the forty miles back home, while his mother and his dying brother rode beside him. Robert died two days after returning home, and it was several weeks before Andrew regained enough of his health to leave his bed.[1]

His mother, Jackson's only remaining relative, died of cholera while helping soldiers in Charleston. Thus, when the war ended, it left Jackson orphaned and alone.

Jackson, like Lincoln, was a self-taught frontier lawyer. He was taken in by his uncles after his mother died and studied law while still in his teens, passing the bar at age twenty. Jackson became engaged in a wild lifestyle of betting, horseracing, and partying before eventually deciding his future lay in the law in the new western territory of Tennessee. He succeeded in being appointed prosecutor in the frontier western district of North Carolina and set out with a group of lawyer friends to bring law to the frontier. On the way, the group narrowly escaped massacre when, as the men slept in a clearing, Jackson noted the number of owl hoots around them—and recognized the hoots as American Indian signals. He and his friends broke camp and traveled through the night. Unfortunately, a group of hunters found Jackson's abandoned campsite and stayed for the night. By morning, all but one hunter had been killed.[2]

This attack was not the only brush with death on the journey west. In 1795 Jackson's party arrived in Jonesborough. In its first court session, Jackson argued with another lawyer, Waightstill Avery, and challenged him to a duel—Jackson's first of many such encounters. Just after sundown, Jackson met Avery outside of town. Both men fired and missed, but Jackson's honor had been restored. He shook hands with Avery and left.[3]

Jackson and his friends left Jonesborough in October 1788 and embarked for the small frontier settlement of Nashville. The town was hazardous. Lewis Robards, whose father-in-law had founded Nashville, took Jackson in to help protect the house from attacks by local tribes.

Jackson served in Congress at a young age. He was Tennessee's first representative in the House, taking office in 1796. He quit after nine months to become a senator, but quit that job after seven months and returned to Tennessee. Jackson became wealthy in 1804 after he bought a plantation in Tennessee called the Hermitage. He already owned nine slaves, but when he left Tennessee to become president, the plantation had more than one hundred slaves.

Jackson was also a self-taught military leader, becoming involved in Tennessee's state militia. He won an 1802 election as the militia's leader, replacing another Revolutionary War figure, John Sevier.

When Jackson took part in the War of 1812, he led a force of militia against the Creek tribe, who had massacred more than four hundred settlers at a fort in Alabama (then part of the Mississippi territory). The Shawnee chief, Tecumseh, encouraged the Red Stick Creek tribe of northern Alabama and Georgia to attack white settlements.

Jackson set off to exact vengeance, and his journey through tribal country left almost nothing standing. He fought the Red Stick group at the Battle of Horseshoe Bend in 1814, killing more than seven hundred. As a result Jackson was offered an official position as major general of the U.S. Army, commanding the Seventh District—Tennessee, Louisiana, and the Mississippi territory. Supported by the government, Jackson demanded twenty-three million acres of land from the Native peoples.

The Creek were forced to acquiesce to Jackson's demands and an agree-ment, the Treaty of Fort Jackson, was signed on August 10, 1814.

Following the treaty, Jackson was called upon to defend New Orleans from the British. On December 2, 1814, Jackson's exhausted army marched into the city and was welcomed by the city's residents. He was a strict officer but was popular with his troops. They said he was "tough as old hickory" wood on the battlefield, and he acquired the nickname of "Old Hickory." However, the citizens became angry when Jackson imposed martial law. Shrugging their complaints off, Jackson confronted sixteen hundred British troops under the command of Gen. John Keane, who marched on the city.

On New Year's Day of 1815, a massive bombardment shook the besieged city but the American defenses held and they inflicted double their own casualties on the British. A week later, on January 8, the battle ended. The British had been defeated, losing over two thousand men, while the Amer-icans had lost only thirteen. It was the biggest, most complete victory in the history of American warfare. By January 19, 1815, the British were gone.

Two years later, in December 1817, Jackson was ordered by President James Monroe to lead a campaign in Georgia against the Seminole and Creek tribes and also to prevent Florida, then owned by Spain, from becoming a refuge for runaway slaves. Critics later alleged that Jackson exceeded orders in his Florida campaign and that it caused an interna-tional incident. However, after Jackson caused the tribes to cease their attacks on behalf of Spain and Britain, as well as forcing Spain to cede Florida to the United States, he was made military governor of Florida.

———

Jackson was ill-tempered, a fierce hater, unbending, dictatorial, and vindictive. During his election campaigns citizens called him a bully and adulterer. He was also was one of the sickliest of American presidents. He had suffered from smallpox during the War of Independence and in the Creek Campaign of 1813 he had to survive on acorns. He also suffered from dysentery. His health problems were not improved by his self-medication, which compounded his ailments. During his first year as president, Jackson suffered from chronic infections that affected his bronchial system and gave him severe headaches and swelling in his legs.

Jackson was extremely sensitive about his honor, engaging in numerous duels in which he used thirty-seven pistols. Consequently, his health was severely affected by the wounds he received from dueling.

During one confrontation with Col. Waightstill Avery, who was acting as opposing counsel during a court case, Jackson had taken exception to words Avery used during the trial and challenged him to a duel. Both men walked away unhurt, but it was thought they had deliberately missed each other.

One of the most famous he fought was the duel in May 1806 against twenty-six-year-old Charles Dickinson, a lawyer and excellent shot. Dickinson had been angry with Jackson over a horse race and the payment of a forfeit fee to Jackson. During the subsequent argument Dickinson insulted Jackson's wife, Rachel.

Rachel Robards had been waiting for her divorce when she met Andrew Jackson at her mother's boarding house. Her first husband had left her for the wilderness, unannounced, and when the statutory time passed with no word, the courts duly declared him dead and Rachel was free to remarry. However, not long after she and Jackson married, the first husband returned to Nashville. Numerous political opponents regularly made disparaging remarks to him and others about Rachel, which had a deleterious effect on Jackson's health. Jackson eventually organized another marriage ceremony when the divorce was again finalized.[4]

Dickinson, who had killed twenty-six men dueling, had written a statement for a Nashville newspaper following the argument criticizing Jackson. Dickinson had called Jackson a "worthless scoundrel . . . a poltroon and a coward."[5]

Jackson responded by writing a formal letter to Dickinson: "Your conduct and expressions relative to me of late," Jackson wrote, "have been of such a nature and so insulting, that it requires and shall have my notice." Dickinson's insults, Jackson wrote, "must be noticed and treated with the respect due to a gentleman. . . . I hope . . . that your courage will be an ample security to me that I will obtain speedily that satisfaction due me for insults offered."[6]

The duel took place on the banks of the Red River at Harrison Mills, Kentucky, as dueling had been outlawed in Tennessee. Jackson, who was a bad marksman, had been advised by his friend Thomas Overton that if he waited to take the second shot he would stand a better chance. General Overton was Jackson's second; Dickinson's, a Dr. Cattlet. A pair of identical pistols owned by Jackson was used. The guns, with seven-inch barrels, were loaded with deadly one-ounce .70-caliber lead bullets.

A distance of twenty-four feet was paced off. The principals took their positions. Dickinson wore a short coat of blue with gray trousers and Jackson wore a bulky dark-blue overcoat and trousers to match. Jackson liked to wear his coats well padded and loose, to hide his extremely narrow shoulders, which emphasized his lean, long body.

Dickinson fired first and hit Jackson in his chest; the bullet lodged only an inch away from his heart. He also suffered two broken ribs and a punctured lung. However, Jackson was still standing as Dickinson asked, "My God have I missed him?"[7]

As the rules of dueling required, Dickinson had to remain in place as Jackson pulled the trigger of his pistol but the hammer stuck. As per the rules, Jackson was allowed a second shot. He raised his pistol, fired, and shot Dickinson, the bullet tearing through his intestines. Dickinson died later that night from his wounds. Jackson had never before killed anyone in a duel, even though he had participated in over one hundred.

Jackson made light of his own wound. He did not want Dickinson's friends to know he was badly hurt. Refusing help, he mounted his horse and, incredibly, rode to Nashville, a distance of forty miles.

Back home, Jackson's doctors told him the wound was serious. Jackson's loose overcoat had deceived the sharpshooter's calculation but, even so, the bullet had shattered the chest wall, breaking two ribs and embedding itself deep in the left lung and probably carrying with it pieces of cloth and fragments of bone.

The heavy lead bullet that remained in Jackson's chest was never removed and created a wound that would never heal. No surgeon of that time dared to remove the ball from its dangerous position near the heart. It resulted in abscesses forming around the bullet causing fever and coughing of blood.[8] After the fatal duel, Jackson was destined to be a semi-invalid for the rest of his life, kept alive only because of his stubborn nature and indomitable will.

On September 4, 1813, Jackson also fought a knife-and-gun battle with Thomas and Jesse Benton, two brothers who lived in downtown

Nashville. The feud began when Jackson had acted as a second when Jesse Benton dueled with William Carroll, who later became governor of Tennessee. Both Carroll and Benton survived the duel but Thomas Benton blamed Jackson for the affair. Benton made threats to kill Jackson who responded by in turn threatening Benton.

The Benton brothers, both of them armed with pistols, arrived in Nashville and registered at the City Hotel, avoiding the Nashville Inn, as the brothers knew Andrew Jackson and his friends always stayed there. Jackson had arrived at the Nashville Inn at around the same time the Bentons arrived in town. News soon spread of what citizens thought would be a violent confrontation. As Jackson and one of his friends, both armed, walked from the inn to the post office they passed near the City Hotel. On their return they saw the Bentons outside the hotel's tavern. Jackson raised his whip to Thomas Benton, shouting, "Now, defend yourself you damned rascal!"

Before Benton could draw his pistol, Jackson pointed his gun. Jesse Benton, however, was behind Jackson and fired his pistol, hitting him in the side. Jackson began firing his weapon, which made a powder burn on Thomas's coat. He was bent forward as Jesse tried to shoot again, but a bystander, James Sitler, shielded Jackson. Jackson's friend John Coffee intervened in the battle but missed Thomas, whose guns were empty. Coffee clubbed him with the handle as Benton fell backward down a flight of stairs. Another friend of Jackson's, Stockley Hays, attacked Jesse with a sword cane, but the blade broke on a button. When Jesse Benton tried to shoot Hays, his gun misfired. The fight ended when the participants backed off after seeing Jackson's prostate form on the ground. He had come close to death, losing a lot of blood, and his left shoulder had been shattered by a slug. Another slug had been embedded against the upper bone of his left arm. Both had been fired by Jesse Benton.

Doctors who rushed to the scene wanted to amputate Jackson's arm but he refused. "I'll keep my arm," he said.[9] Doctors refused to remove the bullet as the earlier bullet was too near the heart. After Jackson became president, he asked a visiting doctor from Philadelphia to remove the bullet in his arm. When the doctor cut his arm open, the bullet dropped to the floor. As Thomas Benton later said, after he became a United

States senator, and also a friend of Jackson's, "I had a fight with Jackson. A fellow was hardly in the fashion then who hadn't."[10]

As the years passed, Jackson did not abandon his penchant for dueling. In 1817, when Jackson was still an active general, he challenged Gen. Winfield Scott to a duel. Jackson had insulted the general by calling him "a hectoring bully" and one of the "intermeddling pimps and spies of the War Department." Scott had accused Jackson of an act of mutiny. Scott declined the challenge on religious grounds, adding that he preferred to risk his life to a better purpose "in the next war."[11]

———————

Following his inauguration ceremonies in March 1827, Jackson invited everyone to celebrate at the White House. Jackson supporters trampled the carpets, sprayed tobacco juice over the floors, climbed chairs, and were raucous and unruly. The president was nearly crushed to death by his supporters and he was forced to escape to another abode.

During the Jackson years, the president kept public hours at the White House, where he would make himself available for petitions and interviews. Jackson said, "No matter how dirty, how drunk, or how muddy, a citizen has a right to see his president."[12]

Public access to the White House had advantages and disadvantages. The steady stream of visitors passing through the White House allowed presidents to campaign without leaving home, but it was a time-consuming job, and as the front door was frequently unlocked by the steward in the morning and not locked again until sundown, all kinds of people entered the mansion.

Visitors to the White House who wished to see Jackson would go to the porter's lodge and sign the visitor's register. The steward would take the visitor's name and give it to a servant, who would take it to the president or his private secretary and nephew, Andrew Donelson. If the person was approved, he or she would be taken up the stairs and announced. If the visitor was well known to Jackson, that person might be taken immediately to see him.[13] Some visitors arrived at the White House without an appointment. The doorkeeper would usually take the visitor's card upstairs to the president. Visits by ordinary citizens were usually brief, but sometimes took up a whole morning of the president's time—office seekers, in particular.

Jackson traveled with his private secretary and his friend Ralph Earl as well as various members of his cabinet. When the president toured New England in 1833 newspapers noted that the president "travels unarmed and unattended, but by his household, by day or night, through a land where every house he sees is his home, and every man he meets is already enrolled in his life guard."[14] However, during the trip, his horse-drawn carriage had just crossed a bridge connecting New York's Battery and Castle Garden, when it collapsed. Jackson was unhurt as he was at the front of the procession.[15]

As with presidents before him, Jackson was also the subject of unconfirmed rumors of conspiracies to remove him from office. One rumor circulated in Washington that a force of five thousand soldiers was forming in Baltimore to overthrow Jackson. The president responded in his characteristic way. He threatened to hang all five thousand and the threat subsided.[16]

Jackson reported he had received over five hundred letters threatening to kill him over the course of his two terms. As soon as he received the letters, he endorsed them and sent them to the *Washington Globe* for publication. One man had written, in February 1834, "Damn your old soul, remove them deposites [*sic*] again and recharter the bank, or you will certainly be shot in less than two weeks and that by myself."[17]

It was not until 2012, however, that historians discovered that Jackson had been threatened by Junius Brutus Booth, the father of Lincoln's assassin.

Junius Booth was a British-born Shakespearian actor during the antebellum period. His three sons followed in his footsteps as actors, including John Wilkes Booth, who would later become notorious as Abraham Lincoln's assassin. He was an alcoholic given to making rash threats and irrational statements while in a drunken state. In 1835 he sent Jackson a threatening letter, which for years had been considered to be a forgery, beginning with the words, "You damn'd old Scoundrel." Booth promised to kill Jackson if the president did not pardon two prisoners, named De Ruiz and De Soto, who had been sentenced to death for piracy. He threatened that if Jackson did not pardon the pirates, "I will cut your throat whilst you are sleeping." He also threatened to have Jackson "burnt at the stake."[18]

————

Andrew Jackson was the first president to be physically assaulted. During the first week of May 1833, Jackson, accompanied by members of his cabinet, left Washington by steamboat for Fredericksburg, Virginia. Jackson was to lay the cornerstone of a monument to George Washington's mother, Mary.

When the steamboat *Sidney* returned and stopped at Alexandria to take on a military company, it was boarded by Lt. Robert Beverly Randolph, a navy veteran of twenty-five years who worked as a purser.

In 1828, when he was serving on board the frigate *Constitution*, Randolph was appointed acting purser by Captain Patterson, replacing John B. Timberlake, who committed suicide when he was drunk. Randolph complained he was responsible for stores that were not actually on hand and it led to accusations against him. After some years, he was investigated by a court of inquiry, which exonerated him from an intentional use of public property but not from the default. The court reported him to be careless or neglectful, though not dishonorable, and that he was "an efficient officer." Although cleared of fraud, the court found him $4,303 in default and censured him for bad bookkeeping. The case was then turned over to the president, who, as commander in chief, had the final say on the punishment. Jackson dismissed Randolph from the navy in spite of the efforts of "influential friends" on his behalf.[19]

Subsequently, Randolph became "aggrieved" at the "wrongs" he had received at the hands of the president and insisted he had been dismissed without just cause.

Despite severe wounds in his side—the result of his duel with Charles Dickinson—Jackson decided to receive visitors during his trip to Fredericksburg. Randolph walked to Jackson's cabin and found the president seated between the dinner table and the berths, reading a newspaper, his pipe clenched in his teeth. As Randolph approached, Jackson excused himself for not standing because of the pain in his side. Randolph took off his glove as Jackson reached out to shake his visitor's hand. Instead of shaking hands, however, Randolph "thrust his hand violently into the president's face," intending to pull Jackson's nose.

The captain of the boat instantly grappled with Randolph, resulting in a broken table. Other passengers came to Jackson's aid, one of them striking out at Randolph with an umbrella. Randolph's friends beckoned to him to leave the boat before the passengers could discover what had happened. When blood was spotted on the president's face, Jackson insisted he was not injured, although he complained that his side pained him more than it did.

"Had I known," Jackson later said, "that it was Randolph who stood before me I should have been prepared for him, and I could have defended myself. No villain has ever escaped me before and he would not, had it not been for my confined situation."[20]

Jackson was angry with his assailant, and one of the passengers offered to kill Randolph. Jackson insisted, "No, sir, I cannot do that. I want no man to stand between me and my assailants and none to take revenge on my account. Had I been prepared for this cowardly villain's approach, I can assure you all that he would never have the temerity to undertake such a thing again."[21]

Jackson believed he had been publicly insulted, and in an article for a newspaper wrote that the assault was "dastardly and cowardly" and was part of a political conspiracy to harm him.[22] Jackson also believed that Randolph's assault would "compel us . . . to go armed, for our personal defense." It could lead, Jackson said, "to what I would sincerely regret, and which never should happen while I am in office, a military guard around the president."[23]

In Virginia, dinners were held by Jackson's political opponents in honor of Randolph, and newspapers split on the issue of whether or not Randolph had gotten away with his assault on the president. Federal authorities were powerless to act, and Virginia refused to do so. Jackson vented his anger at the "disgrace" that Virginia had brought upon itself for failing to act against his assailant. There was a belated effort to bring Randolph to justice five years after the attack took place, but by that time Jackson was no longer willing to press the case against him.

The attack generated little serious effort to change the law against attacking or even assassinating a president. Randolph's assault was instead seen as an aberration that had no direct bearing on the president's security.

————

The first public attempt on a president's life occurred in 1835 when Richard Lawrence, an English immigrant, attacked Jackson on the steps of the Capitol Building. He accosted Jackson with two pistols, both loaded. Neither bullet emerged. The odds were phenomenal that both weapons would misfire.

Lawrence had immigrated to America from England with his parents when he was twelve years old and the family eventually settled in Washington DC. As a young man he made his living as a house painter in Washington, although his true wish was to be a landscape artist.

Lawrence's parents noticed a change in their son's personality around two and a half years before he attempted to shoot President Jackson. He began to utter threats of violence during arguments and would frequently talk to himself and laugh inappropriately. His work suffered and he no longer had any interest in his career. Noticing his strange behavior, his colleagues were afraid to work with him.

Lawrence would also indulge in fantasies. He told people he was the rightful king of England and imagined himself to be King Richard III. Part of his duties, he believed, was to rule over not only England but also the "American colonies." Local children began to call him "King Dick." At other times he would say he was only the heir to the throne and that he owned two great estates in his mother country. He thought that his employment as a painter was beneath his station in life.

In November 1832 and the spring of 1833, Lawrence set out on trips to England, intending to claim his "inheritance," but on both occasions he returned home complaining that England's weather was "too cold" or that the government had conspired against him.

Lawrence did not return to his employment but instead moved in with his sister and her husband, informing them he did not have to work because he would one day become very wealthy. However, he believed that the president's opposition to the Second Bank had denied him the ability to receive a dispensation owed to him by Congress for his various imaginary estates.

Lawrence visited the Capitol on numerous occasions, apparently to check on the progress the government was making to reimburse him. He was noticed by many congressional workers. According to Lawrence, he once approached Vice President Martin Van Buren in the Capitol rotunda and threatened that if he did not receive his money both the vice president and president would "fall."[24]

Despite Lawrence's insistence that he was about to become a wealthy man and did not have to work, he sought intermittent employment as a painter from time to time but always quit when his employers refused to pay him a higher wage than his fellow workers.

Lawrence's sister and her husband soon tired of their unstable relative and his bizarre fantasies. On one occasion Lawrence even accused his sister's maid of laughing at him and threatened to shoot her. He also attempted to bludgeon his sister with a four-pound weight during an argument. The husband informed the authorities and Lawrence was jailed. However, he was soon released after a grand jury refused to indict him, claiming he was not mentally responsible for his actions.

Following his release from jail, Lawrence lodged at a boarding house in the capital. When he consulted a doctor about a minor ailment, the physician came to the conclusion that his patient was "insane."[25] When it came time to pay his rent, Lawrence insisted he would settle his debts as soon as he received the millions of dollars purportedly owed him by the government. During one argument, he threatened to "put a ball" through his landlord's head.[26]

Lawrence continued to seethe with anger and resentment and began to believe that if Martin Van Buren became president on the death of Andrew Jackson, he would receive his "entitlement." In January 1835, Lawrence visited the White House hoping for an interview with the president. He was armed with two pistols. The doorkeeper told him that Jackson would not see him that day but if he returned another time he might be lucky. Lawrence later told authorities that if he had spoken to the president that day and had been refused his money, he would have shot him.

On January 23, Lawrence went to the White House a second time and was taken to see the president. When Lawrence entered Jackson's office, he found the president conversing with a Pennsylvania congressman, Joel

Barlow Sutherland. As Jackson turned to address his visitor, Lawrence requested a check for $1,000 so he could travel to England. Jackson told him he was too busy and he should see him another time. Lawrence left without protest.[27]

Lawrence returned to the White House once more, on the afternoon of January 29, again armed with two pistols. However, after standing at the Pennsylvania Avenue gate, staring at the mansion, he left. But he knew that President Jackson would be attending the funeral the next day at the Capitol for a South Carolina congressman, Warren R. Davis.

The morning of January 30, 1835, was gloomy and damp. Before Lawrence set off for the Capitol he was observed sitting on a chest in his paint shop, holding a book and laughing loudly. Suddenly, he stood up and declared, "I'll be damned if I don't do it."[28]

The two pistols Lawrence carried with him were already loaded. They were powerful enough to put lead balls through inch-thick planks of wood from a distance of seven and a half yards.

Lawrence was waiting in the rotunda of the Capitol when Jackson arrived, but, not wishing to interfere with the funeral, he bided his time. During the service he watched Jackson through a window of Statuary Hall, a semicircular room situated south of the rotunda and separated from it by a short passageway.

As the service was coming to a close, Lawrence crossed the rotunda and hid behind a column out on the East Portico. The East Portico is the main entrance to the Capitol. As the procession filed out, Jackson was accompanied by his Treasury secretary, Levi Woodbury. Jackson leaned on his friend's right arm, walking some distance behind the coffin as the procession went through the door leading out to the East Portico.

Meanwhile, Lawrence drew his pistols from his suit pockets and cocked them before concealing them beneath his overcoat. As Jackson stepped out on to the portico, Lawrence threw his coat to one side and leapt forward, pointing his two percussion-cap pistols at Jackson.

Lawrence fired the first pistol, but the cap, even though it detonated, failed to ignite the powder. Jackson lunged at his would-be assassin with his cane and "ejaculated an emphatic expression," "frightening" his attacker. Years earlier Jackson had described how he typically used a cane to defend himself. He said that a cane swung at head level was easy to deflect and therefore it should be "held like a spear" and assailants should be "punched in the stomach." Jackson went on to describe how he had used the tactic when he fought a man in Tennessee: "Sir, it doubled him up," Jackson said. "He fell at my feet, and I stamped on him."[29]

This time, after Jackson raised his cane to his attacker, Lawrence dropped the pistol. However, the would-be assassin quickly passed the second pistol to his right hand, aimed, and pulled the trigger. The muzzle was said to be touching Jackson's breast. However, once again his pistol misfired. Navy Lt. Thomas R. Gedney pinioned Lawrence and wrestled him to the ground as Woodbury grabbed his collar. Gedney threw him in a carriage and took him to jail. Davy Crockett, who was then a congressman and who had helped to subdue the would-be assassin, said Lawrence was the "damndest villain in the world."[30]

The crowd began to shout, "Kill him. Kill the assassin. Kill him." According to the *Fayetteville Observer*, "[The] excitement that immediately ensued was terrific; the mass in attendance swayed to and fro like waves of the ocean; and hundreds, not knowing what was the actual cause of the alarm, attempted to make a precipitate retreat, to avoid being trampled on."[31]

Unfortunately, when Mississippi senator George Poindexter left the scene of the assassination attempt "precipitously," it led to accusations he had hired Lawrence to carry out the act. Even Andrew Jackson suspected that the senator was somehow involved in the attempt on his life. Despite witnesses coming forward to link Lawrence with Poindexter, the accusations remained unproven and a senate enquiry exonerated the senator.[32]

Jackson was enraged at the attempt on his life. As onlookers saw that the moment of danger had passed and Lawrence had been taken away, Jackson was ushered into his carriage and taken to the White House. By the time he arrived at the Executive Mansion, he had calmed down. In fact, he acted as if nothing had happened at all, and when Vice President Martin Van Buren arrived at the mansion from the scene, he was surprised that the president was calmly conversing with Maj. Gen. Winfield Scott about another matter.

Jackson later commented that he believed Lawrence was put up to it and that the attempted assassination was a conspiracy organized by the Whig Party to stop his plan to destroy the Bank of the United States.[33]

Washington police were asked to test-fire the pistols used by Jackson's would-be assassin. They worked perfectly and were able to drive bullets through an inch-thick wood plank at thirty feet. A former nemesis, Sen. Thomas Hart Benton, said the two pistols were "so well loaded, so coolly handled, and which afterward fired with such readiness, force and precision—missing fire, each in its turn, when leveled eight feet at the President's heart . . . made a deep impression upon the public feeling, and irresistibly carried many minds to the belief in a superintending Providence."[34] Another expert examined the pistols and found them loaded with the "powder of the best quality and the balls rammed tight, but the percussion caps exploded without igniting the powder."[35] The odds against the misfiring of both pistols were estimated to be 1 in 125,000.

During his interrogation by Washington police, Lawrence provided contradictory explanations of why he had attempted to assassinate the president. His reasons ranged from avenging his father's death at the hands of Jackson to the notion that the "tyrant Jackson" had impeded his accession to the English throne.

Lawrence was tried for the attempted assassination in April 1835. During his trial he dressed the part of royalty, sporting a shooting jacket, brown pantaloons, and a black cravat. More than once he interrupted the proceedings to remind the jurors that he was not subject to the jurisdiction of the court. He was indignant that he should be tried by "commoners." "It is for me, gentlemen," he said, "to pass judgment on you and not you upon me."[36]

The case was prosecuted by Francis Scott Key for the District of Columbia. During his trial, psychiatric testimony described Lawrence as having a history of "grandiose, referential, and paranoid delusions." Today Lawrence would undoubtedly be described as a paranoid schizophrenic. It was also revealed that Lawrence's father had been hospitalized for mental problems and an aunt had died insane.[37]

Alternately laughing, crying, and cursing, Lawrence pleaded not guilty by reason of insanity. The jury took just five minutes to agree with him and he spent the rest of his life in jails and hospitals. In 1855 he was one of the first patients admitted to St. Elizabeth's Hospital in Washington DC, where he died on June 13, 1861.[38]

According to Harvard professor Alan M. Dershowitz, "had [Lawrence] been convicted of the crime for which he was charged, he might have lived the last twenty years of his life at liberty—and at risk of trying to kill again."[39]

On April 21, 1835, following the trial, the Washington DC newspaper the *Intelligencer* reported, "It is a notorious fact that this city, being the seat of government, is liable to be visited by more than its proportion of insane persons."[40]

The attack on Andrew Jackson did not inspire any action by Congress to provide protection for the chief executive, however, and Jackson still made himself available to anyone who walked into the White House. The lack of security remained unchanged.

Incredibly, given the clear risks that had been publicized by the Lawrence attack, a thief entered the White House on April 17, 1835, and walked into Jackson's bedroom, where the president was sleeping. The noise awoke the president, who demanded to know who was there and what he wanted. The intruder said he had lost his way and was simply trying to get out of the mansion. Other members of the household were awakened and thought another assassination attempt was in progress. However, after the intruder was seized, it was discovered he was unarmed and that his likely motive was theft, not murder. The thief was locked in the stables until he could be turned over to a magistrate the next morning. However, during the night he escaped through an open window, which was thought to be too high for anyone to reach from the ground.[41]

Jackson's family was shocked by the incident. Jackson's nephew, Andrew Donelson, expressed hope that his uncle would in future "never forget to lock his door when he retires to bed. After the attempts which have been made on his life he should not neglect such precautions as will never permit another to escape immediate and exemplary punishment."[42]

CHAPTER 3

The Antebellum Presidents

I would object on general principles that it is antagonistic to our traditions, to our habits of thought, and to our customs that the President should surround himself with a body of janissaries or a sort of Praetorian Guard, and never go anywhere unless he is accompanied by men in uniform and men with sabers as is done by the monarchs of the continent of Europe.

—Sen. Stephen Mallory, U.S. Senate 1850–61

From the time of George Washington to the presidency of Andrew Jackson, America had been undergoing vast changes. The nation's population had more than doubled in size and hundreds of thousands of Americans had emigrated westward. Cities flourished as new European immigrants arrived. Although this influx of people created jobs and economic prosperity, there were also negative effects. Poverty was increasing, which led to an increase in crime, violence, and rioting in American cities. Along with the spread of crime and the growth in the population came increased threats against American presidents.

There was also the developing fear that disputes and problems between the North and the South would inevitably lead to a war between the states, creating security problems for American leaders.

Southern states first began discussing secession in response to the Nullification Crisis during the Jackson administration in the early 1830s. While it would take almost thirty years before South Carolina became the first state to secede, the antebellum presidents attempted to satisfy all factions in the hope that they could pacify the Southern states enough to keep them from leaving the Union.

During the antebellum years, the tensions between the states led many individuals and politically motivated groups to solve their problems by resorting to presidential assassination.

MARTIN VAN BUREN

Andrew Jackson's immediate successor was fifty-four-year-old Martin Van Buren, the first president to have been born an American citizen. Van Buren is noted as the true founder of Jackson's Democratic Party, having organized it in the 1820s. He had not lived through the revolutionary struggle that created the nation and did not expect Americans would hold the same reverence for him as they had his predecessors.

In 1829, after Jackson won his first term in office, Van Buren became secretary of state, resigning the governorship of New York. In 1832 the first Democratic Party convention nominated Van Buren to be Jackson's running mate. In May 1835, Van Buren became Jackson's handpicked successor and won the Democratic nomination for the presidency by a unanimous vote of the convention. He reaffirmed Jackson's opposition to the Second Bank of the United States and pledged to uphold the rights of slave owners where slavery already existed. However, although he was an expert machine politician, those skills were never transferred to his presidential leadership. His presidency was also unfortunate to occur just as the United States was entering the 1837 depression. Another panic in 1839, caused by a glut in the cotton market, the backbone of the American economy, acted to make him an unpopular president. Van Buren was not up to the job; he did not have a plan for the economy and his opponents nicknamed him "Martin Van Ruin."

As vice president, Van Buren supported Jackson's controversial decision to withdraw funds from the Bank of the United States. With tensions over the issue rising, rumors spread that conspirators were meeting to plan an assassination attempt against the president. In response Van Buren took to carrying a loaded pistol when he presided over the Senate, one of his duties as vice president.[1]

Although Van Buren ushered in an elegant era in the White House, he liked things done in regal style, redecorating the mansion, restricting public access to many rooms, and using a grand carriage. It added fuel to the fire of his opponents who accused the new president of having the "trappings of monarchs" and "monarchical affectations." Van Buren was also accused of wanting to be an aristocrat, although these accusations were essentially untrue.

Van Buren had been a regular visitor to the White House when he was secretary of state and vice president and disapproved of the lack of guards. Although the doorkeeper was a permanent fixture, the guards were not. Monroe's successor, John Quincy Adams, had not hired guards, and Andrew Jackson did not favor them, either. Guards had been employed by James Monroe, although Presidents Adams and Jackson had not continued with the practice. The arrangements had been temporary, as it was generally thought the word "guard" suggested an armed White House, which was antithetical to the idea of an open democratic democracy.

The lessons of the Lawrence assassination attempt should have improved matters. However, as a contemporary noted, shortly after Van Buren took office, "there were neither guards without the gate or sentries within, nor a single servant or attendant in livery anywhere visible. . . . Everyone present acted as though he felt himself to be on a perfect footing of equality with every other person."[2]

But there were some slight improvements to the security of the Executive Mansion. A wooden "watch box" for a sentry was built on the south grounds, at the gate to the President's Garden. During Van Buren's administration the doorkeeper was the only federal employee within the White House. Two government-paid guards sharing around-the-clock patrol duties were also hired. It also became the custom for the doorkeeper to keep firearms in the room off the entrance hall.[3] When he hosted public receptions, the president stationed police officers at all the White House gates to "prevent the intrusion of any improper person."[4] Despite these measures, however, a drunk managed to enter the White House and spend the night on a sofa in the East Room.[5]

The White House guards were supported by the Washington police force that was always available if the situation required. In 1836, the year of Van Buren's election, the Washington police district constables numbered twelve officers and two clerks. The police force was small for a city of its size; in 1830, the total population of Washington was 39, 834. The night watch and foot patrols were rarely seen except in periods of slave unrest, such as during the Nat Turner Rebellion of 1831, and Washington politicians made demands for increases in night patrols and laws aimed to restrict the rights of blacks, free and enslaved, to meet or assemble.[6]

Van Buren's decision to hire guards led to criticism that he had abandoned the American principle of "equality." He replied to such criticisms by saying he was simply keeping "the *mobocracy* from intruding themselves at levees [parties]."[7]

Although Van Buren had restricted access to a number of rooms in the Executive Mansion, it remained open to just about every citizen. At times, friends, near enemies, and total strangers could be seated at the dining table with the president.[8]

However, the president's "public" receptions were not open to the general public. Although announcements were made in local papers that the president would be "home" on a certain date, only "certain elements of society" were welcome.[9] The president stationed police officers at every gate and doorway, not for his own protection but to keep undesirables out. This did not prevent citizens from turning up at the gates of the mansion to gawk. The crowds of "unsavory men and women" would harangue the social elite as they arrived at the White House in their elegant carriages. On occasion they would throw mud at the visitors.[10]

Van Buren eschewed a personal bodyguard, habitually walked to church alone, and rode his horse through the woods near the White House unaccompanied. One observer wrote, "The president walked into the church, unattended by a single servant, took his place in a pew in which others were sitting beside himself, and retired in the same manner as he came, without being noticed to any great degree than any other member of the congregation, and walking home alone, until joined by one or two personal friends, like any other private gentleman."[11]

WILLIAM HENRY HARRISON

Van Buren served one term as president and was heavily defeated for reelection by William Henry Harrison. The former general may have won election as he most resembled Andrew Jackson, but it was the parlous state of the economy that eventually persuaded voters. Harrison was considered by his opponents to be too old to be president and that he was really a "country bumpkin." To offset these criticisms he gave a long, learned speech on a cold Inauguration Day to dispel fears about his age. He caught a cold, which soon turned into pneumonia. He was the first president to die in office.

Harrison was never at any real risk of assassination as he was president for only thirty-one days.

JOHN TYLER

President Tyler was born into an aristocratic Virginia family. Initially a Democrat, his opposition to Andrew Jackson and Martin Van Buren led him to an alliance with the Whig Party. Tyler had been a state legislator, governor, U.S. representative, and U.S. senator before being elected vice president in 1840. When Charles Dickens visited the White House during Tyler's presidency, he described the chief executive as "mild and pleasant in appearance. His remarkable and unaffected, gentlemanly and agreeable manner . . . his whole character and demeanor . . . becomes his station singularly well."[12]

Following Harrison's death, a brief constitutional crisis had arisen over how the succession process was supposed to work, and Tyler was derisively called "His Ascendency" and "His Accidency." There were no clear guidelines for succession. Many thought he was simply a caretaker president who had to defer to Harrison's cabinet in the decision-making process. However, Tyler was his own man with his own agenda. He immediately moved into the White House, took the oath of office, and assumed full presidential powers. He also asserted his right to the presidency, kept Harrison's cabinet on, and told them to resign if they objected to his right to rule.

The "Tyler Precedent" not only ensured the orderly transfer of power in his time, but guaranteed that future "accidental" presidents could govern with authority. The precedent was set into law in 1967 when Congress ratified the Twenty-fifth Amendment to the Constitution, guaranteeing that "in every case of the removal of the President from office or of his death or resignation, the Vice President shall become President."

Historians generally agree that Tyler's presidency was a failure, and his weakness lay in his support for the philosophy that sought the extension and preservation of a slaveholding America.

When he first took office, the new president did not believe he was in any real danger and abandoned Van Buren's security measures. Charles Dickens, commenting on the lack of security wrote, "We entered a large hall and having twice or thrice rung a bell, which nobody answered, walked without further ceremony through the rooms on the ground floor, as diverse other gentlemen . . . were doing very leisurely. . . . We had not waited in this room many minutes before a black messenger appeared and conducted us into another of smaller dimensions where at a business-like table covered with papers sat the president himself. He looked somewhat worn and anxious, and well he might being at war with everybody."[13]

When he visited New York in the 1840s, Tyler proved his republican credentials by appearing without a bodyguard. When he gave his speech, he was introduced with the words, "No mercenary soldier protects [his] person . . . no hired voices cheer his presence."[14] Tyler responded by saying that "God forbid" he would ever have "hired vassals" attending him. He continued with his speech by telling his audience, "My bodyguard I desire to be the people, and none but the people. That is the bodyguard that a plain, republican president of the United States can alone desire to have."[15]

However, President Tyler soon had reason to fear that some of "the people" violently opposed him. Tyler had been forced out of the Whig Party and, for all practical purposes, became a member of the Democratic opposition. It made him a controversial figure. He received numerous insulting and threatening letters, and anti-Tyler signs were put up in the streets of Washington. Additionally, Tyler became more cautious after an increasing number of European assassinations.[16] In response, security measures at the White House were increased and they were the direct result of three incidents.

On a Sunday morning in 1841, as Tyler walked along the south side of the White House grounds, a drunken painter threw stones at him.

On August 16, 1842, Tyler stunned his fellow members of the Whig Party by using constitutional powers to veto a bill to revive the Second

Bank of the United States. He thought the bill was unconstitutional and infringed upon the rights of the states, particularly because of the federal government's power to override a state's objections to hosting a branch bank in its state.

On August 18, 1842, two drunken crowds descended on the White House. The first crowd threw stones and fired shots in the air, shouting "Down with the veto." A second crowd arrived at the house later with a scarecrow-like figure of Tyler that was hung and then set on fire. Similar protests were repeated around the country as news spread about the veto. Some even went so far as to disfigure the front of the White House with black paint. Only one sentry and a doorkeeper stood in the way of the mob.[17]

When shots were fired, Tyler, his family, and the White House staff feared for their lives.[18]

With tensions high, Tyler feared he would fall victim to bombs. One day an unmarked package arrived at the White House. It was discovered in the entrance to the building. White House staff believed it might have contained an "infernal machine," the term used in those days for a bomb. President Tyler and his staff looked at the package but were afraid to touch it. Tyler actually "trembled." Martin Renehan, a doorkeeper, placed the box on a table and as he raised a meat cleaver to open the box, Tyler, who was hiding behind a column, called out, "Martin, are you not afraid?" "No, sir," Renehan replied as he struck the wooden box. As the box fell open, Tyler and his staff saw a model of an iron stove.[19] Fearing his enemies would ridicule him, Tyler warned his staff not to say anything. "If you do," he said, "they'll have me caricatured."[20]

Tyler's response to these incidents was to ask Congress to establish "a police force for the protection of public and private property in the city of Washington" and partly to improve presidential security. Congress argued about how the police officers would be appointed. They feared the police force would become a formidable army if they were appointed by the president, a Praetorian Guard that would allow a president to impose his will in a monarchical way. Sen. John Crittenden of Kentucky objected to the fact that the bill gave the president the power to appoint these police. According to the record of the Senate debates: "It seemed to [Crittenden] that, by subjecting this matter to the control of the President of the United States, it might be metamorphosed into a political guard for the Executive. . . . [Crittenden] thought that it would not be entirely safe to organize such a corps. It was a little sort of standing guard, which might eventually become a formidable army. The seeds sown by this bill would soon germinate, and their full development might overshadow the liberties of the people."[21]

A compromise was enacted. On August 23, 1842, Congress passed an act "to establish an auxiliary watch for the protection of the public and private property in the City of Washington." The force, called the "auxiliary guard," consisted of a captain and fifteen men. Its official function was described as "the protection of public and private property against incendiaries, and . . . the enforcement of the police regulations of the city of Washington." The auxiliary guard was made subject to rules and regulations prescribed by a board consisting of the mayor of Washington DC, the corporation counsel of Washington DC, and the United States attorney for the District of Columbia, "with the approbation of the President of the United States," and was appointed by the mayor of Washington with the consent of the president. They were called "doorkeepers" rather than "guards" or "sentries" to avoid the accusation that it was a "royal bodyguard."[22] The force became the first White House security force and would later form the nucleus of the Washington Metropolitan Police.[23]

The guards were more than mere doorkeepers, however. Their duties were varied and were not specified by the act of Congress. They mingled with the crowds during presidential receptions, carried confidential messages, and met official and household guests at the stage line or train station. They also received all callers in the White House entrance hall, frequently announcing them to the president or his wife. They were also given the powers of investigation and arrest.[24]

Perhaps the closest John Tyler came to being killed during his one-term presidency was during a demonstration of a navy gun, the Peacemaker, on board the navy's newest steam frigate, the USS *Princeton*. According to U.S. Secretary of the Navy Thomas W. Gilmore, the new cannon would be "heard around the world."[25]

On Wednesday, February 28, 1844, the president and four hundred guests, who had been invited by Tyler's friend, Capt. Robert Stockton, boarded the vessel, which was moored in the Potomac River near Washington DC. The guest list included former first lady Dolly Madison and members of Tyler's cabinet.

The Peacemaker was developed by Stockton, who believed that the new weapon—which was made of wrought iron instead of the usual cast iron (considered too brittle for shots heavier than thirty-two pounds)—would demonstrate America's weapon superiority. The gun was purportedly able to fire 216-pound balls. However, it had undergone little testing.

The gun fired twice before guests moved below deck for refreshments and a toast to President Tyler and impromptu singing. However, Captain Stockton was persuaded to fire the gun once more, purportedly by Secretary of the Navy Thomas Gilmer, so he returned to the deck, accompanied by a number of guests. President Tyler was about to join them when his son-in-law, William Waller, began to sing a patriotic song about 1776. The president decided to hang back to listen. As Waller neared the end of the song, a loud explosion was heard. The breech of the gun had exploded and large fragments of metal flew out, killing six men—including Secretary of State Abel Upshur; Secretary Gilmer; and President Tyler's slave, Armistead—and injuring twenty others. Julia Gardiner, whom the widowed president was about to marry, was present on deck when her father, Col. David Gardiner, became one of the casualties.[26] Had Tyler's son-in-law not begun to sing his song, the president would likely have died because his intended place of honor on deck would have been next to the Peacemaker.

Armistead's funeral was held the next day. The funerals of five of the victims of the tragedy were held in Washington DC the following Saturday. Members of Congress boarded carriages at the Capitol and rode up Pennsylvania Avenue to the White House where the bodies had lain in state. A mile-long funeral procession formed behind a military escort as the five hearses, each drawn by a pair of black horses, left the White House. The procession was followed by the president's carriage. Thousands of spectators lined Washington's streets as the procession headed for Congressional Cemetery.

On the way back to the White House, as President Tyler's carriage passed the Capitol, the horses became startled and they began to race

THE ANTEBELLUM PRESIDENTS 47

down Pennsylvania Avenue. As the horses galloped through the market district at Seventh Street, spectators hurled themselves out of the way of the president's carriage. Tyler's son John desperately tried to control the team but he was unsuccessful. When the carriage reached the corner of Pennsylvania Avenue and Fourteenth Street, the site of today's Willard Hotel, an unidentified black man stepped out and stopped the horses, thus saving the president from injury or death.[27]

JAMES POLK

By the end of the 1840s, the president usually saw office seekers every day, and they were taking up an enormous amount of time. Tyler's successor, James Polk, had become "disgusted" with the "passion for office" and of the men who "were engaged in the patriotic business of serving themselves." Polk wrote, "My office was crowded this morning with visitors, most of them seeking military appointments. For the last week I have been greatly annoyed by this kind of importunity. The city is crowded with young men, many of them loafers without merit, seeking military appointments. . . . I am often exceedingly disgusted with the scenes which occur in my office, but keep my temper and endure the painful labor which is imposed upon me with patience. . . . I am almost ready at some times to conclude that all men are selfish, and that there is no reliance to be placed in any of the human race."[28]

James Polk, who was small in stature, usually went unnoticed when he entered a room to greet White House guests. His wife solved the problem by asking the Marine Band to play an old Scottish anthem, "Hail to the Chief."[29]

Although there is no recorded attempt to harm Polk, there were a number of security breaches when he was president. Sometimes a visitor to the president would disturb the privacy of the first family. Mrs. Polk's niece, Joanna Parker, was especially disturbed when she discovered a stranger coming out of the president's office and walking into a private room. "He pretended to miss his way in going from the president's office," Parker wrote, "and came down in the private part of the hall into the parlor. There is but little privacy here. The house belongs to the government and everyone feels at home and they sometimes stalk into our bedroom and say they are looking at the house."[30]

ZACHARY TAYLOR

Zachary Taylor was the Eisenhower of his time—a man without previous political experience who was swept into office on the strength of
his popularity as a war leader. He had a long military career capped by
his victory over General Santa Anna in the battle of Buena Vista during
the Mexican-American War.

Taylor did not hear of his nomination for president until a month
after the convention. Too many people had been writing him threatening letters, so he was refusing to receive any mail at his home in
Louisiana when his letter of notification was sent to him. It went to the
dead letter office. When his silence became alarming, party leaders
sent a second letter, and this time postage was paid by party officials to
ensure he received it.

While Polk tightly controlled visitors to the White House, Taylor kept
his upstairs office wide open and he was easily accessible to anyone who
wanted to walk in and greet him. Taylor was also accessible to visitors
in the evening. One visitor to the White House commented that the
president "mingles with the crowd . . . he has no personal attendants . . .
to stand between him and the people."[31] Taylor would also frequently
leave the Executive Mansion unaccompanied, walk to the local market,
and engage farmers in conversation.

Taylor often descended the stairs to the South Lawn of the White
House, mingling with visitors, who were usually a cross-section of Washington citizens, and listening to the Marine Band. Taylor and his staff
believed it was safe for the president to do so, as they trusted the guards
at the gate to make every effort to prevent "pickpockets, prostitutes,
and gamblers" from entering.

Taylor's public accessibility affected his health and almost killed him
during a rail journey he took in 1849. Rail journeys at the time were
onerous because before each stop on the route, influential townspeople
demanded they had the right to board the train and speak to the president. Accordingly, there were sometimes thirty or forty people vying for
his attention, trying to speak with him and shake hands. His trip was
expected to last a couple of months, but within two weeks the sixty-five-
year-old president became sick and exhausted and his aides persuaded
him to return to Washington.

Taylor also fell ill after attending a July 4, 1850, ceremony at which the cornerstone of the Washington Monument was laid. It was a hot day, and the president consumed large quantities of cold milk and iced cherries while he sat hatless in the sun for hours. After developing a bad stomach, he died five days later after having served only sixteen months as president.

Historians have argued over whether he died of deliberate poisoning of his food or because of his doctors' primitive attempts to treat his discomfort. The idea that Taylor was poisoned started with threatening letters to Taylor's successor, Millard Fillmore, which stated that the new president should be careful or he would meet the same fate as his predecessor, meaning President Taylor. If the allegations were true, it would have made Taylor, not Abraham Lincoln, the first president to be assassinated.

There has been speculation among historians that Taylor, being a foe of extending slavery, was poisoned by proslavery conspirators. However, there are problems with this theory. Taylor was in fact a slave-holding Southerner, although he did not oppose California entering the Union as a free state. Some historians have argued that Taylor had been poisoned by people who saw him as a threat to states' power, which eroded each time a free state joined the Union. But Taylor's successor pursued policies that were indistinguishable from those of the man he shared the party ticket with in 1848. Any conspirator seeking to rid the country of a president who was soft on the question of slavery would have known that in Congress, Millard Fillmore opposed the admission of Texas as a slave state. A further problem is that Congress, not the president, has the power to admit states to the Union.

The suspicions that Taylor had been poisoned arose in part because his symptoms at the time of his death resembled those of arsenic poisoning. Any tests, however, would be problematical as embalmers of the time sometimes used arsenic in their preparation of bodies.

In 1991 Taylor's body was exhumed for tests. A laboratory analysis appeared to lay the controversy to rest after it concluded that only miniscule levels of arsenic had been discovered and it could not have caused his illness, let alone his death. The conclusion of the forensic anthropologist who conducted the examination was that Taylor died of natural causes, perhaps from contaminated food he had eaten or possibly from the treatments, cathartics and laxatives, he received for gastroenteritis and acute diarrhea.

Political scientist Michael Parenti, however, questions this explanation for Taylor's death. He interviewed a number of people involved in the examination and studied reports by forensic pathologists. Parenti concluded that the procedure used to test for arsenic poisoning was fundamentally flawed. A 2010 review of the case stated, "There is no definitive proof that Taylor was assassinated, nor would it appear that there is definitive proof that he was not."[32]

MILLARD FILLMORE

The fifty-three-year-old Millard Fillmore was Zachary Taylor's vice president, and so became president in 1850 after Taylor's sudden death. He was considered to be a hands-off manager and apparently aimed to appease rather than manage. Although he personally opposed slavery, Fillmore signed the Compromise of 1850, which he felt would temporarily pacify both North and South. But the Fugitive Slave Act, a resolution promising federal support for capturing runaway slaves and allowing slaves to be hunted in antislavery states, infuriated Northern abolitionists, lost Fillmore any hope of reelection, and served only to delay the coming Civil War. The Whigs refused to nominate him.

As tensions mounted between North and South, Fillmore sensed personal danger. He became concerned that the White House guards were not efficiently carrying out their duties and became strict with rules. He told the guards that any visitor who did not "conduct himself properly" should be "removed forthwith." He also had a guardroom built at the "president's gate." Guards were armed with "four musketoons fixed with bayonets, each supplied with 20 rounds of ammunition."[33] Fillmore continued with the practice of meeting the public, although he kept the meetings short and businesslike. Like presidents before him, however, he was "deluged by office seekers."[34]

Fillmore was president for two years and 237 days, and, although he had to contend with the usual "crank visitors" to the White House, there are no recorded incidents of assassination plots or assassination attempts during his short presidency.

FRANKLIN PIERCE

Franklin Pierce, who succeeded Fillmore, was known as "Handsome Frank," but he was reviled by all. In 1852 the tenuous strands of the 1850 Compromise were barely holding the nation together. Antislavery groups were angered at the proslavery act. In Kansas Territory the anti- and pro-slavery forces were fighting it out, and Pierce failed to create solutions.

Known as a social man and a drinker, he managed to stay sober during his presidency. His problems with drink probably had their origins in the loss of his three children. Benny was killed, and two others died of disease. Adding to his problems was the death of his vice president, Rufus King, six weeks after the inauguration.

Even before he became president, Franklin Pierce came within a hairsbreadth of losing his life.

Tragedy struck the president-elect on January 6, 1853, two months before he took office. Pierce, along with his wife and his eleven-year-old son, boarded a train in Boston headed for his hometown of Concord, New Hampshire. When the train arrived near Andover, Massachusetts, their carriage slipped off the tracks, toppled down an embankment, and ended up in a field. Pierce and his wife were only slightly injured but when the president-elect climbed out of the carriage, he found his son had been killed. His head had been crushed.

The Pierces never recovered from the tragedy. During his inauguration the new president refused to use the Bible for his swearing-in ceremony, believing God had punished him for his sins. Instead he broke precedent by raising his right hand and affirming, rather than swearing, his loyalty to the U.S. Constitution.

Franklin Pierce believed that Millard Fillmore had instituted "stiff rules" for visitors to the White House, so he relaxed them. He was friendly and frequently asked the guards to show visitors around the "People's House." He was also liked by his staff. The doorkeeper, Charles Cone, said the president "does not keep his manners for the fine folk that come here, but he gives me the compliments of the morning as grandly as he does General Scott."[35] A coachman told White House correspondent Frank G. Carpenter that President Pierce spoke to him "just as freely as to the diplomats who came in their royal liveries."[36]

Pierce would meet White House visitors formally in the Blue Room, accompanied by the marshal of the District of Columbia, who heard each visitor's name and then whispered it to the president. Pierce would shake hands and give a brief pleasantry as the line moved along. However, when Pierce took office he found the White House "besieged" by office seekers who used the place as a "hotel lobby," lounging about in chairs. They were described as "rude and boisterous" when the White House doors were opened each morning, and many had to be "driven out" when the office closed at midday.[37]

Although Pierce made himself accessible to the public, he became the most guarded president to date. He never rode alone and never left the White House unaccompanied. But he liked to ride fast and often galloped through the streets of Washington at night.[38]

The Kansas-Nebraska Act had provoked outrage among Northerners and this contributed to Pierce's increasing unpopularity shortly after taking office. Crowds at the White House, which was always open to the public, had grown over the years and Pierce's friends and political allies feared that someone might take a shot at him. Additionally, he had been receiving a number of assassination threats. He was also surrounded by large crowds when he left the White House grounds. Wishing to shake his hand, crowds often became unruly and he was worried they might contain an assassin.[39]

Accordingly, Pierce was concerned about security at the White House and his own personal security. He was no doubt influenced in his decision because he had observed violence as a military officer and presidential candidate. He had also witnessed the attempted assassination of Andrew Jackson in 1835 and the killing of a friend, Maine congressman Jonathan Cilley, in a duel, as well as fistfights between congressional representatives when he served in the House.[40]

Pierce's response was to hire a bodyguard by the name of Thomas O'Neil, an officer who had served with him as his orderly in the Mexican-American War. During a battle, Pierce had been wounded and Sergeant O'Neil came to his aid. After the war the two men had kept in touch.

The doorkeeper, a federal employee, remained on the White House grounds, while O'Neil, also a federal employee, accompanied Pierce wherever he went, including the president's regular horseback rides. The usual visitor procedures applied. The White House iron gates were opened at 8:00 in the morning and closed at sundown. People wandered along the paths in the White House grounds and many visitors would stare up at the second floor hoping to catch a glimpse of the president and his family.

The president's visitors would be met by Sidney Webster, the president's secretary, who would write his approval or disapproval beside the caller's name. The information was returned to the doorkeeper, who either asked the visitor to leave or ensured he was taken to see the president. O'Neil would sit in a chair in the entrance hall observing visitors who were taken to Pierce's office. He was always within earshot of the president and ready to come to his assistance if required. Pierce thus introduced the two-level security arrangement that characterizes presidential protection today. An outer perimeter of police-type guards secured the Executive Mansion itself, while an inner perimeter—the bodyguard—protected the person of the president.[41]

Each time the president left the Executive Mansion, O'Neil was by his side. When Pierce was in the White House, O'Neil remained within calling distance. However, O'Neil was not with the president when he was out in his carriage. The arrangement led to a security breach in 1854 in which the president was attacked while waiting for his carriage outside the Capitol. Pierce was approached by a young man who shook hands with him and then offered him a drink. When Pierce refused, the young man threw a hard-boiled egg at him, hitting him in the face. The attacker was arrested and taken into custody. During his incarceration the young man attempted suicide by cutting his wrists with a pocket-knife, which provoked sympathetic feelings in Pierce. The president dropped the charges.[42]

Having a personal bodyguard also did not prevent Pierce from being arrested after he ran down an elderly woman, Mrs. Nathan Lewis, with his horse on the streets of Washington in 1853. The president was released after the arresting officer, Constable Stanley Edelin, discovered Pierce's identity.[43]

After Pierce left office in 1857 he returned to New Hampshire a disillusioned man, having failed to deal with what was becoming a civil war in Kansas over the issue of slavery. He blamed Lincoln and other abolitionists for the terrible tragedy of the nationwide Civil War.

Pierce's pro-Southern sentiments were remembered by his neighbors in New Hampshire. He became a critic of Abraham Lincoln during the Civil War and was accused of being a traitor. When word of Lincoln's assassination reached his hometown, a mob marched onto Pierce's property, angry that the former president had not been flying the stars and stripes. Pierce appealed to the mob and they left without harming him. But it was a narrow escape.

JAMES BUCHANAN

James Buchanan served as president in the critical years before the Civil War. Many issues divided the nation but slavery was the main cause of argument. Buchanan personally opposed slavery, but as president he insisted that the Constitution protected it and that laws must be obeyed. When seven of the fifteen states of the Confederacy seceded in 1860–61, Buchanan refused to use force to hold them in the Union. He believed a warlike policy might cause all the slave states to secede, making peace between the North and South impossible.

Historians have generally considered both Buchanan and Franklin Pierce to be poor presidents whose cowardice in handling the South in the years before the Civil War ended the remotest possibility that the United States would be spared the tragedy that ensued. Northerners and Southerners alike blamed them for either not preventing a war or not starting it earlier. Between 1853 and 1861, Pierce and Buchanan revealed personal leadership weaknesses and pro-Southern sympathies.

A severe illness suffered by James Buchanan the day before his inauguration, and the strange circumstances surrounding it, caused many contemporaries to allege that the president had been poisoned. They believed it was an attempt on the part of "Southern Disunionists" to remove Buchanan in order to bring his vice president, John C. Breckenridge, to power. Another theory held that Northerners may have attempted to kill the president because they felt Buchanan was too sympathetic to the South.

Prior to his inauguration, President-elect Buchanan arrived at the National Hotel in Washington DC on January 25, 1857. The very next day people at the hotel began complaining of symptoms of poisoning, which included inflammation of the intestines and a swollen tongue.

One death occurred. The postmortem examination stated that "sufficient arsenic discovered in the stomach [was present] to produce death."

Buchanan himself was affected, and, quite ill, returned to his farm in Pennsylvania. He was sometimes bedridden and his ailments lasted for around six weeks.[44] As presidential inaugurations in the nineteenth century did not take place until March 4, he did not return to Washington until March 2. Buchanan returned to Washington and again checked into the National Hotel.

When Buchanan returned to the hotel, reports of poisoning resumed. In the days surrounding the inauguration, more than seven hundred guests at the hotel, or guests at Buchanan's inauguration parties, complained of illnesses. And as many as thirty people, including some of Buchanan's relatives, died.[45]

It was first believed that rats were the cause. They had purportedly entered the water tanks after they had been poisoned. However, an analysis was made of the food and drink at the hotel and nothing untoward was discovered.[46] The mystery surrounding the alleged attempt to kill Buchanan was never solved.

During his time in office Buchanan would usually sleep until 6:30 a.m. After breakfast he would receive visitors during the morning hours. People were usually lined up around the block for their meeting with the president, which took place in the Blue Room. His afternoons were reserved for his cabinet officers. He would then take an hour-long unaccompanied walk around the streets of Washington, usually through Lafayette Park and up Pennsylvania Avenue. Frequently he would meet friends or other politicians during his walks and he would stop to chat.

Buchanan's steward was a Belgian, Louis Burgdorf, but he was listed as a "doorkeeper" so that his salary could be paid by the government. His doorkeeper duties were in fact carried out by one of the two outdoor watchmen, Thomas Stackpole.[47]

During the summer months, Buchanan resided at the Old Soldiers' Home, which at that time was outside Washington's city limits. It had been founded in 1851 by Gen. Winfield Scott for disabled soldiers. It was on a high elevation removed from the oppressive heat of the city. The president commuted to the White House every day except Sundays, traveling by coach and without guards, although guards were present at the home. During his commute he was usually accompanied by a valet and his secretary. The journey took around a half hour.[48]

It has been assumed that James Buchanan passed through his presidency without any attempts to assassinate him. Yet there is compelling evidence to suggest otherwise. When a group of Civil War army veterans met in Saratoga in 1887, one of them revealed a plot to kill Buchanan that had formed years earlier, in 1858. The unnamed veteran spoke of how Buchanan was hated "intensely" by the Kansas abolitionists. He was accused of "all the crimes charged against the 'Border Ruffians'" and "all the bloodshed that kept the settlers of this newly opened territory in an uproar." Kansas abolitionists believed that if Buchanan could be assassinated, Kansas would fall into their hands.

The well-financed plot was hatched in Lawrence, Kansas, where the veteran had been serving under General Sumner during the border troubles. The man chosen to act as Buchanan's assassin, he said, was a "hard driving . . . muscular . . . desperado."[49]

In the spring of 1858, the "desperado" arrived in Washington to see for himself "the lay of the land." A month or so later he returned to Kansas and reported to his fellow conspirators that the task of killing the president would be "easy," as Buchanan often "loitered" in the grounds of the White House and had been observed unaccompanied on the streets of Washington. The would-be assassin was sure he could kill the president and make his escape back to Kansas, where he was "assured of protection" from the conspirators.

However, as the day of the planned assassination drew near, the veteran tipped off the authorities after hearing plotters discuss the assassination in a Lawrence tavern. Willing to act as a spy, the veteran was given instructions to secure a job as a barkeeper at Winchell's Saloon, situated on Main Street in Lawrence, the tavern where the conspirators met.

At midnight one Saturday, the group of plotters arrived at the saloon and entered one of its rooms, locking the door. On the following Monday, the informant quit his job and reported back to General Sumner and his staff.

In April 1858, the veteran (turned informer) and the would-be assassin arrived in Washington at the same time. The informer followed him around and observed the plotter purchasing a gun for twenty-five dollars. The gun was sent to the would-be assassin's lodgings, which were situated "within gun-shot of the grounds of the White House."[50]

Acting on the information supplied by the veteran spy, President Buchanan, who was "very apprehensive of danger to his life during the last years of his presidency," was told he was in grave danger. The authorities, however, could not arrest the would-be assassin as the evidence was scant. Instead, after discovering he had been a fugitive from justice and had committed a felony in the city two years previously, the would-be assassin was arrested. He was brought to trial on the old indictment and sentenced to four years in the Albany Penitentiary. Before he had completed his prison term, Buchanan had left the White House. When the would-be assassin was eventually released, he was described as a "wreck" and died soon afterward.

When the veteran spy was asked why he had not provided information about the assassination attempt earlier, he answered, "For the same reason, perhaps, that Jefferson Davis did not tell the story of his attempted assassination till now, that I did not see any use of it. But I have all the facts in writing, and they will someday be found among my papers, by which time, it is to be hoped, one or two men yet prominent in Kansas politics, will have passed from the stage."[51]

Another attempt to harm Buchanan was made soon after. Following the election of Abraham Lincoln, in November 1860, the government received information that a group of conspirators, led by rabid secessionist Sen. Louis T. Wigfall of Texas, had devised a plot to kidnap Buchanan during the remaining months of his presidency, with the badly thought-out idea that Buchanan's vice president, John C. Breckenridge, would take over. The plot failed when Buchanan's secretary of war, who had been approached by Wigfall, declined to join in the conspiracy.[52]

When Buchanan left office he told his successor, Abraham Lincoln, "If you are as happy . . . on entering this house as I am in leaving it and returning home, you are the happiest man in this country." Buchanan returned to his Pennsylvania home, Wheatlands, in Lancaster. He was afraid to drive his carriage through town, as he had received threats his house would be burned down. Lancaster Masonic Lodge members stood guard at the home for months until the threat subsided. James Buchanan died there on June 1, 1868, at age seventy-seven.[53]

CHAPTER 4

Protecting Abraham Lincoln

I long ago made up my mind that if anybody wants to kill me, he will do it. There are a thousand ways to getting at a man if it is desired that he should be killed.
—Abraham Lincoln

There was never an hour from the time he entered Washington on the 23 February 1861 to the 15th April 1865, that he was not in danger of his life from violence.
—Ward Hill Lamon, Lincoln's bodyguard and marshal of the District of Columbia.

What can we do to prevent assassination? The President is so accessible that any villain can feign business, and, while talking to him, draw a razor and cut his throat, and some minutes might elapse after the murderer's escape before we could discover what had been done.
—Maj. John Hay, secretary to Abraham Lincoln

From the time he assumed office, Abraham Lincoln was severely abused in the press. Newspapers of the time inspired, and sometimes provoked, assassination attempts against America's sixteenth president. Lincoln was frequently described as a "gorilla," a "half-witted usurper," a "mole-eyed monster with a soul of leather," and the "head ghoul of Washington."[1]

At the beginning of his first term in office, an Alabama newspaper reported that "Mr. Lincoln's life would not be worth a week's purchase after a single gun had been fired against Fort Sumter."[2] The *La Crosse (WI) Democrat* devoted some thirty-two columns of abuse to Lincoln, "the great usurper and widow-maker." Other Democratic papers described Lincoln as a "horse-thief" and a "looter."

Vitriol directed against Lincoln grew during his 1864 reelection campaign. This was not unusual during presidential campaigns, but the idea that a president should be assassinated was something altogether different. The *New York Tribune* declared that to kidnap or kill Lincoln would be "easy." The *La Crosse Democrat* stated, "If Abraham Lincoln should be reelected for another term of four years of such wretched administration, we hope that a bold hand will be found to plunge the dagger into the Tyrant's heart for the public welfare."[3] The *New York Herald* described him as a "joke incarnated."[4]

Lincoln had been a target for assassination since his election in 1860, and at least four plots had been organized to assassinate him. From his election in November 1860 to his death in April 1865, Abraham Lincoln faced constant danger from those hostile to him and to the Union cause.

Although Lincoln was heavily protected—usually by the military escorts that accompanied him on trips outside the White House—and soldiers were billeted on the White House grounds during the war, he initially eschewed personal protection. He often took walks from the White House to the War Department alone and went horseback riding unaccompanied. He insisted there was no danger when he roamed the grounds of the Old Soldiers' Home where he spent the summer months to escape the insufferable Washington heat.

Lincoln had been receiving threatening letters predicting his assassination from the time he was elected president and filed them in a large envelope on which he wrote "Assassination."[5] Lincoln said he "never attached much importance to [threats of assassination]; never wanted to believe any such thing. So I never would do anything about them, in the way of taking precautions and the like. Some of my friends thought differently."[6] "Soon after I was nominated at Chicago [in 1860]," Lincoln told artist Frank Carpenter in March 1864, "I began to receive letters threatening my life. The first one or two made me a little uncomfortable, but I came at length to look for a regular installment of this kind of correspondence in every week's mail, and up to inauguration day I was in constant receipt of such letters. It is no uncommon thing to receive them now; but they have ceased to give me any apprehension."[7]

As soon as Lincoln booked into his hotel room in Washington, prior to his inaugural, he found a threatening and abusive note in his room.[8] "On one occasion," wrote Col. L. C. Baker, head of the National Detective Bureau, "I carried to Mr. Lincoln two anonymous communications, in which he was threatened with assassination. In a laughing, joking manner, he remarked, 'Well, Baker, what do they want to kill me for? If they kill me, they will run the risk of getting a worse man.'"[9] He reasoned that if anyone actually took the trouble to write a death-threat letter, the author was probably not serious in his or her intent.

Lincoln also received numerous letters from admirers, friends, and acquaintances who warned him about the plotting of his enemies. Lincoln's mail was "infested with brutal and vulgar menace, and warnings of all sorts came to him from zealous or nervous friends . . . but . . . it was hard for him to believe in political hatred so deadly as to lead to murder," according to Hay.[10] Typical of the warnings Lincoln received was Horace White's, who was secretary of the Illinois Republican State Central Committee. In a letter dated December 11, 1860, White wrote, "$40,000 had been subscribed in the St. Charles Hotel, New Orleans to procure the assassination of yourself and [Vice President elect Hannibal] Hamlin."[11]

Lincoln secretary, John G. Nicolay, said Lincoln was fully aware his life was in danger from the moment he was elected president. "He knew that incitements to murder him were not uncommon in the South, but as is the habit of men constitutionally brave, he considered the possibilities of danger remote, and positively refused to torment himself with precautions for his own safety; summing the matter up by saying that both friends and strangers must have daily access to him; that his life was therefore in reach of anyone, sane or mad, who was ready to murder and be hanged for it."[12]

Incitements to murder Lincoln, which involved financial gain, were common. Horace Greeley, editor of the *New York Tribune* reported that "substantial cash rewards" were available in the South to anyone willing to assassinate Lincoln before the inauguration. Greeley believed Lincoln was "in peril of . . . death."[13]

Lincoln's first brush with death occurred when he was president-elect. On February 11, 1861, Lincoln boarded an eastbound train in Springfield,

Illinois, at the start of a whistle-stop tour in seventy towns and cities ending in Washington DC. Intelligence communications were reported to Commander of the Army General Scott that a plot to assassinate Lincoln existed. One report stated, "All concurred in the declaration that a plot existed to assassinate President Lincoln and General Scott. They agreed singularly in the details, and sometimes in fixing the same dates for the attempts."[14]

Col. Edward Vose Sumner was also aware of the danger facing Lincoln during the preinaugural period. He wrote to Lincoln's secretary, John George Nicolay, "The political excitement is becoming so intense, that a feeling of personal hostility, and bitterness, is increasing every day. I have heard of threats against Mr. Lincoln, and of bets being offered that he would never be inaugurated. . . . It would most likely be made [at Lincoln's home] at Springfield. Mr. Lincoln's habit of walking about alone at night, gives an opportunity to make the attempt, with a good chance of escaping detection. I would respectfully urge him to carry such arms about him, when walking alone at night, as will make him secure against any crazy fanatics."[15] Others urged Lincoln to avoid particular routes from Springfield to Washington prior to his inauguration.[16]

In fact, there were several attempts to assassinate Lincoln during the journey, including an incident that occurred when the president's train left Cincinnati. A grenade "of the most destructive character" was found in Lincoln's carriage, which was occupied by the president-elect, his friends, and family. It was found on a seat, set to explode in fifteen minutes.[17]

As Lincoln began preparing for his trip, Samuel Morse Felton, president of the Philadelphia and Baltimore Railroad, received information from a reliable source, philanthropist Dorothea Dix, who had been touring the South. She had had many conversations with Southern leaders and discovered there was a definite plot to assassinate Lincoln before he was inaugurated in the hope it would incite a coup d'état.[18]

Felton contacted a private detective, Allan Pinkerton, who had a reputation for being "competent" and "honest."[19] Early in February of 1861, Pinkerton sent two of his best detectives to Baltimore to infiltrate the pro-secessionist groups who he believed would harbor the likely plotters. Lincoln was scheduled to pass through Baltimore on his way to Washington and would not consider any other means of transport or a different route. He was insistent for two reasons. First, his aides were not convinced a plot existed. Additionally, Lincoln did not want to be judged a coward for fleeing from danger.

Pinkerton met up with his agents in Baltimore and hired a suite of offices. He presented himself as a Southern businessman, John H. Hutchinson. The agents, including Harry Davies, Kate Warne, and Timothy Webster, fanned out across the city, mixing with crowds in saloons and hotels to gather intelligence. Davies assumed the character of an ardent antiunion man. Through Davies, who had managed to infiltrate a group of anti-Lincoln secessionists, Pinkerton learned of the "leading man" in the alleged plot, a Capt. Cypriano Ferrandini. He was a hairdresser from Corsica who had immigrated to the United States and established himself as the long-time barber and hairdresser in the basement of Baltimore's Barnum's Hotel. Ferrandini was said to be an admirer of the Italian revolutionary Felice Orsini, a leader of the secret brotherhood known as the Carbonari. In Baltimore, Pinkerton believed, Ferrandini was advocating that the Southern cause should adopt the same tactics as the Italian revolutionary.

During a meeting Davies arranged between Pinkerton and the head conspirator, Ferrandini said Lincoln would never become president and he would use any means to prevent the president from passing through Baltimore. "Never, never shall Lincoln be president," Ferrandini vowed. "He must die—and die he shall. . . . Our plans are fully arranged and they cannot fail. We shall show the North that we fear them not."

"He is a man well calculated for controlling and directing the ardent minded," Pinkerton wrote. "Even I myself felt the influence of this man's strange power, and wrong though I knew him to be, I felt strangely unable to keep my mind balanced against him."[20] Pinkerton said Ferrandini was a fanatic whose "eyes fairly glared and glistened . . . and his whole frame quivered . . . when he spoke of assassinating Lincoln."[21]

Acting on his own findings and those of his agents, Pinkerton was able to discover exactly how Ferrandini and his plotters would kill Lincoln. The president-elect was to enter Baltimore from Harrisburg on February 23, 1861, via the Northern Central Railroad. The conspirators were to kill the president while he traveled from the Calvert Street station to the Washington Depot and, as there would be little or no police protection (the Baltimore police chief was pro-secessionist), the task of assassinating Lincoln was considered to be easy.

"A vast crowd would meet [Lincoln] at the Calvert Street depot," Pinkerton wrote. "Here it was arranged that but a small force of policemen should be stationed, and as the president arrived a disturbance would be created." While the police rushed off to deal with this diversion, he continued, "it would be an easy task for a determined man to shoot the President, and, aided by his companions, succeed in making his escape."[22]

Meanwhile, Harry Davies was taken to a Baltimore house by one of the plotters. There, Ferrandini asked the twenty men in the room to swear allegiance to the cause of Southern freedom and then asked them to draw lots. There were twenty white paper ballots and one marked red in the wooden ballot box in front of them. The conspirator who drew the red ballot would be the main assassin. Anticipating that the nominated assassin would lose his nerve at the last second, Ferrandini had marked eight ballots in red ink.

Pinkerton felt it was now time to warn Lincoln. By February 21, Lincoln was departing New York City for Philadelphia en route to Washington via Baltimore accompanied by Col. Elmer Ellsworth, Col. Edwin V. Sumner, and Ward Hill Lamon, who had appointed themselves as Lincoln's bodyguards.

Pinkerton's plan, agreed to by Lincoln and his aides, would safely bring the president-elect through Baltimore from Harrisburg, Pennsylvania, earlier than expected. In addition, Lincoln would make his approach to the city on a different rail line and arrive at a different station.

On the evening of February 22, telegraph lines to Baltimore were cut at Pinkerton's behest to prevent communications from passing between potential conspirators in Harrisburg and Baltimore. Meanwhile, Lincoln left Harrisburg on a special train and arrived secretly in Baltimore in the middle of the night. His sleeper car was unhitched and drawn by horse to Camden Street station, where it was coupled to a Washington-bound train.

Once Lincoln's rail carriage had safely passed through Baltimore, Pinkerton sent a one-line telegram to the president of the Philadelphia, Wilmington, and Baltimore Railroad: "Plums delivered nuts safely."[23]

On the afternoon of February 23, Lincoln's scheduled train arrived in Baltimore. The large crowd that gathered at the station to see the president-elect quickly learned that Lincoln had already passed by. Even though the rest of the Lincoln party, including Mrs. Lincoln and the children, had been on this train as originally scheduled, they had already left the train in an unscheduled stop several blocks north of the President Street station. No one was ever arrested for participating in the Baltimore Plot.

For the rest of his presidency, however, the story of his sneaking like a coward through Baltimore would be told and retold by his enemies, with particular effect by cartoonists of the day. Newspapers characterized him as a coward who sneaked away from danger, accusing him of betraying an "unrepublican" fear of the "people."[24]

Lincoln decided that in future he would not repeat the behavior and became lax toward his protection. He instructed his aides to disregard threats against his life in letters sent to the White House. He held "an almost morbid dislike for an escort . . . and daily exposed himself to the deadly aim of assassination," according to Lincoln's friend, the journalist Noah Brooks.[25]

Lincoln's life was in the balance a second time in the short period after his election and before his inauguration when a Southerner, Thomas Clements, and an accomplice traveled to Washington from Alexandria, Virginia, with the intent of assassinating the president during the inauguration ceremonies. However, after Clements boasted about his plot he was arrested by Washington police. He told his arresting officers he had arrived a half hour too late to kill the president. His alleged motive was that Lincoln had robbed him of a "large amount of money."[26] Capitol police also arrested a man by the name of Columbus Edelin. He had told a police officer he was going to shoot the president-elect.[27]

———

On March 4, 1861, the day of Lincoln's inauguration, there were sharpshooters on the housetops along Pennsylvania Avenue as President-elect Lincoln and President Buchanan rode slowly to the Capitol. There were squads of cavalry to guard the street crossings along the routes. Riflemen were at the upper windows of the Capitol Building and artillery to the right of the east front. Cannons were also placed outside the Treasury

Building. Fifty riflemen guarded the inauguration platform against any bomb threats and a further 650 men, including marines and state militiamen, acted as reinforcements, assisting in securing the area.

Col. Charles P. Stone was commissioned to ride alongside the presidential carriage to prevent a clear shot at Presidents Buchanan and Lincoln. Infantry units marched behind the carriage to watch the rooftops for snipers and to intercept any would-be assassin from rushing the carriage. Additionally, special police officers were assigned to mingle with the crowds.

Gen. Winfield Scott organized the inauguration security arrangements. Allan Pinkerton and Lincoln's friends and close advisers were all involved in protecting the president. Scott, however, was criticized for the purported excessive security. But he had good reason to be cautious. He had received over 130 letters threatening Lincoln's assassination from fifteen different states.[28] Horace Greeley, who sat behind Lincoln as the new president delivered his inaugural address, said he expected "to hear its delivery arrested by the crack of a rifle aimed at his heart."[29] Within the crowds assembling for the inauguration, there were many who were hostile to the new president. One woman was overheard to remark, "There goes that Illinois ape, the cursed abolitionist. But he will never come back alive."[30]

Lincoln wanted the White House to remain the "People's House" and a symbol of American democracy. He wanted to keep the Executive Mansion open to those who wanted to discuss the war or tour the house, as it showed that the government was confident that the United States would survive. Lincoln also believed that armed guards, dressed in uniform, were a sign of weakness. It would make him look "unmanly," he said, and would invite attack rather than prevent it.[31]

However, a detail of soldiers was deemed necessary to guard the White House and the president. Two weeks after Fort Sumter, there were rumors of an impending attack on Washington. On April 18, 1861, General Scott assigned a group of 120 men from Kansas, called the Frontier Guard, to protect the president and the White House. The guard was billeted in the East Room and wore civilian clothes. If the Confederate army attacked, Lincoln was to be taken to the basement of the Treasury Building for safety. Soldiers were to make a last stand in Lafayette Park across from the Executive Mansion.[32] In late 1862 two companies were assigned to protect the president—the Union Light Guard of cavalry from Ohio, nicknamed the Bucktails, and the 150th Pennsylvania Regiment of infantry—at the insistence of various military leaders.

The Lincoln White House had a doorkeeper, Edward McManus, at the entrance. He had worked at the White House since the time of Zachary Taylor. On the second floor was an usher, Louis Burgdorf, who had also served under James Buchanan. Otherwise, the president, like others before him, had scant personal security.

White House visitors were always a problem, and Lincoln's office staff eventually agreed to intercede to prevent the president from being overburdened. However, as Hay wrote, although his staff tried their best and "strove . . . to erect barriers to defend [Lincoln] against constant interruption . . . he was always the first to break them down."[33] A White House guard, William Henry Crook, who had been a member of the Washington police force for two years before he was assigned to guard Lincoln in 1865, said that "anyone who wished to talk with him could walk up to his office, and after speaking with the doorkeeper go in and meet him. Except when engaged with others, President Lincoln seldom, if ever, declined to receive any man or woman who came to the White House to see him."[34]

Col. Charles Halpine, an aide to Army Chief of Staff Henry Halleck and sometime military aide to Lincoln, was also struck by Lincoln's accessibility. "I have many times entered the mansion," Halpine wrote, "and walked up to the rooms of the two private secretaries, as late as nine or ten o'clock at night, without seeing or being challenged by a single soul. There were, indeed, two attendants—one for the outer door, and the other for the door of the official chambers; but these—thinking, I suppose, that none would call after office hours save persons who were personally acquainted, or had the right of official entry—were, not infrequently, somewhat remiss in their duties." Halpine tried to warn Lincoln about the inadequate security arrangements. However, he reported, Lincoln "heard me through with a smile, his hands locked across his knees, his body rocking back and forth—the common indication that he was amused."[35]

Lincoln also told Halpine that "to betray fear of this, by placing guards or so forth, would only be to put the idea into their heads, and perhaps lead to the very result it was intended to prevent. As to the crazy folks, Major, why I must only take my chances,—the worst crazy people at present, I fear, being some of my own too zealous adherents. That there may be such dangers as you and many others have suggested to me, is quite possible; but I guess it wouldn't improve things any to publish that we were afraid of them in advance."[36]

Lincoln subscribed to the American idea that assassination was only a remote possibility. "Assassination of public officers is not an American crime," he once said.[37] However, at times he did become concerned about the dangers of assassination. In fact he frequently surmised he would not survive his presidency. At other times he treated the subject with disdain.[38]

Ward Hill Lamon, a friend of Lincoln's who spent the war years as marshal of the District of Columbia, held himself responsible for Lincoln's safety. He shared with Commissioner of Buildings Benjamin B. French responsibility for "introducing people to the president and his wife at White House receptions and [keeping] an eye on any suspicious person who came through the door."[39]

Lincoln said that Lamon was a "monomaniac" when it came to his protection.[40] Lamon tried to persuade the president, in the spring and summer of 1862, to allow a military escort to accompany him to and from the White House, but he "persistently opposed my proposition, always saying . . . that there was not the slightest occasion for such precaution."[41] On one occasion Lamon was out walking with Lincoln when a "Confederate sympathizer" grasped the president's hand, "under the guise of friendship," making Lincoln cry out in pain. Lamon "delivered a blow straight in the ruffian's face and felled him to the ground." Lincoln told his friend that the next time he had to hit a man, "Don't hit him with your fist; strike him with a club or crowbar or something that won't kill him."[42]

Lamon was often found by Lincoln's side. On election night of 1864, he armed himself with pistols and bowie knives and prepared to guard Lincoln's bedroom while the president slept. However, he discovered that Lincoln had left the White House with two friends, radical Republican Charles Sumner and Baron Gerolt, the Prussian minister, who, he said, were unable to guard "against an assault from any able-bodied woman."[43] Lamon, frustrated over the president's lack of concern about his safety, even offered his resignation, but it was refused.

Lincoln told Colonel Halpine he was unconcerned about the threats to assassinate him, despite the fact that in the first few days of his presidency he had received news of a Confederate plan to slip a group of men, headed by Benjamin Franklin Ficklin, into Washington to kidnap or kill him.[44]

The problem of "cranks" wishing to see the president was a constant irritant to Lincoln's aides. Some of them succeeded in entering the White House and occasionally into Lincoln's presence before their eccentricities were recognized. However, Lincoln was apparently unperturbed. He liked to talk with people, William M. Thayer, one of Lincoln's early biographers, said. "He could usually get something, if it were only a quaint phrase, even from cranks." Lincoln was "conscious that he sometimes might be running a risk."[45] One day a government official had walked through an unguarded door of the White House. When the official informed Lincoln that his protection was inadequate Lincoln replied, "Well, you know that it is as well to have but one trouble of it. Assassination would be one, but continual dread would make two of it."[46] Lincoln's aides were also aware that even political leaders were threatening assassination. At a private dinner during the first year of his presidency, for example, Sen. James Asheton Bayard of Delaware said he would give $10,000 if the president were to be assassinated.[47]

Even though Lincoln was urged to halt the stream of visitors to the White House, he insisted that the people who called to see him must do so—as they did "not want much . . . they get little and I must see them. [Presidents] moving only in an official circle are apt to become mere official." Lincoln felt "refreshed" during his "public opinion baths." He called them "invigorating" and that no hours of his day were "better employed."[48]

Lincoln's wife, Mary, disagreed with her husband's laissez-faire attitude and was terrified he would be attacked.[49] On one occasion she had been injured when the bolts holding the driver's seat to the carriage she was in had been loosened. It was believed that the target had been

Lincoln, not his wife.[50] Lincoln and his wife were also alarmed when, in February 1862, following the death of their son Willie, intruders set fire to the White House stables, killing Willie's pony.[51] The president knew of his wife's fears. "Mother has got a notion into her head that I shall be assassinated, and to please her I take a cane when I go over to the War Department at nights," he said.[52]

Secretary of War Edwin Stanton was also seriously concerned about Lincoln's habits. As the White House did not have a telegraph office, the president walked to the nearby War Department to receive news about the army in the field. Stanton had advised Lincoln since 1862 not to leave the White House unguarded and regarded his solitary walks as "foolhardiness."[53] Noah Brooks concurred. When he informed Lincoln that walking around Washington was not safe, the president simply laughed and showed Brooks the stick he was carrying.[54]

Stanton continued to worry about Lincoln's safety throughout the war and, in February 1865, took seriously a warning he received from army intelligence that "the president could be seized any reception evening, in the midst of the masses assembled round him, and carried off by fifty determined men armed with bowie knives and revolvers, and once out could be put into a market wagon guarded by a dozen horsemen, and borne off at will—the conspirators having first set a dozen, or twenty hacks in motion to distract attention. Look out for some such dash soon."[55]

After spending years in the White House with sparse protection, Lincoln finally received a personal guard some five months before he was assassinated. Ward Lamon asked for a detail of Metropolitan police officers to be stationed at the White House. On November 3, 1864, Washington police officers Sergeant J. R. Cronin, Alexander (or Andrew) Smith, Thomas F. Pendel, and Alphonse Dunn (or Donn) reported for duty at the White House as "doorkeepers." They were taken to the president's office, given instructions about their security duties, and were told to keep a sharp lookout in different parts of the White House, particularly the East Room and at the door of the president's office. They were to accompany Lincoln whenever he left the White House and were stationed outside Lincoln's private rooms at night.[56] Other officers who served in the detail were William S. Lewis, William Henry

Crook, George W. McElfresh, Thomas T. Hurdle, Joseph Shelton, D. Hopkins, and John F. Parker.

Changes were made occasionally, although the detail was never more than five officers at any one time. The new detail guarded the approach to the president in his office or elsewhere in the building and accompanied him on any walks he might take.[57] The officers were armed with revolvers, and additional firearms were kept in the porter's lodge. When Lincoln moved around Washington he was accompanied by at least one guard. Lincoln tolerated them reluctantly and insisted they remain as inconspicuous as possible.[58]

Concerned about the numerous threatening letters the president was receiving, Lincoln's aides told the guards that everyone in the vicinity of the president should be watched—"even women."[59] Following Lincoln's reelection in 1864, death threats had increased in their intensity—some of the threateners were insisting he would not live through the first year of his second term.

Lincoln acknowledged one such threat from a Polish radical named Adam Gurowski, a former translator at the State Department, who had been "skulking about the White House grounds."[60] Gurowski had criticized the Lincoln administration's policies and it resulted in his dismissal from the State Department. He had also written numerous "rabid" letters addressed to Lincoln and often met him when he went out walking the streets of Washington, although there is no evidence of any conversation between the two men. His diary contained insulting references to Lincoln. According to one of his personal guards, William H. Crook, Lincoln had declared that "as my personal safety is concerned, Gurowski is the only man who has given me a serious thought of a personal nature. From the known disposition of the man, he is dangerous wherever he may be. I have sometimes thought that he might try to take my life. It would be just like him to do such a thing.[61]

Most of the letters threatening assassination arrived by mail from Lincoln-haters in the South. Unlike previous occasions, when Lincoln would make throw-away remarks about his security, he now became more concerned. Lamon responded to the new threats by writing to Lincoln's personal secretary, warning him that the president should not "go out alone either in the day or night time."[62]

Lincoln discussed the threats with Lamon and asked him to "keep a close watch." When Lamon asked, "How close?" Lincoln replied, "Well, I'd prefer that you not sit in my lap. But try to stay as close as possible for just a bit." Many evenings Lamon would sleep on the floor outside Lincoln's bedroom, grasping a pistol and knife.[63]

Shortly after the new guards began work at the White House, Sergeant Cronin chose Thomas Pendel as Lincoln's personal guard. According to Pendel, he walked with the president "everywhere" and was the guard chosen to stand in front of Lincoln's desk when the president received visitors.[64] During Lincoln's walks to the War Department, a two-story building that overlooked Pennsylvania Avenue and the White House, Pendel would notice the many large "boxed" trees en route. He often thought how easy it would be for a would-be assassin to hide behind one of the trees waiting for the president to pass, then to shoot him.[65]

Pendel was aware of the dangers Lincoln faced and was wary of how the president would often be waylaid at the White House entrance by strangers who would "thrust notes into his hands as he passed." Once, when Lincoln and Pendel exited the White House to walk to Secretary Stanton's house, Lincoln told him, "I have received a good many threatening letters, but I have no fear of them." Pendel replied, "Because a man does not fear a thing is no reason why it should not occur." Lincoln agreed.[66]

One day, shortly before his assassination, the president walked over to Secretary Stanton's office in the War Department for a short meeting, accompanied by Pendel. On their way back to the White House they passed a stranger on the stairway of the War Department. The stranger looked at Lincoln and the president returned the look. Pendel said he watched both men intently as the stranger ascended the staircase as they were descending. Lincoln kept his eyes on the man as the stranger reached the head of the stairs and peered over the balustrade, staring at the president "very closely." Pendel said Lincoln "did something unusual for him. He looked at the man very steadily." When Lincoln exited the building he said to Pendel, "Last night I received a letter from New York stating that there would be a man here who would attempt to take my life. In that letter was a description of the man who was said to be anxious to kill me. His size and the kind of clothes he would wear when he would make the attempt were carefully described. The man we just passed agreed exactly with the description in that letter."[67]

On one occasion, bodyguard William H. Crook frustrated the efforts of a man who tried to see Lincoln during the president's visit to City Point. When Crook barred his admission to see Lincoln, the man "made threats against the president," according to Crook. At the time, the man gave his name as "Smith but Crook came to believe later it was John Surrat who he knew before the war when he lived in the same county in Maryland. Surrat joined John Wilkes Booth's conspiracy to assassinate Lincoln in 1865.[68]

Despite the provision of personal guards detailed to accompany Lincoln on his walks to and from the War Department, the president would occasionally "evade" them, according to Crook, and walk to the War Department alone, "around midnight."[69] Sergeant Smith Stimmel, of the president's "mounted bodyguard" detail, said that it was, "a common thing to see him going alone from the White House to the War Department late at night . . . a distance of half an ordinary city block or more . . . densely shaded by trees."[70] One bodyguard would follow Lincoln to the War Department without the president's knowledge.[71]

———

During the summer months Lincoln would take refuge from the insufferable city heat by staying at the Soldiers' Home, which had a higher elevation with cool shaded hills. It was situated around three miles north of Washington along the road to Silver Springs, Maryland, and afforded a panoramic view of the capital. The home was also a wartime retreat for Lincoln from 1862 to 1864. He spent over a quarter of his time as president there, thirteen of his forty-nine months in office. The president usually stayed there from early summer to late autumn and commuted to the White House each day.

Secretary of State Seward differed with Lamon and Stanton over Lincoln's security during his commute to the Old Soldiers' Home. He had no fears the president was in any danger, nor was he concerned about the president's habit of riding between the White House and the Soldiers' Home alone, often at night and without informing anyone. "Assassination is not an American practice or habit," Seward wrote in

July 1862. "Everyday's experience confirms it. [The president went] to and fro from [the Soldiers' Home] on horseback, night and morning unguarded. . . . I go there unattended, at all hours by daylight and moonlight, by starlight and without any light."[72]

However, the dangers to Lincoln were real. Leonard Swett, a fellow Illinois politician and one of Lincoln's friends, was adamant that a personal bodyguard was necessary after he visited the Soldiers' Home with a fellow lawyer, William H. Hanna. Unfamiliar with the area, their carriage driver became lost, and when they discussed the incident with President Lincoln the next day at the White House, they told him they were concerned about the lack of security. Lincoln replied, "I cannot be shut up in an iron cage and guarded . . . no precaution can prevent [assassination]. You may guard me at a single point, but I will necessarily be exposed at others. People come to see me every day and I receive them, and I do not know but that some of them are secessionists or engaged in plots to kill me."[73] When the two lawyers, together with Ward Lamon, challenged Lincoln's attitude about his "recklessness," the president promised he would "look into" the possibility of improving the security measures.

In September 1862, two companies of the Bucktail (Union Light Guard) regiment were detailed as a permanent guard for Lincoln at the Old Soldiers' Home.[74]

In mid-September 1862, "a couple of horsemen" had appeared at the main gate of the Soldiers' Home and asked one of the guards about the president's "comings and goings." The guard reported the incident to Mrs. Lincoln who became alarmed.[75] In early 1862, a Confederate officer, Joseph Walker Taylor, had observed Lincoln's habit of riding alone from the White House to the Soldiers' Home. Taylor had been staying at his uncle's home in Washington after he had been wounded. When he recovered he escaped through Union lines and traveled to Richmond where he met Confederate president Jefferson Davis. Taylor proposed a plan to kidnap Lincoln but Davis rejected the idea, believing the plan might have resulted in the president's assassination, to which he objected. The plan was resurrected in 1864, but by then Lincoln was well protected so it was held in abeyance.[76]

By December 1863, Edwin Stanton was so displeased at the level of protection afforded Lincoln he ordered a cavalry detail, organized by Governor David Todd and specially recruited from Ohio, to act as the president's personal bodyguard. They traveled with Lincoln from the White House to the Soldiers' Home from the spring of 1864 and remained with him until the end of the war.[77] "Our duties were to guard the front entrance to the White House grounds and act as an escort to the President," said Sergeant Smith Stimmel, a member of the detail, "whenever he went out in his carriage or on horseback, as he often did during the summer, but not much during the winter months."[78]

Lincoln was not pleased with Stanton's decision. He told an Illinois acquaintance on a ride from the White House to the Soldiers' Home that his cavalry escort had been detailed against his wishes and that such protection was "futile."[79] Lincoln had a "persistent and often expressed aversion to the presence of guards. . . . I know that he repeatedly sent men detailed to guard him back to their quarters," said Frank Johnson, who was a member of the Eleventh New York volunteer cavalry regiment.[80]

Lincoln protested about the detail to General Halleck. He said that the soldiers' spurs and sabers made so much noise that he was unable to hear his wife speak He said many of the men in the escort appeared to be raw recruits, and he was more afraid of them accidentally discharging their revolvers or carbines than he was of any deliberate attempt to abduct or kill him.[81]

Lincoln's attitude toward his military guard sometimes provoked him into acting irresponsibly. He enjoyed eluding his protectors, a characteristic of all American presidents. He often encouraged his coachman, Francis Burke, to increase the speed of the carriage so as to outrun the escort.[82] "Nearly every day we were made aware of his feelings on the matter," one soldier wrote. Frequently the president would leave the Soldiers' Home in his carriage without informing his escort and they would rush out the gate to catch up with him. When soldiers were posted outside his cottage there, Lincoln angrily dismissed them. The next day they returned but hid behind a large tree. Lincoln saw them and once more angrily dismissed them.[83]

In July 1864, Lincoln's final summer season at the Soldiers' Home, Confederate troops threatened the city's defenses. The Confederate army came within a mile of the Soldiers' Home when it tried to capture Fort

Stevens. The fort was one of a ring of forts built to protect Washington DC during the Civil War. It had to be captured before any Southern attack on Washington could be successful.

As word of the impending attack spread, President Lincoln and his cabinet traveled to Fort Stevens to observe the engagement. Foolishly, Lincoln risked his life as he tried to view the Confederate army's assaults. While the battle was raging, Elizabeth Thomas, whose eighty-eight acres of land had been taken over by the army to build the fort, saw President Lincoln standing on the bank of a newly built trench. Thomas shouted at nearby soldiers warning them the president was exposing himself to enemy fire. "My God," she shouted, "Make that fool get down off that hill and come in here." Immediately after she shouted, one of the officers who had been standing near the president was struck by a Confederate bullet. Lincoln reacted by seeking cover.[84] Others attribute the shouted warning as coming from future Supreme Court Chief Justice Oliver Wendell Holmes, General Wright, or an enlisted man.[85] It was the second time in American history a sitting president had come under enemy fire—the first being President James Madison during the war of 1812.

In the summer of 1864, Lincoln once again came within a hairsbreadth of being shot. He had gone out for a late-night horseback ride in woods near the Soldiers' Home, and at around 11:00 p.m. he heard a shot. He galloped back without his hat. Private John W. Nichols of Company K, 150th Pennsylvania Volunteers, was on guard duty at the gate when he heard the shot and witnessed a bareheaded president riding quickly on horseback toward his cottage. Lincoln told Private Nichols he had fallen off his horse when the shot was fired and he had lost his hat. Nichols and another soldier rode down the twirling driveway of the house toward the main road, where they discovered the president's silk plug hat with a bullet hole through the crown. The bullet would probably have hit Lincoln had his horse not reared up. Lincoln wanted the matter "kept quiet" and the incident was kept out of the newspapers.[86]

Lincoln downplayed the incident and told Ward Lamon that he was "suddenly aroused . . . by the report of a rifle" as he neared the gates of the Soldiers' Home. He said he had been "unceremoniously separated from his eight dollar plug hat" and said he thought it was not an assassination attempt. "I cannot bring myself to believe," he said, "that anyone has shot or will deliberately shoot at me with the purpose of killing me."[87]

Even though Lincoln was guarded by cavalrymen and police officers, his recklessness continued until the end of the war, when he exposed himself to assassination by Confederate sympathizers on trips to Petersburg and Richmond.

———

Lincoln knew that Jefferson Davis, the president of the Confederate States of America, had discouraged all talk of plots aimed personally at Lincoln. However, after documentary evidence of Union attempts to kill or kidnap Davis were discovered in Richmond in 1864, retaliatory plots to kidnap Lincoln were condoned by the Confederate Secret Service.

The risk of assassination by Confederate spies was real, as new discoveries have proven. There was an assassination plan organized by Confederate Secretary of State Judah P. Benjamin. The plan called for explosives expert Sgt. Thomas F. Harney and Col. John Mosby to bomb the White House but it was cancelled at the last minute when Harney was captured by Union troops.[88]

Another alleged plot to kill Lincoln was organized by Luke Pryor Blackburn, a physician, philanthropist, and politician from Kentucky. On April 12, 1865, just days after the last major battle of the Civil War, a Confederate double agent named Godfrey Joseph Hyams claimed Blackburn had plotted to infect Northern cities with yellow fever. According to Hyams, he had agreed to help Blackburn smuggle trunks of clothes used by patients infected with yellow fever into the North's major cities. At the time, it was a common belief that "contaminated" articles could transmit the disease.

Hyams also alleged that Blackburn had filled a valise with shirts and instructed him to deliver it to Lincoln at the White House, saying they were from an anonymous admirer. Hyams claimed he delivered the trunks to the Northern cities as agreed, but did not attempt to deliver the valise to President Lincoln.

The assassination of Abraham Lincoln, just two days after Hyams related his story, led to Blackburn's arrest. Investigators attempted to connect the assassination to Confederate president Jefferson Davis and his Confederate spies. The U.S. Bureau of Military Justice ordered Blackburn's arrest for attempted murder, but an arrest could not be effected because Blackburn was in Canada, beyond the bureau's jurisdiction. The subsequent discovery of the cache of garments and linens in Bermuda convinced Canadian authorities to act. They arrested Blackburn on May 19, 1865, charging him with violation of Canada's neutrality in the Civil War. In October 1865, a Toronto court acquitted Blackburn on grounds that the trunks of garments had been shipped to Nova Scotia, which was out of the court's jurisdiction. A charge of conspiracy to commit murder was dropped after Blackburn's attorney reminded the court that such a charge could only be made if the accused had made an attempt on the life of a head of state.

Historians disagree as to the strength of the evidence against Blackburn, and many of the federal and Confederate records relating to the case have been lost. Writing in the journal *America's Civil War*, navy doctor J. D. Haines noted that the Confederate agents who testified against Blackburn were of dubious reputation.[89]

Historian Edward Steers, however, contends that although the evidence against Blackburn was circumstantial, enough evidence survives not only to prove Blackburn's involvement in the plot, but to show that high-ranking Confederate officials up to and including President Jefferson Davis were aware of, condoned, and financed it.[90]

———

John Wilkes Booth, whose dark hair and dark eyes enhanced his fame as an actor, was a proslavery fanatic who thought President Lincoln was a "tyrant."

His pro-Confederate views had become increasingly pronounced during the war to the point that he had given up acting for full-time plotting. By mid-1864, he began to recruit like-minded co-conspirators for a plot to kidnap Lincoln, a move he hoped would end the war. He made contact with Confederate agents in Canada, who gave him money and put him in touch with others who could help him with his plan. Among these were the members of a pro-Confederate information network in southern Maryland, including Dr. Samuel Mudd. It is not clear how many of the conspirators were aware when Booth's objective changed from kidnapping to murder. Legally speaking, all those involved in such a conspiracy are responsible for the crimes in which it results. Additionally, Confederate involvement in John Wilkes Booth's plot to assassinate Lincoln is difficult to prove, but it is clear that Confederate leaders were prepared to kidnap Lincoln in order to further military objectives.

The murder of Abraham Lincoln on April 14, 1865, was not Booth's first opportunity to kill or kidnap the president. Booth had approached Lincoln on Inauguration Day, March 4, 1865 at the Capitol. He attended the inauguration as a guest of his secret fiancée, Lucy Hale, daughter of the soon-to-be United States ambassador to Spain, John P. Hale. "As Lincoln and other officials passed through the rotunda on their way to the inauguration platform, [Booth] attempted to push through the police lines. Officer John W. Westfall grabbed hold of the man and they struggled. Other policemen quickly came to Westfall's aide and [Booth] gave up his attempt to break through," according to author Frederick Hatch.[91] Booth later wrote in his diary, "What an excellent chance I had, if I had wished, to kill the President on Inauguration Day!"[92]

On April 11, 1865, two days after Lee's army surrendered to Grant, Booth attended a speech at the White House in which Lincoln supported the idea of enfranchising the former slaves. Furious at Lincoln's remarks, he changed his plans from kidnapping to assassination.

Booth's new plans, which were finalized at Mary Surratt's boarding house in Washington DC, called for his co-conspirators, Lewis Powell and David Herold, to kill Secretary of State William H Seward, and for George Atzerodt to kill Vice President Andrew Johnson. Booth would assume the role of the president's assassin when Lincoln and his wife attended a play at Ford's theater, a few blocks from the White House on the evening of April 14.

Maj. Henry Rathbone and his fiancée, Clara Harris, joined President and Mrs. Lincoln for a performance of the play *Our American Cousin.* The president's bodyguard for the evening was Patrolman John F. Parker, a man who proved himself unfit for protective duty. He was supposed to remain on guard in the corridor outside of the presidential box during the entire performance of the play, but he instead strolled down the street to a saloon with Lincoln's footman and coachman. Exactly what John Parker and Charles Forbes were doing, and what orders they had at Ford's Theater, have long been debated. To this day, historians are divided on the issue of whether or not Parker was assigned simply to escort Lincoln to the theater or in fact guard him.

However, even if a police officer had been present, it is questionable, at best, as to whether he would have denied entry to the presidential box to a premier actor such as John Wilkes Booth. Even President Lincoln was aware of the famous actor and enjoyed Booth's performances so much that he sent a note backstage inviting him to the White House so they could meet. Booth, a rebel sympathizer and Confederate spy, evaded Lincoln's invitation. Booth did not give Lincoln a specific reason why he could not visit, but he told friends, "I would rather have the applause of a negro to that of the president." According to the book *Inside Lincoln's White House*, the actor Frank Mordaunt later corroborated the story saying, "Lincoln was an admirer of the man who assassinated him. I know that, for he said to me one day that there was a young actor over in Ford's Theater whom he desired to meet, but that the actor had on one pretext or another avoided any invitations to visit the White House. That actor was John Wilkes Booth."[93]

Around ten that evening, Booth moved toward the door of box seven. He had already drilled a small hole in the door earlier that day and as he observed the president watching the play, he entered the box and saw the high back of the horsehair rocker and the silhouette of a head above it. Booth turned the knob. The door swung open as he saw Lincoln diagonally away to the left, four feet away.

Booth put his derringer behind the president's head between the left ear and the spine and fired. Lincoln's head inclined toward his chest as the assassin exclaimed, "*Sic semper tyrannis!*" Booth quickly turned to Major Rathbone. He dropped his derringer, pulled out a knife and slashed Rathbone across his arm before jumping onto the stage.

When Booth jumped, the spur of his right foot caught in the draped flag. The banner ripped, following him to the stage as he stretched out his hands to take the shock of the fall. Booth's left leg snapped just above the instep, but he regained his composure, ran across the stage, and headed for the wings before hobbling to the back door of the theater. Booth snatched the bridle of his horse from a theater worker and galloped out of the alley. Within half an hour Booth had crossed over the

Navy Yard Bridge and out of the city into Maryland. David Herold made it across the same bridge an hour later and rendezvoused with Booth.

Meanwhile, back in the city, Atzerodt had lost his nerve and failed to kill Vice President Andrew Johnson. Lewis Powell had entered Secretary of State William Seward's house and attempted to stab him to death. However, Seward survived.

On their way to hoped-for sanctuary in Virginia, Herold and Booth stopped at the home of a pro-Confederate doctor, Samuel Mudd, who attended to Booth's broken leg before they continued on their way. During the journey they stopped at Garrett's farm. On April 26 soldiers surrounded the farm's barn, where Booth and Herold had been sleeping, and announced that they would set fire to it if the fugitives would not surrender. Herold surrendered, but Booth refused to come out. A sergeant named Boston Corbett crept up behind the barn and shot Booth, severing his spinal cord, with the bullet wound entering the back of the head about an inch below the spot where Booth had shot Lincoln. He died two hours later.

The remaining conspirators were eventually arrested. Mary Surratt, Lewis Powell, David Herold, and George Atzerodt were tried by court-martial and sentenced to death; Samuel Arnold and Michael O'Laughlen, who played auxiliary roles in the conspiracy, were sentenced to life in prison. Another conspirator, Edmund Spangler, was sentenced to imprisonment for six years. Samuel Mudd was also sentenced to life in prison as a suspected accomplice in the conspiracy. Surratt, Powell, Herold, and Atzerodt were hanged in the Old Arsenal Penitentiary on July 7, 1865.

CHAPTER 5

The Reconstruction Presidents

We warned [President Johnson] to be on his guard when he first started upon this tour, and the pistol shots at Indianapolis now emphasize our warning . . . the danger is more imminent than most persons imagine.
—*New York Herald*, 1866

It seems I was to be attacked [by John Wilkes Booth], and Mrs. Grant's sudden resolve to leave [Washington] deranged the plan.
—Ulysses S. Grant

Quietly, without causing any disturbance in the crowds at inaugural ceremonies— for excitement is always to be avoided—many a queer looking, half-mad fellow has been taken away and kept until the ceremonies were over.
—Veteran detective under Washington Chief of Police Col. William E. Moore, 1893

[William Meyers] said he intended to shoot President-Elect Hayes then proclaim himself president and to be sworn in amid the ringing of bells and the firing of cannon.
—*Washington Evening Star*, July 7, 1881

On the night of Lincoln's assassination, Vice President Andrew Johnson chose to go to bed early. He had been staying at a hotel, Kirkwood House, at Twelfth Street and Pennsylvania Avenue, since his inauguration as vice president the previous month. His friend, Leonard J. Farwell, who worked at the Patent Office, woke Johnson to tell him about the tragedy at Ford's Theater and ordered guards for the lobby. Johnson leaned on Farwell when he heard the tragic news. Soon Johnson's friends arrived and assembled in the hotel's parlor and halls.

Against the advice of his friends, Johnson insisted on going to see Lincoln as the president lay stricken in a bedroom of the Petersen House across the street from Ford's Theater. He arrived at 2:00 a.m. and remained there for thirty minutes before returning to his hotel. At 10:00 a.m. he took the oath of office in the closed parlor after receiving notification that Lincoln had died, becoming America's seventeenth president.

At the time Johnson was sworn into office, he was unaware that he had been a target for assassination in the conspiracy to kill Lincoln. It was part of John Wilkes Booth's plan to decapitate the heads of the U.S. government.

Booth had assigned George B. Atzerodt to kill Vice President Johnson at his hotel. Atzerodt had been enlisted as a member of the conspiracy because Booth planned to flee south following Lincoln's assassination. Atzerodt lived in Port Tobacco, on the south side of the Potomac, and had good knowledge of the area.

Atzerodt was to go to Johnson's room at 10:15 p.m. and shoot him. Earlier that day, Booth had stopped by the Kirkwood Hotel and left a note for Johnson asking if he was at home. The note was later handed to Johnson's personal secretary. Historians have interpreted the note in different ways. One theory suggests that had Atzerodt failed to carry out his assassination mission, the note would implicate Johnson in the Lincoln assassination. Another theory is that Booth was merely trying to ascertain whether or not Johnson would be at the hotel at the time Atzerodt was due to assassinate him. Some historians believe Booth had hoped to secure a pass from Johnson so he could pass through the lines outside the city if he was stopped by guards.[1]

Although Atzerodt had already informed Booth that he would not go through with his role as the appointed assassin of the vice president, he booked into room 126 at the hotel on April 14, having asked for a room immediately under Johnson's. At the appointed time he went downstairs carrying on him a knife and pistol and walked to the bar. Atzerodt engaged in conversation with the barman, Michael Henry, and asked about Johnson's character and behavior. After spending some time in the saloon, eventually becoming drunk, he wandered around the streets of Washington. Nervous and afraid, Atzerodt threw his knife away in the street and made his way to the Pennsylvania House Hotel where he checked into a room and fell asleep.

During the investigation into Lincoln's assassination, a bankbook in Booth's name was found in Atzerodt's room.[2] The failed would-be assassin was eventually arrested, tried with the other conspirators, and hanged.

As the new president would need to give Lincoln's family time to vacate the White House, Johnson was offered a vacant house by Sen. Samuel Hooper. He immediately began to receive visitors at the Hooper house, alone and without bodyguards. Like presidents who came before him, Johnson believed it was the right of all Americans to meet with him.

The shock of Lincoln's assassination did not provoke tighter security at the White House, and the soldiers billeted at the Executive Mansion remained there for security purposes for only a short period. The level of protection reverted to normal because people believed presidents should not fear assassination after the country had returned to "normalcy."

By July 1865, when Johnson moved into the White House, the president's aides felt a "new feeling of security." One of Johnson's aides was so sure the new president should not fear any threats to his life that he fired his pistol out of a White House window—"the five loads I put in my revolver on the day the president died."[3] Although soldiers had been stationed in front of the White House and at its rear, they were soon withdrawn and replaced by police officers appointed during Lincoln's presidency, who acted as "watchmen."[4]

With Johnson's accession to the presidency, the White House security was thus reduced to two doorkeepers and three watchmen, and their duties were entirely to guard the White House.[5] According to former Lincoln bodyguard William Henry Crook, "It was not deemed necessary for President Johnson to be accompanied by personal bodyguards, as President Lincoln had been, for the war was over, and while times of tumult were not entirely gone, yet the positive enmity had begun to disappear between North and South."[6] Crook did not see himself as a "personal guard" in the same way in which he had acted for Lincoln, although he was selected to accompany Johnson whenever the president went to any formal affair. Crook did not for example, accompany Johnson on the presidential "Swing around the Circle" when Johnson visited New York, Albany, Cleveland, and Chicago.[7] And Crook did not feel himself to be Johnson's protector "in the sense that I had felt responsibility for Mr. Lincoln's safety."[8]

Metropolitan police assisted on special occasions to maintain order and prevent the unruly behavior of crowds who assembled near the White House for important events. The only personal protection the president received was from the doorkeepers, who were not especially trained in bodyguard duties. However, the Treasury Department's detective force also performed guard duty at the White House every day.[9]

Johnson reinstated the levee, an open house that allowed visitors to meet President Johnson. During Johnson's first levee, on February 27, 1866, the crowd was so large that guards gave up checking visitors.[10] At his last levee, on February 22, 1869, soldiers were brought to the White House to aid police officers. However, according to a newspaper report of the time, "The crowd was so great that customary regulations could not be enforced. The mass of people became so dense as to be uncontrollable. Policemen stationed at doors were swept away by the throng and carried onward with the living tide."[11]

President Johnson was well aware of the risks he was taking. His predecessor had been assassinated, and as a young Southern congressman from the state of Tennessee, he had witnessed the viciousness of unruly mobs. In April 1861, when Senator Johnson returned to his home in Tennessee at the close of the session of Congress, he had been exposed to violence and burned in effigy in nearly every city in the state. On one occasion a mob entered a railroad car in which he was riding and announced they were about to lynch him. Johnson pointed his pistol at them and they backed away.[12] Another time, a Virginia mob dragged him from the train and attacked him. However, they stopped short of hanging Johnson as they thought that that job belonged to his Tennessee constituents. In future, Johnson began placing a pistol on the lectern when he gave pro-Union speeches.[13]

According to William Crook, "[Cranks] were particularly active during Mr. Johnson's administration. We learned how to handle them—with gloves." Thomas Pendel, who stayed on as the White House doorkeeper after Lincoln's death, related the story of a typical eccentric who purported to be a surgeon of the army. He turned up at the White House, dressed in full uniform, to see President Johnson, and while Pendel and the visitor were talking, Johnson's granddaughter snatched the visitor's card out of his hand and took it to her grandfather. When the president arrived downstairs, the visitor looked at him and "showed his intensity to the full extent." Pendel quickly ushered the visitor to the door.[14]

In October 1865, Robbins Sumner (brother of General Sumner), who worked in Alexandria, Virginia, as a watchman, arrived at the White House demanding to see President Johnson. He was told Johnson would not see him and he was escorted to the front door. After Crook walked with him a short distance, Sumner turned and aimed his pistol at the presidential bodyguard. A soldier, who happened to be walking nearby, grabbed Sumner's arm just in time to prevent him from shooting Crook. Crook believed Sumner's real target was President Johnson.

Sumner was taken to the Fourth Ward police station where he was charged with assault and battery with intent to kill. However, a local judge decided there was no case to answer and simply fined him twenty-five dollars for carrying a concealed weapon. His pistol was confiscated. As Sumner could not pay the fine, he was jailed.[15]

Another would-be assassin turned up at the White House on several occasions to see Johnson but his attempts to get near him were foiled by the doorkeepers. He was identified by the name of "Grapevine" and was armed with a large bowie knife. "Grapevine" was angry with Johnson because he believed he was the rightful president. On his final visit, when he was told the president would not see him, he became irate "like a madman" and threatened to kill Johnson. When he tried to force his way in, Crook arrested him and the would-be assassin was sent to an insane asylum. Crook said, "Episodes of that kind were a frequent occurrence in the White House. We dealt with them quietly and they rarely got into the newspapers."[16]

In September 1866, Johnson traveled around the country on a speaking campaign, between August 27 and September 15, 1866, in which he tried to gain support for his post–Civil War Reconstruction policies. The tour received its nickname, "Swing around the Circle," due to the route that the campaign took: Washington DC, to New York, west to Chicago, south to St. Louis, and east through the Ohio River valley back to the nation's capital.

Johnson undertook the speaking tour in the face of increasing opposition in the Northern states and, in Washington, to his lenient form of Reconstruction in the South, which had led the Southern states largely to revert to the oppressive and racist social system that had predominated before the Civil War. He organized the trip because he believed he could regain the trust of moderate Northern Republicans by exploiting tensions between them and their radical counterparts who had demanded a harsher punishment of the South than the president had planned.

During Johnson's trip to Indianapolis, he was prevented from speaking by an unruly crowd of people who supported the Radical Republicans. The incident was instigated by radical leaders. The unruly crowd smashed torches, tore up banners, and "hissed and hooted" Johnson when he attempted to express his thanks for the welcome he had received in the city.[17] As Johnson began speaking, fights broke out as rioters clubbed opponents and fired pistol shots into the crowd At least two people were killed and several were injured.

The *New York Herald* opined that it should come as no surprise that "one of the pistol shots fired during the . . . riot had nearly killed President Johnson. This is what the radicals have been threatening to do . . . their incendiary ranting and ravings will end in assassination, unless they find some less dangerous mode of getting rid of the man who stands boldly between them and the accomplishment of their revolutionary schemes. We warned the president to be on his guard when he first started upon this tour, and the pistol shots at Indianapolis now emphasize our warning . . . the danger is more imminent than most persons imagine. We shall breathe more freely when the president is once more safe at Washington. His loss to the nation would be incalculable."[18]

Ulysses S. Grant told the *Indianapolis Herald* that there had been a "deliberate attempt" on the life of the president during his visit. President Johnson and his party, including Grant, were staying at a hotel in the city during the visit. When they gathered in one of the rooms booked for the party, a shot was fired from a second-story window on the opposite side of the street from the hotel. The bullet struck a Chinese lantern near where the president was standing and passed within three feet of Grant's head. Local law enforcement agencies made no arrests.[19]

The near miss at Indianapolis was not the last time Johnson's life was threatened by a would-be assassin. On February 10, 1869, a young woman, Annie O'Neill, a former worker at the Treasury Department, entered the White House and concealed herself in the building. Shortly after 8:00 p.m., she was discovered in a White House corridor walking toward Johnson's private apartment. When O'Neill was approached by one of Johnson's aides and asked her business with the president, she replied, "I am sent by God Almighty to kill Andrew Johnson." O'Neill was quickly apprehended and when she was taken into police custody it was discovered she had been armed with a double-barreled pistol, albeit, unloaded.

White House aides told reporters she had been "laboring under an attack of insanity," apparently caused by fear she would lose her entire savings, which had been invested in a "homestead" for her family. She had bought the property, however, when it had been "under a tax title."[20]

Andrew Johnson's efforts to put into effect the more generous policies that Lincoln had advocated with respect to the South came to a head when he dismissed Secretary of War Edwin Stanton, who not only opposed the president but secretly acted as an informant for his bitter enemies. Congress had just passed a law designed to prevent such actions by a president but Johnson rejected it, as it would have damaged the "checks and balances" formulated in the Constitution. Johnson was impeached by Congress but was found not guilty by one vote. However, his credibility and reputation were destroyed and he returned to his home in Tennessee.

––––––––

Ulysses S. Grant had worked hard to help bring the Southern states peacefully back into the Union. Grant did not always agree with Andrew Johnson but did his best to support him. As the presidential election of 1868 drew near, Grant became the popular choice for president. He was the hero who had saved the nation and a soldier who had risked his life on numerous occasions, having had many horses shot from under him during the war. He easily won election and, at the age of forty-six, became the youngest president. However, although he was reelected in

1872, he is judged a failure by historians, mainly because he returned power to the Congress and did not properly control his administration, which was mired in corruption.

The first postwar plot to kill Ulysses Grant occurred in North Carolina, on his return from the surrender of Johnston to Sherman, when the train on which he was traveling was derailed. Grant's coach was the only car on the train, and there was little doubt he was targeted for assassination.[21]

A second attempt was made in southern Indiana in late 1865 when his single-car train was derailed once more. The train left the tracks as it approached a bridge over an eighty-foot drop below. Grant survived the crash and told his aides to say nothing. Grant believed that publicity about assassination attempts would inevitably lead to further attacks.[22]

When John Wilkes Booth heard that General Grant was expected to visit Ford's Theater with President Lincoln on April 14, 1865, he had made up his mind that the Civil War victor would be assassinated along with the president. Grant frequently moved around Washington without a military escort, including the times he attended the theater. On February 10, 1865, Grant had accompanied Lincoln to Ford's Theater to see John Sleeper Clarke in the comedy *Love in Livery*. No military guards were posted at Lincoln's box. A number of people entered the box unchallenged to give the president messages.[23]

On the evening of April 14, 1865, Lincoln had been hoping Grant would accompany him to Ford's Theater, but at the last minute, Grant's wife, Julia, had persuaded her husband they should leave by train for Burlington, New Jersey, to see their children. Besides, Julia Grant did not like Mrs. Lincoln.

Grant and his wife started for the train. As they were driving along Pennsylvania Avenue, a horseman drove past them at a gallop, turned his horse, and approached the carriage once more, looking in. Julia Grant remarked to her husband, "There is the man who sat near us at lunch to-day, with some other men, and tried to overhear our conversation." Grant later said the man was "so rude . . . we left the dining room." The Grants left without finishing their lunch.

Grant believed the stranger outside their carriage was simply curious but he later discovered that "the horseman was Booth. It seems I was to be attacked, and Mrs. Grant's sudden resolve to leave [Washington] deranged the plan."[24]

Julia Grant also believed she and her husband had been followed to the train station during their journey to Burlington. Police investigators later found that someone had tried to force their way into Grant's private carriage, which was locked.

Grant received a letter a few days later from an anonymous source in which the writer confessed he had been detailed to kill the Civil War general after he boarded the train. The writer said he rode on the train as far as Havre de Grace (Maryland) but, as Grant's car was locked, he could not get in. Grant "thanked God he had failed."[25] The purported would-be assassin expressed regret for his actions and was "thankful" he had been prevented from carrying out the assassination of the general.[26]

There is some credible evidence that Michael O'Laughlen, who had participated in the Lincoln conspiracy, was the man who attempted to break into Grant's railway carriage, and also the author of the confessional letter.[27] O'Laughlen was a childhood friend of John Wilkes Booth and they grew up across the street from each other in Baltimore. He joined the Confederate army in 1861 but was discharged in June 1862 for health reasons. He returned to Baltimore to work for his father's feed and produce company.

In August 1864, Booth recruited O'Laughlen to assist in the kidnapping of President Lincoln. On March 15, 1865, O'Laughlen attended a meeting with Booth and fellow conspirators in the Gautier restaurant in Washington DC. At the meeting, a plan was organized for March 17, 1865, whereby Lincoln would be kidnapped after he attended a play on the outskirts of Washington. However, Lincoln altered his plans at the last minute and the plan was abandoned. Another kidnapping plan involved Booth capturing Lincoln at Ford's Theater while O'Laughlen put out the lights in the theater. They abandoned that plan as impractical. After the attempt to kidnap Lincoln failed, O'Laughlen returned to Baltimore.

O'Laughlen was arrested three days after the Lincoln assassination and charged with stalking General Grant with intent to murder him. At the military trial, prosecutors introduced as evidence vague telegrams between O'Laughlen and Booth in an attempt to establish that O'Laughlen was involved in the plan to kidnap Lincoln. Unable to prove their case, O'Laughlen was sentenced to life in prison for his part in the earlier plot to kidnap the president. He was sent to Fort Jefferson, Florida, where he died of yellow fever in 1867.

Historians are divided as to whether O'Laughlen planned to assassinate General Grant. The prosecutors at O'Laughlen's trial said he had been stalking Grant and produced three witnesses who claimed to have seen him at the home of Secretary of War Edwin Stanton on the night prior to the Lincoln assassination; the gathering was attended by General Grant. O'Laughlen's attorney argued before the court that his client had been innocently walking the streets of Washington, observing the victory celebrations.

According to author Bill O'Reilly, "[At Stanton's home] . . . Mike O'Laughlen does nothing to harm the secretary of war. Nor does he bother Grant . . . observers will later remember the drunk in the dark coat and suggest that his intentions were to kill the general and the secretary. Nothing could be further from the truth: the surprising fact is that O'Laughlen is actually here to warn them about Booth." O'Reilly and Dugard maintain that O'Laughlen could not summon up the courage to tell the guests at the party about the Lincoln conspiracy because if Booth were arrested he could implicate O'Laughlen in the aborted kidnapping plot in which he was a participant.[28]

———————

Following Grant's succession to the presidency in 1877, the guards at the White House were released. However, plainclothesmen mingled with the crowds at receptions and they had the authority to search visitors who they believed looked "suspicious." The grounds of the Executive Mansion were guarded by the Metropolitan Police assigned to the White House. Watchmen who worked for the Treasury Department were also added to the security contingent. Coaches parked in the driveway of the mansion were guarded by the police officers, and guests were restricted to certain rooms in the mansion.[29]

President Grant ordered his staff to allow visitor access to the White House three times a week for an hour a day. He would shake visitors' hands before taking his solitary walk to the Capitol and back.[30] Grant would also walk to Secretary of State Hamilton Fish's home in Scott

Square or to the nearby Willard Hotel, which offered him a leather chair in a secluded place in the lobby, where he could watch the comings and goings of the visitors to Washington.[31] William Crook said that the "idea that Grant might meet with assassination . . . when walking alone . . . never occurred to his friends."[32]

Almost every day, when weather allowed it, Grant would go for drives in his light racing buggy. He enjoyed sitting on the edge of his seat and racing past other carriages on the streets of Washington. One day, Grant drove his carriage west on M Street at great speed. He was pulled up by a Washington police officer and arrested. Grant's horse and carriage were briefly impounded. After posting a twenty-dollar bond, he walked back to the White House.[33] Grant would also often take his horse "Jeff Davis" for a ride.[34]

During his presidency Grant was subject to the ravings of "cranks" who would visit the White House. White House guard Henry Kolb related the story of a typical crank, a forty-five-year-old man who arrived at the White House demanding to see the president. When Kolb told him President Grant was not receiving visitors that day, the stranger said he was a member of the House of Representatives. Believing his story, Kolb directed the Congressman upstairs to Grant's reception room.

The visitor told Grant that notwithstanding the fact he had been elected to Congress as a Democrat from the Baltimore district by a "1,000,000 Republican majority," another politician had been occupying his seat at the Capitol. He wanted Grant to accompany him to the Capitol and demand that the usurper be ousted. When Grant refused his request, the stranger threatened him with "dire vengeance." Grant pressed the alarm button to summon his doorkeeper. After a short while, an usher in the reception room called out to Kolb requesting assistance. When Kolb entered the room, he observed the stranger "gesticulating wildly, talking loudly and following the president about the apartment in a very excited manner." The visitor was in a "white heat rage" at President Grant. Kolb observed that Grant was "as cool as a norther," but he had "an angry gleam in his eyes."

After Grant ordered Kolb to "put [the] fellow out," the guard seized the visitor as Grant sat down at his desk, resuming his work. Grant later rebuked Kolb for not being more careful who he allowed into the White

House. "I am not afraid of such fellows," Grant said, "but they annoy me and occupy valuable time, all of which you could avoid by not admitting them." Kolb believed that Grant "narrowly missed being assaulted or perhaps assassinated on that day."[35]

In 1875 Grant announced he would not be seeking a third term as president. Four years later, however, he decided he would like a third term and his name was put forward at the 1880 Republican convention. Grant lost, and James Garfield became the compromise candidate. Julia Grant later came to believe it was all for the best. "I am so glad," she said, "my husband was not nominated in Chicago. . . . If he had been nominated and elected he might have been assassinated by some crank like the one who killed poor General Garfield. It is so disreputable to be put out of life by a crank. To die for sweet revenge is one thing, but to be snuffed out by a worthless crank is ignoble."[36]

––––––––––

The 1876 disputed presidential election was highly controversial, with the Democratic candidate, Samuel J. Tilden, having won the popular vote but losing in the Electoral College to Rutherford B. Hayes. However, in the famous "Compromise of 1877," an informal deal was struck to resolve the dispute, which, in effect, gave Hayes the presidency in return for the new president acquiescing to the Democrats' demand for the withdrawal of federal troops from the South, thus ending Reconstruction. The troops had been in place since the end of the war to support corrupt carpetbag state governments. Hayes also promised to give important positions to Southern Democrats. The compromise, in effect, allowed the nation to enter a seventy-five-year period in which it tacitly permitted white-dominated politics and institutions in a quarter of the states.

Despite this compromise, Tilden's supporters were still angry that their candidate had lost, and the air was filled with threatened recriminations, including public demonstrations and threats made against President-elect Hayes's life as he prepared for the trip to Washington for his inauguration. Some Republicans were also fearful a plot to seat Tilden had been organized, and the group, said to number "30 well-known Republicans," appointed "four stalwart Republicans" to keep guard night and day at Tilden's country home to prevent the

Democrat from going to Washington and "declaring himself President of the United States."[37]

According to White House guard William Crook, some of Tilden's supporters were so violent, "it was common to hear threats made on the streets that they were determined to seat him in the White House if they had to bring an armed force to Washington for that purpose."[38]

Following the disputed election, John S. Mosby, a former Confederate army commander who became a friend of Grant's and worked in the Justice Department, warned the outgoing president "to be careful of his own person" and feared "an effort would be made to assassinate him." Mosby said the language of the Democrats "was now more desperate and more threatening and violent than that of the Southern men on the election of Lincoln in 1860." Mosby feared there would be bloodshed if the Electoral College voted Hayes into office and believed that Democrats were saying that "the first man to be gotten out of the way" would be Grant.[39]

On November 20, 1876, President Grant received a letter warning him he was going to be assassinated. The letter stated, "I beg you to read these lines . . . I overheard a conversation between two men who were plotting your assassination. Said he, the first man, 'Do you think the plan will work?' 'Admirably,' replied the second, 'he was in the habit of walking alone, we can be on the watch and some dark evening when he enters either of the gates of the White House, we can conveniently post ourselves, and then the dagger must do the rest. The first blow must do the work for he is brave and will defend himself.'"[40]

On November 22, the United Order of Bush Rangers in Boston wrote to President Grant adorning the letter with drawings of a skeleton in a casket, a skull and crossbones, a rifle, a pistol and a dagger. The letter stated, "You are a doomed man. You and your assistant thieves will soon be assassinated. I kindly advise you not to be out on dark nights—one of your men is one of our sworn friends—even half your soldiers are on our side. I give you fair warning beware we have got an Association of 10,000 sworn men all over the states beware you sneak thief. Your Doom Blood Blood your Blood Family KKK Your Bitter Enemies."

Another letter, dated November 24, from Long Point, Arkansas, warned Grant, "There were three men in a conversation about the election. One man said President Grant is trying to have Louisiana, South Carolina, and Colorado all returned for Hayes and he knows damn well that Tilden carried all three of them . . . if he does . . . the first thing I will do will be to put a ball through old Grant's head." On November 25, a writer from Atlanta warned Grant, "There is a plan hatched up in Virginia to assassinate you . . . it is to be done by a federal soldier now in your city who is to do it by accident to stumble down and let his gun go off or run a bayonet through you."[41]

Shortly before the inauguration, Grant ordered the prosecution of Donn Piatt, who used "seditious language" in an article he wrote for his newspaper, *The Capital.* Piatt had called Hayes "His Fraudulency" and stated that "somebody ought to assassinate President Hayes on his ride to the inauguration." Piatt was jailed.[42]

Grant was determined to stand fast and warned Tilden's supporters not to make any ill-conceived move in support of their candidate. He said he would make sure Hayes was inaugurated and would not "shirk in his duty," according to White House guard William Crook. Crook believed that Grant's warning put an end to the threats made by Tilden's supporters.[43]

The formal inauguration of President Hayes was organized for Monday, March 5, 1877. However, during the 1876 election, Hayes had received numerous death threats and had escaped assassination when a shot was fired through the window of his home.[44] Grant invited Hayes to stay at the White House until the inauguration. Hayes declined and opted instead to stay with a friend, Sen. John Sherman. Fully aware that the controversial election had angered many of Tilden's supporters, he deputized his son, Webb, to act as his bodyguard and authorized him to carry a pistol at all times that he was with his father.

Grant, fearing a coup, was worried that Tilden's supporters would swear the Democrat into office on the Sunday before the inaugural. Additionally, Hayes's aides believed an assassin might strike at any time. Accordingly, Grant advised the new president to take the oath of office in the White House, in case problems arose during the ceremony at the Capitol. He was the first president to do so, and on Saturday, March 3, 1877, he was sworn into office in the White House's Red Room. Two days later, surrounded by six Secret Service agents acting in an unofficial capacity, Grant and Hayes rode to the Capitol and the president-elect was again sworn into office.

Although there is no definitive evidence that Tilden's supporters entertained the notion of assassinating Hayes, there is credible evidence that the president-elect was targeted for assassination on his Inauguration Day nonetheless. According to an Iowa newspaper, the *Carroll Herald*, the story had "considerable appearance of truth, to the effect that a lunatic was to have assassinated President Hayes on the day of his inauguration. It is said that Mr. Hayes was informed of the affair, and by his request it was kept from the public."[45]

Just before March 4, 1877, a man visited Reverend Father D. Reville, a famous Dominican priest and "orator" who lived in Washington at the time. The man confided in the priest that one of his acquaintances from Illinois, William Meyers, had arrived in the city with the intention of assassinating President-elect Hayes. Meyers was described as a "well-to-do man from Northern Illinois." The priest's visitor said he believed Meyers was "insane" and "determined to carry out his act."

Father Reville, who had been a priest at St. Dominic's Church in Washington, took the man to see a Washington detective by the name of "McDevitt" who in turn advised Maj. A. C. Richards, the Washington police chief. Richards asked McDevitt to look into the matter. He eventually tracked the would-be assassin to the Imperial Hotel. On his way there, McDevitt encountered two Secret Service agents, C. E. Anchist and E. W. Maxwell, and enlisted their assistance. The three men agreed not to reveal their identities but simply question Meyers about his plans. During their conversation Meyers asked the men to join him in his plot to kill Hayes and gave Anchist a twenty-dollar gold coin to purchase a pistol after the agent promised to aide him in the conspiracy.[46]

McDevitt immediately arrested Meyers and, after a search of his room, it was discovered the would-be assassin had gathered "an arsenal of weapons." During questioning at police headquarters, Meyers admitted to his assassination plans. He said he intended to shoot President-elect Hayes, "then proclaim himself president, and to be sworn in amid the ringing of bells and the firing of cannon." Convinced Meyers was insane, the police authorities, "after consultation," sent him to an insane asylum.

Meyers was incarcerated for a period of around six months then released to the supervision of his sons with the assistance of a nurse.[47]

President Hayes was informed of the plot to kill him. He thanked the officers for their diligence and promised to reward them. He arranged for Maxwell to be awarded an appointment as a second lieutenant of the Twentieth Infantry shortly after the inauguration. Unfortunately, Maxwell soon got into trouble. He signed his pay accounts more than once, doubling his pay, and he also received loans with his pay as security when he had already fraudulently overdrawn it. He was sentenced to two years at the Texas State Prison in San Antonio. However, Hayes pardoned Maxwell and he was released from prison one month after he began serving his sentence.[48]

In August 1881, the assassination story was corroborated when an assistant district attorney, Joseph E. Hayden, told reporters he had "saved President Hayes' life" by turning over to the police " a lunatic" who had planned to kill the president on his Inauguration Day.[49]

———

It was the early practice of presidents to hire their own secretaries, and Hayes employed four. His son, Webb Cook Hayes, became the most important. Webb followed his father everywhere and he liaised with members of Congress. He was with his father throughout the day and acted as his personal bodyguard, always armed with a pistol. He was also the official "greeter" at social events and stood next to his father when White House visitors met the president.[50]

Hayes was described by White House guard William Crook as "one of the best-natured men" who ever lived in the White House and a man who was "easily approached by anyone who had an excuse for meeting him."[51]

As Hayes had received so many assassination threats, he gave up the tradition of having concerts on the White House lawn. Access to the White House was curtailed and guards were stationed at external gates outside of the hours of 2:00 to 10:00 p.m. The entrance to the Executive Mansion's main door was provided with a guard station and all visitors had to show some identification before entering. The increased security measures were later relaxed after Hayes's wife, Lucy, asked her husband to allow the "rolling of Easter eggs on the White House lawn," which later became an Executive Mansion tradition.[52]

During Hayes's term in office, there was no diminution in the numbers of so-called cranks who arrived at the White House. Nor did the number of letters threatening assassination abate. A man who thought he was a prophet who controlled the destinies of presidents, for example, sent many letters threatening to kill Hayes. He was eventually apprehended and sent to jail.[53]

"White House Cranks" were said to be numerous, according to a newspaper report, and "almost every day one of them appeared." During Hayes's term in office, thirteen people were arrested for loitering around the White House, and eleven were sent to an asylum. Among them was a "wealthy young woman, from Indiana" and an "older woman," who were both convinced Hayes wanted to marry them. According to a newspaper of the time, "numerous other cranks called [at the White House] but were sent away, being considered harmless."[54]

One day when the president had received "many visitors," including senators, representatives, and cabinet members, he asked if there were any more to see. His secretary told him he had two and one of them was "crazy." Hayes asked him to send in the "sane one." When the visitor entered the president's room, he explained he was "emperor of the world" and he had "come to take possession of the White House and the government." Hayes rang a bell to summon his secretary and said, "If this is the sane one of the two, please have him taken away and send in the maniac."[55]

Hayes was the first president to travel across the United States to the Pacific Ocean. The *San Jose Times* opined, "Nothing so strongly illustrates the true freedom and happy security in the land of liberty . . . than the comparison naturally suggested by the untrammeled movements of our worthy president on his present long journey, when compared with the nervous precautions necessitated in monarchical countries when the crowned head passes through its districts." The newspaper noted that when the Russian emperor traveled on a recent rail journey, "40,000 troops and 10,000 peasants lined the route." "Happily," the newspaper noted, "America has no such terrors for the head of government."[56]

However, there were a number of reports that Hayes had been the victim of assassination attempts during his travels around the country. It was reported, for example, that a man named "Freebolter" had attempted to assassinate Hayes at Muscotah, Kansas, a small railway station on the Union Pacific Railroad near Atchison City. Hayes passed through the area in 1880 on his way back to the White House. Freebolter was arrested and taken to Atchison County Jail.[57]

Hayes lost the 1880 election to James Garfield and left Washington by train for his home in Fremont, Ohio. During the journey the train collided with an unscheduled train going south. Both trains were wrecked and the engineer of the southbound train was killed. A greater tragedy, which would have meant the deaths of not only former President Hayes and his wife but also the other passengers on the train, was prevented from happening by the driver of the Hayes' train, John M. Unglaub, who acted quickly in reversing the engine as soon as he saw the oncoming train. Unglaub was badly injured. Hayes believed he had saved their lives.[58]

CHAPTER 6

James Garfield's Assassination and Chester Arthur's "Near Miss"

Assassination can no more be guarded against than can death by lightning.
—President James Garfield

Rutherford B. Hayes did not seek reelection in 1880, and at that year's Republican National Convention, the choice for presidential nominee had delegates deadlocked between former president Ulysses Grant and James Blaine, a U.S. senator from Maine. On the thirty-sixth ballot, James Garfield, a Civil War general and congressman from Ohio, was chosen as the compromise candidate. His courage on the battlefield, especially at Chickamauga in September 1863, helped garner votes. Chester Arthur was selected as his running mate. In the general election, Garfield and Arthur defeated Democratic nominee Winfield Hancock and his running mate, William English, and took their oaths of office on March 4, 1881.

During the Civil War, President Lincoln and Gen. George B. McClellan agreed that an espionage agency should be formed. Its first head was Allan Pinkerton and it was called the Secret Service. Pinkerton was replaced by Lafayette Baker who later was accused of setting up his own espionage network within the White House, prompting its abolition.

However, at the war's end, in April 1865, one-third of the money in circulation was counterfeit and posed a significant risk to the American economy. As a result, newly appointed Treasury secretary Hugh McCulloch recommended to Lincoln a special commission to investigate the merits of forming a national police force to prevent and eliminate counterfeiting operations. The new agency, not to be confused with the old espionage agency, was also named the Secret Service and was the forerunner to today's organization. The first head appointed was William P. Wood, who later had to resign amid allegations of corruption. In 1867 the agency's mission had broadened to include fraud against the government. Besides the Secret Service, the only other real federal police force at this time was the U.S. Marshals Service. The Secret Service soon began taking over many of the functions in enforcing federal law that the marshals could not handle on their own.

Unlike the federal marshals, who were formed through a specific act of Congress, the new Secret Service operated through the Treasury Department, not Congress, and it received its statutory authority through appropriation bills. Congress kept close watch on the new Secret Service, but as it developed it became increasingly autonomous. Congress tolerated the agency because its investigations were generally successful, certainly during the period 1865 to 1874. However, in 1874, Secret Service chief Hiram C. Whitley was accused by Congress of illegally using the agency's resources in an attempt to frame a prominent Washington politician. The agency was forced to accept the authority of Congress and make reforms, which ultimately improved its standing with senators and representatives.

Other government agencies recognized the efficiency of the Secret Service and requested assistance with their own investigations. Over time the agency took on new jobs, including combating the Ku Klux Klan.[1] Later it would conduct espionage during the Spanish-American War in the mid-1890s and during the First World War. Its main job, however, was prosecuting counterfeiting operations and other forms of fraud.

The agency had also assisted with the security arrangements at inaugural ceremonies. It was not until the Cleveland administration that they were requested to act as presidential guards, but they did so only in a very limited way and in an unofficial capacity.

At the time James Garfield took office, presidential security remained lax, even though he had around one hundred visits by office seekers every day and any White House visitor had access to him.[2] Lincoln's assassination, it was generally believed, was an aberration brought on by the Civil War, and the pathology of assassination belonged only to European corrupt and despotic regimes. America also had "exceptional status," and assassination was "un-American." Such crimes, it was believed, were the result of "un-free" disgruntled citizens who lived in undemocratic nations.

Garfield began his presidency by vigorously challenging the problems facing the Republican administration. One of the gravest problems he sought to resolve was the reform movement started by President Hayes to curtail the power of the Republican Party machine in New York. Known as the "Stalwarts," this faction virtually owned the city by controlling all the patronage. Among these, the richest position was the federal office of the Collector of the Port of New York.

Garfield began his reform efforts by appointing a tough anti-Stalwart to the office. His appointee immediately began attacking the corrupt practices of the customs house. As Garfield expected, the Stalwarts in turn attacked the president, and many vehemently swore vengeance against him.

Garfield had been president for only a few months when he was targeted for assassination. The motive lay not in the political dispute the president was engaged in but centered on the anger of a disgruntled, mentally unbalanced, and insignificant office seeker, Charles Julius Guiteau. The thirty-nine-year-old Guiteau was born in Illinois and from earliest boyhood was erratic, self-willed, and cruel. He described himself as a lawyer, politician, and theologian. He had tried religion, living for six years in a colony of "Bible communists," became a lawyer belonging to the Illinois bar, and had failed when he tried his hand at publishing a New York newspaper. Guiteau cheated people out of their money, moving from city to city, swindling landladies and hotels and whoever would trust him. His plausible manner and knowledge of religious literature gained him admission to the clergy and churches, and nearly all of them suffered more or less from his dishonesty. Shortly before he died, Guiteau's father began to believe that his son's persistent lying and swindling was the result of a "diseased brain."[3]

In 1880 Guiteau became attracted to politics after being laughed at and driven out of the field as a religious lecturer. He turned his attention to politics in the presidential campaign and offered to work for Garfield but was rebuffed, although he did write a speech in support of the candidate.

After the campaign was over, Guiteau felt his efforts had earned him the appointment as U.S. consul in Paris. He thought his endorsement and campaign speeches had secured the election for Garfield.

Former president Grant had had his encounters with Guiteau during the election campaign and described him as looking "seedy and like a dead-beat."[4]

Shortly after Garfield had been sworn into office, Guiteau began to harass White House doorkeepers Thomas Pendel and Alonzo Dunn for access to the president. A White House police officer, Henry Kolb, was the officer who first pointed out Guiteau to Secretary of State James Blaine and warned him that he was a "dangerous crank."[5] A White House doorkeeper, Arthur Simmons, told the *Pittsburgh Press* he remembered Charles Guiteau and the "efforts [he] made to get at President Garfield. He called here at least a dozen times. On one occasion he even got into the president's office under the pretence of being a newspaper man, but was hustled out in time to prevent him doing any damage here."[6] Guiteau had also written a number of threatening letters to Garfield.[7]

Guiteau continued to visit the White House virtually every day during the spring of 1881, pressing his claim for a government job. The doorkeeper of the private secretary's room at the White House said that Guiteau "came day after day" to the White House to see Garfield. The secretary's doorkeeper saw "danger in his eyes" and would not allow him to present his card to the president.[8]

On the May 13, White House doorkeeper William Crook "came into collision with [Guiteau]." Guiteau walked into the reception room and asked for paper to write a message to President Garfield. Dissatisfied with the quality of the paper he received, he became arrogant and haughty and asked Crook, "Do you know who I am?" Guiteau added that he was "one of the men that made Garfield president." Guiteau continued to call at the White House, enquiring about the president's health, then quietly leaving.[9] Snubbed by the doorkeepers, he spent his time sitting on a bench in Lafayette Park, staring at the front door of the White House. Feeling he had been personally affronted, Guiteau decided to seek revenge.[10]

As a strong believer in the spoils system, Guiteau began to reason that by killing Garfield, Chester Arthur, a Stalwart, would become president and end Garfield's reforms. On June 8, Guiteau borrowed fifteen dollars and bought a powerful, pearl-handled, .44-caliber British revolver. He thought it would display well in a museum.

As Garfield had no bodyguard and frequently walked the streets of Washington alone, he became an easy target for the disgruntled office seeker. Guiteau began stalking the president. On the day he bought his pistol, Guiteau followed the president and his wife to the Baltimore and Potomac Railroad depot for their trip to the New Jersey seashore, where they had a summer home. But once again he decided not to assassinate the president. He lost his nerve. He was too touched by the scene of Mrs. Garfield clinging "so tenderly to the president's arm."[11]

Less than a week later, Guiteau saw a newspaper report of the president's itinerary. Garfield had announced to the press his intention of attending the twenty-fifth reunion of his class at William's College in Williamstown, Massachusetts. He would, the papers announced, depart Washington by train on July 2.

According to Thomas Donaldson, a friend of the former president, Rutherford Hayes, "Mrs. Blaine told me yesterday how Garfield escaped being shot at her door. The day before [Garfield's assassination], about 4:00 p.m., Mrs. B., sitting in her window saw the President coming on foot toward her house, behind him [rapidly] walked Guiteau. Mrs. B. walked out to the door and opened it for the President to enter, not caring to wait for a ring and her servant to come. Garfield at once entered without halting and Guiteau missed his chance. Mr. Blaine [and] the President about 5, walked to the White House. Guiteau, who had been waiting, followed them but lacked the nerve to shoot."[12]

———————

On the morning of July 2, 1881, Garfield and Blaine took a carriage from the White House at around 9:00 a.m. to begin the journey to

Massachusetts. Arriving at the railroad station, they walked together into the waiting room of the depot without bodyguards or police protection.

This time Guiteau's nerve did not desert him. He approached Garfield from behind, and from a distance of three feet fired his pistol.[13] Guiteau's first bullet went through Garfield's right arm. Garfield cried, "My God, what is this!" As the president turned to see who had shot him Guiteau fired a second bullet hitting the president in the back and lodging near his pancreas.

As Garfield fell to the floor, the station erupted in screams. Guiteau ran to the station door, heading for his waiting carriage, but his exit was blocked by a Venezuelan diplomat, Simon Camacho. When Guiteau turned and headed for another exit, Robert Parke, a special Washington agent of the Baltimore and Potomac Railroad, seized the assassin. Parke later vaguely recalled having been approached by a "calm, lithe little man who asked a lot of questions." As the president appeared with Blaine, Parke saw the "lithe little man" pull out of his pocket a large bulldog revolver and fire twice. Parke said, "I thought the president was going to die right there. I tried to speak to him but he could not recognize me. Mrs. Sarah E. White, the mistress of the waiting room, rushed up and lifted the president's head into her lap. He vomited a little. The station had been empty but the news spread and soon there were several thousand people about us. They got a Pullman mattress and carried the president to a room upstairs."[14]

After Parke seized Guiteau, police officer Patrick Kearney came to his assistance. Fearful the station crowd was going to lynch him, Guiteau gave up his struggle and told Kearney he wanted to go to jail.[15] As Kearney marched Guiteau out of the station, the assassin kept insisting he had something to say and waved a letter he had written to Gen. William Tecumseh Sherman:

To General Sherman:

I have just shot the President. I shot him several times as I wished him to go as easily as possible. His death was a political necessity.

I am a lawyer, theologian, and politician. I am a Stalwart of the

Stalwarts. I was with General Grant and the rest of our men in New York during the canvass.

I am going to the Jail. Please order out your troops, and take possession of the jail at once.

Very respectfully,
Charles Guiteau.

Kearney took Guiteau to police headquarters for interrogation. However, shortly after they arrived, a mob bent on vengeance had assembled outside the building and it was deemed prudent to send Guiteau to the District Jail.

Following an examination of Garfield's wounds by doctors who had been called to the scene of the shooting, the president was taken to an upstairs room where ten doctors attended him. The paramount consideration, the doctors concluded, was to find the bullet, but they had no idea where it was lodged so they probed the wound. However, in a time when combating disease was in its infancy, they did it with unsterile hands and instruments that started the spread of a virulent infection. Garfield asked to be taken back to the White House and an ambulance arrived. Slowly the carriage made its way to the Executive Mansion.

For a brief period the president began to rally and there was renewed hope for his recovery. But then a decline set in; his condition worsened and the doctors once again probed for the bullet. Unwittingly, all the doctors accomplished was to send infection deeper into Garfield's body. Complaining of increasing pain, the president grew weaker and in desperation the doctors turned for help to Alexander Graham Bell, the inventor of an electrical induction device for locating metals. However, it failed to detect the bullet because, unknown to Bell at the time, the presence of steel springs in Garfield's sickbed blocked the signal.

By September, Garfield insisted he be taken to a cottage at Elberton, New Jersey, a coastal town, where he would escape Washington's sweltering summer heat. He arrived there on September 6. However, his condition was already hopeless, and on the evening of September 18, 1881, Garfield whispered, "My work is done," and lapsed into a coma. He died the next day of the septic poisoning that had been induced by the doctors probing for the bullet. His body had developed a protective cyst around the bullet to neutralize it, and had the doctors not continued probing for the bullet throughout the months since he had been shot, he could easily have survived the assassination attempt. Garfield had been president for less than six months, eighty days of which he was incapacitated by his wounds. It had taken three months for Garfield to succumb to his wounds.

The night President Garfield was shot, a rumor spread that the assassin may have been a "star route" conspirator. The Star Route Frauds scandal involved a lucrative nineteenth-century scheme whereby U.S. postal officials received bribes in exchange for awarding postal delivery contracts in southern and western areas of the country.

At a meeting of the cabinet the same night, Col. James Brooks, who was chief of the Secret Vice Division, was called in and instructed to investigate the alleged conspiracy. He was the first man allowed to interview Charles Guiteau, and he visited the assassin in jail, remaining with him all night. The following day he reported his opinion that the conspiracy story was untrue. According to Brooks, Guiteau "raved all that night, and harped on the one idea that he would be appointed Minister to England or to some other great mission as a reward for his bloody and horrible work."[16]

When Guiteau was taken to the District Jail, he became convinced that Gen. William Tecumseh Sherman would send troops to free him and that Chester Arthur would be "overwhelmed with gratitude."[17] The guards at the jail were soon doubled in anticipation of an attack by a mob of outraged citizens. Twenty-five men had arrived from Baltimore to take part in a proposed lynching of the assassin, but nothing came of it.

A month after Guiteau was arrested and awaiting trial in the heavily guarded jail, a prison guard, William C. McGill Jr., received information from a colleague that Guiteau had been acting suspiciously. McGill feared the assassin was attempting suicide so he unlocked the cell door. When he entered he saw Guiteau holding a makeshift knife he had made with steel taken from his shoes. McGill drew his Smith and Wesson .32 revolver and leveled it at the assassin, demanding he hand over the weapon. Guiteau sprang from his bed and attacked the guard. During the scuffle McGill's coat was cut in several places and the gun accidently discharged when Guiteau briefly had it in his possession. The bullet lodged in the wall across the corridor. An army sergeant and another guard heard the shot and rushed to McGill's assistance. Following a short struggle, Guiteau gave up and shouted, "They are trying to kill me, give me my pistol; it belongs to me."[18]

Two attempts were made on Guiteau's life in the months he spent in jail awaiting trial. In September 1881 there was talk among the soldiers detailed to guard Guiteau about which one of them should be chosen to shoot the assassin when he showed his face at the window of his cell. It was decided that the honor should go to Sergeant John A. Mason, the best shot in Company B, Second Artillery.

On the evening of September 12, three wagonloads of soldiers arrived at the prison from the nearby arsenal to relieve the day guards. Mason was in the first wagon and was observed fumbling with the lock on his rifle. When the wagon reached the jail, Mason jumped out, ran to a small hillock, and took aim. He fired at Guiteau's cell window. The bullet passed by Guiteau's ear, went through his coat, and passed through a photograph of his mother, which was in his pocket. Mason then walked toward the captain of the guard and said, "I wanted to kill that wretch in there and I have been at it for ten days. I hope I have done the work in good style."[19]

Mason was court-martialed at the Washington Arsenal on February 20, 1882. On March 10 he was convicted and sentenced to be dishonorably discharged from the army and given eight years' hard labor. However, public sympathy was with Mason, who had a wife and child. One hundred and twenty thousand people signed a petition asking for leniency and a pardon. It was presented to President Arthur on March 20, 1882. A fund of $11,000 was raised across the country for his wife and child, who were affectionately known as "Betty and the baby."

Mason was unexpectedly pardoned in November 1883 in time for Thanksgiving. He had been imprisoned for twenty months and ten days.[20] After his release, he said, "What had I done? I had been sent to guard an assassin who had murdered our president. What would any man have done under the circumstances? . . . If I had been tried by a jury I would have been acquitted." Mason said he did not regret having fired at Guiteau, but he did "regret having had to put in all this time here, unjustly as I think."[21]

A second attempt to kill Garfield's assassin was made shortly before 3:00 p.m., on November 19, 1881, during Guiteau's trial. The police van returning Guiteau from the courtroom to the jail was approached by a horseman who rode up to the van, peered inside, drew his .32-caliber pistol, and fired. The vigilante missed his mark—the bullet only grazed Guiteau's left arm, two inches below the elbow, making a flesh bruise. Guiteau's coat and shirt sleeve were torn. A witness heard the attacker exclaim, "I have shot the son of a bitch."

A police officer, W. I. Edelin, who accompanied Guiteau, aimed his revolver at the would-be assassin and fired before Guiteau's assailant could get off a second shot. When the horseman made his escape, the coach driver gave chase, giving up only when the tracks of the Baltimore and Ohio Railroad prevented him from continuing.

A manhunt to find Guiteau's attacker followed. A police officer who patrolled the Soldiers' Home saw a man who fitted the attacker's description, and several shots were fired when he attempted to apprehend him. A drunken twenty-nine-year-old William Jones was eventually arrested after hiding out in nearby woods. He was regarded as an eccentric by his neighbors and described as an "attention seeker" who was "mentally unstable."[22]

The public response was immediate. A defense fund of $300 was raised for "Hero Bill Jones," who was nicknamed "the Avenger." He was indicted on November 25, 1881, for assault with intent to kill. However, when he was tried later that month, he was acquitted. It was believed that police officer W. I. Edelin had failed to identify Jones as Guiteau's assailant because he felt sympathy with the gunman. Nearly thirty years later, Bill Jones, by then a farmer, was arrested for the murder of one of his neighbors.[23]

Guiteau's trial began on November 14, 1881. His lawyers tried to argue he was insane, but Guiteau saw himself differently. "I am a man of destiny as much as the Savior, or Paul, or Martin Luther," he announced to the court. Throughout the trial, Guiteau ranted incessantly, invoking God and proclaiming that the American people would be judged harshly if he was found guilty.

The subject of insanity was on trial as much as the assassin. Witnesses were called who described Guiteau's psychological state of mind, his narcissism, and his visions of grandeur. The prosecution challenged every defense witness who attempted to show that the assassin was mad, including a young neurologist, Edward Spitzka, who wrote that Guiteau's "hereditary history, his insane manner, his insane documents and his insane actions were to be committed to any asylum in the land, he would be unhesitatingly admitted as a proper subject for sequestration."[24] However, although the jurors believed Guiteau killed Garfield because he wanted to be infamous, more than one hundred years later, Guiteau's grasp on reality, or lack of it, would no doubt result in his spending life in a mental institution. Psychiatrists would probably diagnose him today as a paranoid schizophrenic.

On January 25, 1882, when the trial ended, the jury decided Guiteau was both sane and guilty. It took them only one hour and five minutes to make their decision. After the verdict was read out in court Guiteau responded:

> I am not guilty of the charge set forth in the indictment. It was God's act, not mine, and God will take care of it, and don't let the American people forget it. He will take care of it and every officer of the Government, from the Executive down to the Marshal, taking in every man on that jury and every member of this bench will pay for it, and the American nation will roll in blood if my body goes into the ground and I am hung.

The judge wasn't buying it, however, and told the assassin as much before handing down the death sentence: "One cannot doubt, that you understood the nature and consequences of your crime or that you had the moral capacity to recognize its iniquity. Your own wretched sophistry, not inspiration overcame the promptings of conscience."[25]

On June 30, 1882, Guiteau was executed by hanging. As the noose was adjusted he exclaimed, "Glory, glory." When the trap door fell, crowds outside the prison cheered.

The public was confused. European assassinations occurred because individuals and groups were angry at the regimes led by monarchical powers who gave little freedom to their subjects. Guiteau had no real axe to grind—he did not have a genuine political agenda apart from supporting the Stalwarts and wanting to see Chester Arthur accede to the presidency. Americans needed a reason and they blamed the spoils system. Garfield's death was the result of a greedy office seeker, the public and press concluded, who acted violently when he failed to persuade the president to appoint him to office.

Although civil service reforms were enacted under President Arthur, the government still failed to act when it came to protecting presidents. Those measures were not introduced until twenty years later after another president, William McKinley, had been gunned down.

Following the shooting, the clear need for increased security for the president did not inspire any positive responses from the press. Typically, the *Boston Evening Transcript* editorialized, "President Garfield was attacked by a solitary individual who had no other weapon than a revolver; and to similar chances rulers in every age have always been exposed. Assassination will have to be much more frequent than they have ever been to destroy the attractiveness of the post of Chief Magistrate for the majority of mankind."[26]

The new president, Chester Arthur, had risen to power through machine politics. In 1871, President Ulysses Grant named Arthur the customs collector for the Port of New York. In an era of political machines and the patronage system of political appointments, Republican political boss Roscoe Conkling, a U.S. senator from New York, was instrumental in helping Arthur obtain the important position, which controlled some one thousand employees. The U.S. Customs House at the Port of New York collected fees imported from foreign countries more than anywhere else in the country.

Arthur, in turn, gave government jobs to Conkling's supporters, who contributed part of their salaries to the Republican Party. In 1878, after Rutherford Hayes became president, he ousted Arthur from the job in an attempt to reform the New York Custom House and spoils system.

But by that time Arthur had become a wealthy man after working for New York's Boss Tweed and Roscoe Conkling.

When Arthur entered the White House, the *New York Times* described him as "about the last man who could be considered eligible to that position, did the choice depend on the voice either of his own party or a majority of the people of the United States."[27] However, Arthur surprised many Americans (and alienated his former friends) by moving past partisanship. He refused to allow Roscoe Conkling to call the tune and in January 1883 gave his support to civil service reform. Accordingly, Congress passed the Pendleton Civil Service Act relieving the president of the responsibility for filling 10 percent of federal jobs, which henceforth would be determined by an examination system. It reduced corruption within the government considerably.

For a brief period following Garfield's shooting, security at the White House was increased, according to the *Boston Globe*. The White House grounds were shut off from the public, and only those visitors holding cards of admission signed by J. Stanley Brown, Garfield's secretary, were permitted to "pass the policeman at the gate." Soldiers "lounged about" the lawn between the White House and the Treasury Department and spent their time in a "very undignified sprawl upon blankets spread over the soft greed sod. The upper and lower yards of the White House were littered with parts of machinery sent to assist in the cooling of [the president's] sick room."[28]

The matter of personal presidential security was dealt with indirectly and belatedly. Presidents had spent an inordinate amount of time meeting office seekers, including Garfield's assassin, Guiteau, so reforms, legislators thought, would partially keep the chief executive out of harm's way. The *Cleveland Herald* opined, "This crime is as logically and legitimately the result of doctrines of Conkling and his followers as the murder of Lincoln was the result of the teachings of Secessionists. It was not the hand of this miserable office seeker that armed the deadly blow at the life of Garfield, but the embodied spirit of selfishness, of love of rule, of all that is implied by 'the machine' and the 'one man power,' in a word, of Conklingism and its teachings."[29]

However, the dangers remained. According to a report in the *Roanoke Times*, "After the tragedy . . . Guiteaus innumerable thronged our streets, alleys, wharfs and principle places."[30] After a man who threatened Vice President Arthur on July 6 was arrested, the *Sacramento Daily Record-Union* opined: "How many men are on the road, converging upon Washington, of course nobody can tell: but it is clear that the crime of Guiteau is developing a large crop of homicidal maniacs, and that it may be necessary in consequence to keep watch upon all public men of any value for some time to come."[31]

The *New York Tribune* predicted that the assassination of Garfield would lead to the president becoming "the slave of his office, the prisoner of forms and restrictions," unlike the ways of previous presidents.[32] However, although the nation was shocked by Guiteau's act, Congress took no action when it came to the president's personal protection. Chester Arthur continued the practice of walking the streets of Washington and New York without a bodyguard or police protection, and at one time he hailed a cab in front of the White House to attend a ceremony at the Washington Navy Yard.[33]

———

During the period after James Garfield was shot and prior to the time of his death, Chester Arthur stayed in New York. After Arthur was sworn in as president, on the day Garfield died, he immediately returned to Washington and spent the interim period before he moved into the White House at the Butler Mansion on Capitol Hill. The house was owned by Arthur's friend, Nevada senator John Jones. Senator Jones and his family had vacated the property to escape the intense summer heat of the capital. The mansion was built of granite, "with spacious rooms, beautifully finished and elegantly furnished." The first floor held offices, and Arthur had his private office on the second floor. He stayed there for "weeks," according to William Crook, and "messengers were constantly going back and forth to and from the president, and all sorts of papers and documents which needed his inspection and signature."[34] He would sometimes commute to the White House each evening after dinner to give instructions as to how it should be decorated and refurbished.

During Arthur's stay at the Butler Mansion, he escaped an assassination attempt, according to an 1888 report in the *Charlotte Democrat*. The newspaper reported that a "shot was fired at a reporter for the *Cincinnati Enquirer* who was sitting talking to Senator John P. Jones" and that "the villain took the reporter for Arthur." The shot came through a window but missed the target. The incident was corroborated in a statement Senator Jones gave to the *Philadelphia Times* many years later.[35]

The assassination attempt was also reported by Smith D. Fry, the Washington special correspondent for the *Roanoke Times*. In an article dated July 3, 1891, the reporter confirmed the incident had taken place, but failed to mention that it was the *Cincinnati Enquirer* reporter who had been mistaken for President Arthur. "One night while sitting in the Butler mansion on Capitol Hill, where he made his residence with Senator Jones for several weeks," Fry wrote, "President Arthur was shot at through an open window; but the fact was kept from the public at the time, although a well-known newspaper man was in the room when the villainy was attempted. The crank was never known."[36]

The shooting incident occurred during the same period that a civil servant reported that two men were plotting to assassinate Arthur. Washington's *Evening Star* reported on September 28, 1881, that the nephew of former 1880 Republican congressional candidate S. P. Bayley filed a sworn statement for the Washington Police Department that he had overheard two men planning Arthur's assassination. The nephew, also named Bayley, was an attaché of the Army Medical Museum in the Surgeon General's Department. He said that around midnight on Monday, September 26, he overheard two men talking on a sidewalk outside his bedroom window. He heard one of the men swear he "would kill the president in one month." Although Bayley said he could identify the men if they were apprehended, no arrests were made, although vigilance around the president was noticeably enhanced.[37]

The second incident that endangered Arthur shortly after he became president occurred on October 31, 1881, when a "well-dressed, powerfully-built man," Dr. John Noetling, a "prominent doctor from Colesville, Snyder County, Pennsylvania," called at the White House and asked to see the new president.[38] White House guard Thomas Pendel told the visitor, "The president is not here. He is in the Butler house on the south side of the Capitol but I do not believe you will be able to see him." Noetling appeared to Pendel to be "rational" and "sensible."

The doctor left but returned two weeks later and took a seat in the main vestibule. One of the ushers tipped Pendel off that the caller was "not right," so Pendel asked for him to be detained until the arrival of Sergeant Densmore, who was in charge of the door at the time. When Noetling saw Densmore, he "started to leave hurriedly." Densmore "caught him by the throat" before he could exit the door. As the two men struggled, two other White House staff came to Densmore's aid. Noetling tried to reach for his pistol but was thrown to the floor and arrested. When they confiscated the seven-shot revolver, they discovered that every chamber was loaded. The guards believed Noetling was there to assassinate the president. Noetling was taken to the police station and later sent home.[39]

When Arthur entered the White House as president, he instructed his doorkeeper to "admit everyone who comes."[40] Visitors had to report to E. S. Densmore, John T. Rickard, or Thomas F. Pendel, all of whom had worked at the Executive Mansion since the Civil War.[41] During Arthur's first reception, on New Year's Day 1882, after the mourning period for President Garfield had ended, the White House was attended by "several thousand" visitors. They were met by Arthur who was without a personal bodyguard or a military guard.[42]

The new president "never hesitated to walk around the city [Washington] alone, unaccompanied by a guard or other attendant," according to White House guard William Crook. However, Arthur's strolls were infrequent, as the president "did not walk a great deal or take any other form of exercise."[43]

Arthur often drove around the city or nearby countryside in his Victoria carriage, usually accompanied by a friend but without a mounted escort or bodyguard. Occasionally he rode his horse. He undertook these activities despite reports that he was so fearful he would be assassinated he had his life insured for $100,000 for the benefit of his family.[44]

The first winter of Arthur's presidency was an "interesting crank season," according to the *Pittsburgh Dispatch*.[45] Hardly a day went by "but a maniac calls and tried to see the president," the *Daily Globe* reported in 1883. From the time of Garfield's assassination until January 1882, seventy-two "cranks" had been arrested in Washington.[46]

Sergeant Densmore usually dealt with the cranks by using persuasion and not resorting to violence or calling for the local police. On one occasion, a typical crank spoke to Densmore and told him he was the "Second Guiteau." Densmore replied that it did not make any difference who he was, he was not going to see the president, and he showed the drunken visitor to the door.[47] Another visitor arrived at the White House claiming he was the "slayer of President Lincoln." He was arrested and sent for psychiatric examination.[48]

However, cranks of a more serious disposition threatened the life of Arthur during his visits to New York City. In October 1882, an eighteen-year-old William Martin called at police headquarters and asked for a permit to carry a pistol. When he was asked what he wanted a pistol for, the young man replied, "To shoot President Arthur." He was arrested and taken to Jefferson Market Court. During the hearing, it was discovered he had just been released from prison for larceny. He was taken to a hospital to determine his sanity.[49]

In November 1883, a hotel detective at the Fifth Avenue Hotel where the president was staying was alarmed when he stopped a man, described as "around 60 years old," who was "prowling about the hotel." When he was approached by the detective, the man said, "I have a duty to perform. I am a Colonel from Kentucky and I have made this trip for the express purpose of shooting President Arthur." He then hurried outside and hailed a cab before the detective could apprehend him. The detective believed the man was not a crank and would have assassinated the president had he been able to see him.[50]

In 1882, Arthur learned he was suffering from Bright's disease, a serious kidney ailment. He kept the condition a secret from the public. His poor health prevented him from actively seeking reelection in 1884. Instead, the Republicans chose Secretary of State James Blaine as their presidential nominee. Blaine was defeated by Grover Cleveland in the general election.

CHAPTER 7

The Attempted Assassination of Benjamin Harrison

The White House attracts cranks like a magnet [and] scarcely a day passes in which [the doorkeeper] is not called upon by the dictates of prudence to stop some suspicious or unpleasant-looking mortal at the gateway to the president's abode.
—*Stark County Democrat*, Canton OH, May 30, 1889

It would be very difficult for any [would-be assassin] to reach the presence of Mr. Harrison. You don't see why, but that is because you never looked about you closely when you have attended a reception at the executive mansion. How many pairs of eyes do you suppose scan you closely while you are passing from the front door to the cloakroom? . . . Every one of these men have had years of experience in detective work. They can tell at a glance the character of each guest who enters. You never saw these men, you say? You don't suppose, do you, that these men are dressed in uniform, with brass buttons and a big silver badge on the lapel of his coat?
—*Pittsburgh Press*, April 30, 1890

Benjamin Harrison was the grandson of the ninth president, William Henry Harrison, and took the oath of office in March 1889, on the year of the nation's Washington Centennial Celebration (commemorating the inauguration of George Washington as the first U.S. president). His presidency was sandwiched between Grover Cleveland's two terms—1885 to 1889 and 1893 to 1897.

Harrison's presidency is noted for a number of issues of historical significance. During his time in office, six new states were admitted to the

Union, more than under any other president. Accordingly, by the time he left the White House, America's population had risen to sixty-seven million.

Benjamin Harrison was widely known as "the human iceberg," so named by House Speaker Thomas B. Reed, although he was one of the best extemporaneous speakers of the day and was known as one of the most patriotic presidents. Theodore Roosevelt said Harrison was "cold-blooded, narrow-minded, prejudiced [and] obstinate." A Harrison biographer has described him as "formal, colorless, and dour . . . a study in inaction, with a limited view of the parameters of his office." He was also described as a "figurehead" for Republican bosses and big businessmen. Accordingly, he developed a reputation for being subservient to party and Congress.[1]

Along with previous presidents Grant, Hayes, Garfield, Arthur, and Cleveland, Harrison did not make "much of a mark on the country," according to historian Robert Dallek. Their presidential campaigns, Dallek noted, "offered no remedies for continuing North-South divisions or for economic and social ills besetting farmers, laborers and recently arrived immigrants."[2]

Nevertheless, Harrison's administration was efficient and free from major scandals, and he greatly enhanced presidential authority by supporting and signing the Sherman Antitrust Act. Presidential authority was also enhanced when he shielded federal officers from prosecution by states when they pursued official duties. He was successful in persuading Congress to pass the Forest Reserve Act, and he sought reciprocal trade agreements, supported a protective tariff, and sought vigorously but unsuccessfully to counter Southern resistance and protect the rights of black voters. Additionally, Harrison was successful in persuading Congress to provide pensions for Civil War veterans, and he modernized the navy, which resulted in a greater world presence for the United States.

Although never officially sanctioned by Congress, the Secret Service was given the task of providing protection for President Harrison during the preinaugural period. Agents were noticed in Indianapolis, and reporters asked Harrison about the alleged security arrangements. The president-elect was furious. He did not like the idea of being guarded and remarked to newspaper reporters that he should assign Secret Service Chief Bell and his detectives "to look after the safety of the [newspaper] correspondents."[3]

When Benjamin Harrison took office, his White House bodyguard was Edson S. Densmore, a Massachusetts citizen who had worked in his local police force. Later Densmore joined the Washington police force and was promoted to sergeant. During Grant's administration he was instrumental in breaking up gambling houses in Washington and arrested "Congressmen, Senators, and Generals." His name became dreaded in Washington. A newspaper's White House reporter described him as a man who was "straight as a grenadier, his head large and magnificently proportioned, [and] his hair has that iron-gray tinge that always gives an air of power." He had the "instinct for detecting criminals."[4]

According to a newspaper report of the time, the White House had become demoralized when Harrison took office. Densmore had resigned his position as chief usher during the first Cleveland administration but was sent for by Harrison to improve the situation. Although still employed by the Fitchburg, Massachusetts, firm he was working for, he promised the president he would look after the security of the White House until the inauguration was over.

After Harrison took the oath of office, however, Densmore remained as a guest and guide of the White House for a few days, as he promised, then acceded to the Harrison family's wishes that he remain as "chief guardian of the president's life."[5]

Densmore mediated between the president and the public and acted as the president's bodyguard outside the White House, but only if specifically requested. He escorted the president to trains and he was always on hand for the chief executive's return to Washington.[6]

Harrison had boasted in one of his speeches that he was proud of the fact that "the chief officer of the nation" went about unattended and that there was no need for an armed body to surround him.[7] However, there were some voices of dissent. In 1888 the *Washington Evening Star* reported that the president "daily exposes himself . . . as it is his custom to take two walks each day, and usually he strolls mostly, when alone, in the back streets of the northern part of the city. He is seldom accompanied by anyone, and he would prove an easy victim for any would-be assassin."[8]

President Harrison was aware of the risks he was taking. After the assassination of Mayor Carter Harrison of Chicago in October 1893, he said, "There is always a risk that a public officer runs; but with the conditions of the country as they are the risk is increased. When in Washington I frequently had the matter in mind and had some discussions upon it. All men must have free open air and an outside world to transact business. I felt rather than sacrifice this I would suffer to be killed."[9]

Around 5:00 p.m. each day, Harrison went driving, usually to the Maryland or Virginia countryside, and usually with a Metropolitan police officer, friends, or his secretary, Elijah Halford. Often, he would drive his green Studebaker landau alone. Although there were plainclothes bodyguards at the White House, they did not usually accompany him.[10] Harrison was, however, always accompanied by presidential aides or cabinet secretaries during his train journeys. In 1891 the president was given train travel privileges and free transportation on the Pennsylvania Railroad. He was supplied with five luxury carriages. The train, which was named the Presidential Special, took him on a nine-thousand-mile, five-week journey to the West Coast.[11]

When Harrison took his strolls in Washington, usually unaccompanied, he would exit at the rear of the White House. On his return he would dress for dinner. During his walks he frequently stopped to converse with Washington citizens.[12] Strangers would often approach him to ask for railroad tickets or assistance in finding employment.[13] On one occasion, in 1891, a "religious crank" had to be arrested for "annoying" the president as he walked the streets of the city.[14]

Harrison's habits contrasted sharply with Grover Cleveland's. Where Cleveland might have been seen occasionally around Washington in his carriage, Harrison was often observed nearly every day on his strolls, usually unaccompanied. John Philip Sousa's autobiography relates the story of Harrison getting caught out in a rainstorm and becoming thoroughly drenched during one of his solo walks.[15] He was described as a "devoted pedestrian." Sometimes he walked in the afternoon accompanied by one of his clerical staff and occasionally went out with his grandson. He was a frequent visitor to Lafayette Park across from the White House and often walked there unaccompanied.[16]

At one point, his staff, feeling a little nervous about Harrison's vulnerability, hired a bodyguard to follow him. Once Harrison became aware of the ruse, he sent the man home and severely criticized his staff for hiring such protection.[17] Harrison "chafed" under the attendance of bodyguards, according to Secret Service agent Capt. Thomas E. Halls.[18] During a trip to Rochester, New York, in May 1892, he was guarded by twelve city detectives and he was not pleased at the innovation as he did not regard it as necessary.[19]

Edson Densmore was responsible for six White House guards, each of whom was "especially selected for his skill as a detective as well as for muscular strength." A police officer attended the single sentry station at the southeast entrance night and day, and a second officer patrolled the North Portico. The north gates were closed at sundown, and small fences restricted pedestrians along pathways in the grounds. During visiting hours tourists would enter by the north door. Under Harrison's instructions the bodyguards were to act as unobtrusively as possible. At times Densmore would have additional security when Colonel Ernst, master of ceremonies at the White House, would also occasionally act as bodyguard to Harrison with the assistance of a naval attaché, Lieutenant Parker.[20]

Densmore was believed to know "just about every crank who lived in the capital." He "seemed to know them by instinct and none get further than the door or the vestibules," an 1892 newspaper story reported. Densmore was considered by one newspaper reporter to be "the most expert judge of cranks in the country," and his "first lieutenant" had "an upper arm" that was "as big as an ordinary man's thigh, and his fellows were all athletes."[21]

Densmore usually took up his duty at the entrance to the White House. When he was confronted with unruly or disputatious visitors, he would "coax and manage" them until they left. He had to send someone either to the insane asylum or the police station nearly every day, according to a reporter for the *Deseret News*.[22]

In dealing with visitors who were mentally unstable or irksome, Densmore would pretend to write notes to the president to humor them. If the visitor persisted, he would ask them to leave a card or a note, which "never reached the president."[23] Many of the White House's strange visitors were religious cranks, including a man who called himself "The Prophet." He said he was mentioned in the Book of Revelations and that he made and unmade presidents. Years before, he had made threats against the life of Rutherford Hayes and was eventually arrested and sent to jail. He continued to visit the White House following his release but was considered to be harmless.[24]

During every White House reception, each guest had to be vetted by Densmore's guards before they could meet the president. The guards patrolled the lobby around the clock. Anyone who made himself "objectionable" would be "disposed of." Two guards always stood close to the president during "entertainments," watching every person shaking hands. If there was any "hostile intent" the visitor was "seized."[25] On one occasion a woman managed to greet President Harrison at a reception and demanded a deed for the entire United States. Harrison told her she could have it if she would pay the taxes on it, and she agreed to the request.[26]

Although Densmore was not on duty overnight, he made the security arrangements for the White House police force. Sometimes he would walk around the grounds as late as midnight and check guard houses in the early hours of the morning. During public receptions in the East Room, Densmore, armed with a pistol, would always be at the president's side. He performed the introductions and many visitors often mistook him for the vice president.

A White House police officer once told a reporter there were numerous individuals he saw who he feared might do President Harrison some harm. Caroline Harrison complained of the "circus atmosphere" in the White House when she found visitors wandering uninvited into the family quarters. The president often complained about his lack of privacy.

However, the security arrangements were believed to be sufficient. When a newspaper reporter asked one of the White House ushers why any person should not be able to assassinate President Harrison at one of his receptions, he received the reply,

> Simply for the reason that it would be very difficult for any individual so inclined to reach the presence of Mr. Harrison. You don't see why, but that is because you never looked about you closely when you have

attended a reception at the executive mansion. How many pairs of eyes do you suppose scan you closely while you are passing from the front door to the cloakroom? Six in all for at every entertainment of any magnitude whatever six men are on duty for no other purpose than to guard and protect the person of the chief executive from harm. Every one of these men have had years of experience in detective work. They can tell at a glance the character of each guest who enters. You never saw these men, you say? You don't suppose, do you, that these men are dressed in uniform, with brass buttons and a big silver badge on the lapel of his coat?[27]

The White House usher believed the president's bodyguards could recognize a would-be assassin in an instant as their "eyes would always betray them." The assassin would be "laboring under a good deal of excitement" and it would "betray him or her to us at a glance."[28]

Throughout Harrison's administration, the White House continued to attract so-called cranks, but by this time their numbers were growing in line with the increasing American population. The Executive Mansion was a "Mecca" to which "all cranks in the country make pilgrimages when they can," the *Sacramento Daily Record-Union* stated.[29] Many cranks were attracted to Washington "like moths fluttering around a candle," according to a Washington journalist.[30] "The White House attracts cranks like a magnet," the *Stark County Democrat* stated, "[and] scarcely a day passes in which [the doorkeeper] is not called upon by the dictates of prudence to stop some suspicious or unpleasant-looking mortal at the gateway to the president's abode."[31]

A White House police officer, who had been on duty at the Executive Mansion at the beginning of Harrison's term, said the majority of cranks fell into distinct categories, including "the self-important, bustling statesman who rushes in as if his business would spoil if delayed a single moment; the weary and sad-eyed candidate who has waited and waited and lost his nerve and his ability to sleep at night, all on account of the office that never comes; the timid and gawking countryman who is not quite sure that he dares walk in an open door, and who stops to ask questions and say he is afraid of intruding; the loquacious fellow who has been always a good Republican and who imagines everybody about the White House is interested in his story and possessed of influence that could help him if it were but exerted in his behalf."[32]

Once in a while a drunk would appear at receptions, but Densmore and his men would grab the offender and summarily eject him from the White House grounds. There was a "regular drill for this performance, and practice makes perfect," the reporter observed.[33] The inebriated man would be passed from guard to guard, "one by one until he reached the gates of the White House."[34] (Densmore died on November 13, 1892, during Harrison's presidency. His White House role was given to Sergeant Decker.)

Harrison made sure he was accessible to the public. He would make surprise appearances in the East Room, which usually took place before his 1:30 p.m. lunch. He would remain for five minutes or so, chatting to visitors, often chatting about the history of the White House.[35] However, the idea that citizens were entitled to roam the White House grounds at will was still prevalent during Harrison's time in office. Some visitors arrived at the White House asking to see the president's rooms on the grounds that they, as the "peoples' representatives," owned the mansion.[36] Many visitors to the White House would take it as a matter of course that they could dine with the president. Frequently, they were offended when their requests were refused.[37]

Harrison was severely criticized by the press and political opponents for having a bodyguard. During a visit to San Francisco, the police department placed a guard of four officers in plainclothes with Harrison, who immediately objected and asked they be dismissed. This did not prevent a Sacramento newspaper from opining that the president's bodyguard was "silly . . . absurd, un-American and wholly unnecessary." In the East, the newspaper stated, "the president needs no bodyguards. He comes and goes about the national capital. . . . He makes trips to New York . . . freely. . . . In fact, the bare suggestion of a bodyguard would reduce the office of president from the American plane to the monarchical level of timidity and fear of the people." The police authorities, the newspaper stated, implied that the West was "infested with desperate characters . . . would-be Guiteaus so swarm among us, assassins and cranks are so numerous upon our streets that we must . . . guard our guests with bodies of armed men."[38]

From the time he was elected president, Benjamin Harrison faced assassination plots and threats to kill him. Like presidents before him, Harrison was the subject of many an ill-considered threat uttered by a fanatic, a mentally unstable individual, or a drunk. And the threats continued even after he had left office. In 1894, for example, a man was arrested in Atlantic City for threatening to kill the former president. He said after his arrest that he had been employed by the government to kill Harrison and that he had come to Atlantic City to raise funds for his assassination plans.[39]

In May 1889, shortly after Harrison's election, New York anarchists "openly counseled" his assassination during a visit to the city. New York police were aware of the threats but did not give the matter "serious concern." Instead, they kept a "watchful eye." A leading New York anarchist, the editor of *Volks Zeitung*, said he was not aware of any assassination plot but opined that it was "a good time for such a thing to happen." An editorial in the anarchist newspaper *Freiheit* stated, "The American cowboy aristocracy is on the eve of a feast at which they propose to drain the foaming bumper of joy. We intend, however, to spill some drops of poison in their nectar. What needs to be done is to relegate the Constitution to antiquity and the Cabinet to history. Down with the Presidency . . . long live social revolution!"[40]

Edson Densmore was responsible for intercepting the numerous threatening letters that were received at the White House. "Hardly a week passes," a newspaper report stated, "but threatening letters are received from cranks and persons who breathe out intimidations and promise swift vengeance."[41] If the writer came from Washington, Densmore would investigate and liaise with the Washington police force. It was believed that Elijah Halford, the president's private secretary, did not forward the threatening letters to the president.[42]

A typical threatener was A. J. Orton, a clerk in the New York Custom House, who wrote menacing letters to President Harrison and other prominent men. He was charged with "sending scurrilous matter through the mails."[43] Another threatener, Newman Atkinson, who lived in Burlington, New Jersey, was arrested for writing a letter threatening to assassinate the president. He was declared insane and sent to the New Jersey State Asylum in Trenton.[44]

Harrison was also the victim of a number of uninvited guests at the White House who managed to break into the mansion. On two occasions, in 1890 and 1891, the president was confronted by men who threatened him.

In 1890 Arthur P. Cunningham worked in the document room of the U.S. Senate. In November of that year he inherited a considerable sum of money, $1,500,000, from an Australian relative. Excited by his good fortune he began drinking heavily, then decided to visit the White House, as he believed the president was responsible for the "recent economic upheaval." Cunningham forced his way into the room where President Harrison was engaged and began "applying to [the president] all the opprobrious epithets he could think of." Harrison called for assistance from one of the White House police officers, who arrested Cunningham. He was charged and found guilty of disorderly conduct.[45]

On the evening of March 22, 1891, Henry Martin, the stepson of Sen. Zebulon Baird of North Carolina, had been dining with friends at a restaurant near the White House. Becoming increasingly drunk and incapable, Martin told his friends he was going to call on President Harrison and "beat the hell" out of him. Accompanying him to the Executive Mansion, Martin's friends soon learned he was serious in his intentions. The drunken Martin climbed a fence at the southernmost extremity of the White House grounds, unseen by guards, as one of his friends alerted White House police.

Harrison was dining with one of his friends, a banker, B. K. Jamieson, and his wife, when they heard the sound of breaking glass. Martin had broken a window and entered the Red Room. White House police officer John Kenny, who was on guard at the entrance to the mansion, heard the commotion and confronted Martin. The intruder stood shirtless, smashing glassware and shouting, "Where is the president? Let me at him and I'll knock hell out of him." Kenny was joined by Officer Dubos, and as they proceeded to tackle the intruder, Harrison walked into the room to provide assistance. Harrison assisted the police officers in tying Martin up. The intruder was then taken to the local police station at Twelfth

Street. When Martin sobered up in the jail, he said he had no memory of the incident. He pleaded guilty and received a suspended sentence.[46]

A further incident of intrusion at the White House occurred during Harrison's presidency, although this time the president was not threatened. Harrison was sitting out on the rear portico one evening talking to Maryland congressional representative Sydney Mudd, when an unnamed man jumped the rail and said he wanted to see the president. Harrison quietly escorted him inside the house and pressed an electric button, which summoned two doorkeepers who promptly ejected the visitor. The man left without knowing he had been conversing with the president.[47]

There had always been rumors of threats to assassinate American presidents, and President Harrison was no exception. Many of the rumors could not be substantiated or were strenuously denied. One rumor occurred when Harrison was president-elect in the winter of 1888. According to a newspaper report, an assassination plot had been arranged by a "gang of villains" but the scheme was discovered by one of Harrison's friends and thwarted. The newspaper stated that the plot had been kept a "dead secret, and it is said that General Harrison and family intended it never be made public. It is believed that the publication of the story will result in a strenuous effort to bring the miscreants to justice."[48] Another newspaper report of the same incident stated that a "close friend" had revealed the plot and that the attempt to assassinate Harrison had occurred in "December 1888."[49]

Although rumors of assassination attempts were prevalent throughout Harrison's presidency, there is compelling evidence that a serious attempt on the president's life definitely occurred in 1890, but was covered up by White House aides.

In March 1890, Sen. George F. Hoar of Massachusetts received a letter demanding he continue to press for an investigation of Southern courts, which the writer believed to be corrupt. The writer said he had served during the Civil War in a Massachusetts regiment and was mustered out as a captain of his company. The letter was "full of vile accusations against prominent and famous Democrats and Republicans alike" in Virginia. It also contained "vile insinuations against the private lives of several of Senator Hoar's colleagues." The threatening letter was posted in Petersburg, Virginia, and was signed "Old Republican soldier."[50]

Senator Hoar became alarmed when he read that the writer vowed that unless some remedy was forthcoming for halting the abuse that had been heaped upon him, he would go to Washington and kill President Harrison. The writer of the letter stated, "Garfield had his Guiteau and Harrison may have—well, the writer is his assassin. I give him but until the 20th of May to live."[51]

Senator Hoar was a friend of Harrison's. In fact, Harrison considered making him secretary of state if John Sherman turned the offer down. He was one of the foremost leaders in the Republican Party—described at the 1880 Republican National Convention as having "integrity" and "impartiality"—and was a fighter against political corruption.

Senator Hoar, although alarmed by the contents of the letter, reasoned the writer was of unsound mind and probably harmless, so he filed the letter away and thought no more about it. Two weeks later, however, a second letter arrived addressed to the senator and this time the writer repeated his threat to kill the president, "on or immediately after May 20th." Hoar handed both letters over to Secret Service chief John S. Bell.

In 1890 the Secret Service did not have official responsibility for the protection of the president. However, the agency was so flexible as to permit it to operate in all the different federal departments who required "detective assistance." Organized in 1865, with an initial appropriation for detecting counterfeiters and investigating other felonies, the Secret Service was maintained by varied appropriations voted under different and misleading captions in Congress. It acquired functions for which no provision was made by Congress, occasionally arousing suspicion. Many in Congress were therefore confused about its role as a federal agency. In 1874 there was a serious scandal whereby the agency appeared at the time to be a political machine, with the agents working for the legislators or other government officers who had caused their appointment.[52]

Bell formally became chief of the service on February 16, 1889. He had earned a reputation as an honest Newark, New Jersey, chief of police before he became a Secret Service agent on June 22, 1885. As chief, Bell often joined his men in making arrests and he often acted as an undercover agent.

Bell was described by one newspaper reporter to be as "picturesque a character as you may meet in the United States. He looks like a Wild

Westerner. . . . He wears his dark hair long; it falls an inch or two over his coat collar . . . [and] he bears a most striking resemblance to the Hon. William F. Cody, better known as 'Buffalo Bill.' . . . In the museum of the Secret Service I noticed portraits of Cody and Bell side by side, and nobody could decide offhand which was which."[53] In fact, John S. Bell was a close friend of William F. Cody and he was often mistaken for the Wild West hero.[54]

Bell assigned a team of two agents to investigate the "Old Republican soldier" who had sent the threatening letters. The lead agent was one of Bell's best, identified as "Agent O'Dwyer," who had been stationed in Pittsburgh and had assisted Chief Bell in capturing a counterfeiting gang, the "Driggs Family."[55]

A few weeks after Bell received the threatening letters, Senator Sherman, also a friend of the president's, received a similar letter threatening the president's life. Once more the writer gave May 20 as the time of Harrison's assassination. Sherman handed the letter to Chief Bell and it proved to hold a clue "to ferreting out the writer."[56]

Meanwhile, the two Secret Service agents tracked down the source of the letters to the town of Petersburg and managed to locate a suspect. He was a small shopkeeper in the Virginia town and was noted among the local people as being "eccentric."

On May 23, the agents followed the shopkeeper to Washington and observed the would-be assassin stationing himself on Pennsylvania Avenue at around 9:30 in the morning. It was known to be part of the route taken by President Harrison on his carriage rides. The shopkeeper was approximately twenty feet away from Harrison as the president passed by. As he attempted to draw his revolver, the assassin was quickly subdued by the agents and taken to police headquarters. Washington police took possession of a .38-caliber Smith and Wesson revolver, together with a number of letters that chronicled the would-be assassin's grievance and the reasons why he had targeted the president for assassination.[57]

During his interrogation, the Virginia shopkeeper confessed "boldly" that he had intended to kill the president. Later, he was quietly adjudged to be insane and was confined to an insane asylum near Richmond.[58]

On November 26, 1890, the by now ex-chief Bell, who had been visiting the capital on business, confirmed the story to newspaper reporters and "verified it in every particular." Bell said he was sorry that the matter had been made public and he "could not imagine from what source" the story emanated as all the people who had known about it had been "sworn to secrecy."[59]

On November 15, the White House responded to the story of the attempted assassination. The president's secretary, Elijah Walker Halford, called Bell's story "absurd" and added, "There is nothing in it." Halford also said he had consulted his diary when he heard the story and noticed that President Harrison had been at the White House all day on May 23, except for an afternoon walk he took with his secretary. Halford said he remembered the day exactly because of the issuance of a presidential directive to hoist the American flag daily over the White House; a custom that had lapsed during the Cleveland years.[60]

However, Halford was known to be especially sensitive to leaks and was described by Washington's *Evening Star* as having "secretive power, which is essentially necessary in a private secretary." The newspaper went on to describe how Halford's secretive nature could be seen in the manner in which he kept his marriage secret from his wife's parents for so long.[61] Additionally, David K. Frasier, of the Lilly Library, has examined a typed transcript of Elijah Halford's diary held in the Volwiler manuscripts. Frasier stated, "It contains no entry for [May 23, 1890] nor is the incident referenced in any 1890 entry."[62]

Senator Sherman denied he had received a letter threatening the president's life. However, if the senator had verified the story, it would have left him open to criticism that he had not forewarned President Harrison of the impending attack.[63] There is no record of Senator Hoar having denied the story. In later years Hoar would be one of the leading congressional representatives calling for improved security for the president. Hoar, who became chair of the Judiciary Committee in the Senate, would present a bill specifying that "any person who shall attempt to kill the President of the United States or any officer thereof, shall be punished with death."[64]

At the time the assassination story leaked, Bell had been replaced as chief of the Secret Service. Ex-chief Bell received some criticism in the press for confirming the story and some critics referred to Bell having been sacked from his job, implying that he had been an incompetent

Secret Service chief.[65] However, the history of Bell's service appears to suggest otherwise. The *Pittsburgh Dispatch* recognized "the efficiency of Chief Bell."[66] The *Washington Critic* characterized him as "a shrewd, searching officer [who] unearthed many dangerous counterfeiters since his incumbency . . . often [taking] a flying trip over the road to superintend operations in person."[67] After Bell's dismissal, the *Pittsburgh Dispatch* editorialized, "The Secret Service has lost one of the best men ever had by the dismissal of Chief Bell."[68] Other newspapers praised the Secret Service chief for being responsible for the convictions of numerous counterfeiters.[69]

There are no detailed records to suggest why Bell was asked to resign after only a year as chief, but there is evidence he was inundated with requests from bankers, businessmen, and federal prosecutors to send agents to investigate counterfeiting and fraud. The same difficulties in operating under limited Secret Service appropriations was experienced by a previous chief, James L. Brooks, who offered his resignation in 1885, although the new treasury secretary refused to accept it. Brooks struggled to operate an agency that was grossly underfunded and eventually decided to retire.[70]

Bell, who had only twenty-eight agents to cover the whole of the United States, did not have the funds to cover these expenses, so he turned them down.[71]

In an article he wrote for the *Pittsburgh Dispatch* after leaving office, Bell stated,

> Just think of it. Twenty-eight men cover this entire country hunting out counterfeits and counterfeiters . . . it is not the general public alone which is ignorant of the fact, but even Senators, Congressmen . . . these men who spend many years at the Capitol have simply amazed me many a time by their rank ignorance of the workings and character of the Secret Service. President Cleveland told me that the Secret Service worried him to death, in view of the fact that so few persons knew anything concerning its workings . . . morning, noon and night [Treasury Secretary Dan Manning] . . . was bothered by Senators and Congressmen for positions for constituents in the service, and, of course, he had to refuse them all, for it would never

do to replace a man who had been 15 years in the service by a man who had no experience . . . in conclusion let me say that the Secret Service is badly in need of more men and a much larger appropriations annually.[72]

Bell had no luck in persuading Treasury Secretary William Windom to supply additional funds. Instead, Windom suggested to Bell that the position of chief of the Secret Service be vacated for one year to make up for the shortfall and provide sufficient funds for the extra investigations that were called for.

It appears that Bell and sitting treasury secretaries had upset a great many influential people. Accordingly, Bell decided that his position was futile. He had done everything in his power to run the service on a meager budget and decided to let the matter rest. However, on June 2, 1890, Bell received a request from Windom to resign. On June 3, 1890, Chief Clerk John Cowie was named acting chief and served for the next seven months. Windom tried to get Brooks to return as chief but he declined the offer. Finally, Windom persuaded Andrew L. Drummond, agent-in-charge of the New York District, to take the job and he became chief on January 2, 1891.[73]

Accordingly, there is reason to suggest Bell was removed from his job, not because of his incompetency but owing to the machinations of influential politicians and bureaucrats whose requests for help from the agency had been turned down.

According to the *Washington Critic*, Bell was asked to resign for an additional reason, beyond the fact that he had upset many powerful individuals—Bell had to "make way for a friend of Russell Harrison's" and the president's son had a candidate in mind, Thomas J. Furlong.[74] It was reported that Treasury Secretary Windom was "satisfied with the job Bell was doing but the White House was not." Against Windom's wishes, he was forced to sack Bell. It was also known that Bell had resisted making the office part of the spoils system as had his predecessor, James Brooks. Bell was also criticized by friends of President Harrison's, who said that Chief Bell had allowed a "notorious counterfeiter" to escape "in the course of some operations in which he took a personal part."[75]

It would appear that the investigation into the attempted assassination of Benjamin Harrison was carried out without the president's knowledge. It also appears that Harrison had no knowledge of the assassination attempt. So the questions remain: If the story was false, why would Bell include in his story information about two of Congress's most powerful figures (and also friends of Harrison's), Senator Hoar and Senator Sherman? Additionally, why would Bell put himself at risk of exposure by referring to an exact date of the attempted assassination and the name of the institution where the alleged, would-be assassin was sent? The institution's records would have been open to scrutiny by congressional investigators. Furthermore, ex-chief Bell must have known that Congress could have called him before a committee at any time to account for his actions and to explain why he corroborated (or leaked) the story.[76]

In 1892 Benjamin Harrison decided to run for reelection as the Republican Party candidate. Grover Cleveland was nominated by the Democrats. During the campaign Mrs. Harrison contracted tuberculosis, so the president cut back on his campaign schedule. In fact, he hardly left her side. Out of respect for Harrison, Cleveland also eschewed campaigning and whiled away most of his hours at his retreat, Gray Gables, his summer home on Cape Cod. On October 25, Caroline Harrison died of complications from the disease. Two weeks later her husband lost the presidential election. Cleveland won with 277 electoral votes. Harrison received 145 votes.

President Harrison did not mind losing. He said, "For me there is no sting in it. Indeed, after the heavy blow the death of my wife dealt me, I do not think I could have stood the strain a reelection would have brought."[77]

1. Individuals or groups who attempted to kill American leaders or threatened assassination can be traced back to the time of George Washington. As president, Washington did not hire personal guards even though he received his fair share of abuse and threatening letters. Popular Graphic Arts Collection, Library of Congress, LC-USZ62–117116.

2. (*opposite above*) In May 1833, Andrew Jackson was assaulted by a naval lieutenant, Robert Beverly Randolph, and in 1835 he was the victim of an assassination attempt by Richard Lawrence, who fired two pistols at him. Both weapons misfired. Popular Graphic Arts Collection, Prints and Photographs Division, Library of Congress, LC-USZ62-2342.

3. (*opposite below*) Vice President John Tyler received news of William Henry Harrison's death in April 1841. Later that year, a drunken painter threw stones at him. On August 18, 1842, two drunken crowds descended on the White House, throwing stones and firing shots in the air. Prints and Photographs Division, Library of Congress, LC-USZ62-5997.

4. (*above*) Inauguration of James Buchanan. When a group of Civil War army veterans met in Saratoga in 1887, one of them revealed a plot to kill Buchanan in 1858. However, as the day of the planned assassination had drawn near, the Civil War veteran tipped off the authorities after hearing plotters discuss the assassination in a Lawrence, Kansas, tavern. Manuscript Division, the Papers of Montgomery C. Meigs, Library of Congress.

5. (*opposite above*) John Wilkes Booth stumbles and falls after shooting President Abraham Lincoln in Ford's Theater, Washington DC, on April 14, 1865. Lincoln was the victim of a number of assassination attempts during his time in office, including a grenade attack and sniper shots. The Alfred Whital Stern Collection of Lincolniana, Library of Congress, Portfolio 5, no. 1, Stern catalog 5075.

6. (*opposite below*) John Wilkes Booth's original plans involved kidnapping Lincoln on the president's way back to the White House from the Soldiers' Home where Lincoln stayed during the summer months. "Extraordinary Lecture by John Surratt: The Real Story of the Assassination of President Lincoln," the *(London) Day's Doings*, January 14, 1871.

7. (*above*) Ward Hill Lamon, a friend of Lincoln's, held himself responsible for the president's safety. Wikimedia Commons.

8. Booth approached Lincoln on Inauguration Day, March 4, 1865, at the Capitol Building (shown here). As Lincoln passed through the rotunda on his way to the inauguration platform, Booth attempted to push through the police lines. Prints and Photographs Division, Library of Congress, LC-USZ62–1676.

9. Andrew Johnson. Ulysses S. Grant said there had been a "deliberate attempt" on the life of President Andrew Johnson during a visit to Indianapolis. A shot was fired from a second-story window on the opposite side of the street to the president's hotel. The bullet struck a Chinese lantern near where Johnson was standing and passed within three feet of Grant's head. Prints and Photographs Division, Library of Congress, LC-DIG-cwpbh-03751.

10. Rutherford B. Hayes. Library of Congress, LC-DIG-cwpbh-03606.

11. A gunman stalked President-elect Rutherford B. Hayes and plotted to kill him during the inauguration ceremonies at the Capitol Building (shown here). Prints and Photographs Division, Library of Congress, LC-USZ62–92463.

12. Charles Guiteau, assassin of James Garfield. Shortly after Garfield had been sworn into office, Guiteau began to harass White House doorkeepers Thomas Pendel and Alonzo Dunn for access to the president. Wikimedia Commons.

13. On the morning of July 2, 1881, James Garfield was approached from behind by Charles Guiteau. The assassin fired his pistol from a distance of three feet. Prints and Photographs Division, Library of Congress, LC-USZ62–7622.

14. Chester A. Arthur was the victim of *two* assassination attempts. The first attempt was made at the Butler Mansion in Washington DC. The second attempt occurred at the White House when a would-be assassin attempted to see Arthur and struggled with White House guards before being subdued. Prints and Photographs Division, Library of Congress, LC-USZ62–13021.

15. Elijah Halford, Benjamin Harrison's secretary. Harrison was unaware of a serious plot to kill him because the president's aides and political friends kept the incident from him and were sworn to secrecy. Bain Collection, Prints and Photographs Division, Library of Congress, LC-USZ6–1387.

Secretary Thurber.

16. Henry T. Thurber, Grover Cleveland's secretary. The assassination attempts against Cleveland were covered up partly due to the intervention of Thurber. *Brockway Center (MI) Weekly Expositor*, March 10, 1893.

17. Grover Cleveland. Prints and Photographs Division, Library of Congress, LC-USZ62–124416.

18. New York Superintendent of Police Thomas F. Byrnes arrested a would-be assassin at Grover Cleveland's home in New York City. Wikimedia Commons.

19. President William McKinley's last speech, given at the Pan-American Exposition in Buffalo, New York, September 1901. McKinley was assassinated later that day by an anarchist, Leon Czolgosz. Library of Congress, LC-USZ62–107867.

20. (*above*) There were at least three occasions when armed assassins breached Theodore Roosevelt's security, placing him within a hairsbreadth of assassination. Two attempts to kill him were made at his summer home, and another assassination attempt occurred at the White House. Prints and Photographs Division, Library of Congress, LC-USZ2–6209.

21. (*opposite above*) Members of the U.S. Secret Service in 1905. Harris and Ewing Collection, Prints and Photographs Division, Library of Congress, LC-DIG-hec-20490.

22. (*opposite below*) Secret Service agents protect Theodore Roosevelt at his Sagamore Hill summer home in Oyster Bay, Long Island, 1908. Bain Collection, Prints and Photographs Division, Library of Congress, LC-DIG-ggbain-02306.

23. Theodore Roosevelt shortly before the October 14, 1912, assassination attempt by John F. Schrank. Bain Collection, Prints and Photographs Division, Library of Congress, LC-DIG-ggbain-10870.

SCHRANK UNDER ARREST

24. John F. Schrank after his arrest. On October 14, 1912, Schrank shot former president and Progressive Party candidate Theodore Roosevelt outside a Milwaukee hotel. Bain Collection, Prints and Photographs Division, Library of Congress, LC-DIG-ggbain-10878.

25. (*above*) William Howard Taft at his inauguration in 1909. The most serious threat to Taft's life occurred in California in October 1911.The plot involved blowing up a long bridge over which the president's train was to pass. National Photo Company Collection, Prints and Photographs Division, Library of Congress, LC-DIG-npcc-18853.

26. (*opposite*) Woodrow Wilson. In 1919 John Rogofsky, who had recently been released from the state mental hospital at Worcester, Massachusetts, tried to gain admittance to Wilson's suite at the Copley Plaza Hotel in Boston. Prints and Photographs Division, Library of Congress, LC-USZC2–6247.

27. (*opposite above*) Warren G. Harding (*center*) with William Howard Taft (*left*) and Abraham Lincoln's son, Robert. The medical director of the Trenton State Hospital in New Jersey, Dr. Henry A. Cotton, reported that one of his patients had stalked Harding in 1922 and had been determined to kill him. National Photo Company Collection, Prints and Photographs Division, Library of Congress, LC-USZ62–96487.

28. (*opposite below*) Calvin Coolidge at the White House with Native Americans following the signing of the 1924 Indian Citizens Act. In 1925 Norman Klein, the leader of a group of anarchists who had previously threatened the lives of John D. Rockefeller, Henry Ford, and Thomas Edison, threatened to kill Coolidge. National Photo Company Collection, Prints and Photographs Division, Library of Congress, LC-USZ62–111409.

29. (*above*) In 1927 the Secret Service became alarmed when Grace Coolidge (*center*) and her agent bodyguard, Jim Haley (*far right*), were "lost" during the president's summer vacation in the Black Hills of South Dakota. Harris and Ewing Collection, Prints and Photographs Division, Library of Congress, LC-DIG-hec-44548.

30. Herbert Hoover and his wife campaigning in Belvidere, Illinois. An anarchist,
Severino Di Giovanni, saw President-elect Herbert Hoover's trip to Latin America
as an opportunity to exact revenge on the United States. Prints and Photographs
Division, Library of Congress, LC-USZ62–64732.

CHAPTER 8

The Plots to Kill Grover Cleveland

Nobody will ever know the extent of my efforts to protect President Cleveland unless he should be assassinated.

—Henry Thurber, private secretary to Grover Cleveland

Grover Cleveland was the only president to serve a split pair of terms, after losing the 1888 election to Benjamin Harrison, despite garnering more popular votes than his opponent. He was a Democrat in a largely Republican nation and his opponents had held the White House since the time of Lincoln.

Cleveland's election to office was partly a protest against the waste and graft that had plagued preceding Republican administrations following the Civil War. He was considered an honest man and gained the public's confidence in both himself and the government in general. However, it was a time of unrest in America—farmers wanted a fairer deal from the railroads and cheaper money, veterans wanted pensions, and reformers wanted better government.

After losing the election of 1888 to Harrison, Cleveland returned to his law practice and lived in New York City, taking the streetcar to work. During this four-year interregnum, the president's friend, New York Police Superintendent Thomas Byrnes, took it upon himself to provide low-level police security, but the former president did not have a personal bodyguard.

Cleveland was returned to office in 1893, a time of panic and depression. In 1893 the bottom had fallen out of almost everything economic. Recovery was three years away. Unemployment climbed to three million and labor troubles dominated his second term. In a time of no social security and no unemployment benefits, the times were hard for working people. Wages kept decreasing and small farmers were in danger of losing their farms. But Cleveland refused to interfere in business matters and rejected calls for unemployment relief. Critics of Cleveland blamed him for not responding in an imaginative and pragmatic way to the depression. Threat levels against the president also grew exponentially, mainly as a result of his handling of the economic crisis.

In 1893, shortly after his second inauguration, Cleveland, his aides, and his personal physician, conspired to cover up the fact he had been suffering from cancer of the mouth. Cleveland had developed a tumor in his jaw that was malignant and larger than his doctors suspected. It was the Philadelphia press who nearly exposed the cover-up when it opined that the president's health after surgery was more serious than anyone would allow. However, the seriousness of the president's health was kept secret for fear it would cause public alarm and was not revealed until 1917.

There is also compelling evidence, revealed here for the first time, that President Cleveland and his staff covered up an assassination attempt made against him during the period when he was out of office but running for a second term as president.

———————

From the time Grover Cleveland first took office in 1885, the idea that any citizen could walk into the White House and shake hands with the president was common knowledge. The tradition had always exposed the chief executive to unnecessary dangers. However, Cleveland's staff was confident the president was amply guarded. Even though it was "apparently easy" to get within the White House itself, it was considered very difficult for anyone to actually approach Cleveland because they would have to "run a gauntlet of doorkeepers, guards at the foot of the stairs and again at the top of the stairs near the entrance to the president's workroom."[1]

The president was guarded by "gentlemanly and neatly dressed ushers" who stood at the entrance to the White House and throughout the building. They "glanced sharply" at each stranger entering the Executive Mansion and "hardly an inch of the building" was not "under the eye of some of them." A telephone was available that could be connected with the Washington police headquarters and armed forces in the Navy Yard.[2]

Cleveland disliked crowds and speechmaking but he refused to curtail public access to the White House. "The White House belongs to the people," he said. "The nation has a right to come in."[3] In the afternoons the president received "all who may desire to pay their personal respects." The receptions were held in the "capacious" East Room and the crowd of visitors consisted of "young and old, white and black, rich and poor, without distinction." The only restrictions in place were prohibitions on "political conversation" or "office seeking."[4]

The ushers were described as men who had some experience of "police work" and several of them were "police officers detailed for the purposes of acting in case of an emergency." There were eight mounted police officers who patrolled the streets around the White House. When Cleveland attended church, there was always a police officer on duty outside. On his afternoon rides he did not go beyond the range of the mounted police. A police officer in uniform always stood duty outside the building and another officer patrolled the grounds to the south of the White House. Two more, in plainclothes, patrolled the grounds.[5]

The first floor of the White House was patrolled by at least six men during business hours, and a police officer, "usually chosen for his size," kept guard outside the president's office. Visitors were inspected by six-foot-tall Edson S. Densmore, who "never used force when diplomacy worked just as well."[6]

If the visitor made it past Sergeant Densmore's keen eye, another usher would enquire about the nature of his or her business with the president. The visitor was then taken upstairs to see the president's private messenger who sat at a small desk. They had to hand their card to him, which would be taken to the president, who was usually standing near the desk that had been presented to him by Queen Victoria. Cleveland stood when he received visitors, believing they would be succinct in their comments if he were standing.

Cleveland usually received callers every day of the week except Sundays and Mondays, when he met with his cabinet in the library. Usually, there was a "score of men waiting to see the president," according to a White House reporter.[7]

Around 4:00 p.m. each day, Cleveland would take a ride in his carriage, the "Victoria," accompanied by his wife and sometimes a friend or relative. At times the president and his wife would first take a stroll around the south grounds of the White House before their carriage ride. The rides varied in distance and locality but usually included a trip to the president's cottage on the Tenallytown road. Returning around 6:00 p.m., Cleveland would have dinner.

Cleveland never strolled around Washington, in part because he did not like to be "stared at." He always traveled by carriage, which provoked his political enemies to compare him to the monarchs of Europe.[8] In 1885 a New York newspaper accused the president of living "in constant fear of assassination" and that he had been advised by friends never to walk the streets or ride in a conspicuous carriage. However, Cleveland's aide, Colonel Lamont, said the story was unfounded and that the president "never supposed that he was in more danger of assassination than an ordinary citizen, and he has never taken any precautions or given the subject any thought . . . his drives have always been in open vehicles and generally through the suburbs."[9]

When Cleveland was president-elect for the first time, it was revealed that the president's aides and friends had provided him with protective guards from a private New York detective agency without his knowledge.

In March 1885, two men, Theodore Wandel and Thomas Craig, had been seen lurking around President-elect Cleveland's home, Towner Mansion, in Albany, New York, for "three or four" days. They had been inspecting the front and rear of the house on Willett Street and had followed Cleveland when he took his morning walks. Their presence had attracted the attention of local police. When the two men refused to divulge their business they were arrested, taken to police headquarters, and interrogated by Albany Police Chief Willard who asked why they did not report to him if they were protecting the president. Wandel and Craig admitted they were private detectives but denied they had been protecting the president. They told Willard they were simply carrying out a job for Inspector Thomas Byrnes, chief of the New York Police Detective Bureau. The Albany police later discovered that Inspector Thomas Byrnes had been placed in charge of presidential security for President-elect Cleveland's March 1885 inauguration.

When Albany police contacted Inspector Byrnes, they were told the men were indeed hired to protect Cleveland. Byrnes said they were "sent by some friends in New York, whose fears for [Cleveland's] safety had been aroused by the reports that many threatening letters had been sent to him by cranks in various sections of the country." The Albany police investigators also learned that the detective agency, which was situated in Broadway, in New York City, was owned by Thomas Craig and was started by Detective Heidelberg, who was on Inspector Byrnes's staff.[10]

———

Cleveland was well aware of the dangers public servants faced. In 1884, when he was governor of New York, and shortly before he was elected president, he had been assaulted by Samuel T. Boone as he walked to his Albany office unaccompanied.

Boone had approached Cleveland on a number of occasions, asking for a pardon for his brother-in-law, Byron B. Fairbanks. Fairbanks had been sent to prison in March 1884 for two and a half years for firing his pistol into a stone-throwing crowd that had assembled at Boone's house on Halloween. A boy, Milo Hopkins, had been seriously injured. During his imprisonment Fairbanks had been declared insane.

On each occasion that Boone had met Cleveland, he had been informed that the district attorney had opposed any clemency for his brother-in-law. On one occasion Boone had accompanied his wife to the governor's office to plead for clemency. Frustrated at Cleveland's position on the matter, Boone's wife threw herself to the floor screaming. Boone then began stalking the governor and at one point declared that Cleveland would never see his inauguration as president. He also threatened to shoot the future president.

Frustrated at not being able to persuade the governor to accede to his wishes, Boone decided to approach him one final time. The governor was on his customary unaccompanied walk, passing through Eagle Street from the Executive Mansion to the Capitol. When he reached the

Medical College on the corner of Lancaster Street, twenty-eight-year-old Boone suddenly confronted Cleveland, saying, "You have killed my wife," and then attempted to strike the governor across the face. Taken by surprise, Cleveland raised his left arm in time to deflect the blow and the side of his face was slightly touched. Boone continued to lash out, "shouting incoherently," but his blows were deflected.

The attacker picked up a rock to strike Cleveland but the governor fended him off, giving his assailant a "fairly good pounding" until a bystander, Dr. George H. Houghton, came to his aid. Houghton seized Boone as the governor continued on his walk to the Capitol. When Dr. Houghton released Boone, the assailant walked to his boardinghouse, where he was later questioned by police.[11]

A detective was immediately sent to guard Cleveland at the Capitol Building when the police learned of the assault, but the governor laughed the incident off and dismissed his guard. Cleveland considered the matter "trivial" and said he could "take care of himself."[12]

During Cleveland's first term, numerous threats to his life were investigated by the Washington Metropolitan Police Department and state and local law enforcement agencies. In August 1885, William Kearney, who owned a farm near Humboldt, Nebraska, and was described as an "insane man," was arrested for threatening to kill Cleveland. Kearney told local police authorities he was on his way to Washington to kill the president because of a "grievance." When he was arrested, Kearney was "well-supplied with money . . . a (Smith and Wesson) revolver and about 75 cartridges."[13]

In June 1887, Swedish immigrant Benedict Krebs, a forty-seven-year-old carpenter from Springfield, Illinois, escaped from an Illinois insane asylum. When he arrived in Washington, he told a hotel clerk that President Cleveland had defrauded him out of $600,000,000 and he was going to shoot his head off with a shotgun when the president attended church the following Sunday. The Columbus Hotel clerk informed the police and Krebs was arrested. He was sent to St. Elizabeth's insane asylum before being returned to Illinois.[14]

In February 1888, forty-nine-year-old Abraham Isaacs, a Polish immigrant armed with a pistol, was arrested on his way to the White House. He claimed the government had robbed him and he had lost thousands of dollars. The police had acted on a tip-off and after scouring the city, eventually arrested him. He told police officers he intended to assassinate the president.[15]

Cleveland had also been the victim of a stalker during his first term. In 1886 he had been stalked by twenty-eight-year-old Nathan Schuler who believed the president owed him a government position since he had spoken in his favor during the 1884 presidential election campaign. In July 1886, Schuler had been arrested for following the president in the Albany Senate Chamber.[16] He was released but turned up again at the funeral for ex-president Chester A. Arthur on November 22, 1886, in New York City, which was attended by Cleveland. He handed his card to a reporter and asked for his assistance in meeting the president. He said he had been the person who was arrested in Albany the previous July and that he meant the president no harm. Handing over his card to the reporter Schuler said, "I do not want to shoot him. I am a friend of his, and I would not hurt him. Please give him my card and tell him so, will you?"[17]

When the funeral services were over, Cleveland stepped into his carriage, waiting for the cortege to move on its return to the city. Cleveland was surrounded by a large crowd. As the president was talking to one of his cabinet officers, his attention was distracted by a scuffle near his carriage. Schuler had been forcing his way through the crowd but was seized by an onlooker. Schuler then drew a revolver from his pocket "but dropped it immediately." "I can't hurt him," Schuler said. "I only want to talk to the president." Schuler then broke away from his captors and escaped into the crowd. President Cleveland laughed the matter off and told reporters he did not think Schuler really meant him any harm. However, Schuler again caught up with the president at the New York Central Depot. A police officer had to pull Schuler away from the president's carriage, but he simply ran to the other side and tried to climb in. When police officers approached him he ran away.[18] By the time of Cleveland's second term, when the depression was beginning to bite, security precautions taken for his protection were said to be "unprecedented."[19]

———

Even before he took office for his second term as president, Cleveland continued to be stalked by mentally unbalanced individuals. On January

14, 1891, during the Harrison presidency, when former president Cleveland was living in New York City, a man threatening to kill him appeared outside his home. When the man was approached by a police officer, he said Cleveland was "no good now. I'm laying for him and if I get a chance I'll get even with him." He was arrested and had to be subdued by three police officers. Later he was adjudged to be "insane."[20]

In March 1893, when Grover Cleveland arrived in Washington to take the oath of office for the second time, his inauguration was described as having "no solemnity, no great display of guns and sailors, no vast and grim armed guard about the incoming ruler." He had a "detective escort," according to the *Sacramento Daily Record-Union*, but "no ostentatious display of the guard."[21]

It was the custom at inauguration time for the chief of the Secret Service to "call his men to Washington." They were usually assigned "simply to the duty of finding out anything that may be significant" and were "mainly on the lookout for suspicious characters" with regard to protecting the president.[22]

Accordingly, the duties of the Secret Service were of "secondary importance to those of Col. William E. Moore, chief of police of the District of Columbia," because the "Secret Service men have no special acquaintance with the class of people who are to be feared on such an occasion, either as possible assailants of the president or as thieves who will prey upon the crowd." Colonel Moore also had the assistance of police forces throughout the country that sent "one detective from each region."[23]

However, within a year, the dangers the new president faced would lead to a larger, yet still informal role for the Secret Service with regard to presidential protection.

In 1894 an army of unemployed, led by Ohio businessman Jacob S. Coxey, marched on Washington, seeking relief. Coxey's "Army of the Commonweal of Christ" was some three hundred strong and reached Washington from Massillon, Ohio, in April, one month after Cleveland's inauguration. The "army" camped at Brightwood Park from April 26 to May 1. The guard at the White House was increased from twelve to twenty-six men, authorized by Henry Thurber.[24]

Friends of Cleveland's were worried about Coxey's Army, and the Washington DC chief of police made it his special duty to ride out to

Woodley, the president's summer retreat in the capital, to see for himself what dangers the president may have exposed himself to. The chief observed Cleveland seated at his writing table in the full light of a lamp, close to a broad window open to the ground. He believed it would have made a tempting target for an assassin who could have "taken deliberate aim from the long avenue between rows of trees which led to the house." The chief made sure two police officers were stationed at Woodley and others at the White House, where the garden gates were now locked. However, it was believed these security measures at the White House were designed as much to protect the first family from curious tourists as they were to secure the safety of the president.[25]

Secret Service chief William Hazen, who had been appointed on February 1, 1894, was ordered by the secretary of the treasury to keep Coxey and his "army" under surveillance. Hazen assigned agents J. W. Cribbs and Schuyler A. Donnella to act as undercover members of Coxey's outfit. The organization collapsed in farce when its leaders and many of its members were arrested for walking on the White House lawn. Coxey was held in jail until June 10, when he was released.[26] After Coxey's Army left the city, Cleveland's private secretary, Henry Thurber, thought it advisable the guard remain strong, "owing to the unsettled condition of the times."[27]

Cleveland's second term was also a time when the corporate giants of industry were wielding enormous power, with the workers fighting back. There were many organizations supporting the workers, including the dying Knights of Labor, a secret fraternal experiment in federating the workingman. One White House visitor, a fanatical follower of the Knights of Labor, actually went to the Executive Mansion to compel President Cleveland at the point of a pistol to recognize the organization.[28]

During the economic crisis it was reported that "cranks . . . [spoke] in the most inflammatory language."[29] The *Deseret Weekly* said that when Cleveland took office, the president found that while the Metropolitan Police guarded the White House, no guard was provided for him. "Upon his request," the newspaper stated, "Cleveland was provided with a plainclothes man by the police department and he was accompanied everywhere by the guard."[30] Following the assassination of Chicago's mayor, Carter Harrison, in late 1893, detectives were said to be "guarding President Cleveland."[31]

Despite these threats to the president's life, Cleveland's political opponents continued to accuse him of "cowardice." The *San Francisco Call* said President Cleveland was "afraid of cranks."[32] A congressman complained in November 1893 that Cleveland was protected by a "muscular-looking horseman, detailed from the police" to act as the president's bodyguard. "This is another evidence," he said, "of the monarchical tendency of this administration."[33] The *Ohio Democrat* said Cleveland was "greatly afraid of cranks."[34] In 1894 Walter Wellman, of the *Copper County Evening News,* exclaimed, "Is the president a physical coward? He is never seen on the streets of Washington as Harrison has."[35]

The *Wichita Daily Eagle* opined,

> The precautions which [Cleveland] now employs to protect himself from bodily attack by the ill-disposed, savor very much of cowardice. . . . Dr. Joseph Bryant, his physician, is accused of being responsible for this terror of the president's. When Mr. Cleveland comes to New York, he has no less than eight detectives in private clothes guarding him. . . . [Cleveland] is protected night and day by Pinkerton men . . . that the president should select Pinkertons, of all detectives . . . to guard him seems simply incredible to the trades unions . . . no chief executive in our history, not even Lincoln at the wildest period of the war, was ever so surrounded by secret guards as is Mr. Cleveland.[36]

It appears there was some truth in the accusation that Cleveland feared assassination. A member of the president's cabinet said,

> It is true the president has a horror of cranks. He dreads them as much as many persons dread snakes . . . it is not surprising either. [Washington] is infested with cranks to a greater extent than anyone knows. Almost daily queer characters are found about the White House . . . it should be remembered that the grounds about the White House are open to the public at all hours of the day. Anyone who wishes may enter them without check. Any insane man or crank or poor deluded mortal with wheels buzzing in his head can walk right up to the door of the White House without molestation. If he has wit enough to conceal his true character, as many of them have, he can enter the mansion and walk right through it.[37]

The president had some support in the press. The *Wheeling Daily Intelligencer* said that the public was "unfavorably impressed" by the security precautions for the president, and many citizens believed he was showing "the white feather." However, the newspaper stated, the "public mind" was wrong and President Cleveland "should be as safe in public as anybody else but the murderous crank mania puts limits on his freedom to surround himself. . . . President Cleveland was right to surround himself . . . with all possible precautions."[38]

During Cleveland's second term, an average of two mentally unstable persons arrived at the White House each day. Most were harmless, but a few were described as violent and potentially harmful to the president.[39]

There were also a number of White House intrusions. In the summer of 1893, a man from Idaho slept in the grounds of the White House for days before he was discovered. When police investigated his background, they found he had sent threatening letters to the president. However, he escaped before police could discover his true intentions.[40]

In September of 1893, twenty-eight-year-old Joseph Washington, who lived in Pennsylvania, managed to enter the first floor of the White House undetected. When he met a White House cook, he told her he wanted to see "My father . . . Mr. Cleveland." As Washington was talking to the cook, a White House police officer approached. Realizing the visitor was of "unsound mind," the officer acted on a pretext and invited Washington into the garden to look for the president. "Your father is out in the garden," the officer said. The police officer took Washington to a sentry box where he intended to lock the intruder up. When they reached the sentry box Washington attacked a White House policeman, Officer Hibble, and grabbed his blackjack, believing it was a pistol. Washington tried to use the blackjack on the officers but was overpowered. After he was arrested he threatened to kill President Cleveland.[41]

In December of 1893 an intruder managed to enter the White House unobserved. He was known as "Washington's Jack the Ripper" because he carved up White House furniture, cut the curtains in the Green Room, and damaged the sofas and chairs. He was never apprehended.[42]

During the economic crisis, threatening letters arriving at the White House were increasing, and by 1894, there were "an unusually large number of cranks" in Washington. An official said, "There are not less than 500 of these fellows at the national capital, and probably 50 of them are of the type as dangerous as the anarchist who threw the bomb in the French Chamber of Deputies." The official opined that it only needed "a slight suggestion to transform their theories into violent acts."[43]

In October 1893, an armed police officer had been positioned outside the president's office specifically to look out for "cranks."[44] He was instructed to admit only members of the cabinet. Other visitors were referred to Thurber, who had a bell handy to summon guards to eject any person who caused a disturbance.[45] The White House watchmen were proud of the fact they could recognize "19 out of 20 cranks," including a man who had to be restrained by six guards when he attempted to go to the second floor after exclaiming that only President Cleveland could cure him of his ailments, which included "lizards, snakes, and rats in his boots." On another occasion, a man opened the front door of the White House and told guards he owned the Executive Mansion and the president should "get out" immediately. He was sent to an insane asylum. During one White House reception, a man disguised himself as a woman and pilfered seven ladies' pocketbooks.[46]

At the beginning of Cleveland's second term, the new administration had to deal with the inevitable attentions of office seekers. A White House clerical employee said that "in those days, as in the early part of every new president's term, the crush of applicants for offices was tremendous" and that such characters were not unusual, especially during the "office-seeking season." There were always a large number of cranks who "did not take their disappointment with the best of grace."[47]

One supplicant had been turned away, but he returned repeatedly to the White House, giving "hard luck stories, each time becoming more incensed his pleas were not being taken seriously." The office seeker began to denounce President Cleveland, becoming "violently abusive" and made daily visits to the White House to plead his case, "rapidly growing more and more violent in his denunciations of the president."[48] During one encounter the president emerged from his private quarters and observed the discussion between a White House clerical employee and the office seeker. As the office seeker noticed the president, he cried out, "Upon what meat does this Caesar feed?"

and began to insult Cleveland. He ended his tirade by asking why no one had yet assassinated the president. The White House police were informed of the incident, but they could find nothing to charge the man with.[49] He was kept under surveillance, but police could find no evidence he was a threat to the president. The White House employee said he had always "been curious . . . whether he ever remotely thought of attacking President Cleveland."[50]

Half the cranks who visited the White House were characterized as "religious maniacs." One man brought a tin box and said it contained a "new religion." Another knelt and prayed on the White House steps. Nearly all of them claimed to have an intimate acquaintance with the president.[51] Another persistent visitor to the White House wanted to convert President Cleveland "to ways of righteousness."[52]

During Cleveland's time in office, one ruse employed by White House guards to deflect cranks was to tell the visitor to go to a certain address in Washington where, they were told, it would be possible to see the president. A note was sometimes handed to them to present to the pretended owner of the house. When they presented the note at the given address, they were locked in a room.[53]

———

In 1893 Cleveland had good reason to fear assassination. Maj. Richard Sylvester, superintendent of the Washington police, who had thirty years of experience in the protection of presidents, said, in 1912, "Cleveland was always the source of great worry for me because of the strenuous times during his administration, and the intense feeling that was engendered [because of the financial situation]."[54]

Although "tramps" were "swarming around" the city and the president's "cranky" mail had increased, security at the White House was deemed sufficient. In December 1893, White House correspondent Frank G. Carpenter said that the Executive Mansion had "never been more carefully guarded than it is today." He believed the police presence on the grounds made it "crank proof." It had a five-foot-high fence, tipped with sharp points, around the grounds and each fence bar was about an inch thick. The White House had eight gates to the park of the Executive Mansion, two on the side next to the Treasury and two facing the State Department. There were also four gates at the front facing Pennsylvania Avenue.[55]

Washington police were constantly on guard in the streets around the mansion. The grounds of the White House itself had thirteen officers to guard it. During the day, the gates were open and parts of the grounds were free to visitors. The front door of the White House had a massive lock, and the vestibule always contained from three to five guards. Some were White House messengers and others police officers in uniform.

The police were under the charge of Cleveland's secretary, Henry Thurber, but Sergeant Decker, who was characterized as the "chief watch dog" of the president, was in day-to-day control. Sergeant Loeffler was a special messenger to the president and also acted as a guard outside the president's office. Assisting him were two black guards, including Arthur, one of Thurber's messengers.[56]

In Cleveland's second term, Civil War veterans were among the many who continued to threaten the president. Veterans were angered that the president had not solved their pension and unemployment crises. In an October 1893 speech at the Round Table Tabernacle in Butte, Montana, Reverend Rounder said he had frequently heard citizens express the wish that "Grover Cleveland ought to die." Rounder said that such comments were "apt to lead some cranks to believe that if he would go to Washington to kill Cleveland and thus place [Vice President] Stevenson in the president's chair that he would become a hero in the eyes of the entire West and all the unemployed."[57]

That same month, Cleveland's friends learned that the man who had assassinated Chicago's mayor, Carter Harrison, had threatened the president over his handling of the economy. Two weeks before he shot the mayor, Patrick Eugene Prendergast wrote to two U.S. senators. The letters indicated that "in his mind he was intensely wrought up against President Cleveland."[58]

In November 1893, a fifty-year-old tailor, angered at the president's inability to solve unemployment, was arrested after showing off his pistol and declaiming he was going to Washington to kill the president.[59] In 1895 a Buffalo man, William Campbell, told his Clyde, New Jersey, jailers he was going to Washington to kill the president so Cleveland would be unable "to do the old soldiers any more harm."[60]

In November of 1893, an Idaho miner had arrived in Washington bent on killing the president. He was angered about the effects of a repeal bill on the mining interests of the West. The would-be assassin intended killing Cleveland if the repeal bill was passed. A Boise, Idaho, restaurant owner, who overheard the miner's threats to kill the president, reported the incident and tracked the would-be assassin to Washington and then to the White House. He saw the miner hanging around the White House grounds and again the following day, lurking around the Executive Mansion. The restaurant owner reported the incident to Washington police and the would-be assassin was arrested.[61]

Also in November 1893, Hiram Collins, of Indiana, wrote to the governor of his state, blaming the White House for "hard times" and demanding "immediate relief." An investigation of Collins's background disclosed he was mentally unstable and had been sending threatening letters to the president. Collins bought a revolver and was about to board an Indianapolis train to Washington when he was arrested. He was incarcerated in the Logansport insane asylum.[62]

In 1895 a man was arrested and jailed after a campaign of vilification against the president. Oliver Gooding had been a police commissioner in St. Louis and prominent in local politics. He would frequently lay two pistols on his desk at the Missouri Legislature and announce he intended to make a speech to fellow legislators. When Gooding moved to Washington in 1893, police detective Joseph Mattingly began following Gooding after hearing that the Missouri politician had voiced strong disapproval of the president. Gooding had been saying he had given "invaluable services" to Cleveland in the 1884 campaign and that the president was ungrateful in not giving him a suitable reward. He said Cleveland had failed to fulfill his promise to make him a brigadier general.

When Mattingly investigated Gooding's background, he discovered the Missouri politician had written two books criticizing Cleveland. He described the president as an "arch-conspirator" who associated with others for the purposes of "destroying him [Gooding]" and to have him "murdered." Gooding was arrested by the Washington DC marshal and his deputies after an intense struggle. At a hearing, Gooding was described as a "second Guiteau" and sent to St. Elizabeth's hospital.[63]

The most shocking threat to the president's life occurred after

Cleveland had completed his first term in office and shortly before he began his second term. During the 1892 presidential election campaign, Cleveland, who had been living at his New York home, went about his business unguarded. However, his friend, Superintendent Thomas Byrnes of the New York Police Department, kept a special watch on the former president.

Cleveland had been dining with his good friend and personal physician Dr. Joseph Bryant. The Cleveland-Bryant friendship had blossomed during the four years of the Benjamin Harrison interregnum, and they lived in close proximity to each other in New York City. Cleveland lived at 12 West Fifty-Fourth Street and Dr. Bryant lived at 54 West Thirty-Sixth Street.

During the campaign Cleveland had received a letter from "a young German," who had recently immigrated to America. The young man had been "ill and unemployed" and asked the former president for help in securing a job as his private professional nurse. Cleveland's secretary wrote back informing him that the former president was not in any need of such services and could do nothing for him.

The young German became increasingly angry that Cleveland could not, or would not, help him. Rebuffed, he decided to kill him. One evening, three weeks before the November 1892 presidential election, he arrived at Cleveland's New York house and asked to see him. As per the rules of the household, he was shown into the parlor by a servant. The former president had just finished dinner with Dr. Bryant and stepped forward to greet his caller when the young man drew a .44 revolver, pointed it at Cleveland, and pulled the trigger. The gun failed to fire. Cleveland rushed toward his assailant, threw his arms around him, and pushed him against a wall. He held him there until Dr. Bryant and the servants assisted in tying up the would-be assassin.

A nearby police officer was called to the house and a phone call was made to Superintendent Thomas Byrnes, who arrived within thirty minutes of the call. When Byrnes arrived at the house, the police officer who had been first on the scene was instructed to "forever to keep his mouth shut concerning the affair."[64] Byrnes took the would-be assassin to his home where he was kept overnight. The following day Dr. Bryant and another physician examined the young German and "took out a certificate of lunacy." By noon Cleveland's assailant had been transported to Bloomingdale Asylum. Cleveland and Bryant decided to cover up the story because it was "likely to stir up a large crop of cranks."[65]

The story of the attempted assassination was confirmed by a "member of Congress" who had been told the story by the doctor who accompanied Dr. Bryant when the would-be assassin was declared insane.[66] According to acclaimed journalist Frank G. Carpenter of the *Deseret Weekly*, "Through Dr. Bryant and Superintendent Byrnes the matter was kept out of the papers and today no one but the president and his most intimate friends know the exact facts of the case."[67] The story was also confirmed by the *Chicago Herald*'s special correspondent in Washington.[68]

The story cannot be confirmed by Secret Service reports of the time, as the agency did not have responsibility for protecting presidents or former presidents.[69] However, it is known that Cleveland had a history of keeping unpleasant facts from the public. When he discovered he was suffering from cancer, he conspired with Dr. Bryant to keep his illness a secret lest it create panic in Wall Street and have a deleterious effect on the nation.

Furthermore, a telling statement by the president's secretary, thirty-nine-year-old Henry Thurber, may add credence to the story of the attempted assassination. It was known that Thurber was, "like his predecessor, Mr. Halford, secretive," according to the *Washington Evening Star*'s White House correspondent. "He seems to possess a wholesome fear of betraying some of the secrets confided to him by his illustrious chieftain, the president," the correspondent wrote.[70] Thurber was said by Frank G. Carpenter to greatly appreciate "the dangers which surround [Cleveland]."[71]

After Cleveland left office, Thurber acknowledged, in part, his role in keeping presidential secrets by telling a newspaper reporter, "Nobody will ever know the extent of my efforts to protect President Cleveland unless he should be assassinated."[72]

In January 1894, as a result of the increase in threatening letters, the president's fearful wife persuaded her husband that the security of the White House should be increased. Cleveland was also alarmed when he found out that the Secret Service had discovered a plot by a group of gamblers in Colorado to assassinate him. The agency had been investigating the activities of the Colorado gamblers when they stumbled onto the plan. Cleveland had become a target for assassination simply because he was the chief executive of the federal government and therefore the person to whom the Secret Service answered. Secret Service chief William Hazen assigned the two Secret Service men who had been investigating the gamblers to the White House for the president's protection. It was characterized not as a "reach for power" but simply an extension of an existing criminal investigation.

The protection arrangements continued in the summer of 1894 when Mrs. Cleveland learned of a plot to kidnap the Cleveland children from their vacation home in Massachusetts, Grey Gables, while the president was in Washington signing bills passed by Congress. Local Buzzard's Bay citizens had informed Henry Thurber that a number of "tramps" had been "lurking" in the area. Thurber was instructed to investigate the rumors and discovered there had been three attempts to enter the property in a period of one week, and that the summer-home guard had to forcibly remove an intruder from the grounds. Mrs. Cleveland persuaded the Secret Service to station three agents there.

When the president arrived, the agents had been at Grey Gables for three weeks and stayed at a hotel in town, with one agent on guard at all times. Cleveland was unaware of the new security provisions until he arrived for his vacation. No detectives guarded Cleveland at the White House. The protection at Grey Gables was on an informal basis, and when the president returned to Washington, the agents were dismissed as the White House was "sufficiently protected by armed policemen." One or more agents were assigned to guard Cleveland at Woodley (his Washington summer retreat), and on his way to and from the residence he was accompanied by a mounted officer.[73]

The White House guard was strengthened to twenty-seven men where before there had been only three or four.[74] In addition, two Secret Service agents rode in a buggy behind the president, but this practice attracted so much attention in the opposition newspapers that it was discontinued at Cleveland's insistence.[75] There were twenty-five patrol officers and two sergeants. Four or five police officers were stationed at the portico and others were stationed within the mansion as long as visitors were present. A newspaper of the time said, "Mr. Cleveland not only keeps off the sidewalks, but seldom goes driving, and when he is seen abroad in one of the White House carriages, he is under the protection of two detectives, who follow him in another vehicle."[76]

Whenever he made the trip between his summer home and Washington, agents accompanied him. They were called "special policemen" to hide their identities as Secret Service agents because Secret Service chief William Hazen had no official authority to provide such protection. In New York, the city's police force was ordered to guard him. According to Thurber, Cleveland knew nothing of these protective measures. However, it is known that when Cleveland discovered that his guards at Grey Gables were Secret Service agents, he made no objection.

There may also have been an additional reason why the president's wife feared for her husband's safety. In 1894, at the height of the depression, there were a number of reports circulating in the press that Cleveland had been the victim of further assassination attempts. In March 1894, a "suspicious looking package" addressed to Cleveland was handed over to Washington police and found to be a bomb.[77]

It was also reported that on October 25, 1894, a would-be assassin tried to shoot Cleveland in New York City. Cleveland had purportedly been on his way to Washington from his vacation home in Massachusetts, and as he passed along a New York street, a man allegedly stepped close to him, pointing a gun. Before he could fire it, however, the president's bodyguard knocked the weapon out of his hand. The would-be assassin was arrested and he was hurried away, "to avoid being lynched by a mob of citizens."[78] On October 30, 1894, the newspaper that had originated the story backtracked, stating, "The report that an assassin tried to shoot the president in New York was a silly canard. The only foundation for it was that a harmless crank sought an interview with him but did not get it."[79] On November 3, the White House issued a denial that the incident had taken place.

The disputed assassination story may have arisen because of another incident that happened on that same day, October 25, 1894. Cleveland was at the home of Dr. Bryant in New York City when a "crank of note," middle-aged and well-dressed Richard Roeder, rang the doorbell of the Bryant residence "violently" at around 9:00 p.m. When the butler answered the door, Roeder demanded to see President Cleveland. When the butler refused him entry, Roeder insisted, claiming his visit was "of extreme national importance."[80] Roeder said he had been trying to see the president for two years in order to "wipe away the stain" that had been "put upon him" by his incarceration in Germany. He said he had challenged Emperor William to a duel and then been put away in an asylum. President Cleveland was the only man who could "wipe away the stain." Dr. Bryant, who had been dining with President Cleveland, came to the door and reasoned with Roeder, telling him it was impossible to see the president at that hour. As he left the house, Roeder promised he would return.[81]

By 1895 the White House was said to be "better guarded than at any time since the Civil War," although threatening letters had been arriving at the White House "lately in greater numbers than have been known for several administrations."[82] The president never saw the letters, which were examined by a White House clerk who either destroyed them or handed them over to White House police for further investigation. These letters were put in a "crank file."[83]

The outside watches at the White House were so arranged that there were never less than six police officers on duty at any time, day or night. The force was distributed to command every avenue of approach to the mansion. Sentry boxes were erected. Automatic alarm signals were fixed in convenient parts of the White House, and the Executive Mansion was now provided with direct telegraphic and telephonic communication with police headquarters, military posts at Washington Barracks, and at Fort Meyer, Virginia, and the Marine Barracks.[84]

However, the new security arrangements were "gradually withdrawn" when Cleveland's political opponents condemned the protective measures. They called the White House "Fort Thurber" in an effort to ridicule Henry T. Thurber, the presidential secretary who initiated the measures.[85] Various congressional representatives were also beginning to accuse the Secret Service of exceeding its mandate. Later, the accusation was supported by Congress, and Chief Hazen was found to have exceeded his authority when he spent funds on that function.[86]

By 1896, Cleveland's final year in office, the problem of cranks arriving at the White House had not abated. The White House guards said the typical crank usually "wanders up to the portico of the White

House in a shifty, nervous manner, gazing vacantly around and betraying his nature to the very watchful eyes at the door." Some visitors were "forcefully ejected," others were persuaded to leave. Guards could use an "electric button" that would summon police officers and a patrol wagon from the Third Precinct if the caller became violent. He would be held until he could be examined by doctors. If the caller was insane, he was sent across the Potomac to St. Elizabeth's hospital or turned over to friends and relatives.[87]

In 1898, Secret Service chief William Hazen had been accused of misappropriating funds and demoted because he had authorized payment for agents who were protecting President Cleveland and his family.[88] But when hostilities broke out between America and Spain, Congress reconsidered its attitude toward the agency. It ordered a detail of four agents operating under an emergency war fund to guard William McKinley, Cleveland's successor, around the clock.[89]

CHAPTER 9

The Anarchists and William McKinley

Revolutionary anarchism seemed to breed individual assassins as well as the demented who would mimic their deeds
—Ellis and Gullo, *Murder and Assassination*

President McKinley is known to be something of a fatalist—as indeed all soldiers are; confidently believing that when the proper time comes he will be ready.
—*Crawfordsville (IN) Daily News-Review*, December 5, 1900

The Secret Service's earlier work in protecting Grover Cleveland was a stopgap response to labor violence, social unrest, and threats against the lives of the president and his family. The protective duties fell outside the realm of the Secret Service's responsibilities because the agency did not yet have the statutory authority to guard the president. But with these measures, the protection afforded Cleveland institutionalized presidential protection for later administrations.

It was not until 1898 that a congressional audit discovered that the Secret Service was diverting funds and agents to protect the president, which caused a storm of criticism from politicians. Congressional criticism was directed at Secret Service chief William Hazen for exceeding his primary mission and he was quickly demoted to field operative. He was replaced by John Wilkie as head of the agency. Wilkie, however, reintroduced the practice of supplying agents to protect the president after the outbreak of hostilities between the United States and Spain, but only on an "emergency basis."[1]

Although the defeat of Spain ended the emergency measures, Wilkie continued to supply agents in response to the increase in assassination threats on the president from anarchists.[2] A small, personal, protective detail of agents appeared at McKinley's side whenever he appeared in public.

————

Following the presidential election of 1896, two detectives accompanied President-elect McKinley from Canton, Ohio, to Washington. Although McKinley was unwilling to accept personal bodyguards he did consent to the distant escort of the two detectives.

Nearly one hundred detectives from all over the country were sent to the capital for the March 1897 inauguration to augment the Washington police force, which was increased by nearly five hundred special police officers. They dressed in plainclothes and carried badges and batons.[3]

One of McKinley's first orders was to reopen the south grounds of the White House to make it a public park after Cleveland had closed it. He also had Cleveland's sentry boxes removed, and the north driveway once more became a public highway for pedestrians.[4] The new president dispensed with the help of Secret Service agents who had guarded Cleveland the previous four years, but that was to change after hostilities opened up with Spain.[5]

When the weather was fine, President McKinley would sometimes take a half hour's walk, unaccompanied by a bodyguard, through the southern portion of the White House grounds. Often he would leave the gate at the western side of the grounds to be joined by Comptroller of the Currency Charles Dawes. Together the men would make the circuit of the Ellipse, south of the grounds. McKinley was warned that the strolls were dangerous, but he ridiculed the idea.[6]

At other times McKinley would walk to Pennsylvania Avenue or Connecticut Avenue, accompanied only by a cabinet member and without the protection of the Secret Service. He would also walk the streets of Washington alone and "stride out the front door of the executive mansion in his quick-paced, erect manner . . . and, if he wandered too far from home, taking a street car back."[7] His carriage rides with his wife took him usually around the streets of Washington or to the Soldiers' Home or Arlington. In the summer before his death, he became the first president to ride in the newly invented automobile. He did not like the experience, however, expecting that the machine would blow up at any minute or the vehicle would become uncontrollable.[8]

A White House aide, John Addison Porter, and Washington's superintendent of police were responsible for the president's protection. Up to the time of the war with Spain, McKinley's personal protection was sparse. According to the *Arizona Republican*, "He went many places without a detective or policeman in sight."[9] This was during the time when McKinley had triweekly receptions in the East Room, which attracted up to a thousand members of the public.

In his first year in office, the president received at least one hundred thousand visitors at public receptions and spoke with fifty thousand people in his office. He shook hands with numerous others in the East Room receptions. McKinley liked to use the "pull-you-along" method of shaking hands to greet as many people as he possibly could. Security was in place for the receptions, which included three Washington DC police officers, messengers, and Sergeant Loeffler, who was in charge of the door and stood behind McKinley at the receptions, "on the lookout for cranks."[10] McKinley did not abandon these receptions until the war with Spain was over.[11]

Gatecrashers were a problem. According to White House guards, "Hundreds of . . . cranks . . . who created disturbances" had been removed from the White House grounds. When the matter was brought to McKinley's notice, he rejected any solutions that were offered because he did not want the White House to be known as "elitist." He was well aware of the public's attitude to such matters. A newspaper report of 1900 describes how "many persons have been heard to comment upon the apparent lack of guards, and have been loud in their praises of a republic where a chief magistrate needed no one to protect him."[12]

Four years before his assassination, McKinley came close to being killed. It was only months after his accession to the presidency that Joseph Bloomfield Jackson, who came from Meriden, Connecticut, sent letters to local newspapers containing threats against "high officials."

Shortly after the letters were sent, Jackson arrived at the gates of the White House and, after a confrontation with one of the guards, shouted "mysterious boasts about what he was going to do to a high official." The White House police on duty stopped Jackson and searched him. He was discovered to be "heavily armed" and carrying a loaded revolver. As the law stated at the time, Jackson could only be charged with vagrancy and carrying a concealed weapon.

The Washington police officers who were on duty at the Executive Mansion believed that had the president driven out that afternoon, instead of being detained by visitors, he would have been shot by Jackson. The police also believed that their actions in confronting Jackson prevented an assassination.[13]

Commenting on the possibility of McKinley's brush with death, the *Milwaukee Journal* opined: "The simplicity characteristic of presidents of the United States forbids the presence of soldiers or guards and the casual stranger can easily step on the portico within a few feet of the [president's] carriage if he is only informed as to when the president will take his outing. The heavy police guard established by Mr. Cleveland was abolished by President McKinley but one or two more occurrences like [Jackson's assassination attempt] and new regulations will be put into force to give the president ample protection."[14]

———

When the war with Spain broke out, the Secret Service was aware that McKinley was "probably in danger."[15] The president received "scores of foolish and threatening letters, from fanatics or mischief-making people."[16] His secretary, George Cortelyou, recorded seventy-three for the months of March and April 1898 alone. Cortelyou was concerned that a sniper could assassinate McKinley from one of the numerous porches of the State, War, and Navy Building, taking aim at the west windows of the White House family quarters.[17]

Chief Wilkie assigned four agents, or "operatives," as they were known, to guard the president around the clock. It was financed through a special emergency war fund authorized by Congress and it was the first legal use of the Secret Service for presidential protection.[18] After the war, Secret Service agents continued to serve at the White House at least part of the time. In addition, agents regularly accompanied McKinley during his travels. With the expiration of the emergency war fund, these activities once again exceeded the Secret Service's statutory authority.

However, Secret Service chief John Wilkie felt obligated to provide the protection anyway. Wilkie justified his decision on the grounds that the president faced danger as there had been a number of assassinations in Europe. The four Secret Service agents assigned to McKinley accompanied him on his walks. Two were always behind him and two in front. When the agents left the White House at the end of the day, they were replaced by a night shift consisting of a police officer in the transverse hall on the main floor and another in the corridor upstairs. White House police officers patrolled the grounds.[19]

The White House police force consisted of fifteen officers divided into three squads of five each—each under the command of a sergeant. At the rear of the White House stood the "watch house" where a clerk and an operator, who managed the telephone in direct communication with police headquarters, worked. Coded signal buttons were in place around the grounds.[20]

George E. Foster was designated as McKinley's personal bodyguard when the president was not in the White House. Foster, who was a former doorkeeper of the House of Representatives and a friend of the president's, traveled in the same railroad carriage, stood on the steps of the railway carriage when McKinley appeared, and stood guard at the door of the car.

During his travels around the country, McKinley was usually accompanied by two Secret Service agents and his valet, Charles "Frenchy" Tharon. Tharon was given the task of guarding McKinley and his wife when they stayed in hotels. The agents traveled ahead of the president to check out venues where he was to appear. In 1899, when the president visited Atlanta, two agents were with him, supported by two Atlanta detectives.[21] The protection of the president was shared equally between the Secret Service and local police.[22]

Security was relaxed following the war with Spain. Often the Secret Service agents were relieved of their duties by local police when the president arrived in a particular city, resuming their duties when the president was ready to leave. Agent Samuel Ireland said, "Since the

THE ANARCHISTS AND MCKINLEY

Spanish war the president has traveled all over the country and met the people everywhere. In Canton he walks up and down without the sign of a secret service man of any kind as an escort. In Washington he walks about the White House grounds, drives out freely, and has enjoyed much freedom from the presence of detectives."[23]

In Pittsburgh, Superintendent of Detectives Roger O'Mara had a set plan for dealing with known troublemakers when the president was visiting. He said he copied Allan Pinkerton's system—remove suspicious persons out of the way. When the president visited Pittsburgh, O'Mara would meet with recognized anarchists and gave them strict orders and a warning that if they were observed anywhere near the president they would be arrested and sent to a workhouse for a lengthy period. O'Mara also locked up those he considered to be dangerous until the president left town.[24]

McKinley's aides were worried that the president sometimes "slipped out of the White House without telling his guards."[25] He would walk the streets of Washington without Secret Service chief Wilkie's knowledge or the knowledge of his agents. The danger, they believed, was outside Washington, when some "Spanish sympathizer" might want to "do the president harm."[26]

In September 1901, weeks before the president was assassinated, George Foster had chased off a "suspicious-looking" visitor to McKinley's Canton, Ohio, home. And, on the very morning he was assassinated, McKinley had risked his life in Buffalo, New York, when he left the house in which he was staying. His bodyguards and the police who were guarding the house were taken aback when he exited the house, and they had to scramble to catch up with him.[27]

Like Cleveland before him, McKinley was open to attacks from the press who criticized the president's tightened security and the fact that he was "surrounded at all times by armed guards." The press accused the president of being "afraid." Cortelyou responded by pointing out that the president went on long walks, frequently accompanied only by friends.[28]

During McKinley's public receptions, "scores of persons" were turned back at the front door of the White House and "scores" of "cranks" would appear at the door each week.[29] Some of the nation's newspapers were unhelpful. An April 10, 1901, edition of the *New York Journal* contained an anti-McKinley editorial that stated, "If bad institutions and bad men can be got rid of only by killing, then the killing must be done."[30]

Arthur Simmons, an African American doorkeeper at the White House during McKinley's time in office, said, "Scarcely a week of President McKinley's sojourn at the White House has passed without an effort being made by some crank to gain an audience with him. We generally manage to either convince them that they want to see some other official of the government or turn them over to the police."[31]

Some "cranks" became violent when they were told they could not see the president. Around twenty were taken into custody each year and either sent to the "workhouse for vagrants" or "discharged on their promise to leave Washington within 24 hours." However, the security arrangements were said to be adequate, as one newspaper account recorded: "In the White House the President of the United States is always perfectly safe, though visitors have imagined there was no police service whatever in force there."[32] In 1900 a newspaper opined that "assassins generally come from the lower walks of life, and Secret Service men have found that there is usually some outward evidence of the evil designs they harbor."[33]

George Cortelyou, McKinley's secretary, worried about the president's safety. He once discovered that one of the guards had been found sleeping on duty in a second-floor bedroom. Public receptions were also troublesome to McKinley's staff. Cortelyou once told the president, "What would happen . . . if some crank got in there with a revolver in his pants?" McKinley brushed off the anxieties about his safety by telling his secretary he had "no enemies," and "Why should I fear?"[34]

However, the real danger McKinley faced was not the constant harassment of White House office seekers and crank visitors to the White House but the incitement among anarchist groups who called for the president's assassination.

Industrialization had created many successes for many individual entrepreneurs, but it also led to great unrest from the masses of low-paid workers, which provoked numerous violent strikes in the 1880s and 1890s. Before the First World War anarchist societies were common in Europe and the United States, and the threat was greatest in countries where the main wealth and power of a nation were confined to an elite class at the expense of the masses. However, anarchism sounded especially mad to Americans, who enjoyed the blessings of modern consumer society as no other people did. They could scarcely understand anyone who wanted to destroy a social order that was good to them. Americans viewed anarchists as "a collection of intellectual crackpots . . . and maladjusted," according to author Scott Miller.[35]

Anarchists advocated the destruction of the whole establishment— the church, the state, and the educational system by "any means" and, more importantly, they insisted that the capitalism that had created discontented workers must be destroyed.

When anarchist leaders became vitriolic in their support for violence the public became alarmed. Leading anarchist Johann Most said, "Violence is justified against tyranny," and Emma Goldman advocated "propaganda of the deed" [i.e., terrorism].[36] Anarchism became "one of the most feared and hated movements in the nation."[37]

American citizens were aware that anarchist groups had published instructions for making bombs and were calling for the overthrow of the American government. Anarchists had been arrested for attacking police officers and they had actively encouraged workers' strikes. In 1881 workers participated in 471 strikes. In 1886 there were 1,411.[38] Americans were shocked when an anarchist attempted to assassinate the leader of the nation's largest steel company.

However, it has been estimated that there were, at most, ten thousand practicing anarchists out of a population of sixty-two million. The majority of them were opposed to killing. According to Scott Miller, "[For anarchists,] bombings and assassinations only soured the public's view of the movement and, more important, were fundamentally at odds with the idealistic hope that anarchism offered. . . . Immigrants . . . were coming to the United States to improve themselves, not to plot against the government."[39]

The American public was also alarmed because four heads of state were assassinated by professed anarchists between 1894 and 1900. The murders were justified and legitimized by the revolutionaries as a moral act in defiance of institutional oppression or undertaken as a practical means to a desired end. French president Carnot was riding through Lyon in 1894 when he was approached by a twenty-year-old Italian anarchist,

Sante Caserio, with a knife concealed in a rolled up newspaper. Caserio stabbed Carnot six times in the stomach. Premier Canovas of Spain was assassinated in 1897 by Michael Angiolillo, another Italian anarchist. In 1898 Empress Elizabeth of Austria was assassinated by twenty-five-year-old Italian anarchist Luigi Lucheni with a sharpened needle file that was four inches long that he had inserted into a wooden handle. However, it was the assassination of King Umberto of Italy in 1900, by Gaetano Bresci, an Italian who had immigrated to the United States with a wife and child, which inspired a young American anarchist, Leon Czolgosz.

In June 1898, in Paterson, New Jersey, Bresci read that King Umberto I had conferred the Grand Officer's Cross of the Military Order of Savoy on Gen. Florenzo Bava-Beccaris. The previous month Beccaris had ordered his troops to shoot down innocent civilian demonstrators in Milan who were protesting at the rising price of bread.

Bresci was a member of an anarchist group in Paterson. When the group decided that the king should die, they drew lots to determine who would carry out the assassination. Bresci won. He saved his money for two years and in May 1900 traveled from his home in New Jersey to an exposition in Paris, bent on assassinating the king. After visiting the exposition he traveled to Italy and discovered that the king would be visiting a sporting event in Monza. Neatly dressed as a "gentleman," Bresci approached the king's carriage after the contest was over and, as the crowd shouted "Long Live the King!" he lifted his short-barreled five-chamber pistol and fired three times, directly hitting the king. Umberto was dead forty-five minutes later. Bresci was found guilty and given life in prison. Ten months later he committed suicide.[40]

Even though the assassin had been vilified in Italy, even by the left, he was praised by anarchists in the United States, including Emma Goldman, a famous anarchist speaker who said Bresci had her sympathy, insisting that the king was "justly put to death."[41]

The Secret Service thought that the vigorous police response to the recent assassinations was compelling anarchists to flee to the United States, placing American leaders in danger.[42] Their fears were warranted. The Secret Service reported that they had investigated numerous plots to kill McKinley, although many originated with unsubstantiated rumor. One alleged plot, for example, involved Giuseppe Costa and thirteen other anarchists who had allegedly been chosen to kill the president in 1900. The group apparently consisted of eleven Italians and three Austrians. They had been selected by an anarchist society, "the Secret Circle," which operated in Naples, Italy, and their orders were to proceed to the United States, France, Germany, and England, their objective being to "strike individual blows at the same time." The Secret Service allegedly learned that the group of fourteen anarchists planned to travel to Washington DC individually "on a certain day." They planned to "surround the president, quietly waiting for an opportunity to strike. . . . The blow was to be struck by a pistol and the knife" and "one of the number, it was certain, would be successful . . . escape was not considered, the men being willing to sacrifice their lives for their principles."[43]

However, Chief Wilkie denied the existence of the plot. He said, "It is true that on August 1 this government was advised that [an anarchist named] Maresca had left Italy for the United States with the purpose of attacking the president," but that he had been detained and then deported.[44]

Another anarchist plot was said to have been foiled when Michael Andunzi traveled to San Francisco where the president was visiting on a tour of the West. In the city, Andunzi met a man and told him about his assassination plans. Unfortunately for Andunzi, the man in whom he confided turned out to be a Secret Service agent and the would-be assassin was arrested. Andunzi could only be charged with vagrancy, however, as there was insufficient evidence to charge him with threatening to kill the president. Additionally, it was reported that the matter had to be "hushed up" because of Mrs. McKinley's illness. Andunzi was given eight months in a San Francisco workhouse.[45]

Although anarchists constituted the major threat to McKinley's life, the president was also targeted by mentally unbalanced individuals. In 1899 E. S. Greensted was arrested in the Arcade Building in Cleveland for threatening to assassinate the president. Greensted was described as "demented," and when he was searched by police, they found a letter that described McKinley as having "prostituted his high office to the Catholic Church." The letter also included a statement threatening the president with death if he did not stop the war in the Philippines.[46]

In 1899 Henry Muller, a "well-educated" German, hated the United

States. He served in the Civil War, suffered epileptic fits after having been shot in the head during battle, and received a disability pension from the government. Muller wrote to the president of the University of Michigan detailing a plan to kill McKinley. The letter was forwarded to the State Department and the threatener was subsequently charged with plotting to kill the president. Muller was arrested in Montreal, Canada, and extradited to the United States. He was found guilty and sentenced to a prison term.[47]

In 1899 Harry Mitchell, who lived in Virginia, traveled to Washington DC with the express purpose of assassinating McKinley. He was tried and found guilty of threatening to assassinate the president. However, after being examined by psychiatrists, he was found to be insane and sent to the Virginia State Hospital. Mitchell was kept there until the time of McKinley's assassination, when he persuaded his doctors he had recovered from his illness. In 1912 he began to send threatening letters to the inventor Thomas Edison demanding "large sums of money under pain of death." He was arrested in Baltimore, Maryland.[48]

————

Leon Czolgosz was a follower of Emma Goldman, the most famous anarchist in America by the late 1890s. In his early years Czolgosz lived a confused and uncertain life. His mother died when he was twelve. He was shy, pious, compulsively neat, a man who abhorred cruelty and a steady worker until he was twenty-three. But then he broke with the church. According to a priest who knew him, Czolgosz had "no religion . . . [Czolgosz] said anarchy was his religion."[49] Czolgosz became moody and remote and suffered a nervous breakdown at twenty-five. He stayed on the family farm, reading and brooding and rarely assisting with the farm's chores.

Following the assassination of King Umberto, Czolgosz became interested in anarchy and socialism. He also became enamored with the assassin Gaetano Bresci. He left the family farm on July 11 without saying good-bye to his father, and then traveled to cities around the Midwest.

Czolgosz adopted an alias, using his mother's maiden name. He called himself "Fred Nieman (i.e., nobody). It was likely that "Niemand" was intended.[50] He tried to join an anarchist group, but his strange behavior

alarmed them and he was considered to be a police spy. The group immediately published a warning to this effect, although the suspicions were not
shared by Emma Goldman who criticized Czolgosz's fellow anarchists.[51]

————

Nine months before President McKinley's assassination, a newspaper,
reflecting on the level of security the president received, stated that
"only by the merest accident could any evil-minded person . . . get
close enough to the chief magistrate to do him any harm." McKinley
was protected at all times, the newspaper reported, "by half a dozen
detectives in plain clothes, who are always at the president's side, [and]
would in all probability disarm the assassin before he could succeed in
accomplishing his purpose. . . . Assassins generally come from the lower
walks of life, and Secret Service men have found that there is usually
some outward evidence of the evil designs they harbor."[52]
   However, this attitude toward McKinley's safety was not shared by
many of the president's aides and some law enforcement officers. Lt.
Joseph Petrosino, who had worked as an undercover officer with the New
York Police Department infiltrating Italian organized crime gangs, gave
warning of the impending assassination of the president. Anarchists in
Europe and the United States, he warned, had become particularly bold
after the assassination of Empress Elizabeth of Austria and had set their
sights on the American president. The Secret Service sought the aid of
Petrosino and for three months he investigated the allegations. Although
he did not unearth a plot, he knew enough to warn the agency that the
president's life was in danger. He had posed as an anarchist in New York,
Paterson, New Jersey, and other places and knew that resolutions had
been passed by anarchist groups that called for McKinley's death. He
told the Secret Service that the president should be intensely guarded
in crowds or better still should not appear in crowds.[53]
   A "department chief in the United States Secret Service" told the
New York Times, after a demonstration in support of Gaetano Bresci in
the city, and only weeks before McKinley's assassination, that "there is
only one safe rule to follow in dealing with them, and that is to take
them seriously. Nine in Ten of them may be only harmless theorists,
but the tenth may be a very dangerous man. We recently had a case

to deal with in which I am convinced we prevented a horrible form of assassination." The agent said the Secret Service had "captured a bomb" and "got the men" who made it but they could not be tried for lack of evidence. The conspirators could have murdered one of the "highest men in the country," the agent said.[54]

After his second inauguration, McKinley planned a six-week trip around the nation. He was scheduled to visit Louisiana, California, and the Northwest, intending to visit the Pan-American Exposition in Buffalo, New York, as well. He left Washington on April 29 by train. However, in California his wife became seriously ill so the president cancelled the remainder of the tour and returned to Washington. His planned speech at the Buffalo Exposition was postponed until September 5 as part of a planned ten-day absence from Canton, Ohio, beginning September 4, 1901.

Planning for the Pan-American Exposition had been ongoing for years but was postponed during the Spanish-American War. When the war ended, preparations went ahead and all the governments of the Western Hemisphere were invited to attend. The major theme of the exposition was the new source of power—electricity.

When McKinley's secretary, George B. Cortelyou, warned the president that his visit to the exhibition's Temple of Music for a ten-minute hand-shaking session with visitors might be dangerous, the president said he had no reason to cancel the event. "Why should I?" McKinley asked. "No one would wish to hurt me."[55] Cortelyou twice took it off the schedule. McKinley restored it each time. Unable to persuade the president to alter his schedule, Cortelyou telegraphed to authorities in Buffalo, asking them to arrange extra security.

On September 4, Czolgosz was present at the railroad station in Buffalo when the president arrived. He approached McKinley, but was noticed by a police officer when he pushed his way through the crowd. The officer pushed Czolgosz back. On Thursday morning, September 5, Czolgosz, gun in pocket, arrived at the fair and secured a place close to the podium where McKinley would give his speech. He considered shooting the president, but felt he could not be certain of hitting his target; he was also being jostled by the crowd. Czolgosz became indecisive about whether or not to commit his act of assassination there and then, but by the time he had made his mind up, the president had left the podium surrounded by his protectors.[56] Czolgosz continued to follow McKinley as the president began his tour of the fair, but was pushed back by officers. Czolgosz saw no further chance at getting close to the president that day, and he returned to his two-dollar-a-week rented room.

On the morning of Friday, September 6, 1901, McKinley visited Niagara Falls before his planned visit to the Temple of Music in the afternoon. Czolgosz tried once more to get near the president but failed.

McKinley's security at the exposition was thought to be sufficient. The Temple of Music guards included soldiers, police officers, exposition guards, and Pinkerton detectives. Usually when the president traveled he was accompanied only by George Foster, but on this occasion Cortelyou had requested that more agents be assigned to protect McKinley. In addition to Foster, agents Samuel Ireland and Albert Gallagher were assigned.

Agent Samuel Ireland said it had been his custom to stand at the president's rear "and just to his left so that I could see the right hand of every person approaching but . . . I was requested to stand opposite the president so that [exposition president] Mr. Milburn could stand at the left and introduce the people who approached. In that way I was unable to get a good look at everyone's right hand."[57]

When Czolgosz arrived at the Temple of Music he joined a long line of visitors who wanted to shake the president's hand. He had concealed his revolver underneath a bandage wrapped around his hand and because McKinley had been greeted by thousands of people waving handkerchiefs or wiping their brows in the late summer heat, it was not noticed by the president's protectors.

A few moments before Czolgosz approached, a man came along with three fingers of his right hand tied up in a bandage and he had shaken hands with McKinley.

George Foster noticed Czolgosz and later said, "I thought he was a mechanic out for the day to do the exposition and wanted to shake hands with the president."[58] Secret Service agent Ireland noticed that Czolgosz "was a boyish-looking fellow with an innocent face, perfectly calm, and I also noticed that his right hand was wrapped in what appeared to be a bandage. I watched him closely but was interrupted by a man in front of him, who held on to the president's hand unusually long. This man appeared to be an Italian and wore a short heavy moustache. He was persistent and it was necessary for me to push him along so that others could reach the president."[59]

At 4:07 p.m., when McKinley reached for Czolgosz's hand, Foster had his hand on Czolgosz's shoulder, about to urge him to move along, when the assassin fired. Agent Ireland said, "Just as he released the president's hand and as the president was reaching for the hand of the assassin there were two quick shots. Startled for a moment, I looked up and saw the president . . . give Czolgosz the most scornful and contemptuous look possible to imagine."[60] The first bullet hit the president in the sternum and, because of a button, did not penetrate deeply. When doctors attended to him, the bullet fell out of his chest. The second bullet, which entered his abdomen on the left side, struck him in the stomach, spilling blood and fatally wounding him.

Following the shots Ireland reached for Czolgosz and caught his left arm. An African American man, James Parker, who was just behind the assassin, struck Czolgosz on the neck with one hand and with the other reached for the revolver. As he was on the floor, Czolgosz tried again to shoot but before he could point it at McKinley again, Parker knocked it from his hand. A soldier, Francis O'Brien, and Buffalo detective John Geary threw themselves on the assassin as they all proceeded to beat him until the president asked that they stop.

Ironically, had McKinley been wearing a newly invented bulletproof vest, which utilized silk as its primary material, it is unlikely he would have succumbed to his wounds. Casmin Zeglen invented the vest after he was inspired by the assassination of Chicago mayor Carter Harrison and patented it in 1898, two years before McKinley's assassination.

Following his arrest a newspaper article was found on Czolgosz's person. It was a story about Gaetano Bresci and the assassination of King Umberto. After Czolgosz was interrogated by the Buffalo police, District Attorney Thomas Penny released a statement about the assassin: "This man has admitted shooting the president. He says he intended to kill: that he had been planning to do it for at least three days, since he came here. He went to the Temple of Music with murder in his heart . . . he says he has no confederate . . . he says he is a believer in the theories expounded by Emma Goldman . . . he does not believe in our government and therefore he deemed it his duty to get rid of the president."[61] For his part, Czolgosz admitted he was an anarchist: "I fully understood what I was doing when I shot the president. I realized that I was sacrificing my life. I am willing to take the consequences."[62]

At 2:15 a.m., on Saturday, September 14, 1901, McKinley died of "gangrene of both walls of the stomach and pancreas following gunshot wounds."[63] He may have lived if the doctors had known where the bullet was lodged. In yet another irony of the events of that day, had his doctors carried him to a display of a new invention—the x-ray machine—only a few yards from where the stricken president lay, they would have been able to locate the bullet and would probably have been able to save his life.[64]

McKinley's attorney general responded to the news of the shooting by saying, "I warned him against this very thing time and time again. I asked him for the country's sake and his own to have a bodyguard when he went out. He refused. He laughed at me. He insisted that the American people were too intelligent and too loyal to their country to do any harm to their Chief Executive. He had supreme confidence in the people."[65]

His predecessor, Grover Cleveland, responded to the news with "stunning amazement that in free America, blessed with a government consecrated to popular welfare and contentment, the danger of assassination should ever encompass the faithful discharge of the highest official duty."[66] However, although McKinley's successor, Theodore Roosevelt, dismissed the idea that "social discontent" was the cause of McKinley's assassination, he nevertheless recognized there was something wrong with American society and asked Congress to address the social problems stemming from "tremendous and highly complex industrial development."[67]

Thomas Pendel, the oldest of the doorkeepers during McKinley's administration, had been at the White House when President Lincoln left for Ford's Theater on the night he was shot and had taken care of Lincoln's son, Tad. He watched as President Garfield was returned to the White House after having been shot at the Sixth Street Station. On hearing the news of McKinley's assassination, he said, "It looks as though we would have to keep the president in a fort and search all visitors before letting them in to talk to him . . . assassination is too easy here."[68]

There was credible but uncorroborated evidence that Czolgosz had not acted alone when he shot President McKinley. John D. Knox, a famer who lived near the Czolgosz home, said he knew Leon and his brother, Waldeck. They sometimes visited Knox at his farm and spoke to him about their "socialist papers." During the presidential campaign of 1900, the two brothers discussed the president. According to Knox, one of the brothers said, "If he [McKinley] is elected he will be shot before he serves out his term. . . . I'd serve John D. Rockefeller the same way if I got the chance." Knox said Czolgosz and his brother "talked violence all the time and I was glad when they went out of the neighborhood. Almost every night there was a crowd of people from the city at their house. . . . Sometimes there would be quite a crowd of them."[69]

However, following his arrest, Czolgosz insisted he had acted alone when he shot the president, and investigators were unable to find sufficient evidence with which to charge any co-conspirator. Emma Goldman was initially a suspect in the purported conspiracy. However, following her arrest she was exonerated and released. She spoke up for Czolgosz, calling him a "Brutus" and McKinley a "Caesar." In December 1919, during a postwar crackdown on radicals, Goldman was one of 249 anarchists and communists deported to Russia. When the famous anarchist arrived in her home country, she was shocked at the tyranny of the new Bolshevik government under Lenin. She became even more resentful of them than she had been about capitalism.

Czolgosz's trial began on September 23, 1901. The jury returned a verdict on the twenty-fourth. He was declared to be to be sane and found guilty. There were no delusions, hallucinations, or any other mental illness. At his sentencing, he said, "There was no one else but me. No one else told me to do it, and no one paid me to do it. . . . I never thought anything about murder until a couple of days before I committed the crime."[70] The night before his execution, Czolgosz was visited by a Polish priest, the Reverend T. Szandinski. The priest asked the prisoner to disavow anarchy. Czolgosz refused. Another priest who visited the assassin said, "It seems hopeless. I have tried in vain to bring Czolgosz to God. . . . He is the most heartless man I ever saw. . . . I think he is so without conscience he will sleep tonight."[71]

On the morning of October 29, 1901, just seven weeks after he shot President McKinley, Leon Czolgosz was taken to the execution room, trembling. When he was put in the electric chair, he said, "I am not sorry. I shot the president. I did it because I thought it would benefit the people, the good working people." His corpse was destroyed by using acid.[72] Rather than furthering the cause of anarchism, Czolgosz had damaged it. Instead of acting as an inspiration for other radicals, he managed to turn the nation against anything that bore any resemblance to "socialism." As a direct result of Czolgosz's act, what became known as the Anarchist Exclusion Act was passed by Congress in 1903.

The assassination of William McKinley in 1901 was a turning point in the history of presidential protection. It provoked calls from politicians and the media to institute full-time protection for the president. Congress informally requested that the Secret Service protect future presidents, but it wasn't until several years later that it voted to fund the effort. Lawmakers' hesitations stemmed not from a lack of concern about the president's safety, but from a deep-seated reluctance to give up a vision of American society's exceptional nature. No one wanted to admit that the president of the United States needed palace guards, as if he were an Old World emperor or king.

CHAPTER 10

The Assassination Attempts against Theodore Roosevelt

The Secret Service men are a very small but very necessary thorn in the flesh.
—Theodore Roosevelt

Mr. Roosevelt stepped out to the porch of his residence. Less than 100 feet away in a buggy stood Weilbrenner with a revolver aimed directly at the president as he stood silhouetted by the light from his library. Within a fraction of a second a bullet would have sped on its way had not the maniac's revolver been knocked from his hand by a Secret Service agent.
—Jacob Riis, friend of Theodore Roosevelt

Forty-two-year-old Theodore ("Teddy") Roosevelt was one of the most colorful of U.S. presidents. He was also its youngest to date. He was widely known for his charge up San Juan Hill, Cuba, during the Spanish-American War, alongside the First U.S. Cavalry, which he organized and dubbed the "Rough Riders." He was fond of what he called "the strenuous life" and enjoyed hunting, boxing, wrestling, and other types of rigorous sports and exercise.

One of Roosevelt's first notable acts when he became president was to ask Congress to cut the power of trusts, earning him his reputation as a "trust buster." He dissolved forty-four monopolistic corporations. Later in his presidency he gave tacit support to rebels in Panama to form a nation independent from Columbia to ensure that the United States could build the Panama Canal, which expanded the power of the U.S. Navy and thus helped the country participate in a more active role in world affairs. Roosevelt was also noted for his efforts to conserve environmental resources across the United States, adding national forests in the West and reserved land for public use. He was the first sitting president to make an official trip outside the United States—when he left to inspect the building of the Panama Canal—the first president to fly in an airplane, and the first president to receive the Nobel Peace Prize, after helping to mediate the Russo-Japanese War.

Roosevelt left office in 1909 after completing two terms as president. Three years later he ran for a third term as an independent candidate and campaigned across the United States. However, he lost the 1912 election to Woodrow Wilson.

It is generally acknowledged by historians that Roosevelt was the victim of only one assassination attempt, which occurred after he left the presidency and was running for a third term as president. In truth, Roosevelt was both stalked and targeted by would-be assassins during his presidency.

———

In 1901, following McKinley's assassination, Roosevelt was sworn into office as America's twenty-sixth president. However, even before he took the oath, Roosevelt bristled at the efforts made to protect him from an assassin's bullet. Roosevelt had gone to Buffalo to confer with members of McKinley's cabinet and they urged the vice president to be sworn in without delay. He demurred and said he would only do so after he visited the president's funeral bier. As Roosevelt entered his carriage, a body of mounted police and national guardsmen surrounded him. He became angry and shouted, "Get back. I want no escort and I will have no escort. I am now on a mission as a private citizen." The police and national guardsmen acceded to Roosevelt's wishes and the new chief executive continued on his journey alone.[1] Nevertheless, the Secret Service continued its unofficial role as the president's protector.

By 1902 the Secret Service was providing full-time protection. Five years later Congress formally approved presidential protection as one of the Secret Service's responsibilities with the passage of the Sundry

Civil Expenses Act for 1907 (enacted in 1906). The Secret Service usually assigned two agents to serve as presidential bodyguards. When the president took extended vacations, the detail increased to eight to allow around-the-clock protection. "Law thus caught up to reality, as the Secret Service finally received express funding to perform the Presidential security function it had assumed twelve years earlier," a White House security review stated.[2]

In 1908 the Secret Service's mission was expanded to include the president-elect. In that same year Roosevelt transferred a number of Secret Service agents to the Department of Justice, which served as a foundation for the Federal Bureau of Investigation (FBI). Congress permanently authorized protection for the president and the president-elect six years later in the agency's appropriations bills.

Up to the time of McKinley, efforts had been made to keep the presence of bodyguards and Secret Service agents a secret. Now they openly fulfilled their duties and the public became well aware of their protective responsibilities.

Many politicians supported the enhancement of presidential security. In his first message to Congress, Roosevelt himself made this his leading recommendation. However, Congress came under severe criticism for not providing for a *permanent* presidential protective detail.

Legislating for an official bodyguard and efforts to make presidential assassination a federal crime allowing for the death penalty provoked dissent within Congress. Some politicians believed that the presence of Secret Service agents would incite would-be assassins (and anarchists in particular). They thought it would "stimulate their bravado." Others disagreed with creating an official bodyguard because of "an American aversion to pomp and ceremony." Additionally, some politicians criticized the move to legislate for the death penalty for presidential attackers. They averred that executing the assassin would give an added incentive for others to complete the deed.[3]

Seventeen bills relating to presidential protection were introduced in Congress but failed to pass. In 1901 a bill introduced by Sen. George Hoar, who had been instrumental in foiling an assassination attempt against Benjamin Harrison, failed mainly because of the age-old argument that the American public believed a presidential guard was "unrepublican."

The bill had passed in the Senate but stalled in the House. Many legislators believed that a presidential guard would not necessarily prevent an
assassination and would "only alienate the president from the people's
affections." Some in Congress claimed that such protection would likely be
"irksome" and would prevent the president from carrying out his duties.[4]

The American press was split on the issue. One newspaper editorialized that a better solution would be to "exclude murderous anarchists
form these shores." It argued for "intelligent precaution [that] would
reduce the danger to the minimum."[5] In 1904 the *Boston Evening Transcript* editorialized, "Seldom has Congress displayed more indifference
to the teachings of experience than its failure, after three presidential
assassinations, to do anything for the better protection of the Chief
Executive, aside from an unimportant section of the new immigration
bill regarding the deportation of an anarchist."[6]

However, Congress had to respond to the public's fears about presidential assassination. The shock of seeing the third president assassinated
since the Civil War mandated it. A compromise of sorts was made.
Although a protective guard had not been officially instituted, there
was no doubt that the president required some form of protection and
no objections were made when Roosevelt's treasury secretary authorized
the head of the Secret Service to protect the president. Chief John Wilkie
complied, even though a lack of congressional authority meant that no
additional funding was forthcoming.

It had not been a foregone conclusion that the Secret Service would
be the agency to implement presidential protection duties. Some in Congress wanted the United States Army to take on the role of presidential
security. However, many in Congress opposed the idea, anxious that
protecting the president would become a pretext for creating a police
state with the army at the helm. When a Senate bill was considered by
the House of Representatives, the language authorizing the army to
create a presidential protection unit was removed. Instead, the House
of Representatives recommended that the Secret Service be given the
responsibility. It was written into a new bill, but the House and Senate
were never able to agree and the bill simply died.[7]

Another Senate bill, proposed in 1902, which made it a capital crime
under federal law to assassinate or attempt to assassinate the president,

included language that directed the secretary of war to select a detail of soldiers to guard the president. In essence, the proposed legislation granted the secretary of war the authority to provide a plainclothes service within the army. The bill was "laughed at."[8]

In 1906 Congress finally passed a bill giving the Secret Service the responsibility for protecting presidents. But it was not until 1913 that Congress authorized the Secret Service to provide permanent protection to sitting U.S. presidents, and in 1917 it provided for the agency to protect presidents' families as well. But the crime of assassinating or attempting to assassinate a president never became federal law until the time of John F. Kennedy's assassination.

———

Maj. Richard Sylvester, superintendent of the Washington police force, who had thirty years' experience protecting presidents, said that it was well known that President Roosevelt "was very careless of protection from cranks and the police received little cooperation from him in their work. . . . [Roosevelt] was such an active, energetic man that it was rather difficult to throw about him the measure of protection that was warranted. . . . I do not think Mr. Roosevelt . . . attracted the attention of more cranks than other presidents although he was very emphatic and he was frequently the center of great excitement."[9] Capt. Thomas E. Halls, who acted as a bodyguard to six presidents, said Roosevelt "scoffed at danger" and frequently eluded his guard "for the pleasure of being alone." Once, Halls said, he found the president walking unattended through a Washington tenement district.[10] Roosevelt took a fatalistic but defensive approach to the subject of presidential assassination and held the belief that if anyone wanted to shoot him he could not be prevented no matter how many guards were around.[11]

Although Roosevelt never gave a thought to the possibility of his assassination, he had confidence in his own ability to protect himself, should the need arise, and objected strenuously to the presence of guards. "I go around," he once said, "and [an assassin] would have to be mighty quick to get the drop on me."[12] Roosevelt also implied that he would strike back if he was attacked. When reporters mentioned the assassination of President McKinley, he responded by saying, "I'll bet

[Czolgosz] would not have shot me twice." The reporters took this to mean that Roosevelt "would have returned an assailant's fire."[13]

In fact, Roosevelt went armed constantly. He never walked the streets without his gun, and the butt of his pistol was observed many times sticking out of his back pocket.[14] He once broke a state law by carrying his concealed weapon when he gave a speech at Harvard. At the twenty-fifth reunion of his Harvard classmates, Roosevelt was escorted to his room by college president Charles William Eliot, who said the president took "a great pistol from his trousers and [slammed] it down on the dresser."[15]

Roosevelt never considered the Secret Service to be bodyguards in the real sense of the word. He thought of them more as aides who could protect his time from office seekers, curious visitors, and the press; and he did not believe they could prevent his assassination.[16] In 1906, in a letter to Sen. Henry Cabot Lodge, Roosevelt wrote, "[The Secret Service detail is] a very small but very necessary thorn in the flesh. . . . They would not be the least use preventing any assault [but it is] only the Secret Service men who render life endurable, as you would realize if you saw the procession of carriages that pass through [Roosevelt's summer home on Long Island's Oyster Bay], the procession of people on foot who try to get into the place, not to speak of the multitude of cranks and others who are stopped in the village."[17]

During the times when the Roosevelts would hold a reception at Sagamore Hill, the Secret Service guard would be augmented by private guards, but this did not prevent the president's wife, Edith, from worrying about her husband's safety. On Monday, September 15, 1902, for example, the Roosevelts invited the citizens of Oyster Bay to an open-air reception, and the president shook hands with at least eight thousand people, anyone of whom could have been a potential assassin.[18]

The agents stationed at Sagamore Hill were concerned that Roosevelt "never [took them] into consideration" and would "[dart] from the house sometimes and [be] well a mile away before [agents could] have a chance to follow him," according to the president's military aide, Archie Butt.[19]

Roosevelt was certainly aware of the risks inherent in running for public office. While governor of New York and a candidate for vice president, he was mobbed near Cripple Creek and was also attacked in

Fort Wayne, Indiana, by a "gang of hoodlums" who tried to break up his meeting. The governor of Indiana considered it serious enough to apologize to him.[20]

————

Roosevelt's secretary, William Loeb Jr., said, "The idea that he is always under the watchful eyes of a guard is annoying to the president; he dislikes it."[21] When the new president first noticed his guards he was "indignant, he didn't want them," as he felt "entirely capable of taking care of himself," according to long-time White House guard William Henry Crook. However, "if they had to accompany him they had to—that was all there was to it," Crook said.[22]

Roosevelt could never relax while his agents "hovered" over him, checking their watches every time he made a move or staring out the windows while he slept. Roosevelt considered them a nuisance.[23] Accordingly, the president refused to have more than one or two agents with him at a time. His wife, however, secretly requested that additional agents be detailed to protect her husband, though they were asked to avoid making their presence noticed. Officially, Roosevelt's detail consisted of five agents.[24]

Roosevelt liked to show himself to the public at every opportunity and he was often seen walking the streets of Washington. William Crook said the president and his agents used to partake in the "Roosevelt stroll," which consisted of a two-hour, ten- or fifteen- or even twenty-mile walk "over hills, through fields and woods; regardless of weather, obstacles in the way, or anything else," through the marshes southwest of the White House.[25] He occasionally rode in automobiles but preferred riding in his carriage, especially his favorite, a Studebaker brougham with glass windows. (It was not until the inauguration of William Howard Taft that automobiles were considered to be safe and dependable transport for a president.)

Roosevelt's detail became frustrated when the president would "escape" from his protectors. He would often slip out of the White House and roam about the countryside "for hours" while his Secret Service agents wondered where he could be. Occasionally, he told them he did not want them present, including the times he went out at night jogging around the Washington Monument. Sometimes a single agent would follow without the president's knowledge.[26]

Roosevelt frequently went horseback riding with his agents, often accompanied by his military aide, Archie Butt, who carried a pistol when he went riding with the president. A number of agents would station themselves on the route he would take, but Roosevelt would often take a diversionary course.[27]

During his outings on horseback Roosevelt would frequently use "trickery," as he called it, to evade his agents, sometimes leading them to Cooper's Bluff, a vertical 150-foot cliff in the countryside around Sagamore Hill, his country residence. Roosevelt would then hide and watch his agents tumble down the cliff looking for him.[28]

Early in his presidency Roosevelt had befriended forty-eight-year-old Secret Service agent William "Big Bill" Craig, who became his personal bodyguard. Craig, a former bodyguard to Queen Victoria, was an immigrant from Britain who formed a special relationship with the president's son, Quentin, with whom he liked to read comic books. Once Roosevelt eluded Craig for two hours by galloping into the woods near his Sagamore Hill estate.[29]

The newspaper reports about these "escapades" so upset Roosevelt's agents that the Secret Service chief had to ask the president not to put his men in such a humiliating position. Roosevelt acceded to their wishes, and toward the end of his second term he relented and kept his agents close.[30]

Roosevelt had many close calls while out horseback riding, walking, or traveling by car, train, or ship. During his African tour in 1900, when he was vice president, he came close to death when he was charged by a large lion. On walks he often slipped and fell, and during a 1904 horseback ride his horse tripped and threw Roosevelt off, resulting in injuries to his head that led to a brush with meningitis. During another outing on horseback the president broke a blood vessel in his inner thigh. While bear hunting in the Mississippi River Bottoms, in 1906, he was attacked by wounded bears and had a narrow escape.[31]

In 1905, on his forty-seventh birthday, Roosevelt faced death in a collision on the Mississippi River when the steamer on which he was traveling crashed with a United Fruit Company boat, sixty miles below New

Orleans. The *Esparta* rammed through Roosevelt's boat, the *Magnolia*, cutting her hull in several places and beaching her.[32] In 1908 President Roosevelt was thrown through a glass window while in a ship collision in the Gulf of Mexico.[33] On June 4, 1908, he was thrown from his horse, which reared and fell backward into Rock Creek. Only Roosevelt's effort to throw himself between the heels of the horse saved his life.[34]

However, Roosevelt's closest brush with death when traveling occurred on September 3, 1902, during a speaking tour of New England. His personal bodyguard and friend, William Craig, was killed when the president's carriage, an open landau, collided with an electric trolley in Pittsfield, Massachusetts. The incident arose because passengers on the electric trolley urged the driver to catch up to the presidential carriage. The two vehicles collided on a bend.

Roosevelt was thrown forty feet and landed on his face at the side of the road, causing black-and-blue bruises and swelling to his face. He also limped from an injury to his left shin. The president brushed off the leg injury but he had to undergo an operation days later to prevent blood poisoning. Four days later, after his return to Washington, he had to have a second operation to drain the wound. The president was in a wheelchair for weeks. The bone in his leg was permanently damaged.

According to one of Roosevelt's biographers, the president escaped death from the trolley collision by "two inches." The other passengers in the carriage, who were also thrown from the vehicle, were injured, including the president's secretary, George Cortelyou, and Governor Murray Crane of Massachusetts. Cortelyou was concussed and the coachman lay unconscious. The trolley car's eight steel wheels, however, had passed over William Craig. He became the first Secret Service agent killed in the line of duty.[35] The trolley car driver was arrested and later sentenced to six months in prison.[36]

Following the incident, Secret Service agent James Sloan Jr. became the agent closest to Roosevelt. Sloan said they "got to be pretty good friends. We used to wrestle on the mat on the second floor of the White House. He was pretty rough—rough about everything, he was a hard rider." Sloan also hiked fifteen to eighteen miles with Roosevelt. "Roosevelt would walk through water and mud," Sloan said, "and come back to the White House looking a mess. Me too."[37] Sloan also accompanied

Roosevelt to church each Sunday morning, following at a discreet distance of twenty-five yards behind him.[38]

————

In 1903 there was a police force of forty-five guards in the buildings and grounds of the White House. A complete police station was built on the southeast end of the new east entrance, replacing the guardhouse. The White House was divided into four subprecincts patrolled each half hour. The guard was divided into three beats of eight hours. Each beat was commanded by a sergeant. Twelve officers were detailed inside the White House led by the chief usher who received his orders from Colonel Bingham, the president's military aide. Roosevelt's secretary, George Cortelyou, was the person responsible for vetting any presidential visitors at the White House. William Loeb succeeded Cortelyou in 1903 and took over his responsibilities.

During receptions an additional sixty police officers guarded the White House and the surrounding streets. One Secret Service agent was posted in the reception room of the new Executive Office Building and another accompanied Roosevelt when he went out for a walk, always keeping a respectful distance. At Washington police headquarters a police officer was detailed to collect suspicious persons found on the White House grounds. They were transported in a patrol wagon and taken to the station across from the post office on Pennsylvania Avenue. After an examination by doctors, they were transported to St. Elizabeth's hospital if they were considered to be mentally unbalanced or harbored violent intent toward the president.[39]

By 1904 William Loeb reported that there were from two to six cranks who visited the White House each day to see the president. Typical of the cranks that arrived at the White House was Daniel Clifford, a one-armed man, armed with a knife, who wanted to keep a promise he said he made to President McKinley for giving helpful advice about handling the Spanish-American War. The same day Clifford arrived at the White House, Ephraim Sellers called to complain to Roosevelt that churches and the Democratic Party were persecuting him. Sellers said he intended to hypnotize the president. Both men were arrested and sent to St. Elizabeth's.[40]

"The trouble with cranks at the White House," Loeb said, "is that President Roosevelt is absolutely fearless, never scents danger in meeting any man, and is ever ready to greet one and all." Loeb said it was for that reason his friends and associates ensured that the president was "surrounded by every safeguard." Loeb added that he had issued instructions to the president's protectors that "mentally unbalanced" people were not allowed to enter the Executive Mansion.[41]

Washington Police Chief Richard Sylvester said there were 204 cases of insanity to come under the observation of the Washington police in 1904, which was an increase of fifty-six cases from the previous year.[42] It was estimated that during Roosevelt's eight years in office, eighty-seven people had been arrested at the White House.[43]

In 1908 there were two hundred of the three thousand patients at St. Elizabeth's Hospital in Virginia who first showed symptoms of insanity during their efforts to reach the president. Many more were sent to their own homes to be cared for by their families or local institutions. Three-quarters of the threateners were foreigners or came from "foreign extraction." France, Germany, and Switzerland supplied most of them, according to the *New York Times*. "Only four are recorded from Russia," the newspaper stated. "And none at all from excitable Italy."[44]

James Sloan said that during his time in the White House under Roosevelt he interviewed many "psychopathic visitors a day." Some were committed to psychiatric hospitals on his recommendation.[45] One such incident occurred during the time the president would receive visitors, from 9:00 to 10:00 p.m. An unidentified man told the usher at the front door that President Roosevelt was expecting him. As he was wearing white tie and tails, the usher thought he would be the kind of person who would have an appointment. The unidentified man gave the usher his card and was then asked to wait in the Red Room. A few minutes after meeting the visitor, a "grim-faced" president called for the usher and told him to remove the man immediately. When he was searched at the White House gates a pistol was found in his back pocket.[46]

Another man traveled all the way from Iowa to ask Roosevelt to help him escape from his enemies who were pursuing him in "airships" and likely at any moment to drop bombs on him.[47]

The president's staff kept the public unaware of the vast amount of threatening letters he received on a daily basis. By the time he left office, letters threatening to either kidnap him or kill him became "an avalanche."[48] Typical of the threateners was B. S. Catchings, who in January 1906 was arrested in a Philadelphia telegraph office for writing threatening letters to the president and his cabinet. He was described as "insane." Another typical threatener was Marcus Flores of San Antonio, Texas, who, in 1907, was arrested in New York and committed to Bellevue Hospital for writing numerous letters to the Pensions Office threatening President Roosevelt's life. He was enraged that the issue of a pension for his brother had not been addressed.[49]

There were also many presidential threateners who publicly voiced their disapproval of Roosevelt, often in a violent manner. Shortly after Roosevelt became president, an army soldier, Frank Rakowski, was sentenced to ten years' imprisonment in the military prison on Alcatraz, in San Francisco, for publicly threatening assassination.[50]

On December 2, 1903, Roosevelt was traveling with a party of guests on a special train to see the Army and Navy football game at Princeton when an iron bolt was hurled at his train. It crashed through the window of the first carriage and fell at the feet of President Hayes's son. No arrests were made.[51]

In 1904 Edward Dalheimer, who lived in Iowa, wrote a letter to Roosevelt threatening to kill him unless he made certain reforms, including having the gold standard changed to diamonds as a medium of exchange. He was also obsessed with the president's daughter, Alice, and wanted to marry her. He was arrested and taken to Sioux Falls for trial where he was found guilty.[52] On May 26, 1906, Robert P. Lewis was arrested at the White House after he had threatened Roosevelt's life. He was sent to an insane asylum.[53] In 1908 Carrie Ade, of New Rochelle, who was described as "insane," was arrested in Louisville, Kentucky, for saying she was going to Washington to assassinate the president.[54]

There were also a number of well-planned assassination attempts that were foiled before they could be implemented. In May 1903 a Swiss citizen, Joseph Barker, was arrested after police were tipped off that he intended to assassinate Roosevelt during a presidential visit to Washington State. Barker had hidden a .44 rifle at a vantage point on the route of the parade in which the president was due to participate. After a manhunt, Barker was captured.[55]

In September 1908, it was reported that a bullet actually whizzed past Roosevelt's ear as he was riding past the estate of his cousin, W. Emlen Roosevelt, on the Cove Road near the president's summer home at Oyster Bay. The president was apparently returning from a ride with a friend when he heard the sound of a gunshot, but he could not see his would-be assassin who had allegedly been hiding in a clump of bushes near the roadside. Roosevelt galloped home and as soon as the Secret Service was informed of the incident, Chief John Wilkie and a contingent of agents scoured the countryside but were unable to find the gunman. Agent-in-charge James Sloan denied the incident had taken place.[56]

However, a few days later, John Coughlin, who had been a patient at a psychiatric hospital in Walpole, Massachusetts, entered the grounds of Sagamore Hill and approached Roosevelt's house. He was spotted by Secret Service agents Sloan and Adams and was arrested after a struggle. He told the agents he wanted to ask the president to send ten thousand troops to Boston to catch "Yeggmen" (a band of robbers) who had terrorized the city. When Coughlin was searched, agents discovered he had been carrying an unloaded .32-caliber Bull Dog pistol. He was taken to the Oyster Bay town hall where he was arraigned before a judge who committed him to the county jail for a psychiatric examination.[57]

Roosevelt was also the victim of stalkers. In 1903 a Chilean, thirty-nine-year-old Jerome Kehl, was described by White House aides as "the most dangerous White House crank." He was in the hardware business in Concepcion until 1895 when he sold his business and began studying with the object of inventing a "floating propeller." He purportedly had forty other inventions underway.

In October 1903, Kehl left Chile and traveled to the United States, arriving in Baltimore on November 16, 1903. On November 19, he booked into a room in Washington's Hotel Engel, situated opposite the Baltimore and Ohio rail depot, with the intention of visiting President Roosevelt at the White House. Kehl wanted the president to assist him in protecting his patents and also to help him form a series of stock companies to manufacture and market them.

On December 23, Kehl arrived at the White House carrying a letter demanding an interview with Roosevelt. "You will be sorry if you do not see me for I will find you and I will get you and kill you," he had written in his letter. Following his departure, Kehl's letter was turned over to the Secret Service who initiated a citywide search for him. At 9:00 p.m. on December 24, 1903, they discovered that Kehl was staying at the Hotel Engel. When acting captain Helan, of the Washington police, together with detectives Weedon and Tyser, arrested him at the hotel, Kehl attempted to draw his pistol from his hip pocket. After a struggle he was disarmed and taken into custody.[58] In January 1904, Kehl was sent to Bellevue Hospital and then handed over to Sir Walker-Martinez, the Chilean ambassador, who organized his deportation from the United States via the steamship *Cacique*, bound for Chile.

However, Kehl was still obsessed with seeing President Roosevelt. Three years later, in November 1906, he learned of the president's visit to Panama and arrived there from Chile. Secret Service agents, who had traveled to Panama before the president arrived to check out the security arrangements, were keeping a close watch on all arrivals at Panama and Colon prior to the president's visit. They spotted Kehl's name on an arrivals list. He was immediately arrested. Doctors declared him insane and he was deported back to Chile.[59]

Like McKinley, Roosevelt was also targeted by anarchists. According to a newspaper report, when Roosevelt took office "everybody knew" he was "a marked man" because of his denunciation of anarchy and anarchists, especially when he voiced this position in his message to Congress on December 3, 1901, three months after the death of William McKinley.[60]

Throughout his presidency numerous plots to kill Roosevelt, the majority of which involved anarchist groups, were investigated by state, local, and federal authorities. In 1903, for example, police at Lincoln, Illinois, suspected that a satchel full of dynamite that had been hidden near the Chicago and Alton Railroad track was planted by anarchists. It was located within a few feet from where Roosevelt was due to leave his train later that day. No arrests were made.[61]

In 1906 six Polish anarchists were tried for assaulting a Polish immigrant, Walter Sealazkiwiez. Sealazkiwiez testified that in May 1906 an anarchist group attempted to raise funds to send one of their members to Washington to assassinate Roosevelt. He said the plan "fell through."[62]

The following month the Secret Service announced they had uncovered a plot by anarchists to kill Roosevelt, as well as the king and queen of Spain.

In 1907 the Secret Service investigated another anarchist plot. The Roosevelts were staying at their Pine Knot, Virginia, retreat at the time, and the news unnerved Roosevelt's wife, Edith, who apparently was unable to sleep and was in "terror-stricken panic." Without informing her husband, she asked Secret Service agents James Sloan and Frank Tyree to guard the house night and day and stay billeted in a nearby farmhouse, but without making themselves known to her husband.[63]

In October 1908 a plot to kill Roosevelt during a safari trip to Africa was foiled. Knowledge of the plot was revealed by "the police authorities of a half-dozen countries." The plot unraveled when Spanish anarchist Fernando Canatrava was arrested for suspected involvement in a plot to kill King Alfonso of Spain. When two Italian anarchists were arrested in Switzerland, police found documents containing information about Roosevelt's African trip. The documents included details relating to dates and routes of the trip as well as the routes and dates of prospective trips of all European leaders. The assassination was purportedly part of "the greatest terrorist uprising Europe had ever seen."[64]

The two most dangerous threats to Roosevelt's life occurred early in his presidency when two men, in separate incidents, attempted to shoot him. In September 1903, Roosevelt came within a hairsbreadth of assassination when Henry Weilbrenner pointed a loaded gun at him. A month later an armed man, Peter Elliott, breached the president's security but was unable to reach Roosevelt.

The first serious assassination attempt occurred at Sagamore Hill, Oyster Bay. Roosevelt's summer home had been fitted with trip wires by Secret Service agents and, because of the constant threat that the president would be attacked by anarchists, every visitor became a potential assassin. Agents turned away everyone who was not on the approved guest list, and although the security arrangements annoyed the president, he adapted to them. On their afternoons off, agents would wander around town looking for potential assassins or "cranks" that might do the president harm. At the time of the September incident, one agent was stationed at the house in daytime and two at night. There were no servants in the house. After the assassination attempt, two agents guarded the house during the daytime and three at night. More importantly, the assassination attempt would lead to a better appreciation by the president of the responsibilities of his Secret Service detail.[65]

Twenty-eight-year-old Henry Weilbrenner Jr. was the son of an immigrant German farmer who owned a seventy-two-acre farm in Syosset, Long Island, New York, about five miles inland from Oyster Bay. He had been born in the outskirts of Berlin and was one of three brothers. The family had sixty-five cultivated acres, a house, and barns and became one of the show farms of the county. However, two bad seasons compelled the Weilbrenners to put the house under two mortgages, which left the family with little equity, and they had to struggle to make ends meet.

In the summer of 1903, Henry's brother William had become unemployed as a result of the building trade strikes and lockouts. He arrived at the farm with his family, which added to Henry's financial burden. Weilbrenner became increasingly depressed and began to suffer "nervous attacks," which rendered him helpless for a day or two. He had also broken up with his girlfriend a few months previously.

Weilbrenner blamed Roosevelt for the family's dire position and would frequently rail against the president as a "man who had promised everything and done nothing." He was also becoming obsessed with the president's daughter and fantasized about marrying her.[66]

Weilbrenner bought a revolver and slept with it under his pillow. Although his mother criticized him for keeping a pistol, Weilbrenner explained to her that neighbors were plotting his ruin. Witnesses observed Weilbrenner practicing with his pistol.

On Tuesday evening, September 1, 1903, shortly after 10:00 p.m., Weilbrenner, dressed in a suit and wearing an old-fashioned derby hat, harnessed a horse and drove his phaeton buggy away. When his brother asked him where he was going, Weilbrenner gave a sullen shake of his head. The family only discovered the purpose of his trip when they later heard the news of his arrest.

When Weilbrenner arrived at Sagamore Hill in his buggy he was stopped by Secret Service agent Stephen Connell. Weilbrenner told

Connell he had an appointment to see the president. Connell refused to allow him to go to the house and told him it was well past the time for visitors. Weilbrenner returned once again but was told to leave. On his third attempt, around 11:00 p.m., Connell asked him what he meant by returning to the house again. Weilbrenner shouted, "None of your business."

At that moment Roosevelt came to the door. The president's silhouette was outlined sharply by light streaming from the library behind him as he watched the confrontation between the two men. As soon as Weilbrenner saw Roosevelt he shouted, "There he is now," lashed his horse, and made a vigorous effort to reach the veranda on which the president stood. However, Connell managed to grab the reins and drag Weilbrenner out of the buggy before slamming him onto the gravel on the drive and, with the assistance of Agent Murphy, took him to the stables. Weilbrenner's revolver was later found on the floor of the vehicle where it had apparently fallen during the struggle.

Weilbrenner told Agents Connell and Murphy that he had come to Roosevelt's home with the intention of killing him. He repeated it several times, saying the president was responsible for the labor difficulties and that Roosevelt had not fulfilled his promise of bringing prosperity to the workingman.[67]

The agents asked the stablemen to guard Weilbrenner. When they returned to the house, they quickly ushered the president back inside lest more would-be assassins lurked nearby.

Agent Connell later told reporters that it was "a narrow escape for Roosevelt. In another second [Weilbrenner] would have fired the gun."[68] The Secret Service characterized the incident as "an attempt on the life of President Roosevelt."[69]

When Weilbrenner appeared in court, however, he omitted anything about wanting to kill the president. He said he had an appointment to see the president to discuss his "impending marriage to Alice Roosevelt."

At first newspaper stories did not report that Weilbrenner had pointed his pistol at the president. That information was only released when Jacob Riis, of the New York Social Betterment Workers, visited the president the next day. He was the only visitor that day and was shocked to learn the president's version of the story.

Riis told reporters about his conversation with the president: "Mr.

Roosevelt stepped out to the porch of his residence. Less than 100 feet away in a buggy stood Weilbrenner with a revolver aimed directly at the president as he stood silhouetted by the light from his library. Within a fraction of a second a bullet would have sped on its way had not the maniac's revolver been knocked from his hand by a Secret Service agent. . . . Roosevelt saw one of his guards dash a revolver out of the hand of a man who an instant later was seized by the collar and dragged from the buggy . . . the agent, with the assistance of a colleague bundled Weilbrenner into the buggy and drove away to the carriage house." The newspaper report also confirmed that Weilbrenner told the agents, "I wanted to kill him. I had my shooting iron ready." Riis also said, "It makes me shudder to think how near the president was to death."[70]

Following a court appearance and an examination by doctors, Weilbrenner was judged to be insane and sent to the King's Park insane asylum near Mineola, Long Island.

The second incident occurred at the White House, one month after the Weilbrenner assassination attempt. Swedish immigrant Peter Elliott tried to gain an audience with Roosevelt and came armed with a pistol and bullets coated with poison.

The thirty-five-year-old Elliott was born Peter Olson and lived in Minneapolis. For years Elliott worked as a machinist and made minor inventions, including a device for "releasing harnesses in fire and police station houses," which netted him a comfortable sum of money. He also made money on another two inventions.

In 1903 he had been a resident of the city for fifteen years and characterized himself as a socialist. Those who knew him described him as an eccentric who loved to give speeches on the streets of the city on economic, sociological, and political subjects. The speeches were sometimes described as tirades against existing social and political conditions in the country.

Elliott wanted a federal appointment and he blamed Roosevelt for not giving him one. He also said he was going to marry the president's daughter, Alice Roosevelt, and kept numerous newspaper clippings of the president. He changed his name from Peter Olson to Peter Olson Elliott in the hope that a more American-sounding name would help him secure a government job.

According to the *Minneapolis Journal*, Elliott "more than once" made threats to harm the president and told friends and acquaintances of his intention of going to the White House and, if Roosevelt would not see him, he would force the president to grant him an interview.

For some time Elliott had been showing signs of mental instability. He began to believe that the Swedish community in Minneapolis was planning to kill him and that the food he ate in restaurants had been poisoned. He also came to believe that the president had been influenced by the Swedish community in not appointing him to a federal position. His roommate, Al Anderson, reported Elliott to the police, telling them his friend was "unquestionably insane." Elliott was referred to the city hospital but did not stay there long. He began to frequent the St. Paul and Minneapolis telegraph offices where he wrote long messages, mostly to the president, leaving them at the window without paying for them. In September 1903, he told Anderson that Roosevelt wanted to see him.[71]

Elliott traveled to Washington in a freight train, after purchasing a Bull Dog five-shooter pistol, and lodged at the city's St. James Hotel on September 30. He wrote a letter to the president requesting an interview and enclosing a photograph of himself. Secretary Loeb read Elliott's letter and concluded the writer was "insane." Loeb informed White House police officers on duty that they should be on guard for him.

When Roosevelt attended church services with his two sons at the Dutch Grace Reformed Church the following Sunday, Elliott took a seat in the gallery. He left the church at the beginning of the communion service and leaned against a fence railing of a house just below the church. When the president emerged, Elliott approached him, hand outstretched. Roosevelt took his hand as Elliott said, "Roosevelt, shake hands with Elliott." Roosevelt shook his hand and said, "I'm glad to meet you," then walked on. Elliott was told to move on by a Secret Service agent.[72]

At 10:00 a.m., on October 5, Elliott appeared at the Executive Offices next to the White House and asked to see the president. When he was asked why he wanted to see President Roosevelt, he replied, "Oh, just for fun. The president sent for me and I just want to see him." After Elliott was told to return the following month, he walked away.

Shortly before 12:00 noon, Elliott walked up to the main door of the

White House, stepped inside, and asked police officer James Cissell if he might see the president. Chief Usher Thomas Stone recognized Elliott as the person he had been warned about by White House door-keepers following Elliott's previous visits. Stone interrupted Cissell and began to humor Elliott, telling him he could not see the president at that time but he might be able to arrange a meeting in a while. Stone and the officers led Elliott through the basement of the White House to the guardroom at the east end of the building, where he was told the president would see him momentarily. While Elliott waited, a call was made for a police van. However, Elliott was becoming increasingly disturbed and began to act violently toward the officers. After a brief struggle he was overpowered and taken to the police van, which was waiting at the southeast gate.

After Elliott was placed in the van, a further struggle ensued. The officers had failed to search him properly before placing him in the van. Elliott drew his revolver from his pocket and aimed it at Officer Cissell. Cissell grabbed his hand and wrenched the weapon away from him as Elliott sustained injuries to his head and face after crashing through one of the van's windows. Cissell sustained a serious cut on his right arm and two inches of flesh were cut out. Cissell then drew his own pistol and fired two warning shots. Elliott was finally subdued and the police van raced to the emergency hospital. After Elliott's and Cissell's injuries were treated, the would-be assassin was taken to the first precinct police station. When Roosevelt learned of the incident he enquired after Officer Cissell's condition.

When Elliot's pistol was examined, it was discovered he had pre-pared the bullets with poison.[73] The Secret Service concluded that the only purpose for coating the bullets in such a manner was to kill President Roosevelt.[74]

Following the incident, Roosevelt's secretary, William Loeb, and Chief Wilkie, of the Secret Service, ordered every Secret Service agent and White House police officer that news of "cranks" was not to be made public.[75] The incident also provoked a revival of talk about new legisla-tion for the protection of the president, and the number of agents in the president's Secret Service detail was increased.[76]

Elliott was sent to St. Elizabeth's for a short time, then to St. Peter

Hospital in Minnesota. However, in November 1903, he escaped, which greatly alarmed the Secret Service.[77] Elliott was captured but later released. On May 23, 1904, he hanged himself from a bridge in South Minneapolis.[78]

———

Roosevelt agonized over leaving the presidency. There was so much more he wanted to do. But true to his word to the American people, he did not run for reelection in 1908. It was a decision that would haunt him for the rest of his life. Instead, Roosevelt decided to handpick his successor, someone he could rely on to carry out his agenda. With William Howard Taft he thought he had the perfect candidate. However, Roosevelt soon became disillusioned with Taft, who allowed many Roosevelt policies to be overturned.

Roosevelt tried to secure the Republican presidential nomination in 1912, after Taft had served one term as president, but he failed. Still confident the American public wanted to see him as president once more, he formed the Bull Moose Party and campaigned across America in the summer and autumn of that year.

Unknown to the president and his aides, he was being stalked by a German-born New York man by the name of John Schrank.

The thirty-six-year-old Schrank was born in Erding, Bavaria, near Munich, and immigrated with his parents to America when he was nine years old and to New York City when he was thirteen years old. Schrank was short, plump, mild-mannered, and a daydreamer. While tending a bar or working as a handyman at his uncle's tenement house, he read a great deal and wrote down his reflections on paper. One of these jottings stated, "I never had a friend in my life."[79]

Schrank dreamed on September 15, 1901, that the late President McKinley pointed at his vice president and said, "This is my murderer. Avenge my death." The German-born saloonkeeper and self-styled poet-philosopher believed he was given a mission by God to kill Roosevelt, but delayed acting on it for eleven years.

In 1906 Schrank sold his New York bar and roamed the city, all the while extolling his new political philosophy he called "The Four Pillars of the Republic." One of these pillars was that presidents should serve no more than two terms in office.

On September 14, 1912, the ghost of McKinley reappeared to Schrank who took it as a sign that he must act to prevent Roosevelt's election and avenge McKinley's death. Armed with a .38-caliber Colt revolver, Schrank began to stalk Roosevelt, who was campaigning in the South. Schrank said, "Not being able to carry out my plan in Charleston, I proceeded to Atlanta, Georgia, thence to Chattanooga, Tennessee, and from there to Evansville, Illinois, and Indianapolis, Indiana, and to Chicago. In each one of these cities I tried to shoot Roosevelt but was unable to waylay him. I decide to shoot him in Chicago and waited for him at the Chicago and North Western Station, but the intended victim did not arrive there. I decided to do the shooting at the Coliseum, but in this case and others, Roosevelt left the building by an entrance other than the one at which I had stationed myself. After the failure at the Coliseum I decided to come to Milwaukee in advance of the party and lay my plans so carefully that I could not fail."[80]

On October 14, Schrank was outside Milwaukee's Hotel Gilpatrick where Roosevelt, having dined, was preparing to motor to the municipal auditorium.

Although Schrank had lost his nerve during earlier chances to shoot Roosevelt, he was determined to act this time. When Roosevelt exited his hotel and stood in his carriage, Schrank drew his gun, aimed it at Roosevelt's head from a distance of seven feet, and fired. However, at the last second, the man standing next to Schrank noticed the gun and deflected Schrank's arm downward.

The bullet hit Roosevelt in the chest. Roosevelt staggered, but did not drop. Slowed by the folded copy of his fifty-page speech and a metal spectacle case, the bullet had not gone far enough into his abdomen. "It takes more than one bullet to kill a Bull Moose," Roosevelt told his aides. When the former president's wound was attended to, doctors decided to leave the bullet in his rib cage.

Hoping to avoid a circuslike trial, the judge in the case encouraged a panel of experts to find John Schrank insane. Instead of jail, he was confined to an insane asylum, Central State Mental Hospital in Waupun, Wisconsin, for life, where he died on December 15, 1943, at the age of sixty-seven.[81]

CHAPTER 11

Targeting William Howard Taft

What difference does it make? If someone should decide to take a shot at me how could he miss?
—William Howard Taft, responding to a warning by Secret Service agents that the corpulent president had exposed himself to assassination

William Howard Taft was an academic and a legal thinker, but it is generally agreed his time in office was not a happy period in his life. He overate. He often fell asleep at his desk. He was, according to Ira T. Smith, who worked in the White House mailroom under nine presidents, from McKinley to Truman, "the most puzzling, and in some ways the most disliked [president]." Smith wrote that although Taft did not lack "charm or intelligence," the public viewed him as a "fat, good-natured smiling man whose administration was not especially good and not especially bad."[1]

Before he became president, William Howard Taft experienced dangers that the inevitable consequences of holding public office brought. When he was secretary of war under Theodore Roosevelt, Taft visited China, Japan, and the Philippines. During his trip he was stalked by a Japanese would-be assassin. The unnamed potential assailant stalked the secretary from Kyoto, and at Kobe he boarded Taft's ship, the USS *Minnesota*. When Taft and his entourage disembarked, the stalker remained onboard, and when he was approached by officials he said he wanted to talk to the secretary and work for him. If Taft refused, he said, he would commit suicide. He was arrested and taken to a local jail.[2]

In 1907 and 1908, Taft's trains were derailed but he was "unharmed and unfazed." During Taft's "Orient Trip," his carriage horses bolted in Manila. Taft's bodyguard grabbed the reins and steered the horses into a ditch.[3]

During Taft's presidential campaign, he escaped injury when a shotgun was fired at the riverboat he was traveling aboard. In July 1908 he took a trip on the Ohio River. When his boat, the *Island Queen,* steamed slowly around the bend in the middle of the river at Dayton, Kentucky, a shotgun was fired by an unknown man who was on a houseboat moored on the Ohio bank. Several shots from the spent charge hit Mrs. Charles B. Russell, who was standing with her husband near the rail of the deck directly below where Taft was passing at the time of the shooting. Mrs. Russell cried out that she had been shot and was taken below deck where it was found she was not seriously injured. One of the shot had penetrated the skin of her left eye and another had struck her on the chin. A number of pellets had pierced her dress. A man standing nearby was also hit but he was not seriously injured. Mrs. Russell's husband said he was standing next to his wife and "none of the shot struck me. It was lucky we were not closer to the Ohio shore. I saw the man plainly, and at first thought him merely an enthusiastic celebrator."[4]

The would-be assassin was never apprehended. Newspapers of the day described the incident as "an attempt . . . to assassinate Taft."[5] The following day a young man, who had been swimming in the Ohio River at the spot where the *Island Queen* was fired upon, was hit. Charles Hawks was swimming at the foot of Whitaker Street when the *Island Queen* passed. Hawk's friends jumped in to rescue him and discovered that a small number of birdshot had been embedded in his face.[6]

Shortly after Taft became president, he visited a friend who resided in a small town and strolled about greeting the local citizenry. When agents remonstrated with him about how he had exposed himself to assassination, the corpulent Taft replied, "What difference does it make? If someone should decide to take a shot at me how could he miss?"[7] However, the Secret Service thought Taft was one of the easiest chief executives to guard because he "followed routes mapped out by the

Secret Service and schedules of appearances," according to veteran agent Capt. Thomas E. Halls.[8]

Taft's Secret Service detail was given orders not to let the president out of their sight beyond the limits of the White House. All the White House servants were told to inform the Secret Service whenever the president was about to leave. However, when Taft went horseback riding or strolling around Washington he would frequently attempt to evade his agents. On one occasion Taft's agents were sitting outside his office when they noticed he was not there. The detail began to search frantically for the president. Finally, Taft was observed strolling near the Washington Monument. He had simply climbed out of a back window of his office.[9] On another occasion, Taft went Christmas shopping alone in the crowded stores along Pennsylvania Avenue and visiting friends, wishing them the compliments of the season.[10]

One day when Taft's secretary noticed he had left the White House, without informing either himself or the president's protective detail, he ordered the agents to find him. The agents finally tracked Taft down after several hours of searching. Agents saw the president and his wife walking toward the White House, drenched in rain. Instead of characterizing the incident as irresponsible, the press merely described it as "the president's high spirits."[11]

Procedures for protecting a president were improved after William McKinley's assassination. When the president accepted an invitation to attend a function outside Washington, a Secret Service agent would precede him and make arrangements for the trip. The advance agent met with local officials to go over every phase of the stay, including hotel or residence, the route of the drive through the city, the seats at the banquet table, the number of vehicles to meet the party, and the local chiefs of police. The Secret Service began to insist that local officials agree to security details in writing to avoid past problems in which local city officials changed plans without informing the White House.

Arrangements were also made with railroad companies concerning the arrival and departure of the trains and entrances and exits to be used. The agency also ensured that a line of local police officers would be present when the president made his way from his carriage or car to the rail station entrance and on to his railway carriage. At formal functions the president's table was higher. Immediately below, agents would take their positions and a number of them would be placed among the guests. If the president remained in a city overnight, an agent would always stand guard outside his room. The Secret Service would keep a card index of noted "cranks" and they expected local police to keep track of them when the president was in town.[12]

New procedures were also introduced for dealing with suspicious packages that arrived at the White House. On one occasion a package had been sent to the executive offices of the White House and placed on the desk of Sherman Allen, one of the White House's assistant secretaries. The package was intended for President Taft. When Allen opened it he discovered a dynamite bomb and the "fuse was sputtering." Allen extinguished the fuse with his hands. Although the story was denied by Allen and Secret Service chief Wilkie, it was corroborated by "other White House officials," the *Boston Evening Transcript* reported.[13]

As with the presidents who came before him, Taft was frequently criticized by the press for having a large security apparatus. When he visited Pittsburgh, in 1909, Taft was guarded by up to three hundred uniformed police officers stationed at stop-off points along his route. Twenty-five plainclothes officers were also on duty. Local newspapers said the heavy guard indicated that Pittsburgh "did not have law-abiding citizens." The size of Taft's protective detail, the *Fredericksburg VA Daily Star* said, was in contrast to Taft's visit to Petersburg, Virginia, where the president "could go unguarded and unprotected by police men from one end of the South to the other, for he would be guarded and protected by the entire citizenship of the South."[14]

Taft was the first president constantly to use White House automobiles instead of horses and carriages, and he was the first president to ride in an official presidential limousine. He became a big auto enthusiast, redesigning the federal stables to make room for a garage and often advising his chauffeur on how to fix mechanical problems. The White House had four automobiles, two Pierce-Arrows, a Baker Electric, and a White Steamer, but his favorite was the Steamer, in which he enjoyed "fast riding."[15] There was also a small landaulet for his wife.[16]

President Taft liked to take automobile rides in the afternoon and the Secret Service followed behind in their own vehicle. Two police officers on bicycles would also sometimes follow him. The bicycles were superseded by motorcycles during his time in office.[17] After New York's Mayor Gaynor was shot in 1910, an agent rode on the step of the president's car. All the agents were armed with .44-caliber pistols and they were under orders to "shoot first and ask questions later."[18]

In 1910 a serious accident occurred when the president was riding in his car in New York. His vehicle was second in a train of five cars, and at Eighth Avenue a trolley that was stopped by a motorcycle police officer surged forward. The president's car swerved but was hit by the trolley and carried a half a block down Eighth Avenue. However, no one was hurt.[19]

——————

The frequency of crank visitors to the White House did not diminish during Taft's presidency. As one newspaper reported, "Scarcely a month of the four years in office of a president of the United States passes that at least one crank . . . does not call at the White House to tell [the president] how the affairs of government should be managed."[20]

The press referred to the constant stream of delusional visitors to the White House as "Dementia Presidentia." The *New York Times* opined that of "the number of men and women who had to see [the president] on missions of real importance, there has never before been anything like so great a number of more or less demented persons trying to break into the president's sanctum. Nor has there been at anytime so many crank letters, or such a lot of crank literature received at the White House. . . . It was freely prophesized that the new administration would see a distinct falling off in this class of visitors but considering how short a time Mr. Taft has been in office, his popularity with the cranks is phenomenal, and it begins to look as if he might eventually outdo his predecessor in that line."[21]

Some suspicious characters arrived at the Executive Mansion armed. In April 1912, a German immigrant who lived in Baltimore, Michael Winter, had applied unsuccessfully to the German ambassador for a letter of introduction to the president. Frustrated that the letter he requested had not been forthcoming, he arrived at the entrance to the White House, ran swiftly up the steps past the doorkeeper, and for a while was lost in the darkness of the hallway from the frantically searching ushers. He was eventually caught and ejected. A few moments later he tried a second time to force his way into the "private part of the executive mansion," and on this occasion he was arrested by the ushers and handed over to White House police. After Secret Service agents searched Winter, they found a clasp knife in his pocket. However, he was considered "harmless" and was released.[22]

There were a number of "nonserious" threats made against Taft, which, nevertheless, caused great anxiety among the president's security detail. In 1910 a "muscular man" called asking to see the president and was recognized as being the same person who had visited the Executive Mansion the previous year armed with two pistols and asking to see the president about a "grievance." The Secret Service was taking no risks on this occasion and he was arrested.[23] In October 1911, the month before Taft was due to visit Minneapolis, fifty-two-year-old Julius Bergerson began to tell his friends he was determined to assassinate Taft. When Bergerson repeated his threats on the morning of the president's impending visit to the city, one of Bergerson's friends, lawyer, I. N. Berson, informed the sheriff's office and Bergerson was arrested and placed in the county jail. After Bergerson was examined by doctors, he was declared to be insane and taken to the state asylum at Rochester.[24]

On Saturday, May 25, 1912, the president was giving a speech in the public square of Rutherford, New Jersey, standing up in his presidential car, when a "projectile" was thrown by an "Italian man" and hit Taft in the face. His agents pushed him back in his seat and immediately ordered the driver of the car to speed away, leaving the crowd of twelve thousand disappointed as the speech had to be canceled. The "projectile" turned out to be a "wad of wet paper." Agents said the package had been deliberately soaked to weigh it down to become heavier.[25]

The Secret Service investigated a number of serious threats to Taft that were foiled, including an alleged attempt by an armed man to breach the president's security when Taft visited Norwich, Connecticut, in July 1909, to attend the 250th anniversary of the founding of the city. As the president mingled with the crowds, a woman screamed out and then fainted. When she was revived she told police officers and Secret Service agents she had observed a man with a revolver concealed beneath his coat attempting to approach the president. "We were crowding up to get a good view of the president," she said, "and were within ten feet of him when a man brushed by me. Of course, it attracted my attention and I was terrified when I saw that he carried his hand under his coat and there was a revolver in it. I screamed and when he saw me looking at him he wormed his way out of the crowd. I thought he was going to shoot Mr. Taft." The woman accompanied Secret Service officers as they searched for Taft's would-be assassin but they were unable to find him.[26]

Three months later another serious breach of the president's security occurred in Portland, Oregon, when Taft was sitting in his presidential car. On October 2, 1909, twenty-seven-year-old Arthur Wright, who came from Lowell, Massachusetts, attended a parade in honor of the president. The parade had reached the corner of Sixth and Morrison near the Portland Hotel where Taft had been staying. Wright, who had a "peculiar manner," attempted to approach Taft's car holding a camera "backward and at his side." Police Captain Bailey ordered him back, but Wright ignored him and continued to approach the president's car, "thrusting his way" through the crowd. Bailey tackled him and felt what he believed to be a gun. Following a struggle Wright was handcuffed and arrested. When he was searched he was found to be carrying a .38-caliber Smith and Wesson revolver and twenty cartridges in his pockets. Police also confiscated a "special policeman star" pinned on his vest and bearing the name of "Lowell, Massachusetts." Wright was taken to the local police station and charged with carrying a concealed weapon. Although Wright insisted he had only wanted to get near Taft to take his picture, interviewing police officers gave "little credence to his answers." He was charged with carrying a concealed weapon.[27]

In 1910 the Secret Service was alerted to a serious threat when Pittsburgh police informed the agency that a plot to kill Taft had been thwarted. Pittsburgh police arrested Miko Shimko after he had murdered a missionary, the Reverend Dr. Frank Skala, after the preacher delivered his Sunday morning sermon. When police searched Shimko's house they found incriminating evidence that he was planning with others to assassinate the president. Taft was due to arrive in Pittsburgh the following Sunday.[28]

During his 1909 tour of the Southwest, prior to a meeting with the president of Mexico, Taft had stopped off at a number of venues to give speeches. On at least two occasions the Secret Service investigated incidents that were deemed to be of a threatening nature. On October 11, 1909, Manuel Romero was arrested after following Taft's car in Los Angles. He was one of six men who had been arrested at an anarchist meeting called to denounce the president.[29]

When Taft arrived in Albuquerque, New Mexico, on October 15, 1909, he was escorted to the Alvarado Hotel, where he was scheduled to speak at a banquet that evening. The chief of police had asked his officers to keep an eye on a particularly suspicious individual who had been suspected of harboring an animus toward the president. Shortly after Taft arrived, a deranged miner, Thomas Thorp, was observed walking toward the hotel carrying a butcher's knife and shouting, "Where is Taft? I want to kill him." Albuquerque police arrested Thorp, who was described as "drunk" and "feeble-minded."[30]

In August 1912, an alleged would-be assassin breached the president's security cordon armed with a knife. Forty-year-old Carolyn Beers, who came from Greenville, Ohio, traveled to Columbus, where Taft was due to deliver a speech at the Ohio Centennial Celebration. At 7:30 a.m., Taft arrived in the city by train and was taken to the Southern Hotel for breakfast, accompanied by two Secret Service agents. When Taft entered the hotel and approached an elevator to take him to his room upstairs, the agents stopped Beers from approaching the president in the elevator. She struggled with them, all the while insisting she was the president's wife and that she was "following him to see he remains true to me. All I have is a sacred knife which I intend to give him. Please let me at him." The agents arrested Beers; and when she was searched at the police station, they discovered she had been concealing "several knives in the folds of her dress," one with a blade three inches long. When she was interviewed, she repeated her claims that she was the president's wife. According to some newspaper reports, she purportedly said she was going to "punish" the president.[31]

There were numerous rumors of plots to kill President Taft that were investigated by the Secret Service and law enforcement authorities, but most of them were never corroborated. In September 1908, for example, Republican presidential candidate Taft received notification of a letter in the hands of the Topeka chief of police that indicated that "four or five suspicious persons" had conspired to assassinate Taft and "implicate some negro men." One of the alleged conspirators, the letter stated, said he was going to shoot the president when he next visited Chicago, "with a rifle from the top of some skyscraper."[32]

In 1910, Taft's aunt, Miss Delia C. Torrey, reported to police that a stranger had visited her home in Millbury, Massachusetts, to tell her he had overheard a conversation in which plotters in Boston had planned the assassination of the president. As the stranger departed, he threatened to kill Miss Torrey if the "matter got into the newspapers."[33] Torrey later denied that the stranger had threatened to kill her, and after police investigated the matter, they traced the stranger to Worcester, but there "the trail ended."[34]

A plot that may or may not have existed was revealed in a 1919 court case. A Department of Justice agent, Pasquale Pignuelo, was indicted and tried for bribery involving "saloon men" who wanted to evade Prohibition. During the trial, he disclosed that when he was working as an agent for the Justice Department, he investigated a plot to kill Taft. However, Pignuelo was "cut short" in his testimony and the details of the alleged plot were never revealed.[35]

In 1911 and 1912, the Secret Service investigated plots to kill Taft that were deemed to be of a more serious nature. The 1911 plot was revealed by an anarchist, John Steele, who said he had been "high enough up" in anarchist circles to "know that President Taft would be killed as soon as he left Washington after Congress closed." Steele and a fellow anarchist, Stuart Moffet, had been arrested for conspiring to assassinate the mayor of Spokane, N. S. Pratt. They were also suspected of murdering a Spokane police officer, Capt. John T. Sullivan. Spokane Captain of Detectives Martin J. Byrnes said, "The plans [to kill the mayor] were to wait until after the city election. . . . Undercover officers heard Steele make his report to Moffet after a visit to the Pratt home in which he was guarded day and night." Taft was due to visit Spokane the following month. Police said they had insufficient evidence to try the men for plotting to kill the president.[36]

In 1912 Pittsburgh police believed that anarchists, "an active colony of reds on the north-side," had chosen anarchist Carlos Ceznar to assassinate President Taft. It was alleged that Ceznar was "commissioned" to go to Altoona during a Taft visit. The plot was allegedly hatched at a meeting at the cobbler's shop of "nihilist Frank" in Spring Garden Avenue. The police reported that lots had been drawn and it fell to Ceznar to "strike the great blow for the cause." Two days before the purported assassination, however, Ceznar was observed looking "morose" and he would not speak to any of his companions. On the Wednesday the purported plot was due to be executed, Ceznar bought a ticket for Altoona at the Pittsburgh Union depot. He left the train at East Liberty station and walked east to Spruce Street, where he threw himself in front of a train. Police suspected Ceznar lost his nerve after starting out on his assassination mission. Fearing to return to his comrades, and in desperation, he killed himself.[37]

In May 1912, a man who had been serving a prison sentence for sending a bomb to Andrew Carnegie's former business partner, Alexander R. Peacock, confessed to his lawyer he too had been part of an anarchist plot to kill Taft. William D. Pastorius said the plot was organized by anarchists because of the president's abrogation of the Russian Treaty. The plans, he said, had been made at the Hotel Navarre in New York by a group of "European anarchists" he had met. Pastorius said he had been a "dupe" and asked his lawyer to pass on the details of the plot to the Secret Service. However, the agency was unable to substantiate Pastorius's claims.[38]

There were also rumored plots to kill Taft when he met with President Porfirio Díaz of Mexico at El Paso in 1909. The two presidents were scheduled to meet at the Mexican-American border town of Juarez, Mexico. At the time, Mexico seethed with revolutionary tensions, which the following year was to drive Díaz out of office.

Prior to the Taft-Díaz meeting, the FBI notified Secret Service chief Wilkie that an informant had made the bureau aware of a plot to assassinate the president.[39] Wilkie assigned agents to Chicago to learn the identity of the anarchists selected to kill Presidents Taft and Díaz. The plot was allegedly discovered when four undercover Secret Service agents, disguised as laborers, attended an anarchist meeting in

Chicago. However, Chief Wilkie told reporters, "Absolutely no plot is known to exist."[40]

However, two days before the presidents met, the Mexican Secret Service observed a "young man," pretending to be a reporter, who had attempted to gain access to a banquet held for President Díaz in Ciudad Juarez. He was stopped and searched, and agents found in one pocket an automatic revolver, which was shaped like a lead pencil. The pistol held seven cartridges. The Mexican police concluded that the gun had apparently been made to order. They said it was designed in such a way that it would have been easily possible for anyone to have mistaken it for a pencil when the hand was closed over the butt.[41]

———

Shortly after Taft's 1908 election, the president decided he needed a place to escape the insufferable Washington summertime heat. For the previous sixteen years, he and his family had vacationed in Canada on the shores of Murray Bay. However, not wishing to break convention by choosing to vacation on foreign soil, he chose Beverley, Massachusetts, situated near the towns of Manchester and Magnolia. The summer retreat proved to be just as attractive to potential presidential threateners.

It was Taft's wife, Nellie, who decided to rent the fourteen-room cottage at Beverly. Stetson Hall eventually became the "summer White House." (In 1911 and 1912, the Tafts moved their summer residence to Parramatta, located a mile from their previous summer home, in a section of Beverley known as Montserrat, after the owners indicated they wanted to tear down the cottage to make an Italian garden.)

When he was president, Taft had the use of the presidential yacht *Mayflower*, with a crew of two hundred, which was moored in the harbor near the cottage. He also had use of a smaller yacht, the *Sylph*, which was used for shorter trips. Whenever Taft took the yachts out, accompanied by guests, an agent accompanied him.[42] A special presidential train was used for his many trips to and from Washington DC during the summer months.

The summer cottage was closely guarded by eight Secret Service agents around the clock. One agent patrolled the front of the house and the other the rear. When Taft went golfing, an agent was always by his side. The president's visitors were asked to wait down the road from the cottage while agents ascertained whether their names appeared in the engagement book.

The August 1910 attempted assassination of New York's mayor, William Gaynor, prompted the Secret Service to tighten security around the Tafts' cottage, which was situated on Woodbury Point. The agents stationed themselves behind bushes and nailed telephones to trees. Occasionally the agents would have to deal with unwelcome visitors, including a number of individuals who had spent time in insane asylums.[43] In 1910 John George Schubell, who lived in Baltimore, Maryland, approached Taft's house armed with a hammer, and when he was stopped and questioned, he told Taft's agents he wanted to see the president to "discuss religious matters." The agents believed Schubell was insane. He was arrested and examined by doctors.[44]

————

The most serious threat to Taft's life, it can be argued, occurred in California in October 1911.Taft was visiting the state for speeches in Los Angeles and Pasadena, accompanied by Sen. John Works and California governor Hiram Johnson.

Almost one hundred explosions, which began in Massachusetts in 1905, had been scattered across the country for the previous six years and resulted in the bombing of the *Los Angeles Times* building and an attempt to blow up Taft's train at Santa Barbara. International Iron Workers president Frank Ryan and fifty-three other union officials were arrested for the "dynamite conspiracy" in which they plotted to destroy the property of employers on nonunion labor.

The plot to kill Taft was discovered by the sheriff of Santa Barbara County, Nat Stewart, who relayed the information about the plot to special detectives of the Southern Pacific Railroad and the Secret Service. The sheriff said the plot involved blowing up a long bridge, the Cartian Viaduct, twenty miles north of Santa Barbara, over which the president's special train was to pass early on the morning of October 16.

A watchman, Abe Jenkins, had been employed by the Southern Pacific Railroad Company to watch the Cartian Bridge at Gaviota, in Santa Barbara County, after a strike of workers was called days before. In the early hours of October 16, Jenkins was patrolling at the Gaviota end of the bridge—which was a huge structure, made of steel, which carried the rails over a semidry stream between Gaviota and El Capean—when he saw a dark form on the latticework of the bridge. He called out, believing the man was a trackwalker, but when the trespasser began to run away Jenkins chased after him. At the edge of the bridge, which was not very high above the river, Jenkins was tackled by a second intruder, who was soon joined by his accomplice who had doubled back. After a struggle, the men broke away as Jenkins began to fire his pistol.

After searching the area, Jenkins discovered twenty-one sticks of dynamite hidden in a section of one of the steel piers near the middle of the bridge. A long fuse was attached to the dynamite and hung from the pier. The watchman also found a further eighteen sticks of dynamite, "of 80 percent potency," in the next pier, similarly arranged. The dynamite was so placed that the would-be assassin could light the fuse as he observed the president's train and then make his escape. There was sufficient dynamite to "blow the train and bridge to bits."

Jenkins telephoned for assistance, and a posse, which included a special team of Southern Pacific detectives, arrived shortly before the president's train was to pass at 5:00 a.m. They were soon joined by Secret Service agent S. W. F. Hines, who had been accompanying the president during the California trip. Abe Jenkins's story was corroborated by section foreman C. F. Brown, who had seen two men leave a late train at Naples and walk toward the bridge, and by a "Mexican herder," who said the two men spent part of the evening in his cabin. Acting on information provided by the herder, the posse headed north into the mountains but they were unsuccessful in apprehending the bombers.

Secret Service agents concluded that there had been "complete evidence" of a plot to kill the president. Arguments that led the Secret Service to suspect it had been an assassination attempt included the fact that if the men had wanted simply to destroy the bridge, they would have used a timing device, which would have precluded their remaining on the ground to be sure the bomb exploded at the proper moment. The agents believed the motive centered on the striking workers' efforts to publicize their anger at businesses that used nonunion labor.[45] Although a reward of $5,000 had been offered by the vice president and general manager of the Southern Pacific Railroad, no arrests were made.[46]

In December 1911, U.S. District Attorney McCormick met with Taft at the White House to discuss the investigation into the attempt to dynamite Taft's train in Southern California during his trip to the West.[47]

Even when Taft left office, he did not become immune to the attentions of would-be assassins. In 1917 a plot, believed to be pro-German in nature, was revealed that included the assassinations of Presidents Wilson, Roosevelt, and Taft as well as Indiana senator Tom Taggart. The plot was discovered after the heart attack death of sixty-year-old Charles G. Mueller, a traveling salesman, who had been staying at Barlow's Hotel in Trenton, New Jersey. Law enforcement officers found a notebook among Mueller's possessions that recorded how the U.S. presidents and the senator were "picked for death," along with information that Mueller intended to blow up ammunition plants.

A loaded revolver was found in his hip pocket and two double-barreled guns in cases were also found. The notebooks did not indicate how the assassinations were to be carried out.[48]

CHAPTER 12

The Stalking of Woodrow Wilson

There is nothing that can be done to guard against such attacks. It seems to me that the police and Secret Service guards are useless if a madman determines to attack a man in public life.

—Woodrow Wilson

Woodrow Wilson, the Democratic Party nominee of 1912, benefited greatly from a split in the Republican Party in the presidential election of that year. When former Republican president Teddy Roosevelt was beaten by Taft for the Republican nomination, he formed the new Bull Moose Party. During the November election he took votes away from Taft, and Wilson won with just 42 percent of the popular vote. Though his political personality was more understated than Roosevelt's, Wilson also took a "big stick" approach to governing and used the powers of the presidency to rein in big business. He helped create the Federal Trade Commission and signed the Clayton Antitrust Act, both of which gave regulators authority to limit the power of large corporations.

When acts of sabotage by German spies and sympathizers broke out in the United States and losses were inflicted on its shipping by German U-boats, it forced America's hand, and Wilson declared war against Germany in 1917.

Although Wilson has been judged by most historians as a "great president," his conception of himself, according to historian Forrest

McDonald, was "little short of messianic." McDonald wrote that "the day after his election, the Democratic national chairman called on him to confer about appointments, only to be rebuffed by Wilson's statement, 'Before we proceed, I wish it clearly understood that I owe you nothing. Remember that God ordained that I should be the next President of the United States.'"[1]

On his arrival at the White House for duty in December 1914, newly appointed Secret Service agent Edmund Starling described the atmosphere as "melancholy" and said that the newly installed President Wilson was subject to fits of deep depression caused by his wife's death a few months before. Starling, who guarded six presidents in his career, admired Wilson the most and soon after the agent's arrival at the White House formed a strong bond with him. Starling also received another surprise when he began his Secret Service career. He noticed that the president's detail could "blandly" ignore the president if he "ordered them to go away."[2]

Starling said that from his doctor to his valet, Wilson's staff was worried about "the boss," as the agents called him, and they all agreed that what he needed was "female companionship." In 1915 the president began to date a widower, Edith Galt. One of Wilson's agents described the president as a "changed man" after he met her. Starling had to accompany the president and Mrs. Galt on their regular walks in Rock Creek Park. "I wanted to look away," he wrote, "but I couldn't. Something might happen."[3]

At night Starling accompanied Wilson on his visits to Mrs. Galt's home. He would wait at the entrance to the house until Wilson reappeared. It was usually never before midnight. Often Wilson would want to walk back to the White House, which displeased Starling as he had to be back on duty early the next morning to take the president golfing. After Wilson married Mrs. Galt, Starling continued to accompany the president and the first lady on their golf trips.

When Woodrow Wilson took office, William J. Flynn was chief of the Secret Service and William H. Moran his deputy. The Secret Service White House detail was headed by Joseph E. Murphy, and Agent Richard Jervis was responsible for presidential trips. In 1914 Wilson's personal protection detail included agents Jack Sly and Edmund Starling. The agents closest to Wilson were "Jimmie" Sloan and Harry Wheeler, who were said to have "never left the president's side until he retired safely to his room in the White House." When Wilson spent the night away from the White House, both men took turns guarding him through the night.[4]

When Starling arrived at the White House he was told by Murphy that the purpose of the president's detail was to "give him the maximum amount of protection with the minimum amount of inconvenience to his private life. When he goes to his living quarters on the second floor of the White House, we don't go with him. But from the time he comes downstairs until the time he goes back up again, he is under our guard."[5] When Wilson stayed at a hotel, the presidential group occupied a complete floor with the president in the center suite and Secret Service agents in the rooms on each side.[6]

A newspaper report in 1913 described the Secret Service agents at the White House as "watchdogs . . . [who] have no regular hours of duty. There are usually two of them close at hand whether the president is asleep or awake. . . . Athletic, alert, and courageous to the limit, these Secret Service men are nevertheless gentlemen in the true sense of the term, distinguished in appearance, their manners polished; their well-fitting clothes of the latest fashion, worn with ease and grace, their conversation correct and interesting."[7]

Since the assassination of William McKinley, the Secret Service had changed the requirements of service to include only applicants "of athletic build and keen intelligence." Wilson's detail consisted of six or so young agents, "the oldest on the sunny side of 30." The president was guarded "every waking hour" but "surrendered his care to the uniformed officers at the executive mansion" when he retired for the night.[8]

During the Wilson years, the Secret Service continued their scrutiny of individuals who requested a personal interview with the president. Senators and representatives in Congress were allowed to enter the executive offices at any time during the morning reception hours and were allowed to bring anyone with them. However, if a senator or representative gave a constituent a letter of introduction, it rested with the president's staff and the Secret Service to allow entry. Knowing that a senator or representative might have written such letters in order to fob off a persistent constituent meant that the Secret Service always looked upon these letters with suspicion. Only well-known senators, governors, or representatives holding important positions of power were automatically granted entry.

The Secret Service noted at the beginning of the Wilson administration that they expected a surge in unstable visitors to the White House who wanted to see the new president. Each change in administration, an unnamed agent stated, "would start the mentally afflicted once again toward the White House." The reason given by a White House source was that "the excitement the change [in administrations] engendered affected people who were mentally unbalanced."[9]

The doorkeeper at the time of the Wilson administration, Pat McKenna, believed that the most "embarrassing and troublesome" and unstable White House visitors were women. According to another White House source, "It is difficult to deal with a woman crank. If she is crossed there is absolutely no telling what sort of a scene she will create." To deal with the problem, the doorkeeper would show the visitor to the reception room and then say the president was too busy to see them. Experience had shown they would soon become tired of waiting and leave.[10]

The Secret Service used two Pierce-Arrow automobiles for presidential car journeys. They were both open-top with right-hand drives, and the presidential seal was embossed on the sides of the cars. Agents rode in the first car with Wilson, with other members of the presidential detail riding in the second car.[11] After taking office, Wilson began to take hour-long drives in the evening. His favorite drives took him to Northern Virginia along a dirt river road next to the Potomac across from Washington. Another favorite route was through Rock Creek Park to the site of the Washington Cathedral.[12] During his drives, Wilson would often become angry with speeders on the road. He once asked his attorney general if he had the power to stop speeding motorists and fine them $1,000. The attorney general advised Wilson it would be politically unwise.[13] Wilson also objected to the two accompanying police motorcycle riders wherever he went, and the security precaution was dropped.[14]

At weekends Wilson liked to sail on the presidential yacht, *Mayflower*, which had been a White House asset since Roosevelt's time in office.[15] He also loved to play golf, and he would frequently visit the Kirkdale Club at Chevy Chase Circle, the Washington Golf and Country Club across the Potomac in Virginia, or the Town and Country Club.[16] On one golf outing his Secret Service detail thought Wilson had become the victim of a bomb plot. Wilson had been walking the links at the Washington Golf and Country Club when Richard Jervis heard a loud explosion coming from a dense wooded area. A huge tree stump landed near the presidential party, and when Jervis ran into the woods to investigate, he came across a local farmer who had been clearing land near the course. The farmer admitted to Jervis he had used too much dynamite.[17]

Before he took office Wilson had little idea of how the White House security apparatus worked. Following his election, he said, "I found to my surprise that it is the interpretation of the law to guard the president-elect even before he is inaugurated."[18] During his first inauguration, Wilson risked danger of being trampled by overzealous crowds when he took it upon himself to interfere with Secret Service procedures for the protection of the chief executive. He saw a vacant space between the reviewing stand and the crowd and ordered the rope barrier taken down so the crowds could draw near him. The space had been cordoned off because the Secret Service wanted to use it as an emergency exit. When the crowds closed in, it endangered not only the president but his agents also.

When President-elect Wilson announced he intended to keep "open house" for all visitors to the White House during his presidency, agents were reportedly amused. "He thinks he will, but he will do nothing of the sort," one agent said. "Such an idea is preposterous and if Governor Wilson had had two hours experience as president or had ever been in the White House offices he would not have made such a ridiculous promise. A president cannot hold 'open house.'" The agent told reporters that such practices would lay the president open to all kinds of "risks and dangers" and that it would interfere with the regular business of the Executive Mansion.[19]

As with presidents before him, Wilson wanted refuge from his bodyguards. On more than one occasion, he left their protection to wander off on his own. According to Secret Service agent Thomas E. Halls, Wilson was "wholly indifferent to his safety."[20]

Wilson usually never got far enough away without his agents catching up with him. But there were times when they were caught out. Occasionally, Wilson would leave the White House for a walk to his bank or to go shopping, without informing his agents. On one occasion he left the White House on his way to the bank frantically pursued by two agents. Wilson tried to lose them by mingling with the crowds outside the Executive Mansion but they soon found him. Wilson later said, "I came very near to getting away that time."[21]

In August 1915, Wilson decided to take a long tour of the Washington streets in the neighborhood of the White House without informing his agents. Wilson's detail, who were playing chess with newspaper reporters in the White House press room, were clearly upset when a uniformed officer told them, "The president is out alone. He's going down toward Fifteenth Street by himself." The agents quickly scrambled, grabbed their coats and hats, and rushed across the White House grounds in a frantic attempt to catch up with the president. The agents found him a short distance from the White House gates, walking briskly and unnoticed by the crowd on the sidewalk. Wilson was reported to be "smiling ruefully" as his detail overtook him.[22]

In July 1916, Wilson once again eluded his bodyguards when he took a trip down the Potomac on the *Mayflower* with his naval aide and physician, Lt. Cmdr. Cary Grayson, who was also Wilson's friend (Grayson was promoted to the rank of rear admiral a month later). The two men slipped away from the Secret Service detail and took a motor launch to Yorktown, Virginia. Both men strolled through the streets unnoticed until a young girl recognized the president and invited them to her house, where they were served cold tea.[23]

On another occasion Wilson left his office without being observed, exited the White House by a side door, and went to the State Department across the street. In a corridor the president met an Associated Press correspondent, Kirke Simpson, and, placing his fingers to his lips said, "Sh-h-h! The Secret Service is hunting for me."[24]

There were times the president asked his agents for more seclusion during his walks, but he knew he could never order them to stay behind at the White House. Instead, they kept a discreet distance behind him.[25] But the times that caused most anxiety for his detail were the trips the president made by train, because Wilson liked to walk around during train stops and greet crowds.[26] According to agent Edmund Starling, "Unscheduled stops and visits to unguarded places are what make fatalism the only friend of the Secret Service man."[27]

———

During Wilson's first term as president, numerous threatening letters arrived at the White House, many from pro-German Americans who were angry that their country was aiding and abetting Britain and her allies. According to Edmund Starling, most of the letters that arrived at the White House were written by people of "unsound mind" and "in the majority of cases the author [had] no intention of taking action."

According to a July 1915 edition of the *Milwaukee Sentinel*, "Cranks flock to Washington in greater numbers, probably, than any other city in the country. Letters from cranks are received by the cartload annually by the Chief of Police, by the White House officials, and by other government representatives."[28]

That same year, Washington's *Sunday Star* also expressed fears that cranks were arriving in the city in increasing numbers. "Since the European war broke out," the newspaper opined,

> many cranks have stormed the White House, who have been mentally disturbed by tales of bloodshed and the great loss of life in Europe. For over a year they have been absorbing all sorts of war material, and it has preyed upon their minds. Naturally of weak mentality, it only took some great disturbance such as the European war, which is constantly written about, talked about, and pictured in all the periodicals, to inflame their defective but receptive minds. . . . These poor, brain harried mental wrecks believe they have some effective plan by which to end the war. Cranks of this class are watched. . . . They plan to end what they term 'wholesale murder' with murder and they have ingenious and diabolical ideas, as a rule, as to ways to put through their project.[29]

The *Star* observed that "a particularly vigilant, and wary, force of secret service men are on duty at the White House in addition to the officers who work under Maj. Pullman of the metropolitan police.

The cranks who visit the White House number the largest of any who invade the capital."[30]

Most threats led to a full investigation by the Secret Service and, if the threat was judged to be serious enough, arrests were made and convictions sought. The coming of war caused increased concern for the protection of the president, and Congress enacted the "threat statute," making it a crime to threaten the president by mail or in any other manner. In 1917 Congress also authorized protection for the president's immediate family. Sentences were often severe. In 1918, for example, Elias Gracely received a thirteen-year prison sentence for saying he planned to kill President Wilson. Gracely, a farmer who lived in Toledo, Ohio, was tried, found guilty, and sent to the federal penitentiary in Atlanta, Georgia.[31]

Another threatener charged under the new law was Pemberton W. Stickrath, who was reported to have said, "President Wilson ought to be killed. It is a wonder someone has not done it already. If I had an opportunity I would do it myself." However, Stickrath insisted his language did not amount to a true threat and that, with President Wilson hundreds of miles away, he posed no danger to the president. Prosecutors disagreed. They argued that in a country like the United States, where the people are sovereign and the president merely their representative, a threat to kill the president "is an affront to all loyal and right-thinking persons, inflaming their minds [and] provoking disorder [and is] akin to treason." The conviction was upheld.[32]

In December 1912, the Secret Service investigated the case of nineteen-year-old Herman Steinberg, who worked for a fruit dealer in New York City. Steinberg was standing in front of a police station when he was approached by one of the station's detectives. Steinberg told the police officer he wanted to shoot the president-elect because "this is not a fit country to live in. . . . I can't go back to Russia so I would rather go to jail." Steinberg was immediately arrested; when searched, he was found to be carrying a revolver. He was charged with violating the "Sullivan law," which prohibited the carrying of dangerous weapons. When Steinberg was arraigned before a judge, his former employer said Stenberg had made previous threats to kill President-elect Wilson, which led to his firing. Steinberg admitted buying the revolver the week previously because "I had made up my mind to kill Wilson." He intended to wait for the arrival of Wilson in Jersey City, after the president-elect returned from his vacation in Bermuda, and shoot him. Steinberg was found guilty and sentenced to a term in prison.[33]

Wilson was also the subject of extortion threats. In 1912 Newark residents twenty-six-year-old Jacob Dunn and his twenty-four-year-old brother, Peter, conspired with forty-two-year-old Seeley Davenport, who lived in Wharton, New Jersey, to extort $5,000 in gold from President-elect Wilson and threatened Wilson with death unless their demands were met. Following an investigation by the Secret Service and postal inspectors, the three men, who were described as "mountain men," were arrested in a deserted patch of mountain woodland, thirty-seven miles from Wharton.

When Jacob Dunn was interrogated by postal inspectors, they discovered handwriting traits linking him to seven letters sent to the president-elect. One of the letters stated, "I am now going to warn you of what we are going to do to you as we did not Teddy or McKinley either they got shot up just the same or if we don't get what we ask from you, you will get the same. . . . If you have $5,000 in gold for this party we will spare your life but if not we will shoot you before you get in the office as sure as your name is Wilson."[34] In May 1913, Seeley Davenport and Jacob Dunn were convicted by a federal jury of sending threatening letters to Woodrow Wilson. They were both given prison terms.[35]

In 1913, Guiseppe Pomaro was arrested for sending a threatening letter to Wilson in which he demanded "$15,000 or it will be the worse for you." The letter was mailed on May 20, 1913, and handed over to the Secret Service. Foolishly, Pomaro had also written his address in the letter. He was identified by police as a member of a "black-hand gang"—the old-fashioned term for the Mafia. Pomaro was arrested in Youngstown and charged with sending a threatening letter to Wilson.[36]

The same month, Richard Lindsay, a Chicago resident, was arrested in Philadelphia after a struggle with Secret Service agents. He had been tracked down by the agency after he wrote to Wilson demanding $300,000 as "remuneration" for having being assaulted by a federal employee.[37]

In the same year, forty-three-year-old Rudolf Malik, an Austrian who had been in the United States for three months, sent a letter to Wilson demanding $300. Malik wanted the money as "an indemnity" for his inability to return to the country of his birth. He was arrested, charged with having "devised and operated a scheme to defraud the president," and indicted by a grand jury on a charge of having mailed a threatening letter to Wilson.[38]

There were also extortion threats to blow up the White House if demands were not forthcoming. In July 1915, the Secret Service investigated a letter sent to the White House by two brothers informing the president they planned to carry on the work of the "man who dynamited the capitol and attempted to kill [financier] J. P. Morgan and blow up ocean liners." The brothers threatened not only the president's life but also the destruction of the White House and two manufacturing plants in Washington.[39]

Wilson received numerous threats to assassinate him emanating from mentally unbalanced individuals. In May 1915, a man from San Francisco arrived at the White House and shouted, "Right after I have been crowned king of Mexico, Holland, and North America." He was arrested and taken into custody. When he was searched, it was discovered he had been armed with a loaded revolver and had several hundred dollars in his possession. Secret Service agent Jervis was not surprised to see him. He remembered the man had written a letter to Wilson before traveling to Washington, informing him of his intended visit.[40]

In 1916, sixty-two-year-old Morris Diamond, who lived in Bay City, Michigan, wrote several letters to Wilson threatening to kill him. Following a Secret Service investigation, Diamond was arrested by Secret Service agent Gabriel De Force, who opined that the letter writer was "insane." Diamond told the agent that mysterious voices were "calling on him to kill the president."[41] He was sent to an asylum, but escaped on October 27, with three other inmates, by breaking down the door of the ward where they were confined and sawing bars. He was captured shortly afterward.[42]

The Secret Service considered three threats to be particularly serious, as they involved the stalking of the president in cities across America and the breaching of the president's security cordon. Had it not been for the arrest of the individuals involved, the president may have been assassinated.

The first incident occurred in November 1912, when Wilson was president-elect. John Cohan, a one-armed man who owned a farm in Casselton, North Dakota, was arrested on a charge of disturbing the peace in Colorado Springs, Colorado. He told one of the arresting police officers that he would kill President-elect Wilson "if he ever got the chance." Cohan had previously been arrested in New Orleans during a visit to the city by Taft on his last tour of the country. Cohan had also been arrested in Chicago when former president Teddy Roosevelt gave a speech there. Police discovered that Cohan had stalked Governor Wilson at a "number of places . . . across the country during the presidential election campaign." During his hearing, Cohan said, "A man like Woodrow Wilson with his political and religious beliefs should never be allowed to take the presidential chair. Yes, I will kill him when I get out of here." Cohan was judged to be insane and sent to an asylum.[43]

The second incident involved twenty-two-year-old Richard Cullen, who was angry at Wilson's "foreign policies." As Wilson rode through the streets of Pittsburgh, Cullen managed to jump onto the running boards of the president's limousine, despite the presence of agents. Agents quickly arrested Cullen before he could reach the president. When he was searched, they discovered he had been carrying a knife with a five-inch blade. Cullen was sent to Mayview Hospital for "observation regarding his sanity."[44]

The third incident occurred in 1919 and involved a man who had recently been released from the Massachusetts state mental hospital at Worcester. John Rogofsky, who called himself the "King of Poland," tried to gain admittance to Wilson's suite at the Copley Plaza Hotel in Boston. Agents blocked his route and Rogofsky was arrested. After he was searched, he was found to be carrying a .32-caliber revolver with sixty rounds of ammunition. Rogofsky was handed over to local police officers. He was arraigned in Central Court but was only charged with "carrying dangerous weapons," even though he admitted to police that he "intended to get the president and save the world" and that he had been instructed by the "Supreme Being" to carry out his mission. Rogofsky was judged to be insane and sent to a mental hospital.[45]

Wilson apparently escaped a serious assassination attempt when an

Indiana man dropped dead before he could carry out his plans. In 1917, sixty-one-year-old Charles G. Mueller lived with his sister in Indianapolis, Indiana. In May he told her he was going to Trenton, New Jersey, to accept an opening as an architect. He had been unemployed for two years after he quit work, complaining of "stomach trouble." Mueller registered at a hotel in Trenton and, as he was walking through the lobby, he dropped dead of an apparent heart attack. When the local coroner searched his body, he discovered a note Mueller had written setting out his plans to kill President Wilson, ex-president Taft, and ex-president Roosevelt. He had also been carrying a loaded revolver in his hip pocket, and two rifles were found in his room.[46]

———————

When Wilson received news of the sinking of the *Lusitania* in 1915 by a German U-boat, he realized that the United States would be faced with entering the conflict in Europe. He needed time to think, so he left the White House alone, unaccompanied by his Secret Service detail. Wilson walked down Pennsylvania Avenue and when he returned, he walked into his study without speaking to anyone.[47]

It was also a trying period for the Secret Service as mail began to arrive at the White House from pro-German Americans who were angry at the aid the United States was providing for Britain and its allies. In the summer of 1915, for example, a twenty-six-year-old German sympathizer, F. H. Juergens, who lived in San Antonio, Texas, sent a threatening letter to Wilson saying he was angry that the United States did not "observe strict and impartial neutrality." He wanted the government to refuse to supply the Allies with munitions. Until his demands were met, the president's life "would be threatened." He was quickly arrested.[48]

In February 1917, Wilson broke off diplomatic relations with Germany, which created some anxiety for the Secret Service, who were arranging tightened security for the president's second inauguration in March. The level of threats reached "a new high," according to agent Starling, and the president's detail was "nervous and apprehensive."[49] In February the Zimmermann Telegram was made public. The document revealed that Germany had offered Mexico the restoration of Texas if the country would declare war on the United States and become Germany's ally.

In April, Wilson asked Congress to declare a state of war. Thereafter soldiers assisted the Secret Service with the security of the White House.

The German government mounted a huge campaign on American soil of "intrigue, espionage, and sabotage unprecedented in modern times by one allegedly friendly power against another," according to historian Christopher Andrew.[50] The main objective of the German campaign was to prevent American industry and finance from supplying Britain and its allies during the First World War.

Edmund Starling said that during the March 1917 inauguration ceremonies, "the mile from the White House to the Capitol was the longest I ever rode." The inauguration took place under the threat of "several bomb threats and assassination plots."[51] In front of the oath platform, there were machine guns and "fear of assassination was in the air," according to the *St. Petersburg Times*.[52] Starling said the heightened security during a time of crisis was "hard on me both physically and mentally, but especially physically. I pray every night for the president's safety and for the courage and wisdom for myself in performing my duty."[53]

Additional guards were hired to patrol the White House grounds and all cars, letters, and parcels arriving at the Executive Mansion were inspected.[54] At night, the large iron gates that opened on the semicircular drive to the entrance were closed. Previously, tourists could walk through the gates and look in the front door. At the west side of the grounds one gate was left open to admit visitors to the executive offices, but it was guarded by police officers.[55]

By 1918 Wilson had eight agents in his protective detail—Joseph E. Murphy, Jack Slye, Arnold Landvoight, John Sullivan, Walter Ferguson, John Fitzgerald, Miles McCahill, and Edmund Starling. By this time William Moran had become chief of the agency.

When Wilson left the White House in his Pierce-Arrow limousine, he was followed by a car with three or four Secret Service agents. In Wilson's car an agent sat beside the chauffeur. The two cars would move at a fast speed and did not stop at intersections guarded by local police officers. During motorcades, agents rode on the running board of the president's car, "one hand holding to the car and the other free to draw a gun," according to agent Starling. When the car moved slowly agents were ordered to trot alongside, scanning the crowds.[56]

When Wilson played golf he would be accompanied by one or two agents, and another six to eight agents would be stationed at points along the golf course. When the president went for walks he would be accompanied by one or two agents, but he never saw a further group of agents who were always within the vicinity.[57]

During the war, which America entered just months after Wilson began his second presidential term of office, he did not mix with people on the streets of Washington as he had previously enjoyed, and he often complained of his "isolation."[58] However, he no longer tried to evade his agents.[59] Instead of drives in the country, he now began to use the *Mayflower* yacht more frequently.[60]

But Wilson still longed for moments when he could take a walk "like an ordinary citizen." In May 1918, when he was staying at the New York Waldorf Astoria, he told Edmund Starling he was tired of the security that surrounded him. Wilson asked him if he could "sneak out the back way." Starling relented but insisted on accompanying him. According to Starling, the president was "like a kid," even though he nearly became a casualty when he stepped in front of a car on Madison Avenue.[61]

Wilson's agents were urged not to join the army because they were told the job of protecting the president was "more important than being a soldier." Their duties during the war were limited to protecting the president and his family. Agents no longer took responsibility for the White House grounds, which were now guarded by the army.[62]

Wilson traveled to Europe in 1919 with a Secret Service escort of ten men to attend the Versailles Peace Conference.[63] During the president's trip, Edmund Starling saved the life of France's prime minister. Starling was in Paris with the president for the peace talks, and was riding in a limousine behind Georges Clemenceau, when he saw a pistol in the hands of a would-be assassin. Starling reacted quickly and shot the assassin in the hand. The bullet meant for the prime minister was deflected, resulting in the bullet hitting Clemenceau's hat.

The Paris trip posed the greatest danger of assassination. Forty counterintelligence agents had been assigned to protect the president during the conference. They spent much of their time focused on site security and thoroughly examined President Wilson's quarters and all surrounding buildings, including checking telephone lines for taps. Counterintelligence officers patrolled the streets surrounding the president's quarters.

Rumors were circulating that Bolsheviks planned protests and may have planned to kill Wilson. To counter these threats, the intelligence agents worked with the French authorities and the U.S. Secret Service. Some agents worked undercover as journalists or as communist activists to convince protest leaders that Wilson might be simply ignorant of their proposals and that petitions, not bullets, was the right course of action.

It was during Wilson's time in Paris that a purported plot by "Bolsheviks" was uncovered when Maj. Herbert O. Yardley, who received the Distinguished Service Medal from the U.S. secretary of war for his cryptographic work, was in charge of the secret American Cryptographic Bureau. Agents had operated secretly to decode messages between representatives of foreign powers. During the period of its existence, 1917 to 1929, the agency decoded more than forty-five thousand messages. Yardley believed that the success of the American delegation to the Washington disarmament conference was because the American delegates were able to read each day at breakfast the secret coded messages that had passed between the staff of the foreign delegations and their governments.

In 1931 he published his memoirs, *The American Black Chamber*, and revealed that a decoded telegram message had fallen into his hands while he was serving with the Peace Commission in Paris. The message disclosed a plot to assassinate the president. Yardley wrote: "The reader may well appreciate the shock I received as I deciphered a telegram which reported an entente plot to assassinate President Wilson . . . by giving him . . . influenza in ice. Our informant, in whom we had the greatest confidence, begged the authorities, 'for God's sake,' to warn the president. I have no way of knowing whether this plot had any truth in fact and if I had, whether it succeeded. But there are these undeniable facts: President Wilson's first sign of illness occurred while he was in Paris and he was soon to die a lingering death."[64]

Yardley's comments appeared to be confirmed by correspondence discovered in the records of the Office of Military Intelligence of the War Department. In *Woodrow Wilson as I Knew Him*, by Joseph Tumulty, Wilson's secretary, there is a reference to a cablegram to Tumulty, who was in Washington, from Wilson's doctor, Rear Adm. Cary T. Grayson, who was in Paris with the president. Grayson stated that poisoning had been suspected but that it was "unfounded." However, Grayson, who could not recall the telegram, said, "I can't throw any light on this. I received many letters in Paris relating all sorts of things that purported to threaten danger to President Wilson and turned all of them over to Chief Moran of the Secret Service who was in Paris but I do not recall anything of the sort told to Major Yardley. Moran denied he had received a report of the plot.[65] Ralph M. Easley, chair of the Executive Council of the National Civic Federation, confirmed the story but said the plot planned for Wilson to be shot from behind a tree in the White House grounds.[66]

The Secret Service investigated numerous plots to kill the president that were planned by not only pro-Germans in the United States but groups of anarchists. In 1925 Samuel Gompers revealed in his autobiography that he had discovered a plot to kill Wilson. Gompers alleged he made a frantic midnight call to the president requesting a meeting to show him a confidential report about a plot to assassinate him.

The plot was allegedly traced to "extreme pacifists" and the information purportedly came from a Secret Service agent, according to Gompers. The agent, he said, was named Garland, who subsequently disappeared and was believed killed by enemies of the United States. Gompers said that he had seen a "typewritten memorandum form Garland" and that when he read its contents he was "horrified." Gompers was filled with "anxiety." When Gompers showed Wilson the memo, he "took his leave" after a few minutes. The following day he was called to a conference with Assistant Secretary of the Navy Franklin D. Roosevelt, New York Police Commissioner Woods, and William G. Flynn, who had become head of the Secret Service. As a result of the meeting, according to Gompers, extra precautions were made to protect Wilson. No further information about the plot was supplied by Gompers but he said that Garland had been in a "highly dangerous venture to obtain information of the inside circles of German propaganda" and that Garland had taken his own life "in that venture."[67]

During the Wilson presidency, anarchists continued to be a major threat to American presidents. In February 1916, the Secret Service assisted Chicago police authorities in tracking down a man who attempted to commit mass murder and threatened Wilson's life. Jean Crones (aka Nestor Don-doglio) was an immigrant and an anarchist from Cologne, Germany. When he arrived in the United States, he drifted around the country working as a chef at various places. In a protest against visiting Catholic leaders, Crones had laced soup with arsenic at a banquet for three hundred people held to celebrate the arrival of the group. Around one hundred became ill, though none died. The group had been saved from death because the soup had been watered down to accommodate extra guests.

The manhunt for Crones involved four hundred men. When police offi-cers searched Crones's apartment, they discovered anarchist literature and a makeshift laboratory. Police already had in custody a colleague of Crones, an Italian anarchist named John Allegrini. Allegrini told police he never believed Crones would commit murder. People reported various sightings of Crones in Chicago, New York, and Boston, but he was never found.[68]

In November 1917, more than one hundred Italian anarchists, most of them miners and shipyard employees, were arrested in Seattle, Portland, Spokane, Tacoma, and various northeastern cities by federal agents. The Italians were members of the Corcola Studi Sociali, an anarchist orga-nization. According to government investigators, the Italians plotted to help Germany in the war by fomenting revolution in Italy to overthrow King Victor Emanuel. Undercover agents who had infiltrated the group said that at the meetings anarchist leaders asked for volunteers to carry out the assassinations of King Victor and President Wilson. However, because there was not sufficient evidence no one was ever charged with plotting to assassinate the president.[69]

When Wilson returned from Europe on board the USS *George Wash-ington* and docked at Boston on February 25, 1919, he was informed that fourteen Spanish immigrants had plotted his assassination when he made a public appearance in Boston the following day. The men intended throwing a bomb at the president. According to the Secret Service, the two men chosen for the assassination attempt were Elario Orestiass and Florieu Madini.[70]

The men had been in the United States for around a year and most of them spent their time promoting the Industrial Workers of the World (IWW) movement and working with several radical socialist groups. The group included Jose Crau, the editor of a Spanish newspaper, *El*

Corsario. All the plotters were arrested in New York. A bomb, described as a "complicated machine," was also discovered among their possessions.[71]

Secret Service agents Frank Francisco and Edward J. Dowd told reporters they had accumulated enough evidence that would prove the men intended to assassinate the president. However, the charges were dropped after federal officials stated there was insufficient evidence to charge the members of the group with plotting to kill Wilson. The anarchists were deported, however, as they were "alien anarchists."[72]

It was an anarchist plot concocted in Leavenworth Prison, however, that led to successful prosecutions. Twenty men had plotted to kill the president. They had drawn lots to determine who would be the assassin. They also vowed to kill the assassin if he failed to carry out the assassination. Pietro (Sam) Peirre had been chosen.

Pierre was an IWW activist during the war and had traveled coast-to-coast preaching revolution. He had also served a prison sentence during the war for violating the Selective Service Act. During his time in prison, Pierre and two fellow anarchists conspired to assassinate Wilson. They agreed that the first prisoner released would carry out the act.[73]

Before Pierre was released on October 14, 1918, he told a cellmate, fellow prisoner and Italian immigrant John Lavullo, that he now had the responsibility of carrying out Wilson's assassination. Pierre was reported to have told Lavullo, "President Wilson should be killed, and I will kill him myself at the first opportunity." Unbeknown to Pierre, however, Lavullo had been loyal to the Allied cause during the First World War. Lavullo immediately informed the prison authorities of the plot and the Secret Service were notified.

When Pierre was released from Leavenworth, he was tracked by the Secret Service from Kansas to Chicago, then to Michigan, and finally to Cleveland, where he was arrested. During his trip he contacted a number of leaders of the IWW.

Pierre was later tried in a federal court in Topeka, in April 1919, and convicted of plotting Wilson's assassination. He was sentenced to three and a half years in prison. However, Pierre appealed his sentence and was released on $7,000 bail pending the outcome of his appeal. Pierre relocated to San Jose, California, but in November 1920 he was arrested by San Jose sheriff George W. Lyle on a charge of larceny.[74]

On December 31, 1920, Pierre lost his appeal. He was ordered to be deported to Italy after he had completed his sentence for plotting Wilson's assassination. As a reward for exposing the plot, Lavullo was paroled from Leavenworth after serving part of his five-year sentence for violation of the Mann Act.[75]

Felled by a stroke, Woodrow Wilson spent much of the last two years of his presidency unable really to work. The stroke turned him into a rigid, often delusional man who condemned all efforts at compromise on American membership of the League of Nations, which he had fought for during his trips to Paris.

Sadly, Wilson fantasized about running for a third term in 1920, but his health prevented him. Even without him as a candidate, the Republicans made him the main issue in the campaign, and they characterized the landslide victory of their nominee, Warren G. Harding, as a repudiation of Wilson and all his works, including membership in the league.

The Secret Service dropped their protection of Wilson almost immediately when his successor took the oath of office. Edmund Starling accompanied him from the Capitol to his new home in Washington DC and then bade him good-bye before the inauguration of Harding had been completed. Wilson lived on for nearly three years after he left the White House. He died on February 3, 1924, from the long-term effects of the stroke.

CHAPTER 13

Harding, Coolidge, and the Secret Service

Mr. Starling . . . I want to make a request of you. I want you to stay with my husband as long as he is president, and go with him wherever he goes. I know he will be safe with you.

—Florence Harding

Sometimes [President Coolidge] would tell the elevator operator to take him to the basement. Then he would try to sneak out the East or the West entrance [to the White House] just to fool me.

—Edmund Starling

Warren G. Harding was inaugurated as the twenty-ninth president of the United States on March 4, 1921. His inaugural speech introduced the famous word "normalcy," in a phrase used to describe his intentions to heal the wounds and disruptions in American life brought about by the First World War. He was going to return a war-weary country to the peace and happiness of a bygone era. Everything would return to normal.

Harding had many admirable traits, including kindness and generosity—but he was basically a weak and inept man, without many talents. He once told reporters at Washington's Press Club, "It is a good thing I am not a woman. I would always be pregnant. I cannot say no."[1]

If it had not been for his capable wife, and a few strong members of his cabinet, his presidency would have been a complete failure. From the time of his entry into politics in Ohio to the time of his death, his career can best be described as mediocre. The Harding presidency is also the tale of a man in over his head, trusting of untrustworthy associates, trying to cope.

During his time as an Ohio state senator, Harding had been noticed by a fellow politician, Harry Daugherty. Daugherty recognized that the novice politician could be a rising star in politics and began to believe he could advance his own public career along the way with the help of Harding's wife, Florence. Harry Daugherty was a schemer and a crook, even though he knew a successful politician when he saw one.

Daugherty and Florence successfully organized Harding's campaign for the U.S. Senate in 1914. The new senator was well liked by his Senate colleagues because his policy of conciliation and compromise was as successful in Washington as it had been in his home state. Harding was always on both sides of an issue, and he waited until the last moment before casting his vote with one side or the other.

Harding appointed his friend Daugherty America's top law enforcement officer—attorney general. Daugherty quickly surrounded himself with nefarious characters and it wasn't long into the Harding presidency before they began developing schemes to enrich themselves. The most corrupt of the group was Jesse Smith, an unofficial member of the Justice Department, who specialized in kickbacks, illegal whiskey distribution, and political favors, all, presumably, with the approval of Daugherty. It all ended in ignominy during the Teapot Dome Scandal.

The scandal concerned a bribery incident that took place in the United States from 1921 to 1924 and involved Secretary of the Interior Albert Bacon Fall. Fall had leased navy petroleum reserves at Teapot Dome, Wyoming, and two other locations in California to private oil companies at low rates without competitive bidding. He was later convicted of accepting bribes from the oil companies and became the first member of a president's cabinet to go to prison. The scandal was regarded as the greatest and most sensational scandal in the history of American politics before Watergate and the presidency of Richard Nixon. However, there is little evidence to show that Harding was aware of the corruption and bribery taking place in his administration and the revelations about the scandals were not publicized until after the president's death in 1923.

President Harding did not like being guarded and said he felt like a
prisoner. He particularly disliked having agents present when he was
playing golf with his friends. On one occasion, during a golf game in
Florida, he deliberately made wild shots so his agents would have to
retrieve the balls in the mosquito-infested undergrowth.[2] He would also
sneak away to take a walk or visit with friends. His agents always found
him.[3] However, although Harding resented the intrusive nature of the
work of the Secret Service, he did not resent their "constant attention,"
agent Edmund Starling said, "He was just sorry it had to be that way."[4]

Harding was also nervous about the presence of agents when he
brought one of his mistresses to the White House.[5] Nan Briton was thirty
years younger than the president. She would be met at the Washington
railroad station by an agent who took her to the White House and she
would wait for Harding in the Cabinet Room. Even though agents were
stationed outside his office window, Harding would make love to Briton
in an office closet. Agents would take care to be on the lookout for Harding's wife. On one occasion Harding was nearly caught in flagrante with
his mistress and she had to be hustled out of the White House before
Florence Harding could catch sight of her.[6]

Briton would eventually become pregnant with Harding's child. He sent
her money but would not acknowledge or accept his responsibility. After
Harding's death she wrote a best seller in 1927 titled *The President's Daughter*. She sued the Harding estate but lost her case in civil courts. Although
Harding's aides always denied the late president's paternity, it was not until
2015 that the allegations were confirmed through DNA testing.[7]

Agent Edmund Starling had little respect for Harding. "He should
never have been President of the United States," Starling said.[8] However, Starling admired the president personally. "He never did anything
more reprehensible than cuss mildly," Starling said, "and play poker
with his friends. However, he was the kindest man I ever knew. But he
was weak, and he trusted everyone."[9] The agent said that Harding was
"ruined by his friends."[10]

During Harding's presidency a White House police force was instituted
at his request. In 1922 Col. C. O. Sherrill of the U.S. Army, who was chief
military aide to the president, urged the enactment of legislation to

create a separate organization from Washington's Metropolitan Police Department, whose duties would be solely to guard the White House. At first military men were considered, but the idea was abandoned when it was realized that frequent changes in personnel would leave the force unable to recognize White House staff. It was also believed that military men would give the impression of a "palace guard."[11]

The White House had been closed to the public since the start of the First World War. Under Harding, the public were once again allowed in. Visitors arrived daily starting at 9:00 a.m. The gates were left open and visitors could walk up to the North Portico without being challenged by White House police officers.

During his short presidency Harding had a routine each day. He had a habit of leaving his office before lunch to greet any visitors who happened to be around. He shook hands with an estimated 250,000 people during his two years in office. On January 1, 1922, when the tradition of a New Year's Day reception was revived after having been suspended during the war, he greeted more than eight thousand visitors to the Executive Mansion.[12] His Secret Service agents, however, were worried. Millions were unemployed, and "agitators" had "acquired large followers." An unnamed agitator announced he would attend the 1922 New Year's reception. His agents urged Harding to wear a bulletproof vest but he refused. Instead agents took extra precautions, requiring all visitors to take their hands out of their pockets, and women were asked not to conceal their hands in muffs. Packages were checked at the door.[13]

Harding was the first president to drive an automobile—previous presidents had chauffeurs. In the summer of 1922, he wanted to drive from the White House to his home in Marion, Ohio, but the Secret Service warned him of the dangers not only of potential assassins but also of the precarious state of the roads, as well as the unreliable nature of automobiles.[14]

In an era of uncertainty, when it came to public transport, Harding's agents were careful to make sure any vehicle the president used was thoroughly examined. During one of Harding's trips he stopped off at Point Pleasant, near Cincinnati, Ohio, the birthplace of Ulysses S. Grant. A cruise was planned on the Ohio River on a steamer, the *Island Queen*. Edmund Starling thought the steamer was "old and rickety" so he arranged for the president to ride in another boat, a War Department tug, the *Cayuga*, which would run parallel to the *Island Queen*. As the two boats sailed alongside each other, the *Island Queen*'s passengers rushed to the port side of the boat to see Harding. The upper deck collapsed and scores of passengers were injured.[15]

The press reported that it was Secret Service policy to keep knowledge of assassination threats away from the president.[16] However, Harding must have been aware of some threats as he sometimes joked about them, adopting a light-hearted attitude. On one occasion he told an audience at the Washington Hotel that he would have written responses (to the threateners) if they had included return postage.[17]

Numerous individuals threatened to kill Harding during his short term in office. They were investigated by the Secret Service and local law enforcement agencies. Many were apprehended and sentenced to prison terms, including inventor Ernest P. Vincent, who, in June 1923, wrote threatening letters to Harding and numerous government officials. He was arrested by Secret Service agents and taken to Bellevue Hospital.[18]

The most serious threat to Harding's life occurred in 1922. The story did not become public until 1933, however, when the medical director of the Trenton State Hospital in New Jersey, Dr. Henry A. Cotton, reported that one of his patients had been determined to kill Harding that year. The plot to assassinate the president, Cotton said, was due to be executed during the time when Harding was vacationing at Pinehurst, North Carolina. The unnamed man was a storekeeper and an unsuccessful inventor who had become bitter against the government.

Armed with two automatic weapons, the would-be assassin followed the president to Pinehurst. However, having read an article concerning Christianity, he told a minister of his "mental conflicts." The minister reported the conversation to a congressman who informed Harding and his wife of the danger. Secret Service agents shadowed the man and when he returned to New Jersey he was arrested near Camden. Dr. Cotton said he was interviewed by agents and the man was admitted to the state hospital and treated for several years. "That man suffered from intestinal trouble," Cotton said. "We have found 80 percent of our mental cases suffer from intestinal toxaemia which poisons the brain." The assassination attempt was kept quiet until Cotton's revelations in 1933.[19]

In 1920 Florence Harding had visited a Washington DC clairvoyant named Madame Marcia. She had predicted that Harding would become president, but "he will not live through his term. It is written in the stars."[20] The prediction proved to be tragically accurate.

By 1923 Harding's popularity began to decline. During the congressional elections, the Republican Party had lost some seats and Harding wanted to make a tour of the western states to lay the groundwork for his next term in office. The Hardings had been looking forward to a trip to the Far West, particularly Alaska. Finally, after Florence's serious illness in the late fall and winter of 1922, and the president's debilitating case of influenza in the winter and spring of 1923, they departed with an entourage in June 1923.As Harding had been receiving several death threats of late, his protection was increased.[21]

The train transporting the presidential party reached Tacoma, Washington, on July 4, after numerous stops and speeches along the way. Harding was clearly weak and tired, and, on some occasions, Harding's wife gave impromptu speeches in his stead from the rear platform of the presidential train.

After four days of sailing, with the fifty-seven-year-old Harding playing bridge most of the way, the ship carrying the group reached Alaska. They made brief stops along the Alaskan coast, and, on the return trip, Harding ate a meal of crabs and butter. When they reached Seattle, Harding faltered while delivering a speech. Future president Herbert Hoover, who had accompanied the president on the trip, quickly came to his aid as the president dropped pages of his manuscript. Harding complained of violent cramps and indigestion and was put to bed.

One of his doctors diagnosed Harding's complaints as a slight attack of ptomaine from the crabs he had eaten. Another doctor, however, thought Harding's ailment had more to it than indigestion. Herbert Hoover telegraphed ahead to San Francisco requesting that another experienced physician he knew meet the train. The party proceeded directly to San Francisco, canceling a scheduled speech in Portland, Oregon. Heart specialist Dr. Charles Minor Cooper also joined the group.

When Harding arrived in San Francisco he refused a wheelchair and walked off the train into a waiting limousine. He was taken to the

Palace Hotel and put to bed immediately. Harding's condition improved and one of the doctors announced that the crisis had passed. However, other doctors were less confident and thought Harding had suffered a heart attack. Despite a short period of rallying from his mystery illness, Harding died on the evening of August 2, 1923.

Within minutes of the president's death, rumors began to circulate. The four doctors who had been caring for Harding for the previous week could not agree on the cause of death. They disagreed on whether Harding's ailments resulted from a stroke, a heart attack, or both, perhaps exacerbated by the ptomaine poisoning that he may or may not have experienced a few days earlier.

Despite the confusion over the cause of death, Florence Harding announced that she did not want an autopsy. Shortly thereafter, Harding's body was embalmed, making any future examination impossible. The affair provoked controversy and many asked whether Harding had been murdered. As Harding had a reputation as a womanizer, it was hinted that Florence Harding had taken revenge for her husband's infidelity by poisoning him.

Of course it is impossible to prove a negative, and because Florence Harding had her husband's papers burned before her own death, a few months later, any research in this area would be inconclusive. The most likely cause of Harding's death is that proposed by Carl Anthony, who suggested that Harding was a victim of medical neglect, or negligent homicide. Considering the unsophisticated state of medicine at the time, this is not so remarkable. The science was not that far advanced from the time of James Garfield, whose death resulted from medical malpractice.[22]

————

Harding's vice president, Calvin Coolidge, who had been at his home in Vermont when news reached him of the president's death, took the oath of office as president of the United States at 2:47 p.m., Eastern Standard Time, on August 3, 1923. The oath was administered by his father, John C. Coolidge, who found the text of the oath in one of his history books.

Coolidge was a figure seen by many contemporary political observers as an unlikely president. He was accused of being lazy and not dynamic enough. The political commentator and humorist H. L. Mencken mocked his daily naps—"Nero fiddled, but Coolidge only snored"—and newspaper columnist Dorothy Parker reportedly asked, "How could they tell?" when his death was announced.

But there was more to Coolidge than met the eye. After the disillusionment of Woodrow Wilson's wartime efforts to bring about a new world order and Warren Harding's scandal-plagued administration, most voters welcomed Coolidge's granite integrity, his evident objection to bureaucratic overspending, and his skepticism of utopian solutions.

On a personal note, Secret Service agent Edmund Starling, who accompanied him throughout his presidency, said Coolidge was "thoughtful, he was intelligent, he was sentimental, [and] he was wise. There were times when he was irascible. . . . But I found him in the large and full portions of existence an admirable and satisfying man, a peaceful and pleasing and loyal friend. . . . I liked him as a man; I loved him as a friend."[23]

Far from being a hapless president who set the stage for the Great Depression, as some historians and political commentators argue, Coolidge presided over a notable golden age. Robert Sobel, for example, published a tribute called *Coolidge: An American Enigma.* In it, he bestowed what has become conservatism's highest commendation—"the last president who believed in a passive executive branch in times of peace and prosperity." George F. Will lamented that Coolidge was "the last president with a proper sense of his office's constitutional proportions."[24] Many of Coolidge's historian critics recognized the virtues of the thirtieth president as well. Henry Steele Commager, for example, an ardent fan of FDR's, said, "Coolidge's virtues were chiefly negative ones, but then, negative virtues are always preferable to positive vices."[25]

————

Coolidge was a dour man, with a masklike face, who used few words. He wanted to project his New England down-to-earth, common-man philosophy. He was known for his brevity of speech. Once when someone bet they could get more than three words out of the president Coolidge said, "You lose." Coolidge was also thrifty and extremely cautious in his spending.

When Coolidge traveled, he did so as inconspicuously as possible, frequently eschewing a private carriage when he traveled by railroad.

He became just another passenger with only a private drawing room to mark him from most of the other passengers.[26] However, he sometimes took a special train, and on one occasion, as the president slept in his personal suite, he was awakened when it traveled through Aberdeen, Maryland, and hit a car. The car had crashed through a barrier and hit the train at a glancing blow. Two soldiers from the Aberdeen Proving Grounds were responsible for the accident.[27]

When Coolidge became president he was often irritated by the close proximity of his agents. However, he made them his companions. They taught the retiring Coolidge, a man unused to the outdoors, to fish and enjoy life in the woods. Colonel Starling also taught him trapshooting, which he enjoyed.

Richard L. Jervis was the agent in charge of Coolidge's detail. A tall, gray-haired man of distinguished appearance, he had been chief of the White House Secret Service detail since the Wilson administration. He became a member of the agency in 1907 while Teddy Roosevelt was president. Thus, he had already guarded the lives of four presidents.

Jervis was responsible for arranging the schedules of the president's protective detail, arranging police escorts and protection, and accompanied Coolidge to the theater, baseball games, official events, train journeys, and vacations. Jervis also rode in the presidential car to and from the Capitol during Coolidge's inauguration in March 1925, after the president had been elected to office in his own right in November 1924. Other members of the detail included George Drescher, Walter Ferguson, James Fitzgerald, and Arnold Landvoight.

Jervis risked his life for Coolidge in more ways than one. In July 1925, the president was on vacation at his summer White House and went sailing with friends. When Coolidge visited Fort Andrews, an island southeast of Boston, Jervis fell into an unprotected lift shaft, dropping about four feet below the floor level. Narrowly escaping a greater fall, Jervis climbed out uninjured.[28]

In fact, a number of accidents involved law enforcement officers who were detailed to guard Coolidge during his presidential trips. On August 15, 1928, Wausau, Wisconsin, police officer Edward Baerwald was performing crowd control duties during a visit by Coolidge when a cable broke, throwing Officer Baerwald to the ground and causing a fatal skull fracture. On November 28 of that same year, Virginia State police inspector Phillip C. Via was escorting Coolidge when he crashed his motorcycle. He died from his injuries a little more than a month later.[29]

Coolidge possessed a mischievous sense of humor and would frequently play pranks on his protective detail. Jervis said the president, whom agents called "the Boss," was "the greatest kidder of them all. . . . Strangely enough he had the greatest sense of humor. He didn't want us to tell him about the workings of the White House. If we tried to he resented it, so we left him alone to do his own finding out." For example, in the early days at the White House, the Secret Service found their charge difficult to watch; he would disappear from his office and reappear while everyone sought him. His White House "hideaway" was not discovered until someone learned of his weakness for pickles. He was often found in the storage room with his "fingers in the pickle jar."[30]

Rising at 7:30 a.m., Coolidge took his customary twenty-minute walk then returned to the White House to eat a breakfast of sausages and wheat cake. He was usually accompanied by at least three agents, one next to him and two more following behind at a discreet distance.[31] His chief form of exercise, however, was riding an electric horse he kept in the White House; he often requested that his Secret Service agents join him in his workout.

One day, Jervis said, Coolidge returned to the White House from an early morning walk and saw an alarm button on the front porch of the White House. Jervis said nothing, remembering the president wanted to find things out for himself. Coolidge pretended he was tired and leaned against the button, pressing it, and then walked hurriedly into the building. "From behind the safety of the living room curtains," Jervis said, "[he] peeked out and saw two policemen tearing across the lawn . . . and finding no one, returned to the guard house. [Coolidge] pushed the button two more times and each time he would, without change of expression, watch the excitement that resulted."[32]

President Coolidge sometimes walked the streets of Washington accompanied by only a single agent, and for much of the time he walked unrecognized. Occasionally, Coolidge would elude his agents by fooling them into believing he was sitting in his office when he was actually strolling out West Executive Avenue. Agent Starling recalled he would wait for Coolidge at the north entrance to the White House to accompany him on his walks around the streets of the capital.

On awakening in the morning he would walk across the upstairs hallway to the Lincoln Room in his long nightgown and slippers. There he would peek out the window to see whether I was on the lawn. . . . Then he would try to sneak out the East or West entrance just to fool me. Everyone on the staff cooperated with me and tipped me off, so I was always able to catch him up. One day I turned the tables on him and hid in the police box on the East side. He came out of the engine room, up the east steps, and passed right by me. I fell into position behind him. When he reached the gate he turned around with a look of glee on his face, thinking he had at last eluded me. "Good morning, Mr. President," I said. He turned and headed for F Street without a word.[33]

After one escape from his agents, Coolidge bragged about his "accomplishments" for weeks. "It was pleasant to feel like a man for a change," he said, "instead of a goldfish."[34]

On one occasion, Coolidge had been walking in downtown Washington when a motorist, fifty-six-year-old Nathan Smith, a retired businessman, drove by as the president stepped from the curb at H Street and Jackson Place. Smith's car nearly hit Coolidge, who was rescued just in time as one of his agents grabbed his arm and pulled him back from the curb. Another agent jumped on the running board of Smith's car and ordered him to the side of the road, where Smith was placed under arrest and handed over to Washington police for violating traffic regulations.[35]

Coolidge and Starling, whom the president always called "the Colonel," became fast friends. By then Starling was assistant chief of the agency. Coolidge liked to hear Starling's stories about life in the Kentucky hills as they took walks together around Washington.[36] The president's walks were mostly window-shopping excursions, but one day Coolidge asked Starling for a loan of ten cents to buy roasted chestnuts. After that, Starling became the president's "banker" on his walks, furnishing him with dimes and nickels for peanuts, magazines, and newspapers. During Coolidge's vacations, which were taken mostly in the Black Hills of South Dakota, Starling would fish with the president. According to Starling,

Coolidge "may or may not have been a great President. That is for history to decide. To me he was fundamentally and primarily something which I treasure above all the things of earth: he was a good man . . . a peaceful and pleasing and loyal friend. His feelings, like his thoughts, ran deep and did not swerve.[37]

Starling also became responsible for the life of the president's son, John Coolidge, after threats were made to either kidnap or murder him. Starling accompanied John to his college at the beginning of the semester in October 1926. He was guarded by Starling during the daytime when he was at classes and in the evening hours. This was the first time a president's son had been so closely watched.[38]

Coolidge's wife, Grace, was also a keen walker. Early in 1927, she was accompanied by Secret Service agent Jim Haley, following a few steps behind her, when she walked the four miles to the Capitol each day when Congress was in session. Haley trailed the first lady eight to ten miles a day in fair weather. She would often take walks to the Tidal Basin as well as to the Capitol and would speak to everyone who approached her.[39]

In 1927 the Secret Service became alarmed when Grace Coolidge and her agent bodyguard, Jim Haley, were "lost" during the president's summer vacation in the Black Hills. The agency was aware of recent bombings of the New York subway system by radicals who were opposed to the executions of Sacco and Vanzetti, and extra precautions had been made to guard the president.[40]

Grace and the agent had wandered off into the woods and were missing for some hours. The agent was described by the press as handsome and young, which led to rumors that they were having an affair. When they were finally found, the president's obvious annoyance was interpreted as jealousy.[41] According to the Calvin Coolidge Presidential Foundation, "There is no evidence whatsoever that Mrs. Coolidge and Haley were having an affair before, during, or after the hike in the woods. In our Special Collections we have a few letters that throw light on this time. . . . A person may read into events and letters what they will, but most believe that Grace's friendship with Haley was platonic, and moreover was a huge support during the turmoil of the White House years, and after as an old friend."[42]

A mail worker at the White House, Ira T. Smith, said that the alleged affair never happened and that the rumors resulted from Coolidge's concern that his White House should be different from Harding's and free from scandal. According to Smith,

> Somehow a small rumor started about Mrs. Coolidge and her Secret Service companion . . . [and] the Secret Service man immediately vanished from the White House detail. . . . The President of course knew that the rumor was ridiculous, but he took no chances on any fingers being pointed at the White House. The President . . . was always on guard against anything or anyone that might attract unfavorable attention toward the White House. Any breath of scandal frightened him, and he never took a chance, probably because the Harding-administration scandals were so vivid in his mind. Several White House employees who were involved in unsensational divorce actions or something of the sort were quietly but quickly shifted to other jobs. The President never waited to see whether there would be gossip; he got rid of the man if anything arose that just might lead to gossip. I think that was what happened in the case of the Secret Service man who accompanied Mrs. Coolidge on her walks.[43]

When Coolidge took office, White House security appeared to become lax. The public were allowed to enter the White House freely during the daytime hours and many visitors would catch a glimpse of the new president emerging from an elevator or from the Executive Office Building next door to the Executive Mansion.[44] It would be many years before presidents were forbidden to sit outside on the North Portico balcony, when Coolidge began the habit of watching cars go by on Pennsylvania Avenue. However, this form of relaxation soon ended not because of any security breaches but because tourists would stop and stare.[45]

The Secret Service considered Coolidge's summer home—White Court, at Swampscott, Massachusetts—a security problem. The estate was unfenced and surrounded by trees and shrubbery, which made it impossible for agents to guard it unaided. In 1925, for the first time in history, Marines were dispatched from the presidential yacht *Mayflower* to guard the property. A number of embassy guards made up the detachment.[46]

Calvin Coolidge had faced threats to his life before he became president. In 1917, when he was governor of Massachusetts, shortly after war was declared on Germany, he received a bomb threat. The threat was purportedly to be carried out during a Sunday service the Massachusetts governor attended. The pastor of the church said efforts were made to persuade Coolidge to stay at home, but he went nevertheless and was "the most composed person in the congregation."[47]

When Governor Coolidge stayed at the Adams Hotel in Boston for a May Day speech, police were tipped off that a man had been "behaving suspiciously " in the room next to Coolidge's and had made a "remark" about the governor. The threatener was arrested and later sent to an insane asylum. The Secret Service considered the possible threat so serious that extra police were called out to boost the president's security.[48]

During Coolidge's time as president, he received many letters threatening his life. In 1925 a rabbi, F. M. B. Browne, a pastor at Temple Zion in New York's Bronx district, sent the president "an avalanche of letters" demanding he be reimbursed for half of the $25,000 he said he spent on Coolidge's presidential reelection campaign. Coolidge made it known he was angered by the threatening letters and Browne was arrested.[49] In 1926 thirty-year-old Clarence Neal, who came from Berkeley, California, was tracked down by postal inspectors and arrested in Oakland, after he sent threatening letters.[50]

In 1928 fifty-year-old Albert Anderson sent a 133-page letter to the president and the Justices of the Supreme Court, demanding $50,000 and threatening them with death if they did not comply.[51] In January 1929, twenty-seven-year-old Abraham Rosenberg, a postal clerk, was eventually arrested after the Secret Service investigated 1,200 letters threatening Coolidge that were purportedly written by the same person over a number of years.[52] When Coolidge visited Miami, "a serious anarchist who needed to be locked up" was arrested for threatening the president. He was sent to an insane asylum.[53]

There were also a number of arrests of individuals who had publicly threatened to kill Coolidge, including an Indiana farmhand, Robert Ferris, who said he would kill him if he were elected president in 1924. Ferris was arrested, held in the county jail in Leavenworth, Kansas, and tried in a federal court the following month and found guilty.[54]

No sooner had Coolidge taken the oath of office than he experienced a serious breach of his personal security. After Harding's death, Coolidge did not immediately move into the White House but stayed at the Willard Hotel on Pennsylvania Avenue, a short distance from the Executive Mansion. He wanted to give his predecessor's wife, Florence, time to move out following her husband's death. One morning in late August 1923, Coolidge was startled when he heard a noise coming from one of the rooms in his suite. A "young man" who was staying in the hotel had broken into Coolidge's room and begun to rummage through the president's clothes. Coolidge noticed that his wallet, a chain, and a charm were missing. He confronted the burglar and told him, "I wish you wouldn't take that. I don't mean the watch and the chain, only the charm. Read what is on the back of it." Written on the back of the charm were the words, "Presented to Calvin Coolidge . . . by the Massachusetts General Court." The burglar looked shocked as he realized he was robbing the president of the United States. When the young man explained he had run out of money and wanted to return home, Coolidge gave him thirty-two dollars as a "loan" and made sure he was not arrested by the Secret Service when he left the room.[55]

In March 1928, White House security was breached when the president hosted the visit of a Hungarian delegation to honor Hungarian patriot Lajos Kossuth. The group was arranging to have their photos taken with the president when three men and a woman, who had slipped past White House police and infiltrated the group, unfurled a banner and attempted to parade in the White House grounds, protesting against the Hungarian Horthy regime and accusing it of mass murder. The protestors were arrested and removed from the White House grounds.[56]

A further incident became an embarrassing moment for the Secret Service when illusionist Harry Blackstone appeared at the White House to entertain the president, friends, and family. Blackstone managed to lift a Secret Service agent's pistol from his pocket during his act.[57]

During Coolidge's presidency the Secret Service was anxious that a number of radical groups would attempt to assassinate the president. For this reason Richard Jervis liaised with local police forces to ensure that known radicals would be "expelled" from the cities Coolidge planned to visit. In 1928 Jervis thought he had stumbled on an assassination plot when Coolidge visited the opening of the Washington baseball season. A bolted door barred the president's exit when he sought to leave the baseball park. Jervis had to force the door open and splintered it as he and Coolidge stepped through the doorway.[58]

————

The two most serious threats to Coolidge's life occurred in 1925 and 1928.

In 1925 Norman Klein was the leader of a group of anarchists who had previously threatened the lives of John D. Rockefeller, Henry Ford, and Thomas Edison. In July 1925, he threatened to kill Coolidge. Following Klein's threat, the Secret Service initiated a nationwide manhunt for Klein, which was specially ordered by the president. Klein was hunted for three months and was finally tracked down to Tampa, Florida, the headquarters of the group. Klein was arrested and charged with threatening the life of the president.[59]

In 1934 Cuban authorities revealed that there had been a plot to kill Coolidge during the president's visit to the island in 1928. Before Coolidge's visit, Secret Service agents were sent there to work with Cuban police in order to make security arrangements. During their stay the agents and local police discovered an assassination plot. The plotters planned to shoot the president from the window of an apartment opposite the presidential palace in Havana.

Agents and Cuban police arrested a Spaniard, Claudio Bouzon, and a Russian, Nosko Yalob, who had rented the apartment. They were left-wing radical leaders. However, a few days after their arrest, Bouzon's right arm was found in shark-infested waters and fished out of Havana Bay. His injuries revealed he had been killed and then thrown into the sea. The Russian plotter was assumed to have met the same fate.[60] Six Cubans were tried for the alleged murders of the purported assassins. One of the six defendants, former army sergeant Jose Sanchez, confessed to the killings and said he had acted directly on the orders of President Machado.[61]

————

At the end of his elected term in office, Coolidge decided not to run for a second term. He issued one of the most famous and briefest political statements in history—"I do not choose to run."[62] The president had lost interest in his job after the death of his son, Calvin Jr., who had developed a blister after playing tennis in the White House grounds without socks or tennis shoes. The blister became infected, worsened, and he developed blood poisoning. The sixteen-year-old died on July 7, 1924. Coolidge said it was on that day that he lost the "power and glory" of the presidency.[63] Others surmise that Coolidge suffered from depression.[64]

Coolidge followed Theodore Roosevelt's precedent of leaving the inaugural ceremonies at the Capitol immediately upon the administration of the presidential oath to his successor. However, Coolidge did not adhere to the usual custom of returning to the White House with the incoming chief executive. He was driven directly from the inaugural platform to Union Station, three blocks away, to travel home by train. He declined a special train in favor of a private car attached to a regularly scheduled train leaving in the early afternoon. He also declined Secret Service protection.[65]

Even after he left office, Coolidge continued to receive threatening letters. In 1930 he received a letter, while he was staying in Santa Barbara, warning him that an "eastern gunman" had "come west" with the intention of taking his life.[66] The letter contained the words, "I would like to warn you that a gunman murderer from the east arrived in Los Angeles and he said 'Mr. Coolidge is going to make the trip back in a coffin.'" When Coolidge found the letter he turned to his bodyguard and said, "Guess this belongs to you." The matter was investigated by police but was never resolved. However, Los Angeles police provided police protection for Coolidge during his stay.[67]

CHAPTER 14

——————

The Argentinean Plot to Assassinate Herbert Hoover

The effect of the Depression on the Detail was acute. Our vigilance had to be doubled; the worries and problems which ordinarily beset us were multiplied. Crank letters, threats, and eccentric visitors reached a new high.

—Secret Service agent Edmund Starling

Herbert Hoover was a geology graduate from Stanford University who became a wealthy mining engineer with his own engineering and financial consulting firm. An expert administrator, he rose to public prominence during World War I, helping repatriate 120,000 Americans from Europe, and then organizing the Commission for Relief in Belgium. He was so successful that Woodrow Wilson asked him to be head of the U.S. Food Administration and director of the American Relief Administration. The organization fed 350 million people in more than twenty countries after the war. He was secretary of commerce during the Harding and Coolidge administrations and oversaw America's economic modernization.

In 1927 Hoover was dispatched by President Coolidge to lead the relief efforts in Louisiana after a great flood. He was highly successful and managed the logistics of feeding and delivering aid and shelter to seven hundred thousand people. The flood helped propel Hoover to the presidency a year later, his first electoral appointment. Unfortunately for Hoover, Wall Street crashed just eight months into his tenure at the White House and the subsequent economic depression broke his presidency and obscured his many accomplishments.

Once the Depression set in, the gloomy and inflexible Hoover lowered taxes and started public works to create jobs but was insistent that the government not institute relief programs. He came across as mean-spirited and a poor communicator, which led the legions of unemployed homeless Americans to call their makeshift shantytowns "Hoovervilles." Perhaps Hoover's greatest policy blunder as president was signing into law a tariff act that fueled international trade wars and made the Depression even worse.

It has often been said that Hoover was a great man, but he was only great before his presidency and after he left office.

On November 6, 1928, the day Herbert Hoover was elected, he did not have any protection from the Secret Service. The new president-elect was at his home in Palo Alto, California, when news of his election was announced, but his detail did not arrive to guard him until the following day. The detail of six agents was introduced to the new president by Chief William H. Moran. They had been stationed along the Pacific coast from Portland to Los Angeles. The first thing the agents noticed was the vulnerability of the Hoover home with its many windows and doors and high hedges around the grounds. The following day, workmen were assigned to erect floodlights.[1]

Shortly after Herbert Hoover was elected, he embarked on a goodwill tour of Latin America and faced his first real threat of assassination. The new president wanted to give the message that America had no designs on new territory or wanted to wage war. The country was only interested in peace and harmony with its neighbors south of the border. William S. (Bill) McSwain, who had been head of Portland's Secret Service office, was assigned as the agent in charge for the trip. The president-elect traveled by battleship visiting Ecuador, Peru, Brazil, Chile, and Uruguay. During his trip Hoover coined the historic phrase "good neighbors." Hoover was due to arrive in Argentina in December 1928.

An anarchist, Severino Di Giovanni, saw Hoover's trip as an opportunity to exact revenge on the United States after two American anarchists,

Nicola Sacco and Bartolomeo Vanzetti, were tried and executed for a murder and armed robbery in Massachusetts. The two Italian immigrants had been accused of murdering a paymaster and an armed guard at a shoe company in South Braintree and stealing $15,000. At the time of Sacco and Vanzetti's arrest, anticommunist sentiment was at its apex after two decades of assassination, bombings, and labor-organized disruption of industry. Although the evidence against Sacco and Vanzetti was inconclusive, they were found guilty and executed on August 23, 1927.

Di Giovanni and his wife had immigrated to Argentina from Italy around 1922. Holding leftist sympathies, Di Giovanni was soon drawn to a group of anarchists and antifascists in Buenos Aires and became involved in spreading anarchist ideals among Argentina's workers and fomenting anarchist agitation among Italian workers. Di Giovanni also became involved in protests against the United States after the arrests of Sacco and Vanzetti and he bombed the U.S. embassy in Buenos Aires. However, he was soon identified and arrested. He was tortured for five days but released for lack of evidence.[2]

On the July 22, 1927, Di Giovanni and two fellow Italian anarchists, Alejandro and Paulino Scarfó, blew up a statue of George Washington, and several hours later exploded a bomb at the Ford Motor Company. On August 15, they attempted to assassinate Eduardo Santiago, the federal police officer in charge of the investigation, by bombing his house. Santiago escaped injury when he left his house to buy a packet of cigarettes.

When President-elect Hoover's visit to Argentina was announced, Di Giovanni plotted to assassinate him and chose Alejandro Scarfó for the mission.

Hoover boarded his train at Santiago, Chile, and crossed the Andes Mountains to Buenos Aires. Scarfó was to install the explosives on the rails over which Hoover's train would pass as it approached the Argentine capital. However, police had rounded up numerous anarchists. After the residence of one of the anarchist's had been searched, a railroad map with Hoover's route marked in red pencil was found along with evidence that incriminated Scarfó. Police also discovered an arsenal of bombs, guns, ammunition, and counterfeit money. Scarfó was immediately arrested and admitted he had planned to assassinate Hoover.

He told police, "Though I am arrested, there will be others who will carry out my plans." He was tried and found guilty of attempting to kill Hoover and was released in 1935.[3]

In January 1931, Di Giovanni was finally arrested, tried, and sentenced to death for his anarchist crimes. He was executed by firing squad on February 1, 1931. He was twenty-nine years old. Before being hit by at least eight bullets, he shouted, "Long live anarchy!"

President Hipólito Yrigoyen of Argentina made a point of meeting Hoover at the railroad terminal, thus sharing any danger the visitors might be in and attempting to efface the national embarrassment felt by Argentina over the anarchists' plans.[4]

Hundreds of guards were deployed throughout the station. Hundreds more policed one hundred thousand of the populace, massed in the station plaza. Three lines of protection had been provided along the station platform, but it did not prevent President Yrigoyen from being pushed about and having his coat ripped. Naval aides kept the president-elect and his wife from being crushed. When the party arrived at the American embassy, a Secret Service agent complained to the Buenos Aires chief of police that he had been robbed of his wallet in the melee. The chief replied, "Well, they got my wristwatch."[5]

No sooner had Hoover returned to the United States for his inauguration than the Secret Service was alerted to an alleged assassination threat. On January 14, 1929, a few days before Hoover arrived in Miami for a fishing trip, the president-elect was targeted by three men who were arrested for threatening to kill him. Miami residents Joseph B. Sommers and Theodore Hill and New York resident Willis Callahan were arrested at a Miami restaurant and charged with "conspiring to do bodily injury to the person of Herbert Hoover and by threats and intimidation to prevent him from taking office as President of the United States."

Three days later the men were arraigned and placed under $10,000 bail, which they could not raise. Assistant U.S. Attorney Louis S. Joel delayed the hearing so he could look for "missing witnesses."[6] Joel failed to produce the witnesses, but those he managed to find could only say Sommers had called Hoover a "nigger lover" and "ought to be killed," saying he "would give a thousand dollars to see Hoover bumped off before the Fourth of July." Callahan allegedly said, "Someone should bump

him off . . . I wouldn't be afraid to do it myself if he came to Miami."
As "no overt act" could be established, the three men were released.
Joseph Murphy, assistant chief of the Secret Service, said he did not
believe there was any plot and described the men as "loud-mouthed
roustabouts."[7] A generation later, when laws were in place to cover overt
threats made against U.S. presidents, a criminal case would have ensued.

Later that year the Secret Service faced yet another purported "train
crash assassination attempt" when Hoover was touring western states. In
October 1929, Hoover's special train had to grind to a stop at a grade
crossing near New Albany, Indiana, after the train driver saw a sedan
being removed from the tracks by Enoch Keller and two other men,
Edward Hopson and George Weir. Keller had gone to the crossing
where the car was placed in the hope of seeing the president's train as
it passed. After Secret Service agents investigated the incident, nineteen-
year-old Charles W. Burdock and forty-three-year-old Young E. Wright
were arrested. They confessed they had placed the car on the tracks
but insisted that they only wanted to collect insurance money and it
was not an attempt to kill the president. They succeeded in convincing
the Secret Service that, ignorant of the president's proximity, they had
plotted merely to collect damages from the railroad. Both men were
tried and sentenced on a lesser charge.[8]

———————

Following his March 1929 inauguration, Hoover continued the tradition
restored by Harding and Coolidge of receiving a "host of public callers," but it was an "ordeal," he said. One ordeal he dreaded was a noon
reception at the White House office, six days in the week, "where any
citizen might shake hands with the President . . . if he passed the Secret
Service inspection for respectability and harmlessness." The average
of thirty to forty persons per day at Theodore Roosevelt's receptions
had increased to between three hundred and four hundred per day
under Coolidge. Hoover soon tired of "wasting a whole hour every day
shaking hands with 1,000 to 1,200 people." Hoover finally decided he
should change the system and ended it, "giving that hour to special
appointments with people from out of town who were in Washington
on matters of importance."[9]

Hoover did continue the custom of New Year's Day White House receptions for the general public. On New Year's morning of 1930, a long line had been waiting since midnight. Before the day was over, Hoover had shaken hands with over nine thousand people. The president concluded that that the custom "might have properly originated with Adams, but that he did not know that the population would increase from 3,000,000 to 130,000,000, nor what changes there would be in transportation for visitors into Washington."[10] According to a report in the *Afro-American*, "There seemed to be more bodyguards and Secret Service men standing about ready to yank the hands of White House callers out of their pockets. They stand about during the audience shifting from one foot to another, fidgeting. The president himself is abrupt."[11]

President Hoover was not universally liked by White House staff. Mrs. Ava Long, the domestic manager of the White House, said she found it much easier to admire the Hoovers than to like them. "Finer people never lived," she said, "but the president and Mrs. Hoover rarely broke through the barrier between those who served and those who are served. During the entire four years that I shared a roof with them, Mr. Hoover spoke to me only four times."[12]

Hoover also had difficulty dealing with the servants—he never looked at them or spoke to one. In fact, the Secret Service was worried that some of the White House staff might attack him. Ike Hoover, the chief usher, "detested" the president.[13]

His relationship with his presidential Secret Service detail, however, was more or less harmonious. He was said to be friendly with them but not "jovial." According to Edmund Starling, "It has been said that [Hoover] resented the supervision of the Secret Service. Perhaps he did, since there were times we had to refuse his requests, particularly his orders to drive more rapidly over dangerous roads. He regarded us, it seemed to me, as a necessary evil, and once he made up his mind that we were thinking always of his welfare we got along all right, though often he heartily wished we were elsewhere."[14]

Hoover spent most weekends at Camp Rapidan, as it came to be known, fishing, walking the trails, building dams and trout pools, and enjoying horseback rides to escape Washington's exhausting summer heat. He had dispatched his secretary, Lawrence Richey, a former Secret

Service agent, together with Col. Earl Long of the Marine Corps, on an exploration of the Blue Ridge foothills in Virginia for the summer camp. It later became part of the Shenandoah National Park. A suitable location at the headwaters of the Rapidan River with an elevation of about fifteen hundred feet was found and a series of log cabins was erected by U.S. Marines, furnishing accommodations for twelve to fifteen guests. It was exactly a hundred miles from the White House.

One of Hoover's favorite guests at Camp Rapidan was the *Des Moines Register*'s political cartoonist, Jay Darling. One Sunday morning, the two men rode their horses through the endless trails and decided to "lose" their Secret Service guards. Hoover had often longed for times when he could be alone and this for him was an opportunity not to be missed. When a side trail ahead turned into the woods, the two men spurred their horses and bolted down the trail. Arriving at an abandoned fire tower, they climbed to the observation deck and watched as frantic agents combed the area looking for them. The agents did not make contact with Hoover for some hours.[15]

Hoover and his wife traveled by car to his country retreat accompanied by a single agent, who sat next to the chauffeur. Hoover had at first a Pierce-Arrow, but in the fall of 1930 it was replaced by a sixteen-cylinder Cadillac limousine. The rest of his Secret Service detail followed in another car.[16]

On one trip to the country retreat, in July 1930, a car driven by Caroline Beach careered past Hoover's car, as well as the follow-up Secret Service car, and then crashed into another car in the president's convoy, which carried the president's secretary, the president's doctor, Joel Boone, and his wife and daughter. Hoover had been returning to the White House from Camp Rapidan.[17]

Following the car crash, extra safety precautions were put into effect for the president's trips to his Virginia retreat. The road to the camp was more thoroughly patrolled to curb speeders, particularly on Sundays when Hoover returned to the White House. A further precaution involved keeping the number of vehicles to a maximum of three.[18]

The Secret Service was also concerned about Hoover's own reckless driving and his penchant for fast cars. He would often drive not at excessive speeds but with "determination," according to Jay Darling.[19] In the year he handed over the reins of power to FDR, Hoover continued driving fast cars around his home state of California. At fifty-eight, he still had "an abundance of energy," according to Darling. In April, May, and June of 1933, he drove more than eight thousand miles. During one visit, when he was camped at the northern end of the Sacramento Valley, Hoover and his son decided to take a drive down the Sacramento Valley turnpike. Entering a flat stretch of road, he opened up the throttle and was stopped by police who remonstrated with him for driving at sixty miles per hour in the middle of the night.[20]

Hoover's White House was witness to the age-old problem of fence jumpers and intruders. A stranger walked into the State Dining Room one night and told Hoover he wanted to talk to him. When the president told him he did not have an appointment, the stranger approached Hoover, declaring, "You better have an appointment with me," before one of Hoover's agents ejected him from the mansion. The president demanded an explanation for the security breach and was later informed that the problem arose because the Secret Service had no official control over the White House police force.[21]

However, according to one of Hoover's Secret Service agents, the incident was not serious and did not constitute a threat to the president's life. Agent George Drescher later described the incident in an interview.

[Mr. Mayer], the big moving picture man was in having dinner with the President. I was over at the Executive Office and Fitzgerald was White House . . . [the intruder] walked right into the State dining room. Well, I won't criticize poor Fitzgerald. I think it was the laxity of the policemen and the . . . doorkeeper. . . . [The intruder has] got to pass the first policeman who's walking up and down out front ; then we've got a policeman inside of the door, with a . . . doorman. I wasn't there—I was over at the Executive Offices—but the minute this started they called me and I rushed on over there. I sent the man down to Gallinger Hospital for observation. He wasn't drinking. It was just laxity, that's all. I talked to him for some time over in the police office in the East Wing before he was sent down to Gallinger Hospital. I said, 'We'll find out what's what.' We could hold him forty-eight hours and we wanted to check what his background was, and so on.[22]

Following the incident Hoover recognized the need for the White House police and the Secret Service to join forces. Hoover wanted the Secret Service exclusively to control every aspect of presidential protection and asked Congress to place the supervision of the White House police under the direction of the chief of the Secret Service. By October 1931, there were forty-seven officers in the White House police force, picked from the ranks of the 1,341-strong Metropolitan Police Force. They were under the command of a captain and directly responsible to the Secret Service officers.[23]

For three years, from 1930, the Secret Service feared that Hoover would be the victim of an assassination attempt, the result of the anger abroad caused by the country's dire economic state. As the Depression set in, criticism of Hoover rose and the president was viewed as a cold, calculating leader who ignored pleas to stem the plight of the American economy and the conditions of millions of unemployed.

There were many false alarms amid the signs that social disruption was imminent. One morning in December 1931, while President Hoover was sitting with his cabinet, a report reached the Secret Service that resulted in police reserves being called to the White House. Motorcycle sirens rang out down Pennsylvania Avenue and reporters wondered what all the fuss was about. Throngs of Washington visitors crowded around the Executive Mansion. When Vice President Curtis left the cabinet meeting, a Secret Service agent joined him, even though the agency was not at that time responsible for a vice president's protection. All was in readiness to meet a reported demonstration by a group of radicals for unemployment relief. However, it was a false alarm.

Three days later, fourteen "hunger marchers" were arrested at the White House as they unfurled their banners demanding help from President Hoover. Their leader, Herbert Benjamin, announced to the press that 1,300 marchers would be arriving in Washington demonstrating for relief. Secret Service chief William Moran responded by calling the demonstrators "communists," after Benjamin said the marchers would "make trouble."[24]

The social effects of the Depression were felt by the Secret Service, and by 1932 security became more complicated. Secret Service agents had to be called in to Washington from around the country in order to buttress White House security. The White House became a "fortress."[25] "Our vigilance had to be doubled," Edmund Starling said. "The worries and problems which ordinarily beset us were multiplied. Crank letters, threats, and eccentric visitors reached a new high. Secret Service agents all over the country were busy checking on the people who felt an inclination to swell the White House mailbags." The mail included letters from people who wanted "to shoot [Hoover]," according to Starling. Most, he said, were written by people of "unsound mind."[26]

Another agent said he had been traveling with presidents since Theodore Roosevelt's time. "Never before," he disclosed, "have I seen one actually booed with men running out into the streets to thumb their noses at him. It's not a pretty sight."[27]

According to Joseph Scott, a Los Angeles attorney who had nominated Hoover at the Chicago Republican convention, Hoover had received more threatening letters than any other president.[28]

Until the end of his time in office, Hoover was the most protected president America had ever seen. When Prime Minister Ramsay MacDonald of Great Britain visited the White House, he was astonished at the extent of the precautions taken to guard Hoover. There were between forty and fifty men assigned to each White House working shift. No one was allowed near the president carrying a package. The gates to the White House were chained and locked, and police officers were stationed at thirty-foot intervals around the Executive Mansion. Two Secret Service agents accompanied the president around Washington. Eight or ten agents provided his protective detail when he went on trips. However, there were numerous agents who were sent ahead from Washington or recruited locally from Secret Service offices around the country.[29]

The heightened security around Hoover first began to show publicly in October 1930 when the president traveled from Washington to Philadelphia, to attend the first World Series baseball games, and on to Pittsburgh and Cleveland, where he gave speeches. He traveled very little in 1931 except to his Rapidan River retreat. He traveled less in 1932, until he became convinced that it was imperative he discard his original plans to campaign for reelection from the White House instead of traveling around the country making speeches.[30]

Hoover did not appear to be worried about the threat radicals and communists posed. His view, however, was not shared by the head of the Secret Service, and William H. Moran was less sanguine. In late November 1931, the chief feared an assassination attempt and quickly assembled a large contingent of police around the White House but nothing came of the threat.[31]

However, a real threat, likely originating from radicals, did exist. The day before the presidential election, an attempt was made to wreck Hoover's train as he was going home to Palo Alto, California. A pilot engine, with a railroad official onboard, had been traveling ahead of the presidential special and was flagged down by a watchman, Paul E. Fish. Fish told the inspector that "a white man" and a "negro" had been attempting to place a bundle of sticks of dynamite at an underpass near Palisade, west of Elko, Nevada, where the Southern Pacific tracks were crossed by the Western Pacific. When Fish confronted the would-be assassins, a gun was leveled at him before the two men ran away. Fish reported, "[I] thought at first they were prospectors but when I shouted the Negro jerked a gun from his pocket and leveled it at me." In the struggle that followed, the "white man" attempted to stab Fish before both men finally broke away and ran. Fish fired four shots as they fled.[32]

The presidential train was delayed by forty minutes as railroad police and Secret Service agents searched the roadbed and vicinity. Twenty additional sticks of dynamite in a sack were found along the Western Pacific right-of-way, four hundred feet from the rails upon which the president's train was to travel. A railroad official said the men "undoubtedly had planned to wreck the Hoover train. It is my belief that the two men intended to blow up a Western Pacific bridge where the tracks of that railroad crosses those of the Southern Pacific in order that the president's special might itself be wrecked should it crash into the wreckage on the bridge."[33] Despite an intense search, the two bombers were never found.[34]

The presence of the Bonus Marchers in Washington in 1932 only increased the Secret Service's assassination fears. Motorcycle police officers were stationed at intervals of seventy-five feet on the sidewalks surrounding the White House, and inside the grounds every light burned. Police were held in reserve in the Treasury Building. In January of that

year a confidential Secret Service memo, entitled "Riot Call Regulations," assigned battle stations for the agents and special police who
could defend the White House from mob attack.[35]

Indicative of these fears was the decision to keep the president in
the White House when Congress was adjourning in July 1932. There
had been earlier attempts by former soldiers to present petitions to
Hoover, none of which succeeded. Pennsylvania Avenue had twice been
cleared of marchers by troops and police officers. The night Congress
adjourned, Bonus Marchers, in a silent line, picketed the Capitol in a
plea for cash payment of the veterans' bonuses.

On July 20, John Pace, a radical leader, together with two of his followers, was arrested after the men tried to enter the White House. A heavy
guard was again thrown around the mansion after Hoover's aides were
informed that two hundred radical members of the Bonus Army had
formed a few blocks away with the intention of marching on the White
House. All gates were closed with the exception of two on the north
side, where additional police officers were placed.[36] Hoover was to pay
his customary visit to Congress to sign last-minute bills. But the Secret
Service advised he not make the trip after they concluded the crowd
was dangerously restless. A few days after Congress adjourned, Hoover
called out the troops to drive the Bonus Marchers from Washington.
The marchers' camp was burned that night while Hoover watched from
the south window across the Washington Monument grounds.[37]

Although Hoover's aides became worried that the Bonus Marchers
constituted a threat to the government, their worries were not shared
by some Secret Service agents. "Generally speaking," Edmund Starling
said, "there were few comments and they had little effect on the [agents']
thinking. The veterans were Americans, down on their luck but by no
means ready to overthrow their government."[38]

During Hoover's 1932 reelection campaign around the country, he
was faced with perhaps the most hostile crowds any sitting president
had ever faced.[39] During speaking engagements in Philadelphia, Cleveland, Boston, and the Carolinas a heavy protective guard was notable.
He received additional protection from local police forces and was
surrounded by his Secret Service detail and other law enforcement
officers continuously.

Hoover's motorcades were often pelted with eggs and rotten fruit. He was heckled while speaking and on several occasions his Secret Service detail prevented attempts to kill him, including capturing a man who approached the president carrying sticks of dynamite. Another citizen angry at the president removed several spikes from the rails in front of Hoover's train.

Just a few weeks before the election, Hoover had accepted a speaking engagement in Des Moines, Iowa, despite having been warned by the Secret Service of a plot by radicals to assassinate him. Additionally, reports indicated that disgruntled farmers meeting in Sioux City were preparing for a hostile demonstration against Hoover.

Osro Cobb, a leader of the Republican Party in Arkansas, who became politically and personally close to the president, recalled that just a few weeks before the 1932 election, Hoover had been standing near a window in the Oval Office, "deep in thought and obviously troubled." Hoover told Cobb about the impending speaking engagement in Des Moines, Iowa, in three days and that the U.S. Secret Service had warned him that it had uncovered evidence of plots by radical elements to assassinate him if he kept it. "Turmoil and uncertainty prevailed in the country," Cobb said, "but there was absolutely no fear in his expression; to the contrary, there appeared to be an abundance of personal courage. Frankly, my heart went out to him, but I pointed out that fate and destiny played a part in the lives of all presidents and that I felt all possible precautions should be taken to protect him but that he should appear and make one of the greatest speeches of his administration. He smiled and said, "Osro, that's what I have already decided to do. Your concurrence is comforting."[40]

The Iowa National Guard lined Des Moines's streets but the demonstration failed to appear. Hoover courageously kept the appointment and he received a warm reception. However, later, when he gave a speech in Detroit, loud booing resulted in a roar from the crowd. For the first time in his long memory, Edmund Starling heard the president of the United States booed. During a demonstration after the speech, mounted police had to charge the crowd.[41]

A week before the election, on a campaign visit to New York and then on to St. Paul, Minnesota, Hoover became convinced he was about to lose his reelection effort when he heard the antipathy of the crowds.

At one point a tomato was thrown at the president. It hit Secret Service agent George C. Drescher on the shoulder. Drescher jumped in front of Hoover. Later the president spoke to Drescher and said, "I'm through—I'm through." Hoover's wife put her arms around her husband, "just as lovely as she could," Drescher said. Hoover was "still suffering the effects of that when he got out there to Stanford. He was a hardy man. . . . It wasn't that he wasn't strong."[42]

Hoover's fears were well-founded when Election Day came around. That evening, November 8, 1932, Hoover's eyes were "bloodshot, his expression registering disbelief and dismay."[43] He was easily defeated by Franklin Roosevelt, winning only six of forty-eight states.

The dangers Hoover faced were not abated after he left office. In January 1933, only a few weeks before he was to hand over the presidency to Franklin Roosevelt, an Italian immigrant, Giuseppe Zangara, allegedly stalked Hoover with the intention of assassinating him. Zangara, an Italian immigrant, hated the rich and believed he was acting for the "poor people of the world."

Zangara told Miami police that he had originally bought his handgun in Miami to take to Washington to shoot Hoover, but because he had heard that the president-elect was coming to Miami, and also because the weather in Washington was cold, he changed his mind and targeted Roosevelt. Zangara also said he could not get off a shot at Hoover because of the president's Secret Service agents, who had been guarding him too well.

Roosevelt had joined a fishing trip to Miami before he went ashore on February 15, 1933, to give an impromptu speech at Miami's Bay Front Park. FDR was in the lead car, a green Buick convertible, of a three-car motorcade. Secret Service agent Gus Gennerich was sitting in the right front seat of the Buick and Marvin H. McIntyre, a press relations aide, sat beside him. Mayor of Miami R. B. Gauthier was sitting next to FDR in the rear seat. A team of five Secret Service agents was in the follow-up car, seventy-five feet behind the president.

FDR did not leave his car when he addressed the crowd. He spoke less than two minutes. As the president slid down into his seat, Chicago's mayor, Anton Cermak, approached the president and FDR shook his hand. Someone on the left-hand side of the car handed Roosevelt a five or six-foot-long telegram, and as the president reached to take it, Zangara started shooting with his nickel-plated .32-caliber double-action revolver. However, Zangara was crushed by the crowd and was unable to aim his pistol with any real accuracy. He had been on a chair firing wildly. A bystander managed to knock Zangara's arm, and this may have saved the president's life. Although the shots missed FDR, a bullet came within two feet of his head. However, Mayor Cermak was hit along with four others in the crowd. Roosevelt told agents to put Cermak in the presidential car and he held the fatally wounded mayor on the way to the hospital.[44]

Zangara, who had apparently been driven half-mad by a stomachache, likely the result of "peptic ulcer disease," pled guilty to four counts of assault and was sentenced to eighty years in prison. When Mayor Cermak died on March 6, Zangara was tried a second time. He pled guilty and received the death sentence. During his trial Zangara said he thought he had a "right to kill [Roosevelt]. . . . I see Mr. Hoover, I kill him first. Make no difference who go get that job. Run by big money. . . . I sorry Roosevelt still alive. . . . I want to shoot Roosevelt."[45]

Before his execution Zangara was incarcerated in Raiford Prison. He had told the warden, Leonard F. Chapman, that he had gone to Washington to shoot Hoover, had waited for ten days outside the White House for an opportunity to shoot the president, but had aborted his plans. However, author Blaise Picchi, while acknowledging Zangara may have wanted to shoot Hoover, believes the assassin did not go to Washington as he said. Picchi wrote, "Assuming that this was true (which is doubtful) it strains belief that he would plan to go back to Washington in the middle of an unusually cold winter—he had often said that cold weather aggravated his stomach pains—to attempt once more to shoot a president whom he had failed even to glimpse. And a president who would be out of office in less than three weeks."[46] According to the author, it is "highly unlikely" Zangara had a gun in Washington "because he bought one just before the shooting in Miami." Picchi argues that the "frugal Zangara" would not have purchased two guns and he did not need two.[47]

Following the attempted assassination of President-elect Roosevelt, the Secret Service detail assigned to guard Hoover was doubled and the uniformed guard around the White House was also increased.[48]

Roosevelt purportedly made no provision at all for Hoover to be protected after the inauguration. Secret Service agents said two agents took him to the train station and "put him on the train." According to Secret Service agent George Drescher, the president's secretary called the mayor of New York, and the mayor of New York arranged for police protection for him in New York City.[49]

On March 24, 1933, a few days after Hoover left office and retired to his California home, situated on the Stanford University campus, he was once again the subject of a security breach when a fifty-five-year-old mentally ill man, William Campogiani, a former wrestler and janitor, arrived at his house armed with a .38 revolver. He was prevented from entering when a Hoover employee subdued him and handed him over to local police. The Secret Service believed he was mentally ill and released him but kept him under surveillance. A spokesman for the agency said the would-be assassin was "under the delusion that he was involved in big business deals with former presidents Coolidge and Hoover."[50]

Afterword

Notoriety, the Copycat Effect, and Presidential Secrecy

There have been exciting incidents in the secret history of inaugurations, and more than once there is every reason to believe that the life of the president-elect has been preserved by means of the vigilance of his private guard.
—A veteran detective under Washington Chief of Police Col. William E. Moore, 1893

[William Meyers] said he intended to shoot President-Elect Hayes then proclaim himself president and to be sworn in amid the ringing of bells and the firing of cannon.
—*Washington DC Evening Star*, July 7, 1881

Angry people seeking notoriety of all degrees find the stage they want at the White House.
— Hugh Sidey, veteran White House correspondent, 1995

It is generally accepted that had the assassination attempts against U.S. presidents chronicled in this book succeeded, the course of American history would have changed.

The Presidential Succession Act of 1792 stipulated that the next in line to become president after the vice president was the president pro tempore of the Senate. Had Andrew Johnson been assassinated on his trip to Indianapolis, for example, Lafayette S. Foster would have become president, as there had been no law allowing Johnson to appoint a vice president after Lincoln's assassination. If the assassination attempts against Chester A. Arthur had succeeded, the sitting president pro tempore of the Senate, Thomas F. Bayard, would have become president.

The succession law was changed in 1886. The next in line to succeed to the presidency after the vice president became cabinet members in order of the creation of the office. Had the assassination attempts against William McKinley succeeded, his vice president, Garret Hobart, would have become president, and it is possible there would never have been a Teddy Roosevelt presidency and also no William Howard Taft presidency. Had the pre-1905 assassination attempts against Roosevelt succeeded, former Lincoln secretary John Hay would have taken office. (The presidential succession laws were changed once more in 1947, when the Speaker of the House became next in line for succession after the vice president.)

———

Most would-be presidential assassins in the nineteenth and early twentieth centuries harbored multiple motives, including bringing attention to a personal or public problem, avenging a perceived wrong, ending personal pain, saving the country or the world, or developing a special relationship with the target. Many, like Richard Lawrence, Peter Elliott, and John Schrank, suffered from mental illnesses and were imbued with irrational and delusional thoughts centered on the president. As historian David Herbert Donald wrote, assassins were "with few exceptions . . . single individuals, mostly social misfits, suffering from obsessions and delusions."[1]

Some would-be assassins appeared to have genuine political motives, including the many presidential threateners who were members of, or who had some form of affiliation with, political organizations—especially anarchists, Southern sympathizers, and members of racist organizations. Although their ideologies may have been loathsome to the majority of citizens, their violent goals cannot be characterized as irrational. Indeed, the majority of individuals who stalked and plotted against American presidents during this period in American history could not be described as psychotic and completely out of touch with reality. Even though some were clearly suffering from a personality disorder of some form, they knew the difference between right and wrong and were able to adapt and conform, for the most part, to society, at least until they committed their violent acts.

Most presidential assassins during this period had been seriously disturbed in their young lives. According to one of John Wilkes Booth's first biographers, Benn Pitman, as a child the future assassin was "a wild young lad, handsome in appearance like all the Booths, but, also like them, erratic and unpredictable."[2] Charles Guiteau's father believed that his son's persistent lying and swindling was the result of a "diseased brain." Leon Czolgosz became moody, remote, and suffered a nervous breakdown at twenty-five. He told his police interrogators after he shot McKinley, "I never had much luck at anything and this preyed upon me. It made me morose and envious."[3] Roosevelt assailant Henry Weilbrenner suffered from "nervous attacks" and depression.

Assassins often had poor interpersonal relationships. They were unable to work steadily at interesting or well-paying jobs and were characteristically rejected by friends, acquaintances, members of the opposite sex, and even political groups or countries to which they swore allegiance.

Because of their inherently low opinion of themselves, presidential assassins kept failing at one task or another and they used their failures as proof that society was plotting against them. Rather than admit they were woefully inadequate and that they should change their ways, they frequently built up defensive hostility against others and insisted they were persecuted by others. Consequently, they blamed their employers, government officials, and other authority figures, including the president. The "Old Republican soldier" who attempted to shoot Benjamin Harrison, for example, had become paranoid, accusing "Virginia politicians" of "heaping abuse" on him. He saw his murderous plans as a way to solve his problems.[4] Henry Weilbrenner had broken up with his girlfriend and blamed Theodore Roosevelt for his family's impoverishment.[5] Friends of Roosevelt stalker Peter Elliott described him as an "eccentric" who thought the Swedish community in Minneapolis was trying to poison him. Elliott was also a narcissist who believed he deserved a federal appointment and blamed the president for refusing him one.

However, a central and overriding motive for many presidential assassins and would-be assassins has been a craving for notoriety after having lived a life of relative obscurity. As a result they have unconsciously attempted to "gate-crash" into immortality, believing their memories would be ennobled on earth and they would be gratefully remembered by their countrymen for eons to come.

Before he assassinated Abraham Lincoln, Booth told friends, "I'll be the most famous man in America." He coveted celebrity. "I must have fame, fame! . . . What a glorious opportunity for a man to immortalize himself by killing Abraham Lincoln," he said, two years before his crime.[6] Leon Czolgosz felt isolated and worthless and gave himself an alias—"Fred Nieman" (Fred Nobody). Czolgosz was a "nobody" wanting to be a "somebody." Although clearly delusional, William Meyers, the would-be assassin of Rutherford B. Hayes, believed he would become a hero after he assassinated the president-elect. He planned to proclaim himself president and be "sworn in amid the ringing of bells and the firing of cannon.[7]

The prosecutor at Charles Guiteau's trial said the assassin "had an inordinate desire for unholy notoriety, that his vanity was boundless."[8] During the trial Guiteau proclaimed, "Some of these days instead of saying 'Guiteau the assassin,' they will say 'Guiteau the patriot.'"[9] Another Guiteau prosecutor said he was a "deadbeat, pure and simple. Finally he got tired of the monotony of dead-beating. He wanted excitement of some other kind and notoriety, and he's got it."[10] Many who knew Guiteau best during his life were convinced that his primary inspiration was "a morbid insane desire to do something which would impress his name upon history, no matter how infamous the deed."[11]

Author Candace Millard recognized Guiteau's craving for infamy when she wrote, "Guiteau had little thought for the crime he had just committed. . . . His mind was too preoccupied with the celebrity that awaited him . . . he believed he was about to shake off the poverty, misery, and obscurity of his former life, and step into the national spotlight."[12] Guiteau even had his shoes shined because he was aware of the attention he would be receiving during his trial.[13] Millard also noted that Guiteau was "in fact, happier now than he had ever been" after he shot President Garfield and he "had long thirsted for fame and recognition." The assassin felt that the "intense interest in his life and the frenzy of activity that surrounded him at the District Jail was not terrifying but thrilling."[14] Reporters who visited Guiteau at the jail were "sickened by the arrogance and enthusiasm with which he recounted his plans to murder the president," Millard wrote. One newspaper reporter present at the trial said Guiteau's "vanity" was "literally nauseating."[15]

In 1891 the *Robinson Constitution* recognized that infamy was central to the motives of presidential assassins. The newspaper editorialized, "[The cranks'] object in getting into the White House is usually for the purpose of saving the country or 'removing' the President of the United States, thinking that by assassinating the president they will benefit the country and immortalize themselves, even as did Brutus, Booth, and others. An immortality of infamy to these poor deluded creatures is better than no immortality at all. It is doubtful if there has been a single week in the past ten years that some one of these cranks has not shown up either at the Capitol, the [Washington] Monument or the White House seeking to jump from the top of one of the former or kill the occupant of the latter."[16]

As a reporter in the early 1890s observed, "The cause of so many cranks flocking to Washington is that they hear and read so much of Washington that it keeps working upon their diseased imaginations."[17]

Throughout American history, presidential aides and law enforcement officers have been aware of the dangers of the copycat effect on presidential assassination. The copycat theory was first conceived by a criminologist in 1912, after newspapers in London gave extensive coverage of the brutal crimes of Jack the Ripper in the late 1800s, which led to a wave of copycat rapes and murders throughout England.

The copycat effect can be seen in a wider context by the way the number of homicides increases significantly after well-publicized crimes. As early as 1905, a Washington DC police officer recognized the copycat effect when crimes were publicized. "It is now an accepted fact," he said, "that almost any form of crime seems to take on an epidemic phase upon repetition . . . a few years ago there was an epidemic of candy poisoning cases. . . . If publicity is given to the visit of one crank to the White House, cranks from all over the country head toward the capital. . . . It is a fact that since publicity of these visits has been withheld . . . these visits have largely decreased."[18]

The copycat effect with regard to presidential assassination involves the mimicking of the behavior of past assassins by unstable individuals who look to assassins of the past for inspiration. The phenomenon also includes the increase in assassination threats following any well-publicized attempts to harm the president. Each assassination or assassination attempt has produced a domino effect—their echoes playing on delusional minds leading to another threat or planned attack.

Assassination "contagion" was noted by the *Roanoke Times* in 1891. Prior to the Garfield assassination, copycat events were little noted because they were only reported locally or regionally. "After the [Garfield shooting] tragedy," the newspaper reported, "Guiteaus innumerable thronged our streets, alleys, wharfs and principle places."[19]

Within days of the Garfield assassination, Vice President Chester Arthur had been threatened. Following the would-be assassin's arrest the *Sacramento Daily Record-Union* opined, "How many men are on the road, converging upon Washington, of course nobody can tell: but it is clear that the crime of Guiteau is developing a large crop of homicidal maniacs, and that it may be necessary in consequence to keep watch upon all public men of any value for some time to come."[20]

The officials' fears were well-founded. Following Garfield's assassination, between forty and fifty "cranks" were arrested in Washington. Most of them were sent to St. Elizabeth's Insane Asylum on "physicians' certificates."[21]

When Mayor Harrison of Chicago was assassinated in 1893, the *Lewiston Daily Sun* reported that "a number of irresponsible and half-crazy persons are seen wandering about the White House from time to time. . . . It is well understood here that every time a crank kills a prominent man, or attempts to do so, and the particulars find their way into the newspapers, a large and miscellaneous crop of cranks is stirred up to the surface of society."[22] According to assassination experts Albert Ellis and John Gullo, Chicago mayor Carter Harrison's assassin, Patrick Eugene Joseph Prendergast, was "an illiterate fellow . . . with a craving for notoriety."[23]

Following the second attempt on Roosevelt's life, by Peter Elliott, forty-four-year-old John Decker entered the White House soon after the doors were opened on the morning of October 7. He was arrested by a White House police officer after causing a "disturbance."[24] Decker was pronounced insane and taken to an asylum.[25] The incident was judged to be so serious that the police officer who arrested Decker received a commendation for his work.[26]

The 1898 assassination of King Humbert of Italy by Gaetano Bresci had inspired William McKinley's assassin, Leon Czolgosz. Czolgosz became enamored with the king's assassin. He kept a copy of a newspaper article about Bresci in his pocket. It was discovered after his arrest. He read it over and over again as he brooded on his plans to kill the president. Czolgosz also bought the same pistol as Bresci—a silver-plated Iver Johnson .32-caliber revolver. Czolgosz even copied Bresci when he hid his gun in a handkerchief. The "bandaged-hand trick" had been used by Bresci to kill King Umberto, although the king's assassin had used a bunch of flowers instead of a handkerchief.[27]

John Schrank's shooting of ex-president Roosevelt in 1912 also inspired copycat attempts. One of Roosevelt's doctors at Oyster Bay believed the attempt on Roosevelt's life had "stirred up cranks" and was responsible for the increase in the number of threatening letters.[28]

Schrank's assassination attempt incited others to "finish the job." Roosevelt's doctor, W. G. Fallow, who lived near the president at Sagamore Hill, received a letter of warning from John A. Waldron, appointments clerk in the governor's office in Albany, New York. Waldron said a man had attempted to force his way into Mercy Hospital in Chicago where Roosevelt was taken following the Schrank assassination attempt. According to Waldron, the would-be assassin had been a prisoner at Clinton Prison during the Roosevelt administration and at that time had written a letter to the president in which he had threatened to kill him. He again announced his intention when he was denied admission to the hospital and threatened to follow Roosevelt to his home. The would-be assassin was eventually arrested and sent to an insane asylum.[29]

The copycat effect was noted by numerous White House officials over the years. In 1910 the *Pittsburgh Press* stated that the attempted assassination of New York mayor William J. Gaynor would inspire copycat assassination attempts on the life of William Howard Taft. The newspaper stated that "the Secret Service operatives have redoubled their vigilance. . . . It has been the experience of the guards that publication of such an outrage . . . serves to give further incentive to cranks all over the country and the president becomes a shining mark for the eccentric or lunatic."[30]

———————

It is hardly surprising that U.S. presidents and their aides in the nineteenth and early twentieth centuries had a history of concealing assassination attempts from the American public. Hiding unpleasant facts was a modus operandi of most presidential administrations. The Harrison administration covered up plans to depose the Queen of Hawaii. The illnesses suffered by Presidents Arthur and Cleveland while in office were kept secret. In Arthur's case, he suffered from Bright's disease, which eventually led to his death after leaving office. The public was told he was suffering from a mild case of malaria, and Americans were unaware he nearly died on a trip to Florida when his kidneys began to fail. He told the press he was "perfectly well." During Cleveland's second term, the American public were unaware he was suffering from cancer of the jaw. That fact was not revealed until 1917.[31]

In addition, attempts to assassinate presidents have been omitted from "insider" memoirs. Historian William Seale noted that watchmen, guards, and ushers were "often silent out of respect for the privacy of those who benefited them. Through the White House past, those who have known the most usually wrote the least. Presidential employees high and low learn one truth from the outset, or their time at the White House is brief: only one public figure occupies the White House, and that is the president; even his family members enjoy the spotlight only at his pleasure."[32]

When Ulysses Grant was general in chief of the armies of the United States, he told his aides to say nothing after he survived two attempts on his life. Grant believed that publicity about assassination attempts would inevitably lead to further attacks.[33] White House guard William Henry Crook said that there was a policy of withholding information about the "frequent occurrence" of violent incidents at the White House. They were dealt with "quietly and they rarely got into the newspapers."[34]

In 1877, Rutherford B. Hayes requested that the story of William Meyers's assassination attempt be "kept from the public."[35] In 1881, Sen. John Jones had asked a Cincinnati journalist to keep the story of the attempt on the life of Chester Arthur a secret. Jones said, "Mr. Arthur must never hear of this, and above all, the public must never hear of it. I consider that Mr. Arthur's life is in your hands. If you publish this incident other cranks will repeat tonight's attempt."[36] Secret Service chief John S. Bell said that the people who had known about the assassination attempt on Harrison had been "sworn to secrecy."[37]

Grover Cleveland's friend, Police Superintendent Thomas Byrnes, warned a police officer who arrived at Cleveland's home following an attempt on the former president's life to "forever . . . keep his mouth shut concerning the affair."[38]

Theodore Roosevelt's private secretary, William Loeb, feared that the assassination attempt made by Henry Weilbrenner on the life of the president would have the effect of "arousing all the mental freaks who hold the president responsible for everything that happens."[39] The North Carolina *Wautauga Democrat* stated, "It has also been discovered that the publicity given any such incident at the White House always brings other crazy men in search of the president and Secretary Loeb has now issued orders that henceforth all such incidents are to be withheld from the public."[40]

After an intruder had been caught in the White House in 1912, a newspaper noted that White House officials were reluctant to give details of the incident because it would inspire "others of the same caliber in like action."[41]

In 1912 the *Boston Evening Transcript* responded to government denials that a bomb had been sent to the White House by opining, "It has always been the policy of the Secret Service and the White House officers to deny publicity to any incident which savors of an attempt at violence upon the president."[42]

———

From the inception of the American republic there have been difficulties in protecting the president and the problem has resided in the nature of the president's job. On the one hand, the president had to be "one of the people" and as such should not be surrounded by a "palace guard." Presidents and presidential candidates required attention from a constituency who voted them in or out of office, and therefore chief executives have struggled with conflicting roles—maintaining contact and accessibility with the public along with protecting themselves.

Accordingly, as we have seen, presidents took incredible and sometimes foolhardy risks to fulfill this ideal. The American people gradually came to recognize that adequate protection was indeed necessary, but not until three presidents had fallen victim to assassins.

Additionally, presidents and presidential aides came to believe that any attempt on the president's life would inspire others, and therefore, as far as possible, such acts must be kept from the public. In a free and democratic society, presidential aides in the nineteenth and early twentieth centuries found this to be a difficult task, although a few, like Benjamin Harrison's secretary Elijah Halford and Grover Cleveland's secretary Henry Thurber, had some success.

It is unlikely that we will ever know the full extent of assassination attempts on American presidents. Some Secret Service files are missing from the National Archives and many reports of alleged assassination attempts were never investigated, either by the Secret Service, Congress, or other government agencies. However, as this book, and my previous book, *Hunting the President*, have demonstrated, numerous assassination attempts have been made against nearly every president, from the time of George Washington to the present day. Most of them have been ignored by historians and presidential biographers.

NOTES

PREFACE

1. "Cranks that Visit the White House," *Minneapolis Journal,* October 14, 1901, 4.
2. "Danger for Presidents," *Boston Evening Transcript,* September 10, 1901, 7.
3. Crook, *Through Five Administrations,* 93.
4. *Carroll City (IA) Herald,* August 10, 1881, 1.
5. J. Smith, *Grant,* 462.
6. Frank G. Carpenter, "The President a Brave Man," *Deseret Weekly,* December 16, 1893, 820.
7. "Mr. Thurber's Public Service," *Washington Evening Times,* March 12, 1897, 4.
8. "Larger Guard for Roosevelt," *New York Evening World,* September 3, 1903, 1.
9. "Cranks at the White House," *Washington Times,* October 7, 1903, 6.
10. "Passing of the Crank," *Copper Country Evening News,* April 7, 1897, 4.

1. GUARDING THE EARLY PRESIDENTS

1. Matthew Algeo, "The Incredible Walking President," *Harry Truman's Excellent Adventure,* http://www.trumanroadtrip.com/articles/article/6829750/120407.htm.
2. Seale, *President's House,* 1:5.
3. Seale, *President's House,* 1:92.
4. Seale, *President's House,* 1:5.
5. R. Ellis, *Presidential Travel,* 228.
6. R. Ellis, *Presidential Travel,* 168.
7. Bruce Hoffman et al., *Security in the Nation's Capital,* 9.
8. Seale, *President's House,* 1:93.
9. Whitcomb and Whitcomb, *Real Life at the White House,* 20.

10. R. Ellis, *Presidential Travel*, 3.
11. R. Ellis, *Presidential Travel*, 2.
12. "The Presidential Job," *Deseret Weekly*, July 18, 1896, 1.
13. "Threat of Impeachment Hounded Washington," *Nevada Daily Mail*, June 30, 1974, 4.
14. Dallek, *Hail to the Chief*, xiii.
15. R. Ellis, *Presidential Travel*, 104.
16. Garrison, *Treasury of White House Tales*, 15.
17. Andrew, *For the President's Eyes Only*, 6.
18. Fiske et al., *Presidents of the United States, 1789–1894*, 20.
19. Henry, *What They Didn't Teach You*, 6.
20. Henry, *What They Didn't Teach You*, 15.
21. "Irishman Thomas Hickey Executed for Plotting against Washington," *Irish Echo*, February 2011, http://irishecho.com/2011/02/226-years-ago-irishman -thomas-hickey-executed-for-plotting-against-washington.
22. "Michael Lynch and Thomas Hickey Committed to Prison," American Archives, series 4, vol. 6, p. 1406, http://lincoln.lib.niu.edu/cgi-bin/amarch /getdoc.pl?/var/lib/philologic/databases/amarch/.18040.
23. Teddi DiCanio, "Sergeant Thomas Hickey Court Martial 1776," JRank Law Library, Notable Trials, http://law.jrank.org/pages/2365/Sergeant-Thomas -Hickey-Court-Martial-1776.html.
24. William Mitchell, "The Plot to Kill Washington," *Family Weekly Magazine*, February 19, 1961, 4; and Barbara Rowes, "George Washington Supped Here and Nearly Died from the Peas, But Fraunces Tavern Is Still Serving," *People* 13, no. 8 (February 25, 1980).
25. See: Teddi DiCanio, "Sergeant Thomas Hickey Court Martial 1776," JRank Law Library, Notable Trials, http://law.jrank.org/pages/2365/Sergeant -Thomas-Hickey-Court-Martial-1776.html.
26. "Secret Service Report on Historical Information on Past Attacks and Assassinations Relating to American Presidents," Warren Commission Exhibit No. 2549, 774, http://www.history-matters.com/archive/jfk/wc/wcvols/wh25 /pdf/WH25_CE_2549.pdf.
27. Hodge, *U.S. Presidents and Foreign Policy*, 21.
28. R. Ellis, *Presidential Travel*, 6.
29. "Secret Service Report on Historical Information on Past Attacks and Assassinations Relating to American Presidents," Warren Commission Exhibit No. 2549, 774, http://www.history-matters.com/archive/jfk/wc/wcvols /wh25/pdf/WH25_CE_2549.pdf.
30. Garrison, *Treasury of White House Tales*, 188.
31. Bernstein, *Thomas Jefferson*, 147.
32. David, *American Colonization Society*, 40.

33. Garrison, *Treasury of White House Tales*, 39.

34. Henry, *What They Didn't Teach You*, 14.

35. R. Ellis, *Presidential Travel*, 6.

36. R. Ellis, *Presidential Travel*, 26.

37. R. Ellis, *Presidential Travel*, 102.

38. Watson, *Life in the White House*, 249.

39. See the section entitled "Protection of the White House Complex and the President in the Nineteenth Century," from chapter 4 ("The Evolution of Presidential Security") in Federation of American Scientists, *Public Report of the White House Security Review*, http://fas.org/irp/agency/ustreas/usss /tlpubrpt.html.

40. Seale, *President's House*, 1:145.

41. Whitcomb and Whitcomb, *Real Life at the White House*, 44.

42. Seale, *President's House*, 1:159.

43. Whitcomb and Whitcomb, *Real Life at the White House*, 44.

44. Whitcomb and Whitcomb, *Real Life at the White House*, 44.

45. "The White House 150 Years Old, Rich in History and Tradition," *Milwaukee Journal*, August 18, 1944, 1.

46. See the section entitled "Protection of the White House Complex and the President in the Nineteenth Century," from chapter 4 ("The Evolution of Presidential Security") in Federation of American Scientists, *Public Report of the White House Security Review*, http://fas.org/irp/agency/ustreas/usss /tlpubrpt.html.

47. Marrin, *Old Hickory*, 24.

48. Whitcomb and Whitcomb, *Real Life at the White House*, 54.

49. Garrison, *Treasury of White House Tales*, 40.

50. Whitcomb and Whitcomb, *Real Life at the White House*, 53.

51. Whitcomb and Whitcomb, *Real Life at the White House*, 53.

52. "Secret Service Report on Historical Information on Past Attacks and Assassinations Relating to American Presidents," Warren Commission Exhibit No. 2549, 774, http://www.history-matters.com/archive/jfk/wc/wcvols/wh25 /pdf/WH25_CE_2549.pdf.

53. "Guarding Harrison," *Pittsburgh Press*, April 30, 1890, 1.

54. "The Crop of Cranks," *Lewiston Daily Sun*, 1893, 1.

55. R. Ellis, *Presidential Travel*, 112.

2. FIRST ATTACK ON AN AMERICAN PRESIDENT

1. Brands, *Andrew Jackson*, 26.

2. "Andrew Jackson," History Channel, http://www.history.com/topics/us -presidents/andrew-jackson.

3. "Andrew Jackson in a Gun Fight," *Past Now*, September 4, 1813, https://

pastnow.wordpress.com/2013/09/04/september-4-1813-andrew-jackson-in-a
-gun-fight/.

4. Dantan Wernecke, "My God! Have I Missed Him?" Teaching American History, May 27, 2012, www.teachingamericanhistory.org.

5. American History, http://www.let.rug.nl/usa/biographies/andrew-jackson
/jacksons-duel-with-charles-dickinson.php.

6. Garrison, *Treasury of White House Tales*, 19.

7. Dantan Wernecke, "My God! Have I Missed Him?" Teaching American History, May 27, 2012, www.teachingamericanhistory.org.

8. Whitcomb and Whitcomb, *Real Life at the White House*, 64.

9. "Andrew Jackson in a Gun Fight," *Past Now*, September 4, 1813, https://
pastnow.wordpress.com/2013/09/04/september-4-1813-andrew-jackson-in-a
-gun-fight/.

10. Whitcomb and Whitcomb, *Real Life at the White House*, 65.

11. Marshall and Manuel, *From Sea to Shining Sea*, 185.

12. Garrison, *Treasury of White House Tales*, 40.

13. Seale, *President's House*, 1:258.

14. R. Ellis, *Presidential Travel*, 103.

15. Tom Patterson, "Presidential Road Trips Tainted by Tragedy," CNN, undated, http://edition.cnn.com/2008/TRAVEL/09/30/roadtrips.presidential/index
.html?eref=rss_travel.

16. "Andrew Jackson," What, When, How, http://what-when-how.com/conspiracy
-theories-in-american-history/jackson-andrew/.

17. Donovan, *Assassins of American Presidents*, 74.

18. Katie Freeman, "Letter Threatening Jackson's Life Determined to Be Written by Father of Man Who Killed Lincoln," *Knoxville News Sentinel*, January 25, 2009, 4.

19. "The First Attack on an American President," *Indiana State Sentinel*, January 14, 1880, 9.

20. "The First Attack on an American President," *Indiana State Sentinel*, January 14, 1880, 9.

21. "The First Attack on an American President," *Indiana State Sentinel*, January 14, 1880, 9.

22. Cole, *Jackson Man*, 181.

23. R. Ellis, *Presidential Travel*, 104.

24. Donovan, *Assassins of American Presidents*, 65.

25. Donovan, *Assassins of American Presidents*, 66.

26. Clarke, *American Assassins*, 197.

27. Shore et al., "White House Cases: Psychiatric Patients and the Secret Service."

28. Donovan, *Assassins of American Presidents*, 65.

29. "Andrew Jackson," American Presidents, http://www.americanpresidents .org/presidents/president.asp?PresidentNumber=7.

30. "A Look at Those Who Try to Kill," *Spokane Spokesman Review*, May 23, 1972, 4.

31. "Richard Lawrence—The Assassin," *Fayetteville Observer*, June 21, 1866, 1.

32. "Richard Lawrence—The Assassin," *Fayetteville Observer*, June 21, 1866, 1.

33. "Assassination," The Free Dictionary, http://legal-dictionary.thefreedictionary .com/Assassination+attempt.

34. Jon Grinspan, "Trying to Assassinate President Jackson," March 24, 2014, American Heritage, http://tiny.cc/MIkUA.

35. Burstein, *Passions of Andrew Jackson*, 202.

36. "Randolph's Career—Pulling Jackson's Nose," *Reading Eagle*, July 8, 1899, 2.

37. Clarke, *American Assassins*, 198.

38. Shore et al, "White House Cases: Psychiatric Patients and the Secret Service."

39. Dershowitz, *America on Trial*, 100.

40. J. Hoffman, "Psychotic Visitors to Government Offices in the National Capital," 571–75.

41. Remini, *Andrew Jackson*, 397.

42. Remini, *Andrew Jackson*, 398.

3. THE ANTEBELLUM PRESIDENTS

1. Garrison, *Treasury of White House Tales*, 40.

2. Widmer and Schlesinger, *Martin Van Buren*, 127.

3. Seale, *President's House*, 1:240.

4. Singleton, *Story of the White House*, 261.

5. Whitcomb and Whitcomb, *Real Life at the White House*, 75.

6. "The Metropolitan Police Department, District of Columbia," Washington DC Genealogy Trails, http://genealogytrails.com/washdc/lawsprisons /historyofpolicedept.html.

7. Garrison, *Treasury of White House Tales*, 40.

8. Seale, *President's House*, 1:219.

9. Seale, *President's House*, 1:220.

10. Seale, *President's House*, 1:220.

11. Widmer and Schlesinger, *Martin Van Buren*, 127.

12. "Tyler and Lincoln," *Fredericksburg (VA) Free Lance–Star*, June 1, 1929, 4.

13. "The Inaugural Pageant—From Washington to Hoover," *Fredericksburg (VA) Free Lance–Star*, February 7, 1929, 5.

14. R. Ellis, *Presidential Travel*, 103.

15. Grant Calder, "Protecting the President: 'My Bodyguard I Desire to Be the People,'" *Huffington Post*, April 9, 2012.

16. Seale, *President's House*, 1:241.

17. "Protection of the White House Complex in the Twentieth Century," External Threats, www.trinity.edu/jdunn/whitehouseattacks.htm.

18. Whitcomb and Whitcomb, *Real Life at the White House*, 86.

19. Seale, *President's House*, 1:240.

20. Whitcomb and Whitcomb, *Real Life at the White House*, 87.

21. *Public Report of the White House Security Review*, http://fas.org/irp/agency/us treas/usss/t1pubrpt.html.

22. Hoffman et al., *Security in the Nation's Capital*, 2; and "Secret Service Report on Historical Information on Past Attacks and Assassinations Relating to American Presidents," Warren Commission Exhibit No. 2549, 774, http://www.history-matters.com/archive/jfk/wc/wcvols/wh25/pdf/WH25_CE_2549.pdf.

23. Seale, *President's House*, 1:241.

24. Seale, *President's House*, 1:24.

25. Garrison, *Treasury of White House Tales*, 22.

26. Whitcomb and Whitcomb, *Real Life at the White House*, 90.

27. Ann Blackman, "Fatal Cruise of the Princeton," Military.com, Navy History, September 2005, http://www.military.com/NewContent/0,13190,NH_0905_Cruise-P1,00.html.

28. Thomas V. DiBacco, "Risk of Attacks on White House Just Part of the Price a President Has to Pay," *Baltimore Sun*, May 28, 1995.

29. Whitcomb and Whitcomb, *Real Life at the White House*, 96.

30. Seale, *President's House*, 1:264.

31. Whitcomb and Whitcomb, *Real Life at the White House*, 105.

32. Parenti, *History as Mystery*, 209–39.

33. Garrison, *Treasury of White House Tales*, 41.

34. Seale, *President's House*, 1:303.

35. Seale, *President's House*, 1:323.

36. Frank G. Carpenter, "As Told by Servants," *Washington Evening Star*, March 3, 1894, 1.

37. Seale, *President's House*, 1:307.

38. Frank G. Carpenter, "As Told by Servants," *Washington Evening Star*, March 3, 1894, 1.

39. Seale, *President's House*, 1:309.

40. Seale, *President's House*, 1:309.

41. Melanson, *Secret Service*, 133.

42. Whitcomb and Whitcomb, *Real Life at the White House*, 119.

43. "Franklin Pierce," POTUS, http://www.potus.com/fpierce.html.

44. Whitcomb and Whitcomb, *Real Life at the White House*, 127.

45. Robert McNamara, "Was President Buchanan Poisoned at His Own

Inauguration?" http://history1800s.about.com/od/crimesanddisasters/ss
/failed-assassinations_3.htm.

46. *Nebraska Advertiser,* April 9, 1857, 3; and "Attempt to Poison President Buchanan at the National Hotel the Day before His Inauguration in 1857," *Stark County Democrat* (Canton OH), October 12, 1882.
47. Seale, *President's House,* 1:336.
48. Seale, *President's House,* 1:354.
49. "A President's Escape—How Kansas Man Plotted to Kill Buchanan," *Los Angeles Herald,* August 28, 1887, 11.
50. "A President's Escape—How Kansas Man Plotted to Kill Buchanan," *Los Angeles Herald,* August 28, 1887, 11.
51. "A President's Escape—How Kansas Man Plotted to Kill Buchanan," *Los Angeles Herald,* August 28, 1887, 11.
52. Hatch, *Protecting President Lincoln,* 21.
53. Whitcomb and Whitcomb, *Real Life at the White House,* 128.

4. PROTECTING LINCOLN

1. Dallek, *Hail to the Chief,* xiii.
2. Hatch, *Protecting President Lincoln,* 23.
3. Randall and Currant, *Lincoln the President,* 368.
4. Dallek, *Hail to the Chief,* xiii; "Villains Who Ran for President," *Milwaukee Journal,* November 21, 1951, 8.
5. Hatch, *Protecting President Lincoln,* 10.
6. Stashower, *Hour of Peril,* 85.
7. Bryan, *Great American Myth,* 58.
8. Hatch, *Protecting President Lincoln,* 21.
9. Bryan, *Great American Myth,* 59.
10. Stashower, *Hour of Peril,* 84.
11. Hatch, *Protecting President Lincoln,* 12.
12. Stashower, *Hour of Peril,* 90.
13. Stashower, *Hour of Peril,* 174.
14. Hatch, *Protecting President Lincoln,* 11.
15. Hatch, *Protecting President Lincoln,* 11.
16. Hatch, *Protecting President Lincoln,* 12.
17. Hatch, *Protecting President Lincoln,* 14.
18. Hatch, *Protecting President Lincoln,* 15.
19. Hatch, *Protecting President Lincoln,* 15.
20. Stashower, "The Unsuccessful Plot to Kill Abraham Lincoln," 155.
21. Stashower, *Hour of Peril,* 154.
22. Stashower, "The Unsuccessful Plot to Kill Abraham Lincoln."

23. Stashower, *Hour of Peril*, 312.

24. R. Ellis, *Presidential Travel*, 106.

25. R. Ellis, *Presidential Travel*, 106.

26. Randall and Currant, *Lincoln the President*, 369.

27. "The American Century," *Miami News*, February 19, 1961, 1.

28. Navarro, *Country in Conflict*, 59.

29. Stashower, *Hour of Peril*, 16.

30. "Abraham Lincoln's First Inauguration," Lincoln Online, http://www
    .abrahamlincolnonline.org/lincoln/education/inaugural1.htm.

31. R. Ellis, *Presidential Travel*, 106.

32. Steers, *Lincoln Legends*, 183.

33. Bryan, *Great American Myth*, 60.

34. Crook, *Memories of the White House*, 27.

35. Bryan, *Great American Myth*, 61

36. Bryan, *Great American Myth*, 61.

37. Guelzo, *Abraham Lincoln*, 428.

38. Randall and Currant, *Lincoln the President*, 370.

39. "Ward Hill Lamon, 1828–1893," Mr. Lincoln's White House, http://www
    .mrlincolnswhitehouse.org/inside.asp?ID=61&subject ID=2.

40. Holzer, *Lincoln Mailbag*, 195.

41. Steers, *Blood on the Moon*, 22.

42. "Ward Hill Lamon, 1828–1893," Mr. Lincoln's White House, http://www
    .mrlincolnswhitehouse.org/inside.asp?ID=61&subjectID=2.

43. Whitcomb and Whitcomb, *Real Life at the White House*, 139.

44. Carpenter, *Six Months at the White House*, 66.

45. Bryan, *Great American Myth*, 61.

46. Randall and Currant, *Lincoln the President*, 370.

47. Hatch, *Protecting President Lincoln*, 25.

48. Whitcomb and Whitcomb, *Real Life at the White House*, 138.

49. Seale, *President's House*, 1:370.

50. O'Brien, *Secret Lives of the U.S. Presidents*, 7.

51. Thomas DiBacco, "Rise of Attacks on White House Just Part of the Price a
    President Has to Pay," *Baltimore Sun*, May 28, 1995.

52. "The White House Grounds and Entrance: Security," Mr. Lincoln's White
    House, http://www.mrlincolnswhitehouse.org/inside.asp?ID=78&
    subjectID=3.

53. Crook, *Memories of the White House*, 1.

54. Whitcomb and Whitcomb, *Real Life at the White House*, 139.

55. Randall and Currant, *Lincoln the President*, 369.

56. R. Ellis, *Presidential Travel*, 107.

57. Crook, *Memories of the White House*, 1.

58. Pendel, *Thirty-Six Years in the White House*, 11.

59. Pendel, *Thirty-Six Years in the White House*, 11.

60. "The Only Woman Who Called President Lincoln a Fool," *Afro-American*, August 30, 1952, 11.

61. Crook, *Memories of the White House*, 18.

62. Hatch, *Protecting President Lincoln*, 25.

63. "Lincoln and His Bodyguard," Past in the Present, https://pastinthepresent .wordpress.com/tag/ward-hill-lamon/.

64. Pendel, *Thirty-Six Years in the White House*, 11.

65. Pendel, *Thirty-Six Years in the White House*, 27.

66. Pendel, *Thirty-Six Years in the White House*, 11.

67. Pendel, *Thirty-Six Years in the White House*, 28.

68. Russell Woodard, "Lincoln's Bodyguard and His Relics" *Brockton (MA) Enterprise*, February 9, 1910, 2.

69. "White House Vets," *Washington Evening Star*, April 24, 1903, 2.

70. "The White House Grounds and Entrance: Security," Mr. Lincoln's White House, http://www.mrlincolnswhitehouse.org/inside.asp?ID=78 &subjectID=3.

71. "Men Who Knew Lincoln," *Washington Sunday Star*, January 15, 1922, 1.

72. Pinsker, *Lincoln's Sanctuary*, 50.

73. "Downstairs at the White House," Mr. Lincoln's White House, http://www .mrlincolnswhitehouse.org/inside.asp?ID=27&subjectID=3.

74. Donald, *We Are Lincoln Men*, 141.

75. Pinsker, *Lincoln's Sanctuary*, 51.

76. Steers, *Blood on the Moon*, 26.

77. Steers, *Blood on the Moon*, 22.

78. "The White House Grounds and Entrance: Security," Mr. Lincoln's White House, http://www.mrlincolnswhitehouse.org/inside.asp?ID=78&subjectID=3.

79. Randall and Currant, *Lincoln the President*, 370.

80. "Spokane Man Member of Lincoln's Bodyguard," *Spokane Press*, May 1910, 15.

81. Pinsker, *Lincoln's Sanctuary*, 60.

82. Bryan, *Great American Myth*, 62.

83. Pinsker, *Lincoln's Sanctuary*, 60.

84. "The Only Woman Who Called President Lincoln a Fool," *Afro-American*, August 30, 1952, 11.

85. Holzer, *Lincoln Mailbag*, 335; Shappell Manuscript Foundation, "Oliver Wendell Holmes . . . ," June 14, 1922, http://www.shapell.org/manuscript.aspx ?get-down-you-damn-fool-abraham-lincoln-battle-of-fort-stevens.

86. Pinsker, *Lincoln's Sanctuary*, 60.

87. Steers, *Blood on the Moon*, 24.

88. Feinman, *Assassinations*, 20.

89. "Luke P. Blackburn," Absolute Astronomy, Encyclopedia, http://www.absolute astronomy.com/topics/Luke_P._Blackburn.

90. Steers, *Blood on the Moon*, 46–47.

91. Hatch, *Protecting President Lincoln*, 40.

92. Kauffman, *American Brutus*, 174.

93. "Was Abraham Lincoln a Fan of John Wilkes Booth?" Civil War Saga, June 20, 2012, www.civilwarsaga.com/abraham-lincoln-was-a-fan-of-john-wilkes-booth.

5. THE RECONSTRUCTION PRESIDENTS

1. Donovan, *Assassins of American Presidents*, 272.

2. Whitcomb and Whitcomb, *Real Life at the White House*, 143.

3. Seale, *President's House*, 1:427.

4. Crook, *Memories of the White House*, 64.

5. *Report of the U.S. President's Commission on the Assassination of President John F. Kennedy*, commonly referred to as the Warren Commission Report. See appendix 7, "A Brief History of Presidential Protection," 507.

6. Crook, *Memories of the White House*, 63.

7. Crook, *Memories of the White House*, 64.

8. Crook, *Memories of the White House*, 64.

9. Seale, *President's House*, 436.

10. Garrison, *Treasury of White House Tales*, 42.

11. Garrison, *Treasury of White House Tales*, 42.

12. "Andrew Johnson Dead," *New York Times*, August 1, 1875, http://www.ny times.com/learning/general/onthisday/bday/1229.html.

13. O'Brien, "Andrew Johnson," (chapter 17) in *Secret Lives of the U.S. Presidents*.

14. Pendel, *Thirty-Six Years in the White House*, 57.

15. "Attempt to Shoot Officer at the President's," *Daily National Republican*, October 12, 1865, 2.

16. Crook, *Through Five Administrations*, 92.

17. "The Radical Riot at Indianapolis—What Comes Next?" *Philadelphia Daily Evening Telegraph*, September 13, 1866, 2.

18. "The Radical Riot at Indianapolis—What Comes Next?" *Philadelphia Daily Evening Telegraph*, September 13, 1866, 2.

19. "Attempt to Assassinate the President," *Lexington (MO) Weekly Caucasian*, September 26, 1866, 4.

20. "The Excitement at the White House, *Glasgow Herald*, March 1, 1869, 6.

21. J. Smith, *Grant*, 462.

22. J. Smith, *Grant*, 462.

23. Steers, *Lincoln Legends*, 183.

24. Stephens, *Commanding the Storm*, 54.

25. Stephens, *Commanding the Storm*, 54.

26. Mappen, *There's More to New Jersey*, 79.

27. McFeeley, *Grant*, 224–25.

28. O'Reilly and Dugard, *Killing Lincoln*, 138.

29. Seale, *President's House*, 1: 476.

30. Garrison, *Treasury of White House Tales*, 42.

31. Grant was frequently pestered by petitioners at the hotel, which gave the name "lobbyists" to the political lexicon; Hugh Sidney, "The Presidency: Outsize Slippers for Mr. Lincoln," *Time*, August 25, 1986, http://content .time.com/time/static/sitemap/29_8_1.html.

32. Crook, *Memories of the White House*, 93.

33. Garrison, *Treasury of White House Tales*, 82.

34. Pendel, *Thirty-Six Years in the White House*, 68.

35. *New York Mail and Express*, January 7, 1888, 2; and "Three Troublesome Cranks," *Madison Times*, January 7, 1888, 4.

36. "Gossip above Politics," *Milwaukee Journal*, April 14, 1884, 1.

37. "Guarding the President," *Sacramento Daily Record-Union*, March 14, 1893, 6.

38. Crook, *Memories of the White House*, 123.

39. Simon, *Papers of Ulysses S. Grant*, 24.

40. Simon, *Papers of Ulysses S. Grant*, 24.

41. Simon, *Papers of Ulysses S. Grant*, 25.

42. *Bismarck Weekly Tribune*, March 14, 1877, 2.

43. Crook, *Memories of the White House*, 124.

44. Cummins, *Anything for a Vote*, 120.

45. *Carroll City (IA) Herald*, August 10, 1881, 1.

46. "The Project to Assassinate Hayes," *Washington Evening Critic*, July 7, 1881, 3

47. "The Project to Assassinate Hayes," *Washington Evening Critic*, July 7, 1881, 1.

48. "Pardoned by the President," *Washington Evening Star*, April 26, 1880, 1.

49. *Daily Cairo (IL) Bulletin*, August 3, 1881, 4.

50. Wead, *All the President's Children*, 181.

51. Crook, *Memories of the White House*, 109.

52. Garrison, *Treasury of White House Tales*, 111.

53. *Deseret News*, March 9, 1894, 4.

54. "Assassination of President Garfield," *Quebec Daily Telegraph*, July 5, 1881, 6.

55. "Passing of the Crank," *Copper County (MI) Evening News*, April 7, 1897, 4.

56. R. Ellis, *Presidential Travel*, 103.

57. "Attempted Assassination of President Hayes," *Sedalia (MO) Weekly Bazoo*, November 9, 1880, 2.

58. "Fatal Railroad Accident," *Boston Evening Transcript*, March 7, 1881, 2.

6. GARFIELD'S ASSASSINATION, ARTHUR'S "NEAR MISS"

1. Charles Lane, "In the 19th Century a Different Secret Service, But Not without Controversy," *Washington Post*, October 1, 2014.

2. "How Doctors Killed Garfield," CBS News, July 5, 2012, http://www.cbsnews.com/news/how-doctors-killed-president-garfield/.

3. A. Ellis and J. Gullo, *Murder and Assassination*, 235.

4. Simon, *Papers of Ulysses S. Grant*, xxv.

5. "Dangerous Cranks, *Omaha Daily Bee*, December 28, 1887, 4.

6. "Many Cranks Turned Down," *Pittsburgh Press*, September 8, 1901, 4.

7. Crook, *Through Five Administrations*, 270.

8. *Deseret News*, 16 January 16, 1897, 1.

9. Crook, *Memories of the White House*, 268.

10. Seale, *President's House*, 1:520.

11. R. Ellis, *Presidential Travel*, 109.

12. "The Memoirs of Thomas Donaldson," Rutherford B. Hayes Presidential Center, dated 1881–93, http://www.rbhayes.org/hayes/content/files/donaldsontc/donaldson18811893.htm.

13. "The Earlier Assassins," *Time*, November 29, 1963, http://content.time.com/time/magazine/article/0,9171,875364,00.html.

14. "Heroes: 1881 Man," *Time*, July 13, 1931, http://content.time.com/time/subscriber/article/0,33009,741999,00.html.

15. Millard, *Destiny of the Republic*, 158.

16. "Ex-Chief Brooks," *San Francisco Call*, April 8, 1892.

17. Millard, *Destiny of the Republic*, 159.

18. "Guiteau," *New York Evening Post*, August 18, 1882, 1.

19. "The Shot at Guiteau," *Deseret News*, September 17, 1881, 1.

20. "When President Garfield Was Shot," *Milwaukee Journal*, December 27, 1927, 10.

21. "Sergt. Mason Released," *New York Times*, November 27, 1883, 5.

22. "Another Shot at Guiteau," *Hartford Weekly Times*, November 23, 1881, 1.

23. Newton, *Age of the Assassins*, 144.

24. A. Ellis and J. Gullo, *Murder and Assassination*, 235.

25. "Charles Guiteau: The Assassin," History Rat, https://historyrat.wordpress.com/2011/04/24/charles-guiteau-assassin/.

26. "White House Notes," *Boston Evening Transcript*, July 18, 1881, 2.

27. Brinkley and Dyer, *American Presidency*, 233.

28. "White House Notes," *Boston Evening Transcript*, July 18, 1881, 2.

29. Millard, *Destiny of the Republic*, 197.

30. Smith D. Fry, "Cranks in Washington," *Roanoke Times*, July 3, 1891, 6.

31. "Assassin No. 3," *Sacramento Daily Record-Union*, July 7, 1881, 2.

32. *Report of the U.S. President's Commission on the Assassination of President John*

F. *Kennedy,* commonly referred to as the Warren Commission Report. See appendix 7, "A Brief History of Presidential Protection," 508.

33. *Report of the U.S. President's Commission on the Assassination of President John F. Kennedy,* commonly referred to as the Warren Commission Report. See appendix 7, "A Brief History of Presidential Protection," 508.

34. Crook, *Memories of the White House,* 159.

35. *Charlotte Democrat,* July 20, 1888, 3.

36. Smith D. Fry, "Cranks In Washington" *Roanoke Times,* July 3, 1891, 6.

37. "Alleged Plot to Assassinate President Arthur," *Washington Evening Star,* September 28, 1881, 1.

38. "Another Crank at the White House," *Memphis Daily Appeal,* November 1, 1881, 1.

39. Pendel, *Thirty-Six Years in the White House,* 123.

40. *National Tribune,* December 3, 1881, 4.

41. "President's Favorites," *Abbeville Press and Banner,* June 4, 1884, 4.

42. Crook, *Memories of the White House,* 165.

43. Crook, *Memories of the White House,* 162.

44. *Interior Journal,* December 9, 1881, 4.

45. "White House Cranks," *Pittsburgh Dispatch,* April 14, 1891, 12.

46. "Much in Little," *Gettysburg Compiler,* January 25, 1882, 2.

47. "The Cranks Who Visit the White House to See Arthur," *St. Paul (MN) Daily Globe,* March 30, 1883, 1.

48. *Carroll City (IA) Herald,* May 28, 1884, 1.

49. *Ottawa Free Trader,* October 11, 1882, 2.

50. "Hunting the President—A Crank Proposes to Shoot Arthur," *New North-West,* Montana, November 30, 1883, 2; and "Glory on the Gallows," *Toronto Daily Mail,* November 28, 1883, 2.

7. ATTEMPTED ASSASSINATION OF HARRISON

1. N. Miller, *Star Spangled Men,* 68.

2. Dallek, *Hail to the Chief,* 3.

3. "Harrison's Hair," *Pittsburgh Dispatch,* February 24, 1889, 1.

4. "Guarding the President," *San Francisco Call,* December 13, 1891, 1.

5. "A White House Guard," *Kentucky New Era,* January 9, 1892, 3.

6. "A White House Guard," *Kentucky New Era,* January 9, 1892, 3.

7. "Silly Precautions," *Sacramento Daily Record-Union,* April 28, 1891, 2.

8. "A Startling Story," *Washington Evening Star,* December 21, 1888, 7.

9. "Ex-President Harrison's Views on the Assassination," *San Francisco Morning Call,* October 30, 1893, 1.

10. Whitcomb and Whitcomb, *Real Life at the White House,* 204.

11. R. Ellis, *Presidential Travel,* 138.

12. Seale, *President's House*, 1:559.

13. "No Cranks Need Apply," *Aurora Daily Express*, March 1, 1895, 1.

14. "A Religious Crank," *The Dalles (OR) Times-Mountaineer*, December 19, 1991, 1.

15. Gary Larreategu, "The President's Life Is in Peril" *Statesman*, October–December 2004, http://indianatalks.com/site/2014/10/the-presidents-life-in-peril/.

16. "White House—Secret Service and Military Aides," Old and Sold.com, http://www.oldandsold.com/articles31n/white-house-history-14.shtml.

17. Gary Larreategu, "The President's Life Is in Peril" *Statesman*, October–December 2004, http://indianatalks.com/site/2014/10/the-presidents-life-in-peril/.

18. "President Hard to Keep Guarded," *Gettysburg Times*, July 12, 1926, 2.

19. "Guarded by Detectives," *Spokane Daily Chronicle*, May 30, 1892, 1.

20. *Aurora Daily Express*, March 1, 1895, 1.

21. "A White House Guard," *Kentucky New Era*, January 9, 1892, 3

22. "They Worked for Presidents," *Deseret News*, March 9, 1894, 8.

23. "A White House Guard," *Kentucky New Era*, January 9, 1892, 3.

24. "They Worked for Presidents," *Deseret News*, March 9, 1894, 8.

25. "White House Cranks," *Hartford Weekly Times*, October 19, 1893, 10.

26. "White House Cranks," *Hartford Weekly Times*, October 19, 1893, 10.

27. "Guarding Harrison," *Pittsburgh Press*, April 30, 1890, 1.

28. "Guarding Harrison," *Pittsburgh Press*, April 30, 1890, 1.

29. "The President's Duties," *Sacramento Daily Record-Union*, November 11, 1890, 1.

30. "Capital City Chimes," *Robinson Constitution*, March 18, 1891, 1.

31. "Cranks at the White House," *Stark County Democrat* (Canton OH), May 30, 1889, 3.

32. *Stark County Democrat* (Canton OH), May 30, 1889, 3.

33. "The President's Duties," *Sacramento Daily Record-Union*, October 11, 1890, 1.

34. "White House Cranks," *Hartford Weekly Times*, October 19, 1893, 10.

35. Seale, *President's House*, 1:579.

36. "Toiler for the Nation," *Boston Evening Transcript*, September 13, 1890, 10.

37. *Aurora Daily Express*, March 1, 1895, 1.

38. "Silly Precautions," *Sacramento Daily Record-Union*, April 28, 1891, 2.

39. "A Threat Against Ex-President Harrison," *Glasgow Herald*, July 6, 1894, 7.

40. "Suppress Anarchy," *Chatham Republican*, May 14, 1889, 1.

41. "A White House Guard," *Kentucky New Era*, January 9, 1892, 3.

42. "Capital City Chimes," *Robinson Constitution*, March 18, 1891, 1.

43. *Semi-Weekly Interior Journal*, August 13, 1889, 2.

44. *Pennsylvania Evening Herald*, September 21, 1892, 4.

45. "Rich Develops a Fool," *Rock Island (IL) Daily Argus*, November 18, 1890, 2

46. Gary Larreategu, "The President's Life Is in Peril," *Statesman*, October–December 2004, http://indianatalks.com/site/2014/10/the-presidents-life-in-peril/.

47. "Where the Crank Abounds," *Omaha Daily Bee*, February 15, 1896, 10.

48. "The Latest Sensation—An Attempt to Assassinate Harrison," *Los Angeles Daily Herald*, December 21, 1888, 1.

49. "A Startling Rumor," *Mexico Weekly Ledger*, December 27, 1888, 1.

50. "A Second Guiteau—How An Attempt to Assassinate Harrison Failed—The Crank Went to Washington and Was Ready to Shoot When Arrested," *Pittsburgh Press*, November 16, 1890, 1.

51. "A Follower of Guiteau," *Democratic North-West*, November 27, 1890, 6.

52. "Varied Work of the Secret Service," *The New London (CT) Day*, March 2, 1909, 11.

53. "Chief Bell of the Secret Service and His Counterpart, Buffalo Bill," *Pittsburgh Dispatch*, June 5, 1890, 4.

54. "After a Webster Head," *Bismarck Weekly Tribune*, October 25, 1889, 3.

55. "Coniackers Caught—Ex-Chief Bell Tells the Story of the Capture of the Driggs Family," *Pittsburgh Dispatch*, December 28, 1890, 10.

56. "A Second Guiteau—How An Attempt to Assassinate Harrison Failed—The Crank Went to Washington and Was Ready to Shoot When Arrested," *Pittsburgh Press*, November 16, 1890, 1.

57. "A Would-Be Guiteau—The Story of an Attempt to Kill President Harrison Last May," *Weekly Press*, November 19, 1890, 2, and "The President's Narrow Escape," *New York Times*, November 16, 1890, 2.

58. "The President's Narrow Escape," *New York Times*, November 16, 1890, 2.

59. "A Follower of Guiteau," *Democratic North-West*, November 27, 1890, 6.

60. "A Would-Be Guiteau—The Story of an Attempt to Kill President Harrison Last May," *Weekly Press*, November 19, 1890, 2.

61. "The New Private Secretary," *Washington Evening Star*, March 4, 1889, 6.

62. Email to the author, December 18, 2014. See the Lilly Library, Volwiler mss, 1898–1958, http://webapp1.dlib.indiana.edu/findingaids/view?brand=general&docId=InU-Li-VAB8654&doc.view=print.

63. "Mr. Bell's Story Doubted," *New York Times*, November 17, 1890, 1.

64. "Real Imperialism at Home," *Spokane Spokesman Review*, December 10, 1901, 1.

65. "Mr. Bell's Story Doubted," *New York Times*, November 17, 1890, 1.

66. *Pittsburgh Dispatch*, July 17, 1889, 1

67. "Chief Bell," *Washington Critic*, April 14, 1890, 2.

68. "The Topical Talker," *Pittsburgh Dispatch*, June 5, 1890, 4.

69. "Uncle Sam's Sleuth," *St. Paul Globe*, December 19, 1888, 4.

70. Bowen and Neal, *United States Secret Service*, 179.

71. John S. Bell, "The Secret Service," *Pittsburgh Dispatch*, December 21, 1890, 4.

72. John S. Bell, "The Secret Service," *Pittsburgh Dispatch*, December 21, 1890, 4.

73. Bowen and Neal, *United States Secret Service*, 183.

74. "Chief Bell's Resignation," *Washington Critic*, April 24, 1890, 1.

75. "A Pair of Guesses," *Fort Worth Daily Gazette*, June 5, 1890, 1.

76. John S. Bell's Secret Service papers are missing from the National Archives. The repository holds only Bell's reports for June 22, 1885, to February 15, 1888 in "Daily Reports of U.S. Secret Service Agents, 1875–1936," https:// eservices.archives.gov/orderonline/start.swe?SWECmd=Login&SWEPL=1 &SRN=kmmRFPnpzZZgHMVa6tThKcoaDAsAoehU540EnwiaH5Eb&SWETS =1409309810584; Jennifer E. Capps, Vice President of Curatorship and Exhibition at the Benjamin Harrison Presidential Site informed the author that there are no references to the assassination story in the presidential site's resources. Email to the author, October 10, 2014; Agent O'Dwyer, who arrested Harrison's would-be assassin, is not mentioned in the list of agents in the National Archives' "Daily Reports of U.S. Secret Service Agents, 1875– 1936." However, O'Dwyer's role as a Secret Service agent is corroborated here: http://chroniclingamerica.loc.gov/lccn/sn84024546/1890–12–28 /ed-1/seq-10/#date1=1836&index=1&rows=20&words=Bell+Chief+JohnS +Secret+Service&searchType=basic&sequence=0&state=&date2=1922&prox text=Secret+Service+Chief+John+S.+Bell&y=14&x=7&dateFilterType=year Range&page=1. There is no doubt he was a Secret Service agent, as Bell confirms. Additionally, O'Dwyer is mentioned in a letter by William F. Cody. The agent was hired for an unspecified job by the Wild West showman at the behest of Bell (see Cody's letter in Blackstone, *The Business of Being Buffalo Bill*, 9).

77. Algeo, *President Is a Sick Man*, 53.

8. PLOTS TO KILL CLEVELAND

1. "The Crop of Cranks," *Lewiston Daily Sun*, November 6, 1893, 4.

2. "Cleveland's Habits," *Bridgeport Morning News*, January 1, 1887, 1.

3. Whitcomb and Whitcomb, *Real Life at the White House*, 194.

4. "Cleveland's Habits," *Bridgeport Morning News*, January 1, 1887.

5. "Capital Gossip—The Mecca for Cranks and How They Are Watched," *Bridgeport Morning News*, April 13, 1886, 1.

6. "Washington Cranks," *Middlebury Register*, August 27, 1886, 5.

7. "Capital Gossip—The Mecca for Cranks and How They Are Watched," *Bridgeport Morning News*, April 13, 1886, 1.

8. "Cleveland's Habits," *Bridgeport Morning News*, January 1, 1887, 1.

9. "Cleveland Fears Not Assassination," *St. Paul Globe*, May 8, 1885, 1.

10. "Guarding Mr. Cleveland," *New York Times*, March 3, 1885, 1.

11. "Off for the White House," *New York Times*, March 3, 1885, 2.

12. "Off for the White House," *New York Times*, March 3, 1885, 2.

13. *Deseret News*, August 12, 1885, 2.

14. "Gunning for a President," *San Francisco Call*, July 4, 1887, 1.

15. "Cleveland's Nemesis," *Sacramento Daily Record-Union*, February 3, 1888, 2.

16. "Probably a Crank," *New York Times*, July 23, 1886, 4.

17. "Only a Crank—Attempt upon the President's Life," *Louisville (KY) Courier-Journal*, November 22, 1886, 2.

18. "Only a Crank—Attempt upon the President's Life," *Louisville (KY) Courier-Journal*, November 22, 1886, 2.

19. "Methods Employed to Guard the President," *Meriden (CT) Morning Record*, August 8, 1898, 6.

20. "An Insane Skulker," *Pittsburgh Dispatch*, January 16, 1891, 1.

21. "Guarding the Presidents," *Sacramento Daily Record-Union*, March 14, 1893, 6.

22. "Guarding the Presidents," *Sacramento Daily Record-Union*, March 14, 1893, 6.

23. "Guarding the Presidents," *Sacramento Daily Record-Union*, March 14, 1893, 6.

24. Pendel, *Thirty-Six Years in the White House*, 151.

25. "Methods Employed to Guard the President, *Meriden (CT) Morning Record*, August 8, 1898, 6.

26. Bowen and Neal, *United States Secret Service*, 183.

27. Pendel, *Thirty-Six Years in the White House*, 151.

28. J. Hoffman, "Psychotic Visitors to Government Offices in the National Capital."

29. "Protection for President," *Boston Evening Transcript*, October 6, 1903, 2.

30. Frank G. Carpenter, "White House Watch-Dog," *Deseret Weekly*, December 16, 1893, 819.

31. "Homicidal Mania in America," *Sydney Morning Herald*, November 3, 1893, 5.

32. "Afraid of Cranks," *San Francisco Call*, November 23, 1895, 2.

33. "Cleveland's Bodyguard—One More Evidence of the Monarchical Tendency," *San Francisco Morning Call*, November 15, 1893, 1.

34. "A Mysterious Crank," *Ohio Democrat*, November 25, 1893, 4.

35. Walter Wellman, "An Excess of Caution," *Copper County Evening News*, February 4, 1894, 1.

36. "Needless Caution," *Wichita Daily Eagle*, November 22, 1894, 8.

37. Walter Wellman, "An Excess of Caution," *Copper County Evening News*, February 4, 1894, 1.

38. "The President's Safety," *Wheeling (WV) Daily Intelligencer*, 6 January 1894, 4.

39. "White House Cranks—Lunatics against Whom President Is Guarded," *Hartford Weekly Times*, October 19, 1893, 10.

40. Frank G. Carpenter, "White House Watch-Dog," *Deseret Weekly*, December 16, 1893, 819.

41. "Crank Calls at White House—Wished to Shoot Cleveland and Seize the President's Chair," *Lewiston Daily Sun*, September 29, 1893, 1.

42. "White House Watch-Dog," *Deseret Weekly*, December 16, 1893, 819.

43. "Maine Protests," *Lewiston Evening Journal*, January 10, 1894, 1.

44. "White House Cranks," *Washington Evening Standard*, October 14, 1893, 12.

45. "White House Cranks—Lunatics against Whom President Is Guarded," *Hartford Weekly Times*, October 19, 1893, 10.

46. "White House Cranks—Lunatics against Whom President Is Guarded," *Hartford Weekly Times*, October 19, 1893, 10.

47. "Danger for Presidents," *Boston Evening Transcript*, September 10, 1901, 7.

48. "Danger for Presidents," *Boston Evening Transcript*, September 10, 1901, 7.

49. "Watching a Suspect," *Wichita Daily Eagle*, September 14, 1901, 2.

50. "Danger for Presidents," *Boston Evening Transcript*, September 10, 1901, 7.

51. "White House Cranks—Lunatics against Whom President Is Guarded," *Hartford Weekly Times*, October 19, 1893, 10.

52. "To Convert Cleveland," *Milwaukee Journal*, June 8, 1894, 6.

53. "Washington Cranks," *Middlebury Register*, August 27, 1886, 2.

54. "Guard for Roosevelt," *New York Times*, October 16, 1912, 4.

55. Frank G. Carpenter, "White House Watch-Dog," *Deseret Weekly*, December 16, 1893, 819.

56. Frank G. Carpenter, "White House Watch-Dog," *Deseret Weekly*, December 16, 1893, 819.

57. "Mr. Rounder on Cranks," *Anaconda Standard*, October 30, 1893, 4.

58. "Harrison's Assassin," *Sacramento Daily Record-Union*, October 31, 1893, 1.

59. "An Armed Crank," *San Francisco Call*, November 23, 1893, 8.

60. "Humored a Crazy Veteran," *Rock Island (IL) Argus*, June 25, 1895, 2.

61. "Grover in Danger," *Yellowstone Journal*, November 6, 1893, 1.

62. "More Cranks Locked Up," *Washington Evening Star*, November 17, 1893, 1.

63. "Gooding Declared Insane," *San Francisco Call*, April 2, 1895, 2.

64. "A Startling Revelation," *Laurens Advertiser*, October 3, 1893, 1.

65. "A Startling Revelation," *Laurens Advertiser*, October 3, 1893, 1.

66. "The Crop of Cranks," *Lewiston Daily Sun*, November 6, 1893, 4.

67. "The President a Brave Man," *Deseret Weekly*, December 16, 1893, 820.

68. "A Startling Revelation," *Laurens Advertiser*, October 3, 1893, 1.

69. There are no records of the assassination attempt in presidential biographies or in records in the Grover Cleveland Presidential Library.

70. "No Time for Fun," *Washington Evening Star*, November 18, 1893, 1.

71. Frank G. Carpenter, "White House Watch-Dog," *Deseret Weekly*, December 16, 1893, 819.

72. "Mr. Thurber's Public Service, *Washington Evening Times*, March 12, 1897, 4.

73. "No Cranks Need Apply—They Are Not Allowed to Approach the President," *Aurora Daily Express*, March 1, 1895, 3.

74. Marvin Miller, *American Dream*, 448.

75. *Report of the U.S. President's Commission on the Assassination of President John F. Kennedy*, commonly referred to as the Warren Commission Report. See appendix 7, "A Brief History of Presidential Protection," 509.
76. "White House—Secret Service and Military Aides," Old and Sold.com, http://www.oldandsold.com/articles3ln/white-house-history-14.shtml.
77. "Narrow Escape for Cleveland," *Bismarck Weekly Tribune*, March 2, 1894, 1.
78. "Attempted Assassination," *Hopkinsville Kentuckian*, October 26, 1894, 2.
79. *Hopkinsville Kentuckian*, October 30, 1894, 2.
80. "An Exaggerated Rumor," *Daily Kentucky Era*, October 26, 1894, 1.
81. "A Crank's Call," *Clinton (IA) Sunday Morning Age*, October 26, 1894, 1.
82. "Afraid of Cranks," *San Francisco Call*, November 23, 1895, 2.
83. "No Cranks Need Apply—They Are Not Allowed to Approach the President," *Aurora Daily Express*, March 1, 1895, 3.
84. "Afraid of Cranks," *San Francisco Call*, November 23, 1895, 2.
85. "Protection for President," *Boston Evening Transcript*, October 6, 1903, 2.
86. Bumgarner, *Federal Agents*, 46.
87. "Where the Crank Abounds," *Omaha Daily Bee*, February 15, 1896, 10.
88. Bumgarner, *Federal Agents*, 44–45.
89. Melanson, *Secret Service*, 26.

9. THE ANARCHISTS AND MCKINLEY
1. R. Ellis, *Presidential Travel*, 111.
2. McCann, *Terrorism on American Soil*, 26.
3. "Guardians of the President's Safety," *Washington Evening Times*, February 25, 1899, 6.
4. Whitcomb and Whitcomb, *Real Life at the White House*, 217.
5. "The President's Danger," *Valentine Democrat*, May 13, 1897, 6.
6. "Averse to Bodyguard," *Honolulu Republican*, September 18, 1901, 8.
7. Morgan, *William McKinley and His America*, 313.
8. S. Miller, *President and the Assassin*, 293.
9. "Guarded by Detectives," *Arizona Republican*, February 20, 1899, 7.
10. Frank G. Carpenter, "Gossip about the President," *Deseret News*, December 7, 1897, 8.
11. "Guarded by Detectives," *Arizona Republican*, February 20, 1899, 7.
12. "President's Guard—Means of Protection against Assassins," *Crawfordsville (IN) Daily News-Review*, December 5, 1900, 2.
13. "After McKinley—Man with a Gun Arrested at Door of the White House," *Milwaukee Journal*, September 21, 1897, 1.
14. "After McKinley—Man with a Gun Arrested at Door of the White House," *Milwaukee Journal*, September 21, 1897, 1.
15. Seale, *President's House*, 1:630.

16. "Methods Employed to Guard the President," *Meriden (CT) Morning Record*, August 8, 1898, 6.

17. Seale, *President's House*, 1:630.

18. See the section entitled "Protection of the White House Complex and the President in the Nineteenth Century," from chapter 4 ("The Evolution of Presidential Security) in Federation of American Scientists, *Public Report of the White House Security Review*, http://fas.org/irp/agency/ustreas/usss/tl pubrpt.html.

19. Seale, *President's House*, 1:630.

20. "President's Guard—Means of Protection against Assassins," *Crawfordsville (IN) Daily News-Review*, December 5, 1900, 2.

21. "Guarded by Detectives," *Arizona Republican*, February 20, 1899, 7.

22. "Guarding Life of McKinley," *Stark County Democrat* (Canton OH), August 21, 1900, 8.

23. "God Bless Our President," *Deseret News*, September 7, 1901, 1.

24. "Every Moment Spent Seeking Assassins," *Pittsburgh Press*, September 8, 1901, 24.

25. Whitcomb and Whitcomb, *Real Life at the White House*, 213.

26. "Guarded by Detectives," *Arizona Republican*, February 20, 1899, 7.

27. Newton, *Age of the Assassins*, 300.

28. Seale, *President's House*, 1:630.

29. "Many Cranks Turned Down," *Pittsburgh Press*, September 8, 1901, 4

30. S. Miller, *President and the Assassin*, 5.

31. "Many Cranks Turned Down," *Pittsburgh Press*, September 8, 1901, 4

32. "President's Guard—Means of Protection against Assassins," *Crawfordsville (IN) Daily News-Review*, December 5, 1900, 2.

33. "President's Guard," *Clinton (IA) Sunday Morning Age*, September 9, 1900, 3.

34. Whitcomb and Whitcomb, *Real Life at the White House*, 217.

35. S. Miller, *President and the Assassin*, 247.

36. S. Miller, *President and the Assassin*, 109.

37. S. Miller, *President and the Assassin*, 77.

38. S. Miller, *President and the Assassin*, 108.

39. S. Miller, *President and the Assassin*, 246.

40. S. Miller, *President and the Assassin*, 263.

41. S. Miller, *President and the Assassin*, 264.

42. *Report of the U.S. President's Commission on the Assassination of President John F. Kennedy*, commonly referred to as the Warren Commission Report. See appendix 7, "A Brief History of Presidential Protection," 509

43. "Guarding Life of McKinley," *Stark County Democrat* (Canton OH), August 21, 1900, 8.

44. "Anarchists Arrested," *Lewiston Daily Sun*, August 20, 1900, 1.

45. "Plot to Kill President in California," *San Jose (CA) Evening News*, September 10, 1901, 1.
46. "Threatens President's Life," *Washington DC Evening Star*, March 9, 1899, 2.
47. "Plotted to Kill the President," *San Francisco Call*, March 14, 1899, 8.
48. "Threatens Edison; in Cell," *New York Times*, October 26, 1912, 1.
49. S. Miller, *President and the Assassin*, 77.
50. Newton, *Age of the Assassins*, 308.
51. S. Miller, *President and the Assassin*, 288.
52. "President's Guard," *Clinton (IA) Sunday Morning Age*, December 9, 1900, 3.
53. "Petrosino a Terror to Criminal Bands," *New York Times*, March 14, 1909, 1.
54. "Not Held as an Anarchist," *New York Times*, August 19, 1900, 1.
55. Whitcomb and Whitcomb, *Real Life at the White House*, 217.
56. S. Miller, *President and the Assassin*, 299.
57. "God Bless Our President," *Deseret News*, September 7, 1901, 1.
58. Whitcomb and Whitcomb, *Real Life at the White House*, 217.
59. "God Bless Our President," *Deseret News*, September 7, 1901, 1.
60. "God Bless Our President," *Deseret News*, September 7, 1901, 1.
61. "God Bless Our President," *Deseret News*, September 7, 1901, 1.
62. McCann, *Terrorism on American Soil*, 26.
63. S. Miller, *President and the Assassin*, 323.
64. "Frequently Asked Questions about Dead Presidents: How Did Each President Die?" Python.net, http://starship.python.net/crew/manus/Presidents/faq/causes.html.
65. "Averse to Bodyguard," *Honolulu Republican*, September 18, 1901, 8.
66. Grant Calder, "Protecting the President: My Bodyguard I Desire to Be the People," *Huffington Post*, September 4, 2012.
67. Jefferson Decker, "Anarchy in the USA," *In These Times*, November 24, 2003.
68. "More Care in Future," *New York Times*, September 7, 1901, 1.
69. "Bullets Not Poisoned," *Carroll City (IA) Herald*, September 25, 1901, 1.
70. S. Miller, *President and the Assassin*, 326.
71. S. Miller, *President and the Assassin*, 329.
72. Newton, *Age of the Assassins*, 308.

10. ASSASSINATION ATTEMPTS AGAINST ROOSEVELT

1. "Mad Man and the President—Intended to Kill Mr. Roosevelt," *New Zealand Herald*, October 17, 1903, 2.
2. See the section entitled "Protection of the White House Complex and the President in the Nineteenth Century," from chapter 4 ("The Evolution of Presidential Security") in Federation of American Scientists, *Public Report of the White House Security Review*, http://fas.org/irp/agency/ustreas/usss/tlpubrpt.html.

3. "Protection for the President," *Boston Evening Transcript*, October 6, 1903, 11

4. R. Ellis, *Presidential Travel*, 113.

5. "Real Imperialism at Home," *Spokane Spokesman Review*, December 10, 1901, 4.

6. "Protection for the President," *Boston Evening Transcript*, October 6, 1903, 11.

7. "Protection for the President," *Boston Evening Transcript*, October 6, 1903, 11.

8. "Protection for the President," *Boston Evening Transcript*, October 6, 1903, 11.

9. "Guard for Roosevelt," *New York Times*, October 16, 1912, 1.

10. "President Hard to Keep Guarded," *Gettysburg Times*, July 12, 1926, 2.

11. "Miracle That Roosevelt Had Not Been Shot Before," *Spokane Spokesman Review*, October 16, 1912, 3.

12. Whitcomb and Whitcomb, *Real Life at the White House*, 231.

13. "Miracle That Roosevelt Had Not Been Shot Before," *Spokane Spokesman Review*, October 16, 1912, 3.

14. "Theodore Roosevelt: Assassination Attempt," of 1912, Dr. Zebra, http://www.doctorzebra.com/prez/z_x26a_g.htm.

15. Whitcomb and Whitcomb, *Real Life at the White House*, 231.

16. R. Ellis, *Presidential Travel*, 122.

17. Redmond and Lodge, *Roosevelt*, 223–24.

18. Redmond and Lodge, *Roosevelt*, 223–24.

19. Redmond and Lodge, *Roosevelt*, 223–24.

20. "Guard for Roosevelt," *New York Times*, October 16, 1912, 1.

21. "Crank Visitors at the White House," *Minneapolis Journal*, June 3, 1904, 7.

22. Crook, *Memories of the White House*, 283.

23. Morris, *Rise of Theodore Roosevelt*, 122.

24. Seale, *President's House*, 1:696.

25. Crook, *Memories of the White House*, 283.

26. Whitcomb and Whitcomb, *Real Life at the White House*, 231.

27. Seale, *President's House*, 2:728.

28. Morris, *Rise of Theodore Roosevelt*, 123.

29. Morris, *Rise of Theodore Roosevelt*, 123.

30. Arthur W. Dunn, "Guard President from All Cranks," *Washington Evening News*, July 22, 1915, 6.

31. "The Colonel's Many Escapes," *Boston Evening Transcript*, October 15, 1912, 2.

32. "The Colonel's Many Escapes," *Boston Evening Transcript*, October 15, 1912, 2.

33. Whitcomb and Whitcomb, *Real Life at the White House*, 227.

34. "The Colonel's Many Escapes," *Boston Evening Transcript*, October 15, 1912, 2

35. Morris, *Rise of Theodore Roosevelt*, 142.

36. Whitcomb and Whitcomb, *Real Life at the White House*, 228.

37. "Jimmie of the Secret Service Due to Retire," *Sarasota Herald Tribune*, June 22, 1945, 2.

38. Whitcomb and Whitcomb, *Real Life at the White House*, 231.

39. "Under Watchful Eyes," *Washington Evening Star*, February 21, 1903, 28.

40. "Two Cranks Arrested at White House," *San Francisco Call*, December 3, 1903, 6.

41. "Crank Visitors at the White House," *Minneapolis Journal*, June 3, 1904, 7.

42. "Roosevelt Source of Worry to Police," *Reading Eagle*, October 16, 1912, 17.

43. "During Roosevelt's 8 Years in Office 87 People Were Arrested at the White House," *Walla Walla (WA) Evening Statesman*, May 7, 1909, 6.

44. "Bothered by Many Cranks," *New York Times*, September 8, 1908, 1.

45. "Jimmie of the Secret Service Due to Retire," *Sarasota Herald Tribune*, June 22, 1945, 2.

46. Tully, *Treasury Agent*, 352.

47. "Bothered by Many Cranks," *New York Times*, September 8, 1908, 1.

48. Seale, *President's House*, 2:736.

49. "Bothered by Many Cranks," *New York Times*, September 8, 1908, 1.

50. "Rakowski the Anarchist Will Arrive Today," *San Francisco Call*, January 27, 1902, 7.

51. "Guard for Roosevelt," *New York Times*, October 16, 1912, 1.

52. "Man Arrested for Threatening President Roosevelt," *Saint Paul Globe*, September 28, 1904, 5.

53. "The Colonel's Many Escapes," *Boston Evening Transcript*, October 15, 1912, 2.

54. "Bothered by Many Cranks," *New York Times*, September 8, 1908, 1.

55. *Washington DC Columbia Carrier*, May 29, 1903, 2

56. "Armed Crank at Oyster Bay, *Fredericksburg (VA) Free Lance–Star*, September 10, 1908, 1.

57. "The Secret Service Report," *New York Times*, September 8, 1908, 1, and "Guard for Roosevelt, *New York Times*, October 16, 1912, 1.

58. "Dangerous White House Crank," *New York Sun*, December 25, 1903, 1.

59. "Crazy Man Is Still after the President," *Albuquerque Citizen*, November 8, 1906, 1.

60. "Miracle That Roosevelt Had Not Been Shot Before," *Spokane Spokesman Review*, October 16, 1912, 3.

61. "Plot to Kill President," *Bemidji (MN) Daily Pioneer*, June 5, 1903, 1.

62. "Plot to Kill Roosevelt," *Hartford (KY) Republican*, June 29, 1906, 2.

63. Whitcomb and Whitcomb, *Real Life at the White House*, 231.

64. "Plot to Assassinate Roosevelt Revealed by Anarchist's Arrest," *Montgomery Tribune*, October 2, 1908, 2.

65. "More Guards for the President," *Utica Herald*, September 3, 1903, 1.

66. "Larger Guard for Roosevelt," *New York Evening World*, September 3, 1903, 1.

67. "Larger Guard for Roosevelt," *New York Evening World*, September 3, 1903, 1.

68. "Larger Guard for Roosevelt," *New York Evening World*, September 3, 1903, 1.

69. "Latest News," *Maysville (KY) Daily Public Ledger*, September 1903, 1.

70. "More Guards for the President," *Utica Herald*, September 3, 1903, 1, and "More Guards for President—New Light on Matter—Executive's Peril from Weilbrenner's Pistol Greater Than at First Reported," *Utica Herald—Dispatch*, September 3, 1903, 1.

71. "Elliott Is in Insane Asylum," *Minneapolis Journal*, October 6, 1903, 2.

72. "Armed Insane Man at White House," *Deseret News*, October 5, 1903, 1.

73. "During Roosevelt's 8 Years in Office 87 People Were Arrested at the White House," *Walla Walla (WA) Evening Statesman*, May 7, 1909, 6.

74. "Strange Types That Make White House Their Mecca," *New York Times*, September 19, 1909, 1.

75. "President in Peril," *Toledo Blade*, October 8, 1903, 5.

76. "White House Cranks," *Toledo Blade*, October 15, 1903, 8.

77. "Elliott Is in Insane Asylum," *Minneapolis Journal*, October 6, 1903, 2.

78. "Lunatic Suicides," *St. John (New Brunswick) Daily Sun*, May 24, 1904, 3.

79. "Long Trailed Roosevelt," *Boston Evening Transcript*, October 15, 1912, 3.

80. "Theodore Roosevelt and the Assassin's Bullet," *Milwaukee Journal*, May 19, 1972, 22.

81. "Theodore Roosevelt and the Assassin's Bullet," *Milwaukee Journal*, May 19, 1972, 22.

11. TARGETING TAFT

1. Smith and Morris, *Dear Mr. President*, 6.

2. "Taft in Orient," *The New London (CT) Day*, October 7, 1907, 4.

3. Bromley, *William Howard Taft and the First Motoring President*, 183.

4. "Attempt Made to Assassinate Taft," *Hawaii Evening Bulletin*, July 29, 1908, 1.

5. "News of the Week," *Kentucky Citizen*, May 5, 1910, 1.

6. "Taft Escapes Shot Fired by Boatman," *San Francisco Call*, July 30, 1908, 1.

7. "Taft the Target," *Milwaukee Journal*, November 13, 1946, 2.

8. "President Hard to Keep Guarded," *Gettysburg Times*, July 12, 1926, 2.

9. "Secret Service Guard President Day and Night," *St. Petersburg Evening Independent*, March 2, 1925, 2.

10. Whitcomb and Whitcomb, *Real Life at the White House*, 245.

11. R. Ellis, *Presidential Travel*, 122.

12. "Guarding the President-Elect," *Pittsburgh Gazette Times*, January 5, 1913, 6.

13. "Story of Plot to Kill President Taft Denied," *Boston Evening Transcript*, July 18, 1912, 1.

14. "Guarding President Taft," *The Daily Star*, May 31, 1909, 2.

15. Seale, *President's House*, 2:749.

16. Garrison, *Treasury of White House Tales*, 204.

17. "President Closely Guarded during Brief Visit Here," *Pittsburgh Press*, October 24, 1914, 2.

18. "Guarding President Carefully Since Shooting of Gaynor," *Pittsburgh Press*, August 11, 1910, 4.

19. Bromley, *William Howard Taft and the First Motoring President*, 183.

20. "Crank Visitors to White House, *Walla Walla (WA) Evening Statesman*, May 7, 1909, 6.

21. "Cranks Who See the President—Strange Types That Make White House Their Mecca," *New York Times*, September 19, 1909, 1.

22. "Crank Tries to Force Way to President," *Pittsburgh Press*, April 13, 1912, 1.

23. "Crank after Taft—Armed Man with a Grievance Arrested at White House," *Fredericksburg (VA) Free Lance–Star*, June 18, 1910, 2.

24. "Is Jailed for Threat to Kill President Taft, *Meriden (CT) Morning Record*, October 25, 1911, 1.

25. "Wad of Wet Paper Thrown at Taft," *Providence Evening Tribune*, May 29, 1912, 1.

26. "Plot Laid to Kill Taft?" *Tacoma Times*, July 8, 1909, 1.

27. "Man Carrying Camera and Revolver Tries to Get Close to Taft," *Seattle Star*, October 2, 1909, 1.

28. "News of the Week," *Kentucky Citizen*, May 5, 1910, 1.

29. "Bold Anarchists May Be Deported," *Spokane Daily Chronicle*, October 11, 1909, 16.

30. "I Want to Kill Taft," *Youngstown Vindicator*, October 15, 1909, 1.

31. "Woman Attempts to Assassinate Taft with Knife," *Tacoma Times*, August 29, 1912, 1; "Woman Tries to Attack President," *Milwaukee Sentinel*, August 29, 1912, 1; and "Taft Has Busy Day in Columbus," *Pittsburg Gazette Times*, August 30, 1912, 6.

32. "Plot to Kill Taft," *Richmond (VA) Times Dispatch*, September 8, 1908, 2.

33. "Queer Man Tells of Alleged Plot to Kill President," *Miami Metropolis News*, October 10, 1910, 7.

34. "Aunt Delia's Visitor Was Harmless," *Providence Evening Tribune*, October 10, 1910, 3.

35. "Plot to Kill Taft Revealed at Trial," *New York Evening World*, December 2, 1919, 3.

36. "Tells of Plot to Assassinate Taft," *Cambridge (OH) Guernsey Times*, March 7, 1911, 1.

37. "Plot to Murder President Taft?" *Montreal Gazette*, September 28, 1912, 1.

38. "Plot to Kill Taft Told by Prisoner," *Washington Times*, May 26, 1912, 10.

39. Reppetto, *American Police*.

40. "Alleges Anarchist Plot," *San Francisco Call*, October 16, 1909, 1.

41. "Arrest Youth with Queer Gun," *Middletown (OH) Daily News-Signal*, October 18, 1909, 1.

42. "Guarding President Carefully Since Shooting of Gaynor," *Pittsburgh Press*, August 11, 1910, 4.

43. "Crank Stopped at Beverley—Wanted to See President, He Said, on Pension Matter," *Beaver (PA) Daily Times*, August 17, 1910, 8.

44. "Arrest Caller at Taft Cottage," *Chicago Tribune*, July 31, 1910, 5.

45. "Dynamite Mines Menaced Taft," *New York Times*, October 17, 1911, 1.

46. "Dynamite Plot against Taft Worries Officials," *Meriden (CT) Daily Journal*, October 17, 1911, 2.

47. "Reports to President on Dynamite Probe," *Milwaukee Journal*, 9ecember 9, 1911, 2.

48. "Plot to Kill President Is Believed Revealed," *Yellowstone News*, May 5, 1917, 1.

12. THE STALKING OF WILSON

1. Klein, *Blood Feud*, 167.

2. Starling, *Starling of the White House*, 34.

3. Starling, *Starling of the White House*, 34.

4. "President Closely Guarded during Brief Visit Here," *Pittsburgh Press*, October 24, 1914, 2.

5. Starling, *Starling of the White House*, 31.

6. Starling, *Starling of the White House*, 32.

7. "Guarding the President-Elect, *Pittsburgh Gazette Times*, January 5, 1913, 6.

8. "Young Secret Service Men Guard the President," *Clinton (IA) Mirror*, March 17, 1917, 6.

9. "Wilson Can Not Keep Door Open," *Troy Northern Budget*, November 24, 1912, 1.

10. "Wilson Can Not Keep Door Open," *Troy Northern Budget*, November 24, 1912, 1.

11. Starling, *Starling of the White House*, 33.

12. Seale, *President's House*, 2:802.

13. Whitcomb and Whitcomb, *Real Life at the White House*, 256.

14. E. F. Dorsey, "President Has Much Pleasure Eluding Guards," *Pittsburgh Post-Gazette*, August 7, 1915, 10.

15. Seale, *President's House*, 2:802.

16. Starling, *Starling of the White House*, 40.

17. Bowen and Neal, *United States Secret Service*, 159.

18. "Secret Service Men for Wilson," *Lewiston Evening Journal*, November 7, 1912, 10.

19. "Wilson Can Not Keep Door Open," *Troy Northern Budget*, November 24, 1912, 1.

20. "President Hard to Keep Guarded," *Gettysburg Times*, July 12, 1926, 2.

21. Whitcomb and Whitcomb, *Real Life at the White House*, 259.

22. E. F. Dorsey, "Secret Service Men Dog Steps of President," *Ludington Daily News*, August 10, 1915, 5.

23. "Woodrow Wilson Visited Peninsula Twice," *Daily Press*, June 28, 1992, http://articles.dailypress.com/1992-06-28/news/9206260181_1_grayson-s-sunday-school-james-monroe-president-woodrow-wilson.

24. Kirke Simpson, "Efficient Guard over President," *Norwalk Hour*, December 16, 1932, 19.

25. "Young Secret Service Men Guard the President," *Clinton (IA) Mirror*, March 17, 1917, 6.

26. E. F. Dorsey, "President Has Much Pleasure Eluding Guards," *Pittsburgh Post-Gazette*, August 7, 1915, 10.

27. Starling, *Starling of the White House*, 50.

28. "Fearless Sleuths Guard President," *Milwaukee Sentinel*, July 7, 1915, 10.

29. "Cranks Flock to Capital from All Parts of Country," *Washington Sunday Star*, July 11, 1915, pt. 4, 5.

30. "Cranks Flock to Capital from All Parts of Country," *Washington Sunday Star*, July 11, 1915, pt. 4, 5.

31. "Threatened President; Must Serve 13 Years," *Washington Times*, April 21, 1918, 3.

32. Alexander, *Place of Recourse*, 99.

33. "Lad Threatens Wilson and Lands in Lock-Up," *Pittsburgh Gazette Times*, December 13, 1912, 1.

34. "Demanded $5,000 from Gov. Wilson," *The New London (CT) Day*, December 11, 1912, 1.

35. *Spokane Daily Chronicle*, May 21, 1913, 1.

36. "Threatening President Wilson," *Hawera and Normanby Star*, June 9, 1913, 7.

37. "Chicago Man Sends Threatening Letters," *Reading Eagle*, May 24, 1913, 1.

38. "Austrian Threatens Wilson," *Marion (IL) Daily Republican*, July 2, 1915, 1.

39. "Plot to Slay the President," *Marion (IL) Daily Republican*, August 3, 1915, 3.

40. "Cranks Flock to Capital from All Parts of Country," *Washington Sunday Star*, July 11, 1915, pt. 4, 5.

41. "Threatens to Kill Wilson," *Seattle Star*, September 20, 1916, 1.

42. "Wilson Annoyer Escapes," *New York Times*, October 28, 1916, 1.

43. "Planned to Kill Woodrow Wilson," *Lewiston Saturday Journal*, November 23, 1912, 1.

44. "Crank Is Arrested—Jumped Running Board, Wilson Auto," *Meriden (CT) Morning Record*, October 21, 1916, 1.

45. "Intended to Kill President, Says Crank at Boston, to Save World," *Pittsburgh Press*, February 25, 1919, 1.

46. "Had Plan to Kill Wilson," *New York Times*, May 1, 1917, 1.

47. Whitcomb and Whitcomb, *Real Life at the White House*, 259.

48. "Wilson Threatened: Suspect Arrested," *Pittsburgh Times*, August 5, 1915, 9.

49. Starling, *Starling of the White House*, 83.

50. Andrew, *For the President's Eyes*, 31.

51. Seale, *President's House*, 2:806.

52. "Guardian of President Reflects on 24 Years," *St. Petersburg Times*, November 12, 1968, 6.

53. Seale, *President's House*, 2:822.

54. Seale, *President's House*, 2:815.

55. "Guard the President As Never Before," *Milwaukee Journal*, February 21, 1918, 12.

56. Starling, *Starling of the White House*, 121.

57. Seale, *President's House*, 2:815.

58. Seale, *President's House*, 2:813.

59. "Guard the President As Never Before," *Milwaukee Journal*, February 21, 1918, 12.

60. Whitcomb and Whitcomb, *Real Life at the White House*, 258.

61. Whitcomb and Whitcomb, *Real Life at the White House*, 260.

62. Seale, *President's House*, 2:815.

63. *Report of the U.S. President's Commission on the Assassination of President John F. Kennedy*, commonly referred to as the Warren Commission Report. See appendix 7, "A Brief History of Presidential Protection," 512.

64. "Plot to Poison Wilson Disclosed by Yardley," *Milwaukee Journal*, June 1, 1931, 3.

65. "Plot to Poison Wilson Disclosed by Yardley," *Milwaukee Journal*, June 1, 1931, 3.

66. "Marked for Death in Wilson Plot," *New York Times*, February 28, 1925, 1.

67. "Book Reveals Plot against War Head," *Palm Beach Daily News*, February 28, 1925, 2; "Secret Service Men Guard the President Day and Night," *St. Petersburg Evening Independent*, March 2, 1925, 2.

68. Pacyga, *Chicago*, 196.

69. "Plot to Kill President Is Charge Made," *Bannington (VT) Evening Banner*, November 28, 1917, 1.

70. "New York Police Uncover Plot to Kill President," *Eugene Register-Guard*, February 24, 1919, 5.

71. Hagedorn, *Savage Peace*, 121.

72. "14 Spaniards Held in Alleged Plot to Assassinate Wilson," *St. Petersburg Evening Independent*, February 24, 1919, 1.

73. "Wilson Death Plotter Is Deported," *Washington Times*, December 31, 1920, 5.

74. "Local Man Plotted Wilson's Death," *San Jose Evening News*, November 24, 1920, 1.

75. "Loyalty to Wilson Rewarded," *New York Tribune*, April 25, 1920, 10.

13. HARDING, COOLIDGE, AND THE SECRET SERVICE

1. "A Policeman in the House," *Time*, March 11, 1946.

2. Whitcomb and Whitcomb, *Real Life at the White House*, 269.

3. "President's Bodyguard to Change Responsibility," *Painesville Telegraph*, February14, 1933, 2.

4. Starling, *Starling of the White House*, 191.

5. Other mistresses of Harding have included Carrie Philips, Rosa Hoyle, Augusta Cole, Maize Haywood, and Blossom Jones.

6. Whitcomb and Whitcomb, *Real Life at the White House*, 271.

7. "DNA Shows Proof behind 1920s Presidential Sex Scandal," CBS News, August 13, 2015, http://www.cbsnews.com/news/dna-shows-truth-behind-20s-presidential-sex-scandal/.

8. Starling, *Starling of the White House*, 167.

9. Starling, *Starling of the White House*, 171.

10. Starling, *Starling of the White House*, 167.

11. Bowen and Neal, *United States Secret Service*, 155.

12. Whitcomb and Whitcomb, *Real Life at the White House*, 265.

13. Raymond Clapper, "Listening in at Washington," *Palm Beach Daily News*, March 1, 1925, 1.

14. Whitcomb and Whitcomb, *Real Life at the White House*, 265.

15. Starling, *Starling of the White House*, 186.

16. Raymond Clapper, "Listening In At Washington," *Palm Beach Daily News*, March 1, 1925, 1.

17. Michael Miller, *Old School Warrior*, 141.

18. "Harding Threatened; Man Arrested Here," *New York Times*, June 17, 1923, 1.

19. "Harding Death Plot Revealed," *Reading Eagle*, February 16, 1933, 3.

20. Whitcomb and Whitcomb, *Real Life at the White House*, 264.

21. Cook, *Presidential Leadership by Example*, 185.

22. "Poisoning the President? Florence Harding and her Husband's 'Strange Death,'" CarlAnthonyonline.com, August 2, 2011, http://carlanthonyonline.com/2011/08/02/poisoning-the-president-today-in-flotus-history-august-2-1923/.

23. "A Policeman in the House," *Time*, March 11, 1946.

24. Jacob Heilbrunn, "The Great Refrainer—Coolidge by Amity Shales," *New York Times*, February 14, 2013.

25. "The Presidency by Hugh Sidey: Old Cal Makes a Comeback," *Time*, August 15, 1983.

26. "Stories of Coolidge Reveal Kindly Human Nature Known to Friends," *Deseret News*, January 6, 1933, 2.

27. "Coolidge Special Train Smashes Auto," *Rochester Evening Journal*, November 2, 1926, 1.

28. "President Sails Off Coast Aboard Yacht Mayflower," *Meriden (CT) Morning-Record*, July 10, 1925, 4.

29. "The Colonel C. W. Woodsen Memorial Gallery," Virginia State Police, http://www.vsp.state.va.us/memorial_gallery.shtm.

30. "Stories of Coolidge Reveal Kindly Human Nature Known to Friends," *Deseret News*, January 6, 1933, 2.

31. "Stories of Coolidge Reveal Kindly Human Nature Known to Friends," *Deseret News*, January 6, 1933, 2.

32. "Coolidge Greatest Kidder Say Secret Service Head," *The New London (CT) Day*, November 23, 1935, 1.

33. "A Policeman in the House," *Time*, March 11, 1946.

34. Walter Winchell, "More Info on Secret Service," *St. Petersburg Times*, November 13, 1950, 18.

35. "Coolidge Barely Escapes Being Hit by Auto: Pulled Back by His Guard: Driver Arrested," *New York Times*, September 21, 1925, 1.

36. "Stories of Coolidge Reveal Kindly Human Nature Known to Friends," *Deseret News*, January 6, 1933, 2.

37. Starling, *Starling of the White House*, 272.

38. "Secret Service Man Guarding President's Son," *Lewiston Daily Sun*, October 16, 1926, 6.

39. Charles P. Stewart, "Secret Service Man Has Task of Keeping up with First Lady," *Sarasota Herald-Tribune*, January 22, 1927, 4.

40. "Blasts Wreck Subway Stations in New York," *Painesville Telegraph*, August 6, 1927, 1.

41. Seale, *President's House*, 2:878.

42. Calvin Coolidge Presidential Foundation, "Grace Coolidge and the Secret Service Man," http://www.calvin-coolidge.org/grace-coolidge-secret-service man.html.

43. Smith and Morris, *Dear Mr. President*, 131.

44. Seale, *President's House*, 2:853.

45. "Stories of Coolidge Reveal Kindly Human Nature Known to Friends," *Deseret News*, January 6, 1933, 2.

46. "Marine Guard for Coolidge," *Florence (AL) Times*, June 5, 1925, 8.

47. "Coolidge Unmoved by Vicious Threat," *Bend (OR) Bulletin*, January 26, 1925, 1.

48. "Coolidge Menaced," *Pittsburgh Press*, May 1, 1920, 2.

49. "Coolidges Have Aged Rabbi Arrested after Letters," *St. Petersburg Evening Independent*, March 11, 1925, 27.

50. "Crank Arrested—Sent Threats to Coolidge Officers Claim," *Windsor, Ontario, Border Cities Star*, August 21, 1926, 5.

51. "Threatening Coolidge," *Pittsburgh Press*, February 27, 1928, 1.

52. "Postal Clerk Held for Crank Letters," *Pittsburgh Press*, January 3, 1929, 2.

53. "Miami's Own Whirligig," *Miami News*, April 3, 1936, 1.

54. "Threat to Kill Coolidge Lands Man in Prison," *Victoria Advocate*, July 22, 1924, 1.

55. Shales, *Coolidge*, 259; "The Presidency by Hugh Sidey: Old Cal Makes a Comeback," *Time*, August 15, 1983.

56. "Anti-Horthy Parade Stopped at Capitol," *Pittsburgh Press*, March 20, 1928, 4.

57. "In Search of the Perfect Illusion," *Spokane Spokesman Review*, November 20, 1979, 15.

58. "Secret Service Close Guard over President," *Pittsburgh Press*, March 3, 1929, 9.

59. "Threats Made on President," *Florence (AL) Times*, July 31, 1925, 1.

60. "Plot Revealed to Kill Coolidge," *Pittsburgh Post-Gazette*, June 29, 1934, 1.

61. "Plotted to Kill Calvin Coolidge," *Spokane Daily Chronicle*, June 29, 1934, 1.

62. "The Presidency by Hugh Sidey: Old Cal Makes a Comeback," *Time*, August 15, 1983.

63. Gould, *American First Ladies*, 266.

64. "Calvin Coolidge: How Depression Killed a President," Hub Pages, November 10, 2010, http://thebolesfamily.hubpages.com/hub/Calvin-Coolidge-How-Depression-Killed-a-President.

65. "White House Guard Dead," *Milwaukee Journal*, December 27, 1945, 17.

66. "Letter of Warning for Coolidge," *St. Petersburg Evening Independent*, February 25, 1930, 1.

67. "Letter Says Attempt on His Life Is to Be Made," *Milwaukee Sentinel*, February 25, 1930, 1.

14. ARGENTINEAN PLOT TO ASSASSINATE HOOVER

1. James L. Wright, "Safety Assured for Mr. Hoover—Secret Service Agents Dog the President-Elect's Footsteps," *Milwaukee Journal*, November 15, 1928, 3.

2. "Hoover Train Speeds on as Guards Watch," *Pittsburgh Press*, December 13, 1928, 2.

3. "Hoover Train Speeds on as Guards Watch," *Pittsburgh Press*, December 13, 1928, 2.

4. "National Affairs—Hoover Progress," *Time*, December 24, 1928.

5. Hoover, *Memoirs of Herbert Hoover*, 212.

6. "National Affairs: Hoover in Miami," *Time*, February 4, 1929.

7. "Three Mouthy Men Are Given Liberty—Made Threats against President-Elect Hoover, according to Secret Service Men," *Norwalk Hour*, January 26, 1929, 13.

8. "Thwart Alleged Plot Wreck Special Train of President Hoover," *Ludington Daily News*, October 22, 1929, 1.

9. Hoover, *Memoirs of Herbert Hoover*, 212.

10. Hoover, *Memoirs of Herbert Hoover*, 212.

11. "Hoover Photos Are as Scarce as His Race Appointments," *Afro-American*, January 18, 1930, 2.

12. Seale, *President's House*, 2:900.

13. William Leuchtenburg, "President Herbert Hoover," C-Span, December 16, 2008, http://www.c-span.org/video/?c387781/clip-president-herbert-hoover.

14. Starling, *Starling of the White House*, 284.

15. "Woman Crashes into Automobile of Hoover Party," *Washington Reporter*, July 14, 1930, 3.

16. James L. Wright, "Safety Assured for Mr. Hoover—Secret Service Agents Dog the President-Elect's Footsteps," *Milwaukee Journal*, November 15, 1928, 3.

17. "Woman Crashes into Automobile of Hoover Party," *Washington Reporter*, July 14, 1930, 3.

18. "New Safety Measures for Hoover's Outings," *Lawrence Journal-World*, July 24, 1930, 1.

19. Wert, *Hoover, the Fishing President*, 202.

20. Wert, *Hoover, the Fishing President*, 220.

21. Whitcomb and Whitcomb, *Real Life at the White House*, 293.

22. Herbert Hoover Presidential Library, Oral History Interview with George C. Drescher, a member of the White House Secret Service detail prior to, during, and after Herbert Hoover's presidency, by Director Raymond Henle, June 1, 1967, http://www.ecommcode2.com/hoover/research/historical materials/other/drescher.htm.

23. "Washington Most Policed City," *Tuscaloosa News*, October 15, 1931, 4.

24. "The Presidency: Red Scare," *Time*, December 7, 1931.

25. Whitcomb and Whitcomb, *Real Life at the White House*, 294.

26. Starling, *Starling of the White House*, 289.

27. William E. Leuchtenburg, "Keep Your Distance," *New York Times*, November 29, 2008.

28. "Says Hoover Threatened in Letters," *Border Cities Star*, October 7, 1932, 1.

29. Seale, *President's House*, 2:902.

30. Leo R. Sack, "Hoover Bodyguard Feared Assassination for 3 Years, Kept Constantly on Watch," *Pittsburgh Press*, February 16, 1933, 2.

31. Lisio, *President and Protest*, 58.

32. "Attempt Made to Wreck Hoover Train in Nevada," *Ellensburg Daily Record*, November 8, 1932, 1.

33. "Attack Guard for Hoover's Train in West," *Lewiston Evening Journal*, November 8, 1932, 1.

34. "Attempt Made to Wreck Hoover Train in Nevada," *Ellensburg Daily Record*, November 8, 1932, 1.

35. Dickson and Allen, *Bonus Army*, 52.

36. "Bonus Vets at Capitol; Seek to See Hoover," *South-Eastern Missourian*, July 20, 1932, 1.

37. Leo R. Sack, "Hoover Bodyguard Feared Assassination for Three Years, Kept Constantly on Watch" *Pittsburgh Press*, February 16, 1932, 2.

38. Starling, *Starling of the White House*, 296.

39. Whitcomb and Whitcomb, *Real Life at the White House*, 294.

40. J. Smith, *FDR*, 290.

41. Leo R. Sack, "Hoover Bodyguard Feared Assassination for Three Years, Kept Constantly on Watch" *Pittsburgh Press*, February 16, 1932, 2.

42. Herbert Hoover Presidential Library, Oral History Interview with George C. Drescher, a member of the White House Secret Service detail prior to, during, and after Herbert Hoover's presidency, by Director Raymond Henle, June 1, 1967, http://www.ecommcode2.com/hoover/research/historical materials/other/drescher.htm.

43. "William Leuchtenburg: Obama Should Keep His Distance," History News Network, November 29, 2008.

44. Picchi, *Five Weeks of Giuseppe Zangara*, 20–29.

45. Picchi, *Five Weeks of Giuseppe Zangara*, 150.

46. Picchi, *Five Weeks of Giuseppe Zangara*, 200.

47. Picchi, *Five Weeks of Giuseppe Zangara*, 79.

48. "Hoover Guard Doubled," *Montreal Gazette*, February 16, 1933, 11.

49. Herbert Hoover Presidential Library, Oral History Interview with George C. Drescher, a member of the White House Secret Service detail prior to, during, and after Herbert Hoover's presidency, by Director Raymond Henle, June 1, 1967, http://www.ecommcode2.com/hoover/research/historical materials/other/drescher.htm.

50. "Gun Toter Seeks Hoover," *Spokane Spokesman Review*, March 25, 1933, 2.

AFTERWORD

1. David Herbert Donald, "Why Lincoln Died," Boston.com, November 21, 2004, http://www.boston.com/ae/books/articles/2004/11/21/why_lincoln _died/?page=full.

2. A. Ellis and J. Gullo, *Murder and Assassination*, 233, 235.

3. S. Miller, *President and the Assassin*, 304.

4. "A Follower of Guiteau," *Democratic North-West*, November 27, 1890, 6.

5. "Larger Guard for Roosevelt," *New York Evening World*, September 3, 1903, 1.

6. "Those Dangerous Loners," *Time*, April 13, 1981.

7. "The Project to Assassinate Hayes," *Washington DC Evening Star*, July 7, 1881, 1.

8. "The Great Argument Resumed, *New York Times*, January 25, 1882, 1.

9. "Charles Guiteau: The Assassin," History Rat, https://historyrat.wordpress .com/2011/04/24/charles-guiteau-assassin/.

10. "Guiteau and the Assassination of President Garfield," Awesome Stories, https://www.awesomestories.com/asset/view/Guiteau-and-the-Assassination -of-President-Garfield.

11. "The Murder of Garfield," *Gettysburg Compiler*, September 17, 1901, 1.

12. Millard, *Destiny of the Republic*, 159.

13. "How Doctors Killed Garfield," CBS News, July 5, 2012, http://www.cbsnews .com/news/how-doctors-killed-president-garfield/.

14. Millard, *Destiny of the Republic*, 213.

15. Millard, *Destiny of the Republic*, 213.

16. "Capital City Chimes by 'Calypso,'" *Robinson Constitution*, March 18, 1891, 1

17. "Capital City Chimes by 'Calypso,'" *Robinson Constitution*, March 18, 1891, 1

18. "Psychology and Criminology," *Washington Evening Star*, November 11, 1905, 12.

19. Smith D. Fry, "Cranks in Washington," *Roanoke Times*, July 3, 1891, 6

20. "Assassin No. 3," *Sacramento Daily Record-Union*, July 7, 1881, 2

21. "The 'Crank' Question," *New York Times*, January 4, 1882, 1.

22. "The Crop of Cranks," *Lewiston Daily Sun*, November 6, 1893, 4.

23. A. Ellis and J. Gullo, *Murder and Assassination*, 236.

24. "Another Arrest at White House," *Milwaukee Journal*, October 7, 1903, 1.

25. "White House Cranks," *Toledo Blade*, October 15, 1903, 8.

26. "Policeman Commended," *Washington Evening Star*, October 8, 1903, 2.

27. Newton, *Age of the Assassins*, 292.

28. "Threats Made to Murder Colonel," *Daily Missourian*, October 26, 1912, 1.

29. "Threats Made to Murder Colonel," *Daily Missourian*, October 26, 1912, 1.

30. "Guarding President Carefully since the Shooting of Gaynor," *Pittsburgh Press*, August 11, 1910, 4.

31. Shenkman, *Presidential Ambition*, 234–48.

32. Seale, *President's House*, 2:721.

33. J. Smith, *Grant*, 462.

34. Crook, *Through Five Administrations*, 93.

35. *Carroll City (IA) Herald*, August 10, 1881, 1.

36. *Charlotte Democrat*, July 20, 1888, 3

37. "A Follower of Guiteau," *Democratic North-West*, November 27, 1890, 6.

38. "A Startling Revelation," *Laurens (SC) Advertiser*, October 3, 1893, 1.

39. "Larger Guard for Roosevelt," *New York Evening World*, September 3, 1903, 1.

40. "Washington Letter," *Wautauga (NC) Democrat*, October 22, 1903, 1.

41. "Crank Tries to Force Way to President," *Pittsburgh Press*, April 13, 1912, 1.

42. "Story of Plot to Kill President Taft Denied," *Boston Evening Transcript*, July 18, 1912, 1.

BIBLIOGRAPHY

The Secret Service prepared two short histories of its law enforcement role, each of which includes a helpful description of the agency's presidential protective function: *Moments in History, 1865–1990* (Department of the Treasury, Washington DC: U.S. Government Printing Office, 1990) and *Excerpts from the History of the United States Secret Service 1865–1975* (Department of the Treasury, Washington DC: U.S. Government Printing Office, 1978). Although memoirs by former Secret Service directors and special agents listed below contain only limited specific information concerning the Secret Service's operations, they nonetheless provide vivid portrayals of the challenges faced by those entrusted with the protection of the president.

Of special note is *The President's House*, William Seale's remarkable and comprehensive study of life at the White House. This book was the chief source of information regarding security arrangements in the nineteenth century prior to the Secret Service's assumption of the protective function. It was helpful in describing subsequent decades as well. In addition, *The President's House* astutely discusses the historical tension between security and democratic openness at the White House.

"Abraham Lincoln's First Inauguration." Abraham Lincoln Online. http://www.abrahamlincolnonline.org/lincoln/education/inaugural1.htm.

Abrams, Herbert L. "The Contemporary Presidency: Presidential Safety, Prosecutorial Zeal, and Judicial Blunders: The Protective Function Privilege." *Presidential Studies Quarterly* 31, no. 2 (June 2001): 323–37.

Ackerman, Kenneth D. *Dark Horse: The Surprise Election and Political Murder of President James A. Garfield.* Falls Church VA: Viral History Press, 2011.

Alexander, Roberta Sue. *A Place of Recourse: A History of the U.S. District Court for the Southern District of Ohio.* Athens: Ohio University Press, 2005.

Algeo, Matthew *The President Is a Sick Man*. Chicago: Chicago Review Press, 2012.

Andrew, Christopher. *For the President's Eyes Only: Secret Intelligence and the American Presidency from Washington to Bush*. New York: HarperCollins. 1995.

Assassination. True Crime Series, edited by Time-Life Books. Fairfax VA: Time Life Education, 1994.

Baughman, U. E. *Secret Service Chief*. New York: Harper and Brothers, 1962.

Bell, J. Bowyer. *Assassin: Theory and Practice of Political Violence*. Piscataway NJ: Transaction Publishers, 2005.

Bernstein, R. B. *Thomas Jefferson*. New York: Oxford University Press, 2005.

Blackstone, Sarah J. *The Business of Being Buffalo Bill: Selected Letters of William F. Cody*. Westport CT: Praeger, 1988.

Borum, Randy, Robert Fein, Bryan Vossekuil, and John Berglund. "Threat Assessment: Defining an Approach for Evaluating Risk of Targeted Violence." *Behavioral Sciences and the Law* 17, no. 3 (1999): 323–37.

Bowen, Walter S., and Harry Edward Neal. *The United States Secret Service*. New York: Popular Library, 1961.

Brands, H. W. *Andrew Jackson: His Life and Times*. New York: Anchor, 2006.

Brandus, Paul. *Under This Roof: The White House and the Presidency*. Lanham MD: Rowman and Littlefield, 2015.

"A Brief History of Presidential Protection." Appendix 7 of *The Report of the U.S. President's Commission on the Assassination of President John F. Kennedy*. Washington DC: U.S. Government Printing Office, 1964.

Brinkley, Alan, and David Dyer, eds. *The American Presidency*. Boston: Houghton Mifflin, 2004.

Bromley, Michael L. *William Howard Taft and the First Motoring President*. Jefferson NC: McFarland, 2007.

Brower, Kate Andersen. *The Residence: Inside the Private World of the White House*. New York: HarperCollins, 2015.

Bryan, George S. *The Great American Myth: The True Story of Lincoln's Murder*. New York: Carrick and Evans, 1940.

Bumgarner, Jeffrey B. *Federal Agents: The Growth of Federal Law Enforcement in America*. Westport CT: Praeger, 2006.

Burstein, Andrew. *The Passions of Andrew Jackson*. New York: Vintage, 2004.

Cain, S. "The Psychodynamics of the Presidential Assassin and an Examination of the Theme/Graphic Variables of His Threatening Correspondence." *Forensic Sciences International* 19, no. 1 (January–February 1982): 39.

Carpenter, Francis Bicknell. *Six Months at the White House with Abraham Lincoln*. Gloucester UK: Dodo Press, 2010.

Clarke, James W. *American Assassins: The Darker Side of Politics*. Princeton NJ: Princeton University Press, 1982.

———. *Defining Danger: American Assassins and the New Domestic Terrorists.* Piscataway NJ: Transaction Publishers, 2007.

Cole, Donald P. *A Jackson Man: Amos Kendall and the Rise of American Democracy.* Baton Rouge: LSU Press, 2010.

Coleman, Loren. *The Copycat Effect: How The Media and Popular Culture Trigger the Mayhem in Tomorrow's Headlines.* New York: Paraview Pocket Books, 2004.

Cook, Paul David. *Presidential Leadership by Example: A Presidential and First Ladies Report Card for the Future Millennium.* Bloomington: Xlibris, 2001.

Crook, William Henry. *Memories of the White House: The Home Life of Our Presidents from Lincoln to Roosevelt. Being Personal Recollections of Colonel W. H Crook.* Boston: Little, Brown, 1911.

———. *Through Five Administrations: Reminiscences Of Colonel William Henry Crook, Body-Guard to President Lincoln.* New York: Harper Brothers Publishers, 1907.

Cummins, Joseph. *Anything for a Vote.* Philadelphia: Quirk Books, 2015.

Dallek, Robert. *Hail to the Chief: The Making and Unmaking of American Presidents.* New York: Oxford University Press 1996.

David, John S. *The American Colonization Society and the Founding of the First African Republic.* Bloomington: iUniverse, 2014.

Dershowitz, Alan. *America On Trial: Inside the Legal Battles That Transformed Our Nation.* New York: Warner Books, 2004.

Dickson, Paul, and Thomas B. Allen. *The Bonus Army: An American Epic.* London: Walker Books, 2006.

Donald, David Herbert. *We Are Lincoln Men: Abraham Lincoln and His Friends.* New York: Simon and Schuster, 2004.

Donovan, Robert J. *The Assassins of American Presidents.* London: Elek Books, 1956.

Elliott, Paul. *Assassin! The Bloody History of Political Murder.* London: Cassell Illustrated, 1999.

Ellis, Albert, and John Gullo. *Murder and Assassination.* Fort Lee NJ: Lyle Stuart, 1971.

Ellis, Richard J. *Presidential Travel: The Journey from George Washington to George W. Bush.* Lawrence: University Press of Kansas, 2008.

Fein, Robert, and Bryan Vossekuil. "Assassination in the United States: An operational Study of Recent Assassins, Attackers, and Near Lethal Approachers." *Journal of Forensic Sciences* 44, no. 2 (March 1999): 321.

Feinman, Ronald L. *Assassinations, Threats, and the American Presidency: From Andrew Jackson to Barack Obama.* Lanham MD: Rowman and Littlefield, 2015.

"The Fifties and Ike: A Conversation with Stephen Ambrose. " *Humanities* 18, no. 5 (September/October 1997). http://www.neh.gov/news/humanities /1997–09/ambrose.html.

Fiske, John, Carl Schurz, William E. Russell, Daniel C. Oilman, and William
    Walter Phelps. *The Presidents of the United States, 1789–1894.* New York:
    Appleton, 1894.
Frey, Bruno S. "Overprotected Politicians." Center for Research in Economics,
    Management and the Arts. Working Paper No. 2007-7. http:// www.crema
    -research.ch/papers/2007-07.pdf.
Garrison, Webb. *A Treasury of White House Tales.* Nashville: Rutledge Hill Press,
    1996.
Goode, Stephen. *Assassination!* Danbury CT: Franklin Watts, 1979.
Gould, Lewis L. *American First Ladies: Their Lives and Their Legacy.* New York:
    Routledge, 1996.
Guelzo, Allen C. *Abraham Lincoln: Redeemer President.* Grand Rapids MI: Eerd-
    mans, 2002.
Hagedorn, Ann. *Savage Peace: Hope and Fear in America, 1919.* New York: Simon
    and Schuster, 2008.
Hamilton, Nigel. *American Caesars: Lives of the U.S. Presidents—From Franklin D.
    Roosevelt to George W. Bush.* London: Bodley Head, 2010.
Hatch, Frederick. *Protecting President Lincoln: The Security Effort, the Thwarted
    Plots, and the Disaster at Ford's Theater.* Jefferson NC: McFarland, 2011.
Hayward, Steven F. *The Politically Incorrect Guide to the Presidents: From Wilson to
    Obama.* Washington DC: Regnery, 2012.
Helferich, Gerard. *Theodore Roosevelt and the Assassin: Madness, Vengeance, and the
    Campaign of 1912.* Guilford CT: Lyons Press, 2013.
Henry, Mike. *What They Didn't Teach You in American History Class.* Santa Monica:
    R&L Education, 2014.
Hewitt, Christopher. *Understanding Terrorism in America: From the Klan to Al
    Qaeda.* London and New York: Routledge, 2003.
Hodge, Carl Cavanagh, ed. *U.S. Presidents and Foreign Policy.* Santa Barbara CA:
    ABC-CLIO, 2006.
Hoffman, Bruce, Peter Chalk, Timothy E. Liston, and David W. Brannan.
    *Security in the Nation's Capital and the Closure of Pennsylvania Avenue: An
    Assessment.* Washington DC: RAND Corporation, Public Safety and Justice
    Research Program, 2002. http://www.rand.org/pubs/monograph_reports
    /MR1293-1.html.
Hoffman, Jay L. "Psychotic Visitors to Government Offices in the National Capi-
    tal." *American Journal of Psychiatry* 99 (1943): 571–75.
Holden, Henry. *To Be a Secret Service Agent.* Minneapolis: Motorbooks Interna-
    tional, 2006.
Holzer, Harold. *The Lincoln Mailbag: America Writes to the President, 1861–1865.*
    Carbondale: Southern Illinois University Press, 1998.

Hoover, Herbert. *The Memoirs of Herbert Hoover: The Cabinet and the Presidency, 1920–1933*. New York: Macmillan, 1952.

Hurwood, Bernhardt J. *Society and the Assassin: A Background Book on Political Murder*. London: Parents Magazine Press, 1970.

Hyams, Edward. *Killing No Murder: A Study of Assassination as a Political Means*. London: Nelson, 1969.

Jeffrey-Jones, Rhodri. *The FBI: A History*. New Haven: Yale University Press, 2007.

Jones, Benjamin F., and Benjamin A. Olken. "Hit or Miss? The Effect of Assassinations on Institutions and War." National Bureau of Economic Research. NBER Working Paper No. 13102, May 2007. http://www.nber.org/papers/wl3102.

Joynt, Robert J., and James F. O'Toole. *Presidential Disability: Papers and Discussions on Inability and Disability among U.S. Presidents*. Rochester: University of Rochester Press, 2001.

June, Dale L. *Introduction to Executive Protection*. Boca Raton FL: CRC Press, 1998.

Kaiser, Frederick M. *Direct Assaults against Presidents, Presidents-Elect, and Candidates*. Washington DC: Congressional Research Service, Library of Congress, June 7, 2008.

Kauffman, Michael W. *American Brutus: John Wilkes Booth and the Lincoln Conspiracies*. New York: Random House, 2004.

Kirkham, James F., Sheldon G. Levy, and William J. Crotty. *Assassination and Political Violence: A Staff Report to the Commission on the Causes and Prevention of Violence*. New York: Bantam/Matrix Books, 1970.

Kittrie, Nicholas N. *Rebels with a Cause: The Minds and Morality of Political Offenders*. Boulder CO: Westview Press, 2000.

Klein, Edward. *Blood Feud*. Washington DC: Regnery, 2014.

Kuhn, Ferdinand. *The Story of the Secret Service*. New York: Random House, 1957.

Larson, Kate Clifford. *The Assassin's Accomplice: Mary Surratt and the Plot to Kill Abraham Lincoln*. New York: Basic Books, 2008.

Leuchtenburg, William E. *The American President: From Teddy Roosevelt to Bill Clinton*. New York: Oxford University Press, 2016.

Lisio, Donald J. *The President and Protest: Hoover, MacArthur, and the Bonus Riot*. Bronx: Fordham University Press, 1994.

Mappen, Marc. *There's More to New Jersey than the Sopranos*. New Brunswick: Rivergate Books, 2009.

Marrin, Albert. *Old Hickory: Andrew Jackson and the American People*. Westminster: Dutton Children's Books, 2004.

Marshall, Peter, and David Manuel. *From Sea to Shining Sea*. Grand Rapids MI: Revell, 2009.

Matusky, Gregory, and John P. Hayes. *The U.S. Secret Service*. New York: Chelsea House, 1988.

Mayman, Daniel M., and Melvin Guyer. "Not Guilty by Reason of Insanity Defense." *Legal Digest* 36, no. 1 (2008).

McCann, Joseph T. *Terrorism on American Soil: A Concise History of Plots and Perpetrators from the Famous to the Forgotten.* Boulder CO: Sentient Publications, 2006.

McFeeley, William S. *Grant: A Biography.* New York: W. W. Norton, 2002.

McKinley, James. *Assassination in America.* New York: Harper and Row, 1977.

Megargee, Edwin I. "A Psychometric Study of Incarcerated Presidential Threateners." *Criminal Justice and Behavior* 13, no. 3 (September 1986): 243–60.

Melanson, Philip H. *The Secret Service: The Hidden History of an Enigmatic Agency.* New York: Basic Books, 2005.

Meloy, J. Reid. "Stalking and Violence." In *Stalking and Psychosexual Obsession,* edited by J. Boon and L. Sheridan. Hoboken NJ: John Wiley, 2002.

———. "Approaching and Attacking Public Figures: A Contemporary Analysis of Communications and Behavior." In *Threatening Communications and Behavior: Perspectives on the Pursuit of Public Figures.* Washington DC: National Academies Press, 2011.

Meloy, J. Reid, and Cynthia Boyd. "Female Stalkers and Their Victims." *American Journal of Psychiatry and the Law* 31, no. 2 (2003).

Meloy, J. Reid, Lorraine Sheridan, and Jens Hoffman. *Stalking, Threatening, and Attacking Public Figures: A Psychological and Behavioral Analysis.* New York: Oxford University Press, 2008.

Millard, Candice. *Destiny of the Republic: A Tale of Madness, Medicine, and the Murder of a President.* New York: Anchor, 2012.

Miller, Marvin. *The American Dream: Shadow and Substance—A Collector's Pictorial History of America's 200 Years.* Covina CA: Classic Publications, 1976.

Miller, Michael. *The Old School Warrior.* New York: Create Space Independent Publishing, 2012.

Miller, Nathan. *Star Spangled Men: America's Ten Worst Presidents.* New York: Simon and Schuster, 1998.

Miller, Scott. *The President and the Assassin: McKinley, Terror, and Empire at the Dawn of the American Century.* New York: Random House Trade Paperbacks, 2013.

Morgan, H. Wayne. *William McKinley and His America.* Syracuse NY: Syracuse University Press, 1963.

Morris, Edmund. *The Rise of Theodore Roosevelt.* New York: Random House Trade Paperbacks, 2001.

Munsey, Christopher. "Psychology Secrets behind the Service." *APA Monitor* 39, no. 8 (September 2008): 26. http://www.apa.org/monitor/2008/09/secrets.aspx.

National Geographic. *Inside the U.S. Secret Service.* Episode 8 of the Inside series. DVD, 2004.

Navarro, Bob. *The Country in Conflict*. Bloomington: Xlibris, 2008.

Newton, Michael. *Age of the Assassins: The Loners, Idealists, and Fanatics Who Conspired to Change the World*. London: Faber and Faber, 2012.

O'Brien, Cormac. *Secret Lives of the U.S. Presidents*. Philadelphia: Quirk Books, 2009.

Oliver, Willard M., and Nancy E. Marion. *Killing the President: Assassinations, Attempts, and Rumored Attempts on U.S. Commanders-in-Chief*. Westport CT: Praeger, 2010.

O'Reilly, Bill, and Martin Dugard. *Killing Lincoln*. New York: St. Martin's Griffin, 2015.

O'Toole, James F. *Presidential Disability*. Rochester: University of Rochester Press, 2001.

Pacyga, Dominic A. *Chicago: A Biography*. Chicago: University of Chicago Press, 2011.

Parenti, Michael. *History as Mystery*. San Francisco: City Lights Publishers, 2001.

Parr, Jerry. *In the Secret Service: The True Story of the Man Who Saved President Reagan's Life*. Carol Stream IL: Tynedale, 2013.

Pendel, Thomas F. *Thirty-Six Years in the White House: A Memoir of the White House Doorkeeper from Lincoln to Roosevelt*. Carlisle MA: Applewood Books, 1902.

Petro, Joseph, with Jeffrey Robinson. *Standing Next to History: An Agent's Life inside the Secret Service*. New York: Thomas Dunne Books, 2005.

Phillips, Robert T. M. "Assessing Presidential Stalkers and Assassins." *Journal of the American Academy of Psychiatry and the Law* 34 (2006): 154–64.

Picchi, Blaise. *The Five Weeks of Giuseppe Zangara*. Chicago: Academy Chicago Publishers, 1998.

Pietrusza, David. *1920: The Year of the Six Presidents*. New York: Basic Books, 2007.

Pinsker, Matthew. *Lincoln's Sanctuary: Abraham Lincoln and the Soldiers' Home*. New York: Oxford University Press, 2005.

Piszkiewicz, Dennis. *Terrorism's War with America: A History*. Westport CT: Greenwood Publishing Group, 2008.

"Political Assassination: Regicide's Risk—Killing a Leader Doesn't Always Work." *Economist*, May 17, 2007.

Pontius, Anneliese A. "Threats to Assassinate the King-President While Propitiating Mother." *Journal of Analytic Psychology* 19 no. 1, (1974): 38–53.

Randall, J. G., and Richard Nelson Currant. *Lincoln the President: Last Full Measure*. Champaign: University of Illinois Press, 1999.

Redmond, Charles F., and Henry Cabot Lodge. *Roosevelt: Selections from the Correspondence to Henry Cabot Lodge*. Cambridge MA: De Capo Press, 1971.

Reich, Walter, ed. *Origins of Terrorism*. Washington DC: Woodrow Wilson Center Press, 1998.

Reilly, Michael F. *Reilly of the White House*. New York: Simon and Schuster, 1947.

Remini, Robert V. *Andrew Jackson and the Course of American Democracy*. New York: Harper Collins, 1984.

Report of the U.S. President's Commission on the Assassination of President John F. Kennedy. Washington DC: U.S. Government Printing Office, 1964.

Reppetto, Thomas. *American Police: A History 1845–1945*. New York: Enigma Books, 2011.

Roosevelt, Theodore. *Special Message [Relative to Secret Service] Communicated to the House of Representatives on January 4, 1909*. Washington DC: Government Printing Office, 1909.

Rothstein, David A. "Presidential Assassination Syndrome." *Archives of General Psychiatry* 11, no. 3 (September 1964): 245–54.

Savory, Tanya. *Abraham Lincoln: A Giant among Presidents*. Berlin NJ: Townsend Press, 2010.

Schafer, Stephen. *The Political Criminal: The Problem of Morality and Crime*. New York: Free Press, 1974.

Seale, William. *The President's House*. 2 vols. Washington DC: White House Historical Association, 1986.

Sebastian, Joseph A., and James L. Foy. "Psychotic Visitors to the White House." *American Journal of Psychiatry* 122 (December 1, 1965): 679–86.

Seidman, David. *Secret Service Agents: Life Protecting the President*. New York: Rosen Publishing, 2002.

Shales, Amity. *Coolidge*. New York: Harper, 2013.

Shenkman, Richard. *Presidential Ambition: Gaining Power at Any Cost*. New York: HarperPerenial, 2000.

"The Sharpshooter Who Guards the President." *Popular Science* 169, no. 1 (July 1956).

Shogan, Robert. *The Double-Edged Sword: How Character Makes and Ruins Presidents, from Washington to Clinton*. Boulder CO: Westview Press, 1999.

Shore, David, Richard Filson, Ted S. Davis, Fuillermo Olivos, Lynn DeLisi, and Richard Jew Wyatt. "White House Cases: Psychiatric Patients and the Secret Service." *American Journal of Psychiatry* 142, no. 3, (March 1985).

Simon, John Y., ed. *The Papers of Ulysses S. Grant*. Vol. 28, *November 1, 1876–September 30, 1878*. Carbondale: Southern Illinois University Press, 1994.

Singleton, Esther. *The Story of the White House*. Charleston: Bibliobazaar, 2009.

Smith, Jean Edward. *Grant*. New York: Simon and Schuster, 2001.

———. *FDR*. New York: Random House Digital, 2007.

Smith, Ira T., with Joe Alex Morris. *Dear Mr. President: The Story of Fifty Years in the White House Mail Room*. New York: Julian Messner, 1949.

Smith, Merriman. *Merriman Smith's Book of Presidents: A White House Memoir*. New York: W. W. Norton, 1972.

Sobel, Robert. *Coolidge: An American Enigma*. Washington DC: Regnery, 2000.

Sparr, Landy F. "Personality Disorders and Criminal Law: An International Perspective." *American Journal of Psychiatry and the Law* 37 no. 2, (2009): 168–81.

Spitzberg, Brian H., and William R. Cupach. "What Mad Pursuit? Obsessive Relational Intrusion and Stalking Related Phenomena." *Aggression and Violent Behavior* 8 (2003): 345–75.

Starling, Edmund W. *Starling of the White House.* New York: Simon and Schuster, 1946.

Stashower, Daniel. *The Hour of Peril: The Secret Plot to Murder Lincoln before the Civil War.* New York: Minotaur Books, 2013.

Stashower, Daniel. "The Unsuccessful Plot to Kill Abraham Lincoln." *Smithsonian Magazine,* February 2013.

Steers, Edward. *Blood on the Moon: The Assassination of Abraham Lincoln.* Lexington: University Press of Kentucky, 2005.

————. *Lincoln Legends: Myths, Hoaxes, and Confabulations Associated with Our Greatest President.* Lexington: University Press of Kentucky, 2009.

Stephens, John Richard. *Commanding the Storm: Civil War Battles in the Words of the Generals.* Guilford CT: Lyons Press, 2012.

Swanson, James L. *Manhunt: The 12-Day Chase for Abraham Lincoln's Killer.* New York: William Morrow, 2006.

Takeuchi, Jane, Fredric Solomon, and W. Walter Menninger, eds. *Behavioral Science and the Secret Service: Toward the Prevention of Assassination.* Division of Mental Health and Behavioral Medicine, Institute of Medicine. Washington DC: National Academies Press, 1981.

Tully, Andrew. *Treasury Agent.* Lake Oswego OR: eNet Press, 2012.

Updegrove, Mark K. *Second Acts: Presidential Lives and Legacies after the White House.* Guilford CT: Lyons Press 2006.

United States Secret Service Fiscal Year 2009 Annual Report. http://www.secretservice.gov/annualreport.shtml.

Vowell, Sarah. *Assassination Vacation.* New York: Simon and Schuster, 2005.

Watson, Robert P., ed. *Life in the White House: A Social History of the First Family.* Albany: State University of New York Press, 2004.

Wead, Doug. *All the President's Children.* New York: Atria Books, 2004.

Wert, Hal Elliott. *Hoover, the Fishing President: Portrait of the Private Man and His Life Outdoors.* Mechaniscsburg PA: Stackpole Books, 2004.

Whitcomb, John, and Claire Whitcomb. *Real Life at the White House: 200 Years of Daily Life at America's Most Famous Residence.* New York: Routledge, 2002.

Widmer, Ted, and Arthur M. Schlesinger. *Martin Van Buren.* The American Presidents Series: The 8th President 1837–1841. New York: Times Books, 2005.

Wilkie, Donald W. *American Secret Service Agent.* New York: Frederick A. Stokes, 1934.

Willets, Gilson. *Inside History of the White House: The Complete History of the Domestic and Official Life in Washington of the Nation's Presidents and Their Families.* New York: Christian Herald Bible House, 1908.

Wilson, Frank J., and Beth Day. *Special Agent: 25 Years with the American Secret Service*. London: Frederick Muller, 1966.

Wilson, James Grant, ed. *The Presidents of the United States 1789–1894*. London: Gay and Bird, 1895.

Winchester, James H. "They Guard the President." *Boy's Life*, December 1962.

Youngblood, Rufus W. *20 Years in the Secret Service*. New York: Simon and Schuster, 1973.

Zitek, Brook et al. "Assessment and Management of Patients Who Make Threats against the President in the Psychiatric Emergency Service Psychiatric Services." *Psychiatric Services* 56 no. 8 (August 2005):1017.

INDEX

Indian Removal Act, 21

insanity. *See* mental illness (motive)

Intelligencer (newspaper), 37

Ireland, Samuel, 158–59, 167–68

Isaacs, Abraham, 138–39

Jackson, Andrew: attempts to assassinate, 32–37, 52; duels fought by, 23, 25–28; health problems, 24–26; marriage, 25; military service, 14, 23–24; personality of, 20, 24; presidency of, 20–21, 39; security under, 3–4, 28–29, 31; threats against, *fig.* 2, 29–32

Jackson, Elizabeth, 21, 22

Jackson, Joseph Bloomfield, 156–57

Jackson, Robert, 22

Jamieson, B. K., 125

Jefferson, Thomas, 2–3, 5, 10–11

Jenkins, Abe, 205–6

Jennings, Paul, 11

Jervis, Richard L., 209–10, 212, 217, 235–36, 241–42

Joel, Louis S., 247

Johnson, Andrew: *fig. 9*; attempts to assassinate, *fig. 9*, 78, 80, 81–83, 86–87; security for, 83–84; threats against, 84–85

Johnson, Frank, 74

Johnson, Hiram, 205

Jones, Blossom, 298n5

Jones, John, 112–13, 268–69

Jones, William, 108

Jouett, Jack, 11

Juergens, F. H., 219

Kearney, Patrick, 104–5

Kearney, William, 138

Kehl, Jerome, 184–85

Keller, Enoch, 248

Kenny, John, 125

Ketchum, Isaac, 8

Key, Francis Scott, 36

kidnapping plots: against Abraham Lincoln, 73, 76–78, 89–90; against Calvin Coolidge's son, 238; against George Washington, 7–9; against Grover Cleveland's children, 150; against Thomas Jefferson, 10–11

King, Rufus, 51

Klein, Norman, 242

Knox, John D., 169–70

Kolb, Henry, 91–92, 102

Kossuth, Lajos, 241

Krebs, Benedict, 138

La Crosse (WI) Democrat (newspaper), 58–59

Lamon, Ward Hill, *fig. 7*, 58, 63, 67–68, 69, 70–71, 73, 75

Landvoight, Arnold, 220, 235

Lavullo, John, 225–26

Lawrence, Richard, *fig. 2*, 20, 32–37

legislation: criminalizing threats against presidents, 176, 215; inadequacy of, 31–32; on presidential protection, 174–76, 215; for presidential succession, 42, 261–62

letters (death threats): received by Abraham Lincoln, 59–60, 70–72; received by Benjamin Harrison, 124–25, 126–28; received by Calvin Coolidge, 240, 243; received by Grover Cleveland, 152; received by Herbert Hoover, 253; received by Theodore Roosevelt, 183; received by Ulysses Grant, 93–94; received by William McKinley, 156–57; received by Woodrow Wilson, 216–17

Lewis, Robert P., 183

Lewis, William S., 69

Mitchell, Harry, 164
Moffet, Stuart, 202
Monroe, James, 4, 5, 14–16, 24
Moore, William E., 81, 140–41
Moran, William H., 209, 220, 223, 245, 252, 254
Mordaunt, Frank, 79
Mosby, John S., 93
Most, Johann, 161
motives, x, 262–65; mental illnesses, 109, 182, 211, 262, 263; notoriety, x, 263–65; political, 262. *See also* anarchist movements
Mudd, Samuel, 77, 80
Mudd, Sydney, 126
Mueller, Charles G., 207, 219
Muller, Henry, 163–64
Murder and Assassination (Ellis and Gullo), 154
Murphy, Joseph E., 209, 220, 248

Native Americans, *fig. 28*, 21, 23–24
Neal, Clarence, 240
newspapers: attacking Abraham Lincoln, 64; criticizing security as excessive, 197; opposition to presidential security, 123, 175; role in assassination attempts, 58–59
New York Herald (newspaper), 59, 86
New York Journal (newspaper), 159–60
New York Times (newspaper), 111, 198
New York Tribune (newspaper), 59, 112
Nichols, John W., 75
Nicolay, John George, 60, 61
Noetling, John, 113–14
notoriety (motive), x, 263–65

O'Brien, Francis, 168
O'Dwyer (Secret Service agent), 128, 286n76
Ohio Democrat (newspaper), 142

O'Laughlen, Michael, 80, 89–90
Old Soldiers' Home, 55–56, 59, 72–76
Olson, Peter, 186, 189–92, 263
O'Mara, Roger, 159
O'Neil, Thomas, 52–53
O'Neill, Annie, 87
O'Reilly, Bill, 90
Orestiass, Elario, 224–25
Orton, A. J., 124
Overton, Thomas, 25–26

Pace, John, 255
Panama Canal, 172–73
Pan-American Exposition, *fig. 19*, 166–68
Parenti, Michael, 50
Parke, Robert, 104
Parker, Dorothy, 234
Parker, James, 168
Parker, Joanna, 47
Parker, John F., 70, 78–79
Pastorius, William D., 203
Peacemaker (gun), 45–46
Peirre, Pietro (Sam), 225–26
Pendel, Thomas F., 69, 71, 85, 102, 113–14, 169
Pendleton Civil Service Act, 111
Pennsylvania Railroad, 119
Penny, Thomas, 168
Petrosino, Joseph, 165
Philips, Carrie, 298n5
Piatt, Donn, 94
Picchi, Blaise, 258
Pierce, Benny, 51
Pierce, Franklin, 51–54
Pierce, Jane, 51
Pignuelo, Pasquale, 202
Pinkerton, Allan, 61–63, 65, 99, 159
Pitman, Benn, 263
Pittsburgh Dispatch (newspaper), 130–31

Sanchez, Jose, 242
San Francisco Call (newspaper), 142
San Jose Times (newspaper), 97
Santiago, Eduardo, 246
Scarfó, Alejandro, 246–47
Scarfó, Paulino, 246
Schrank, John, *fig. 24*, x, 192–93, 267
Schubell, John George, 205
Schuler, Nathan, 139
Scott, Joseph, 253
Scott, Winfield, 15, 28, 35, 55, 61, 65
Sealazkiwiez, Walter, 185
Seale, William, 268
secession, 38–39, 54
Second Bank controversy, 21, 32, 39, 43–44
Secret Service: *fig. 21, fig. 22*; agent physical requirements, 210; beginning of presidential protection duties, 100, 154–55; counterfeit duties, 100, 130–31; covering up threats, xii, 128–32, 269; establishment of, 99–100; functions of, 127; funding for protection duties, 171; increasing presidential protection duties, 140, 149–50, 153, 173–74, 175–76; John Bell's dismissal from, 130–31; protecting Benjamin Harrison, 117–18; protecting Calvin Coolidge, 235–39, 241–42; protecting Grover Cleveland, 149–51, 152; protecting Herbert Hoover, 245, 249–57, 258–59; protecting Rutherford Hayes, 94–95; protecting Theodore Roosevelt, 177, 178–79, 181, 186–87; protecting the president's family, 176, 238; protecting Warren Harding, 229–31; protecting William McKinley, 155, 157–59, 162–63, 165–66; protecting William Taft, 195–98, 204–5; protecting

Woodrow Wilson, 209–14, 219–22, 223–25, 226; and the White House police force, 149–51
security (presidential): for Abraham Lincoln, 59, 65–72, 74; during the antebellum period, 40–41, 43–45, 47, 52–53; balanced with accessibility, 269–70; for Chester Arthur, 111–12; of the early presidents, 14–15; for Herbert Hoover, 253; impact of assassinations on, 101, 110, 111–12, 171, 196–97; legislation for, 174–76, 215; opposition to, 1–2, 4, 18–19, 142–43, 156, 171, 174, 197; for Theodore Roosevelt, 176–79; two-level security, 53; for William Taft, 196–97. *See also* bodyguards (presidential); Secret Service
security (White House): under Andrew Johnson, 83–84; in the antebellum period, 40–41, 43–45, 47, 50, 52–53; under Benjamin Harrison, 120–23; under Calvin Coolidge, 239; under the early presidents, 3–4, 9, 11, 15–17, 37; following James Garfield's shooting, 111; under Grover Cleveland, 134–37, 141–43, 145–46, 150–51, 152–53; under Herbert Hoover, 253; physical security measures, 11, 15; under Rutherford Hayes, 96; under Theodore Roosevelt, 181; under Ulysses Grant, 90; under William McKinley, 156; under Woodrow Wilson, 220–21. *See also* White House
Sellers, Ephraim, 181
Seward, William H., 72–73, 78, 80
Shelton, Joseph, 70
Sherman, John, 94, 128, 129
Sherrill, C. O., 229–30